Advancements in Computer Vision and Image Processing

Jose Garcia-Rodriguez
University of Alicante, Spain

A volume in the Advances
in Computer and Electrical
Engineering (ACEE) Book Series

Published in the United States of America by
    IGI Global
    Engineering Science Reference (an imprint of IGI Global)
    701 E. Chocolate Avenue
    Hershey PA, USA 17033
    Tel: 717-533-8845
    Fax: 717-533-8661
    E-mail: cust@igi-global.com
    Web site: http://www.igi-global.com

Library of Congress Cataloging-in-Publication Data

Names: Garcia-Rodriguez, Jose, 1970- editor.
Title: Advancements in computer vision and image processing / Jose
  Garcia-Rodriguez, editor.
Description: Hershey, PA : Engineering Science Reference, [2018] I Includes
  bibliographical references.
Identifiers: LCCN 2017049755I ISBN 9781522556282 (h/c) I ISBN 9781522556299
  (eISBN)
Subjects: LCSH: Computer vision.
Classification: LCC TA1634 .A284 2018 I DDC 006.3/7--dc23 LC record available at https://lccn.
loc.gov/2017049755

This book is published in the IGI Global book series Advances in Computer and Electrical Engineering (ACEE) (ISSN: 2327-039X; eISSN: 2327-0403)

British Cataloguing in Publication Data
A Cataloguing in Publication record for this book is available from the British Library.

All work contributed to this book is new, previously-unpublished material.
The views expressed in this book are those of the authors, but not necessarily of the publisher.

For electronic access to this publication, please contact: eresources@igi-global.com.

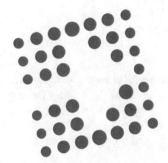

Advances in Computer and Electrical Engineering (ACEE) Book Series

ISSN:2327-039X
EISSN:2327-0403

Editor-in-Chief: Srikanta Patnaik, SOA University, India

MISSION

The fields of computer engineering and electrical engineering encompass a broad range of interdisciplinary topics allowing for expansive research developments across multiple fields. Research in these areas continues to develop and become increasingly important as computer and electrical systems have become an integral part of everyday life.

The **Advances in Computer and Electrical Engineering (ACEE) Book Series** aims to publish research on diverse topics pertaining to computer engineering and electrical engineering. **ACEE** encourages scholarly discourse on the latest applications, tools, and methodologies being implemented in the field for the design and development of computer and electrical systems.

COVERAGE

- VLSI Design
- Optical Electronics
- Chip Design
- Applied Electromagnetics
- Electrical Power Conversion
- VLSI Fabrication
- Qualitative Methods
- Computer Architecture
- Microprocessor Design
- Analog Electronics

IGI Global is currently accepting manuscripts for publication within this series. To submit a proposal for a volume in this series, please contact our Acquisition Editors at Acquisitions@igi-global.com or visit: http://www.igi-global.com/publish/.

Titles in this Series

For a list of additional titles in this series, please visit:
https://www.igi-global.com/book-series/advances-computer-electrical-engineering/73675

Free and Open Source Software in Modern Data Science and Business Intelligence...
K.G. Srinivasa (CBP Government Engineering College, India) Ganesh Chandra Deka (M. S. Ramaiah Institute of Technology, India) and Krishnaraj P.M. (M. S. Ramaiah Institute of Technolog, India)
Engineering Science Reference • ©2018 • 189pp • H/C (ISBN: 9781522537076) • US $190.00

Design Parameters of Electrical Network Grounding Systems
Osama El-Sayed Gouda (Cairo University, Egypt)
Engineering Science Reference • ©2018 • 316pp • H/C (ISBN: 9781522538530) • US $235.00

Design and Use of Virtualization Technology in Cloud Computing
Prashanta Kumar Das (Government Industrial Training Institute Dhansiri, India) and Ganesh Chandra Deka (Government of India, India)
Engineering Science Reference • ©2018 • 315pp • H/C (ISBN: 9781522527855) • US $235.00

Smart Grid Test Bed Using OPNET and Power Line Communication
Jun-Ho Huh (Catholic University of Pusan, South Korea)
Engineering Science Reference • ©2018 • 425pp • H/C (ISBN: 9781522527763) • US $225.00

Transport of Information-Carriers in Semiconductors and Nanodevices
Muhammad El-Saba (Ain-Shams University, Egypt)
Engineering Science Reference • ©2017 • 677pp • H/C (ISBN: 9781522523123) • US $225.00

For an entire list of titles in this series, please visit:
https://www.igi-global.com/book-series/advances-computer-electrical-engineering/73675

701 East Chocolate Avenue, Hershey, PA 17033, USA
Tel: 717-533-8845 x100 • Fax: 717-533-8661
E-Mail: cust@igi-global.com • www.igi-global.com

List of Reviewers

Manikandababu C. S., *Anna University, India*
John-Alejandro Castro, *University of Alicante, Spain*
Miguel Cazorla, *University of Alicante, Spain*
Harini Datti, *Vidya Parishad College of Engineering, India*
Enrique Dominguez, *University of Malaga, Spain*
Magnus Johansson, *Lünd University, Sweden*
Sajid Khan, *Universiti Malaysia Sarawak, Malaysia*
Aravind Kumar Madam, *JNTU Kakinada, India*
Andrew Lewis, *Griffith University, Australia*
Sergiu-Ovidiu Oprea, *University of Alicante, Spain*
Sergio Orts-Escolano, *University of Alicante, Spain*
Alexandra Psarrou, *University of Westminster, UK*
Razieh Rastgoo, *Semnan University, Iran*
Peter Roth, *Graz University, Austria*
Geetika Singh, *MCM DAV College for Women, India*
Victor Villena, *University of Alicante, Spain*

Table of Contents

Section 2
Image Processing

Section 3
Recognition Systems

Detailed Table of Contents

Section 1
3D Robotics Vision and Surveillance Systems

Alberto Martín Florido, Universidad Rey Juan Carlos, Spain
Francisco Rivas Montero, Universidad Rey Juan Carlos, Spain
Jose María Cañas Plaza, Universidad Rey Juan Carlos, Spain

Visual localization is a key capability in robotics and in augmented reality applications. It estimates the 3D position of a camera on real time just analyzing the image stream. This chapter presents a robust map-based 3D visual localization system. It relies on maps of the scenarios built with the known tool RTABmap. It consists of three steps on continuous loop: feature points computation on the input frame, matching with feature points on the map keyframes (using kNN and outlier rejection), and 3D final estimation using PnP geometry and optimization. The system has been experimentally validated in several scenarios. In addition, an empirical study of the effect of three matching outlier rejection mechanisms (radio test, fundamental matrix, and homography matrix) on the quality of estimated 3D localization has been performed. The outlier rejection mechanisms, combined themselves or alone, reduce the number of matched feature points but increase their quality, and so, the accuracy of the 3D estimation. The combination of ratio test and homography matrix provides the best results.

Chapter 2

John Alejandro Castro Vargas, University of Alicante, Spain
Alberto Garcia Garcia, University of Alicante, Spain
Sergiu Oprea, University of Alicante, Spain
Sergio Orts Escolano, University of Alicante, Spain
Jose Garcia Rodriguez, University of Alicante, Spain

Object grasping in domestic environments using social robots has an enormous potential to help dependent people with a certain degree of disability. In this chapter, the authors make use of the well-known Pepper social robot to carry out such task. They provide an integrated solution using ROS to recognize and grasp simple objects. That system was deployed on an accelerator platform (Jetson TX1) to be able to perform object recognition in real time using RGB-D sensors attached to the robot. By using the system, the authors prove that the Pepper robot shows a great potential for such domestic assistance tasks.

Chapter 3

Swati Nigam, SP Memorial Institute of Technology, India
Rajiv Singh, Banasthali University, India
A. K. Misra, SP Memorial Institute of Technology, India

Computer vision techniques are capable of detecting human behavior from video sequences. Several state-of-the-art techniques have been proposed for human behavior detection and analysis. However, a collective framework is always required for intelligent human behavior analysis. Therefore, in this chapter, the authors provide a comprehensive understanding towards human behavior detection approaches. The framework of this chapter is based on human detection, human tracking, and human activity recognition, as these are the basic steps of human behavior detection process. The authors provide a detailed discussion over the human behavior detection framework and discuss the feature-descriptor-based approach. Furthermore, they have provided qualitative and quantitative analysis for the detection framework and demonstrate the results for human detection, human tracking, and human activity recognition.

Chapter 4

Registration of multiple 3D data sets is a fundamental problem in many areas. Many researches and applications are using low-cost RGB-D sensors for 3D data acquisition. In general terms, the registration problem tries to find a transformation between two coordinate systems that better aligns the point sets. In order to review and describe the state-of-the-art of the rigid registration approaches, the authors decided to classify methods in coarse and fine. Due to the high variety of methods, they have made a study of the registration techniques, which could use RGB-D sensors in static scenarios. This chapter covers most of the expected aspects to consider when a registration technique has to be used with RGB-D sensors. Moreover, in order to establish a taxonomy of the different methods, the authors have classified those using different characteristics. As a result, they present a classification that aims to be a guide to help the researchers or practitioners to select a method based on the requirements of a specific registration problem.

Section 2
Image Processing

This chapter addresses the problem of processing hyperspectral images (HI) and sequences leading to high efficiency implementations. A new methodology based on the application of cellular automata (CA) is presented to solve two different processing tasks, the segmentation and denoising of HI and sequences, respectively. CA structures present potential benefits over traditional approaches since they are computationally efficient and can adapt to the particularities of the task to be solved. However, it is necessary to generate an appropriate rule set for each particular problem, which is usually a difficult task. The generation of the rule sets is handled here following a new methodology based on the application of evolutionary algorithms and using synthetic low-dimensionality images and sequences as training datasets, which results in CA structures that can be used to process HI and sequences successfully, thus avoiding the problem of lack of labeled reference images. Both processing approaches have been tested over real HI providing very competitive results.

Chapter 6

Bhavneet Kaur, Chandigarh University, India
Meenakshi Sharma, Chandigarh University, India

Image segmentation is gauged as an essential stage of representation in image processing. This process segregates a digitized image into various categorized sections. An additional advantage of distinguishing dissimilar objects can be represented within this state of the art. Numerous image segmentation techniques have been proposed by various researchers, which maintained a smooth and easy timely evaluation. In this chapter, an introduction to image processing along with segmentation techniques, computer vision fundamentals, and its applied applications that will be of worth to the image processing and computer vision research communities has been deeply studied. It aims to interpret the role of various clustering-based image segmentation techniques specifically. Use of the proposed chapter if made in real time can project better outcomes in object detection and recognition, which can then later be applied in numerous applications and devices like in robots, automation, medical equipment, etc. for safety, advancement, and betterment of society.

Section 3
Recognition Systems

Chapter 7

Thontadari C., Kuvempu University, India
Prabhakar C. J., Kuvempu University, India

In this chapter, the authors present a segmentation-based word spotting method for handwritten documents using bag of visual words (BoVW) framework based on co-occurrence histograms of oriented gradients (Co-HOG) features. The Co-HOG descriptor captures the word image shape information and encodes the local spatial information by counting the co-occurrence of gradient orientation of neighbor pixel pairs. The handwritten document images are segmented into words and each word image is represented by a vector that contains the frequency of visual words appeared in the image. In order to include spatial information to the BoVW framework, the authors adopted spatial pyramid matching (SPM) method. The proposed method is evaluated using precision and recall metrics through experimentation conducted on popular datasets such as GW and IAM. The performance analysis confirmed that the method outperforms existing word spotting techniques.

Chapter 8

Human skin detection and face detection are important and challenging problems in computer vision. The use of color information has increased in recent years due to the lower processing time of face detection compared to black and white images. A number of techniques for skin detection are discussed. Experiments have been performed utilizing deep learning with a variety of color spaces, showing that deep learning produces better results compared to methods such as rule-based, Gaussian model, and feed forward neural network on skin detection. A challenging problem in skin detection is that there are numerous objects with colors similar to that of the human skin. A texture segmentation method has been designed to distinguish between the human skin and objects with similar colors to that of human skin. Once the skin is detected, image is divided into several skin components and the process of detecting the face is limited to these components—increasing the speed of the face detection. In addition, a method for eye and lip detection is proposed using information from different color spaces.

Chapter 9

Most matching or verification phases of fingerprint systems use minutiae types and orientation angle to find matched minutiae pairs from the input and template fingerprints. Unfortunately, due to some non-linear distortions, like excessive pressure and fingers twisting during enrollment, this process can cause the minutiae features to be distorted from the original. The authors are interested in a fingerprint matching method using contactless images for fingerprint verification. After features extraction, they compute Euclidean distances between template minutiae (bifurcation and ending points) and input image minutiae. They compute then after bifurcation ridges orientation angles and ending point orientations. In the decision stage, they analyze the similarity between templates. The proposed algorithm has been tested on a set of 420 fingerprint images. The verification accuracy is found to be acceptable and the experimental results are promising. Future work will enhance the proposed verification method by a new template protection technique.

Preface

Computer vision interest have grown dramatically in the last years. Smartphones, autonomous cars, computer games or social robotics are only a few examples of the impact of computer vision and image processing methods in everyday life. The appearance of low cost cameras and the increase in the computers processing capabilities made possible that thousands of researchers around the world develop sophisticated algorithms to process images and videos in real time with applications in computer science, education, security, government, engineering disciplines, software industry, vehicle industry, medical industry, and other fields.

Moreover, the field has seen an enormous progress in the last decade with the introduction on new algorithms and very powerful computer hardware. This progress has also been extended to a number of very dissimilar areas such as human computer-interaction, multimedia, robotics, automation, medicine and surveillance to name a few. Computer vision has seen very successful application in autonomous machines. This has been possible not only by the improvement of computer hardware but from the development of new very efficient algorithms.

Until a few years ago, fundamental problems affected computer vision that makes most algorithms not viable for real time application. This has started to change dramatically. Over the last few years we have seen an enormous growth of very successful practical implementation of computer vision. Furthermore, some of them have exploited mass production of proprietary hardware to make the deployment of impressive applications at very reduced costs. This has also been possible due to a number of significant breakthroughs in the underlying algorithms and techniques, including feature detectors, classifiers and a large variety of very efficient machine learning algorithms. For example, in the context of computer vision, object recognition is the process of detecting and identifying objects in images or video sequences as well as determining their pose, that is, their positions and orientations. This task is still one of the hardest challenges of computer vision systems so that multiple approaches have been taken and implemented over many years of research in the field. Traditionally, object recognition systems made use of bidimensional images with intensity information. Those systems apply machine learning and matching algorithms which are based either on significant features of the objects or their appearance. However, technological advances made during last years have caused a huge increase in the use of tridimensional information in the field of computer vision in general and, in particular, in object recognition systems; this is due to the capability of acquiring real-time 3D data and efficiently process all this information. Together with the technological development of tridimensional information acquisition systems, another key factor in the evolution of the 3D object recognition field is the creation and development of computing devices which are able to process, in an efficient manner, the huge amount of data representing the tridimensional information provided by range sensors. In this sense, the continuous improvements introduced in the fields of General Purpose computation on GPUs (GPGPU) and low power consumption parallel computing devices.

Advancements in Computer Vision and Image Processing is an edited collection of contributed chapters of interest for researchers and practitioners in the fields of computer vision and artificial intelligence. The target audience of this book includes scientist, engineers and students interested in getting a comprehensive background in the rapidly developing field of computer vision.

It is impossible to select a number of papers to cover all the recent progress in computer vision and image processing. Nevertheless, we have chosen a number of fundamental aspects of the field that are addressed in a very comprehensive manner in this book. The material presented is intended to be a fundamental first step towards understanding the main challenges involved in computer vision applications.

This book presents a comprehensive introduction and the latest development to the fields of computer vision and image processing and its applications to different fields. Written by leading researchers in the field, the volume consists of nine chapters that describe state-of-the-art research in the area. We have organized the chapters in three sections: the first one cover four works related with 3D robotics vision and surveillance systems, the second one includes two papers that present different segmentation techniques, to conclude with three articles related with recognition systems applied to faces, fingerprints or handwritten documents.

SECTION 1: 3D ROBOTICS VISION AND SURVEILLANCE SYSTEMS

Martín-Florido, Rivas-Montero, and Cañas-Plaza presents a robust map-based 3D visual localization system. It relies on maps of the scenarios built with the known tool RTABmap. It consists of three steps on continuous loop: (a) feature points computation on the input frame (using SIFT), (b) matching with feature points on the map keyframes (using kNN and outlier rejection) and (c) 3D final estimation using PnP geometry and optimization. The system has been experimentally validated in several scenarios. In addition, an empirical study of the effect of three matching outlier rejection mechanisms (radio test, fundamental matrix and homography matrix) on the quality of estimated 3D localization has been performed. The outlier rejection mechanisms, combined themselves or alone, reduce the number of matched feature points but increase their quality, and so, the accuracy of the 3D estimation. The combination of ratio test and homography matrix provides the best results.

"In Object Recognition Pipeline: Grasping in Domestic Environments," Castro-Vargas. Garcia-Garcia, Oprea, Orts-Escolano, and Garcia-Rodriguez made use of the well-known Pepper social robot to grasp small objects in domestic environments. They provide an integrated solution using ROS to recognize and grasp simple objects. That system was deployed on an accelerator platform (Jetson TX1) to be able to perform object recognition in real time using RGB-D sensors attached to the robot. Furthermore, a brief analysis of the robot's ability to perform grasping tasks has been carried out. OpenRave was used as a tool for automatic generation of grasping points with custom joint definitions for the Pepper's hand. In this regard, it can be concluded that the whole system works reasonably well for simple objects of an appropriate size for the robot's hand.

Nigam, Singh, and Misra provide a comprehensive understanding towards human behavior detection approaches. The framework of this chapter is based on human detection, human tracking and human activity recognition, as these are the basic steps of human behavior detection process. They provide a detailed discussion over the human behavior detection framework and discuss the feature descriptor based approach. Furthermore, they provided qualitative and quantitative analysis for the detection framework and demonstrate the results for human detection, human tracking and human activity recognition.

Morell, Saval-Calvo, Villena, Azorín, García-Rodríguez, Cazorla, Orts-Escolano and Fuster-Guillo, propose a taxonomy of the different 3D registration methods classified those using different characteristics. The result is a classification that has a first level according to the application, registration type, data used as input and other characteristics, which subdivides in the second level in a more detailed description. The aim of this classification is to help the reader to select a method based on the requirements of a specific registration problem. Due to the high variety of methods, they have made a study of the registration methods, which use RGB-D sensors in static scenarios. This study pretends to cover most of the expected aspects to consider when a registration has to be used with RGB-D sensors

SECTION 2: IMAGE PROCESSING

Priego and Duro describe a methodology for applying Cellular Automata to hyperspectral data in order to address different processing tasks. The first one of these tasks is the segmentation of still hyperspectral images, aiming to transform the hyperspectral datacubes into modified versions that are easier to process by, for example, subsequent classification methods. Once this approach has been analyzed and validated, the applicability of CAs to hyperspectral data is pushed to a higher complexity level by introducing the temporal dimension in the processing of sequences of multi-temporal hyperspectral images. In this the case, the cellular automata structures deal with the denoising problem by taking into account the inter-dimensional diversity by jointly processing the spatial, spectral and temporal information of multi-temporal image sequences.

The chapter "Role of Clustering Techniques in Effective Image Segmentation" by Kaur and Sharma explains the role of various clustering based image segmentation techniques. Both pros and cons are discussed for each method. On the basis of the study made, it has been identified that nearly all methods require a prior user initialization, which automatically becomes a major limitation of clustering techniques. Thus, there is a need of a careful and an appropriate decision making while selecting a method based on the availability of data and user desires. Such a useful yet challenging limitations are discussing in detailed that need to be resolved soon for better results. Lastly, recent updates in the clustering technique have been covered for better visualization of the field.

SECTION 3: RECOGNITION SYSTEMS

Thontadari and Prabhakar propose segmentation-based word spotting technique using a Bag of Visual Words powered by Co-HOG features aimed to reduce the dimension of feature vector. In order to include spatial distribution of visual words information to the BoVW framework, they adopted Spatial Pyramid Matching (SPM) method, which recaptures spatial distribution of visual words information by creating a spatial pyramid bins.

Hajiarbabi and Agah discusses a number of novel methods in the fields of skin detection, texture segmentation, and face detection in color images. A combination of neural networks was designed and developed in order to detect the human skin. The designed networks increase the detection rate of human skin compared to that of the other methods in this field. Deep learning that was used for skin detection.

The results show that deep learning has better performance in terms of recall and accuracy, compared to other methods which include rule based methods, Gaussian method, and neural network. In addition, an algorithm was proposed, implemented, and evaluated in order to locate the eyes and lips in an image using color information. This methodology was combined with another method for finding faces in the images using the locations of eyes and lips.

In "A Secured Contactless Fingerprint Verification Method Using a Minutiae Matching Technique," Djara, Assogba, and Vianou present a contactless fingerprint verification method using a minutiae matching technique, based on the alignment between template images acquired by a contactless system and input images acquired by the same way. Contactless images have been acquired and stored in a database during an enrollment step. The first stage in an Automatic Fingerprint Verification procedure is to extract minutiae from fingerprints. The extracted features are ridge bifurcation, ridge ending and ridges orientations.

In conclusion, this book summarizes the advances in some of the most active topics in computer vision like robotics vision that allows mobile robots to navigate in indoor and outdoor environments and interact with humans and other robots or mobile vehicles. Other field of interest with special attention in the last years due to the global threat that represents terrorism are the surveillance systems. The investment of governments and private institutions in security put the research in the area in first positions of computer vision applications. Transversal to any applications are the image and video processing techniques that extract interesting information from visual data that permits the construction of higher level vision systems from a set of applications that range from simple image filtering to complex video coding and compression systems that use communication applications like video chats or video streaming. Finally, recognition systems provide information to interpret different elements present in images and videos. This is without doubt one of the most active fields in computer vision. Due to the availability of cheap High-Performance Computing (HPC) systems based of GPU and recent advances and rediscover of neural networks in the form of deep neural networks. The most important milestone regarding deep learning: the Convolutional Neural Network (CNN). This special kind of deep network was designed to process data in form of multiple arrays and gained popularity because of its many practical successes. This was due to the fact that they were easier to train and generalized far better than previous models. The alliance of HPC with Deep learning provided researchers with a powerful tool that surpassed traditional recognition systems in image a video and even improve human skills to distinguish elements in visual data.

Acknowledgment

The editor wishes to acknowledge the valuable help of reviewers and colleagues that helped to disseminate and carry on the project.

This work has been funded by the Spanish Government TIN2016-76515-R and TIN2017-89069-R grants for the COMBAHO and MOVI4DHUBO projects, supported with Feder funds.

Section 1
3D Robotics Vision and Surveillance Systems

Chapter 1
Robust 3D Visual Localization Based on RTABmaps

Alberto Martín Florido
Universidad Rey Juan Carlos, Spain

Francisco Rivas Montero
Universidad Rey Juan Carlos, Spain

Jose María Cañas Plaza
Universidad Rey Juan Carlos, Spain

ABSTRACT

Visual localization is a key capability in robotics and in augmented reality applications. It estimates the 3D position of a camera on real time just analyzing the image stream. This chapter presents a robust map-based 3D visual localization system. It relies on maps of the scenarios built with the known tool RTABmap. It consists of three steps on continuous loop: feature points computation on the input frame, matching with feature points on the map keyframes (using kNN and outlier rejection), and 3D final estimation using PnP geometry and optimization. The system has been experimentally validated in several scenarios. In addition, an empirical study of the effect of three matching outlier rejection mechanisms (radio test, fundamental matrix, and homography matrix) on the quality of estimated 3D localization has been performed. The outlier rejection mechanisms, combined themselves or alone, reduce the number of matched feature points but increase their quality, and so, the accuracy of the 3D estimation. The combination of ratio test and homography matrix provides the best results.

DOI: 10.4018/978-1-5225-5628-2.ch001

INTRODUCTION

Cameras are ubiquitous sensors today. They are prevalent on laptops, smartphones and on mobile robots. Extracting information from visual data is not an easy task. One important piece of information that can be extracted on real time from mobile cameras is their 3D localization. Visual localization is the problem of estimating the camera pose from the image flow.

Localization can be used, for instance, in a robot to decide its right behavior. Like in robotic vacuum cleaners as Roomba 980 model. The low-end models just deploy a random coverage navigation algorithm because they only have noisy odometry to estimate their position at home. The high-end models are equipped with cameras and visual localization algorithms. This allows smarter coverage navigation algorithms which clean faster and in a more methodical way. It has been also used in other very different robots like drones or humanoid at the RoboCup. Most interesting robots have cameras.

In smartphones and tablets, it can be used for Augmented Reality and Mixed Reality applications. Knowing the 3D position of the phone some virtual objects can be realistically drawn over the camera image on real time. One interesting example of this is the Tango project from Google. One sample commercial application is IKEA Place app, developed in conjunction with Apple. The new Software Development Kits for Augmented Reality from Google (ARcore) and from Apple (ARkit) take benefit from visual localization technology.

Another use of visual localization is to calibrate the extrinsic parameters of the cameras of a motion capture system. This was a problem in our lab, where a motion capture system is used to track the people position over time. That system uses several RGBD cameras installed on the monitored scenario. In order to compute proper estimations, the position of all the cameras of the system must be accurately known before start. Every time the motion tracking system is going to be installed on a new scenario, it has to be calibrated, that is, the 3D position of all its cameras has to be estimated. The old calibration procedure was manual, pattern based, slow and error prone. A 3D pattern was placed on a certain position of the new scenario, it was observed in the camera images and several relevant points were manually matched. This delivered an estimated 3D position that was also manually refined. The visual localization system proposed on this chapter provides a fast, robust and automatic calibration mechanism. No 3D pattern is needed at all.

Self-localization has been an active topic on robotics since many years ago. Laser based solutions and particle filters provided good and robust estimations (Thrun et al, 2001).

But laser sensors are expensive. Cameras are cheap and widespread sensors, and they are common equipment onboard most robots. New vision based self-localization algorithms were also created (Dellaert et al, 1999). Some of them require previous knowledge of the scene in terms of a map or a collection of beacons. Others, like Visual SLAM (Simultaneous Localization and Mapping) algorithms, calculate the 3D motion of a camera in real-time without prior information of the environment, creating at the same time a map of its surroundings. In addition, the same problem was addressed on the computer vision community, named there the Structure From Motion problem. In that context the real-time operation does not use to be a hard requirement. Visual localization has been one of the main challenges in computer vision and robotics since the early 2000s.

In visual SLAM some interesting concepts appear beyond accuracy and real-time operation like loop closure and relocalization. The relocalization refers to the capability of recovering the right position once the system gets lost by an occlusion, a perception failure or a bad estimation. The loop closure refers to the behavior of the estimation when the camera returns to a previously visited place. The 3D estimations must be the same, but it is usually not the case as the visual localization algorithm may accumulate errors.

This chapter proposes a robust algorithm to locate in 3D a single RGB camera on a given scenario, whose 3D map is available. This map does not include any beacon at all, just a collection of keyframes and their 3D locations, like those built by RTABmap tools from RGBD sensors such Kinect. It provides absolute position on the map. The algorithm has been implemented and it is open source software available on a public repository. The effect of several matching filters on the quality and robustness of the 3D estimate has been also studied. The algorithm has been experimentally validated in different real scenarios where RTABmap maps have been generated.

Next section of this chapter presents the most illustrative localization algorithms. Third section presents the proposed system, describing its steps. Fourth section shows several experiments performed with the implementation of the proposed algorithm. Finally, some conclusions are sum up.

BACKGROUND

First SLAM approaches - known as MonoSLAM - were developed in the 2000s (Davison, 2003), (Davison et al, 2007), and were based on extended Kalman filters that updated camera pose and map elements in each iteration, what increased execution time and limited the number of features tracked.

Afterwards, optimization methods such as PTAM (Klein & Murray, 2007) proved to be more accurate and efficient than filter based approaches, especially when handling thousands of points (Strasdat et al, 2012). The main contribution of this paper was splitting up camera tracking and mapping in two separated threads, becoming aware that real-time was only mandatory for tracking purposes. Most of visual SLAM algorithms have followed PTAM structure, maintaining tracking and mapping separated and focusing on improving accuracy and efficiency.

According to how they extract information from images, SLAM algorithms can be divided into two types: (a) Feature-based (indirect) methods: This method was originally developed in PTAM, extracting features from images and matching them in consecutive frames. Thus, camera motion is obtained minimizing the reprojection error of 3D points. (b) Direct methods: Contrary to feature-based methods, direct methods use directly intensity values in the image and minimizes the photometric error to calculate camera motion. This kind of methods generate denser maps than feature-based methods but are less efficient.

Many SLAM algorithms require using fast processors or even GPUs to work in real time, creating dense maps and achieving low localization errors. However, these algorithms don't behave properly within devices with less computation capabilities, such as cell phones or unmanned aerial vehicles (UAVs).

Parallel Tracking and Mapping (PTAM) (Klein & Murray, 2007) was the first visual SLAM approach capable of handling thousands of 3D points in real-time. This approach extracted features from images using FAST corner detector algorithm (Rosten & Drummond, 2006) and matching these features in different frames to obtain their 3D position. It also proposed a method to efficiently generate and store a 3D map, saving in memory only some important frames (Keyframes). However, the system proposed was quite simple and it wasn't able to manage large scale maps.

Following PTAM main scheme, that is, splitting mapping and tracking, (Strasdat et al, 2011) proposed an algorithm that detected loop closures and could handle large maps, while ORB-SLAM (Mur-Artal et al, 2015) improved accuracy using ORB descriptors (Rublee et al, 2011) instead of FAST features. However, these approaches need fast processors to work in real-time.

Direct methods were first applied to visual SLAM by (Newcombe & Davison, 2010), looking for dense maps instead of feature-based sparse maps created by previous SLAM approaches, but they needed GPUs to work in real-time. Other authors improved efficiency and accuracy using direct methods in following years DTAM (Newcombe et al, 2011) LSD-SLAM (Engel et al, 2014) and specially DSO (Engel et al, 2016), that achieved real-time tracking by reducing map density.

Meanwhile, SVO (Forster et al, 2014) proposed an efficient hybrid method capable of running at double real-time speed in slow processors. However, this algorithm was designed to use down looking cameras, losing camera tracking easily in other situations.

There are several tools with different algorithms used to generate 3D maps: visual-sfm (McCann, 2005), GraphSLAM (Lu & Milios, 1997), (Thrun & Montemerlo, 2006), RTABmap (Labbe & Michaud, 2014), Pix4d (Kung et al., 2011), etc. RTAB-Map (Real-Time Appearance-Based Mapping) (Labbe & Michaud, 2014) is a SLAM algorithm for RGB-D sensors which is based on graphs, on GraphSLAM. Despite GraphSLAM is an offline algorithm, thanks to a new memory management the authors have achieved real time performance (Labbe & Michaud, 2011). In addition, it also allows map building across several sessions, which it is useful for big maps.

RTABmap was chosen to be the baseline of the proposed robust localization system due to several advantages: (a) the project is open source (https://introlab.github.io/rtabmap/), so any modification can be included as well as any additional feature, (b) it includes most of state-of-art localization algorithms, (c) their authors provide a ready-to-use software tool for map building and (d) it has support for several input devices, such as stereo cameras and RGBD sensors. Combining color images and depth information RTABmap computes very accurate position estimations and maps.

In the generated graph the nodes store odometry information for each map place. They also store RGB images, Depth images and visual words (Dorian & Juan, 2012). The edges store rigid 3D transformations between nodes. There are neighbor edges, which are added between two consecutive nodes, and loop closure edges, which are added when the algorithm detects that the camera is in a previously visited place.

For detecting previously visited places a bag-of-words approach (Sivic & Zisserman, 2003) is followed. It employs a Bayesian filter to test the loop closure hypothesis over the set of previous images, computing the likelihood from the SURF (Bay et al, 2008) features as visual words.

For 3D position estimation of a new frame a previous RGB image is selected using the visual words and it is registered with its corresponding depth image. For each 2D feature point its 3D position is computed using the camera intrinsic parameters (K matrix) and the measured depth at that pixel. When a loop closure is detected, the set of feature points matchings is used with RANSAC (Fischler & Bolles, 1981) to compute the rigid 3D rotation and translation. If the number of inliers of that transformation is above a certain threshold, then it is accepted as valid loop closure and a new edge is added to the map.

The obtained graph is optimized with the TORO algorithm (Tree-based netwORk Optimizer) (Stachniss et al, 2007) using nodes and edges as restrictions. When a loop closure is detected some odometry errors may be introduced and propagated through the nodes. TORO algorithm minimizes such errors and improves the graph coherence.

To keep real time operation as the size of the map (the number of nodes) increases, a smart memory organization is included in RTABmap. It has a Short-Term Memory (STM), a Working Memory(WM) and a Long-Term Memory (LTM). New nodes are always inserted in STM which has a bounded maximum size. When such maximum is reached the oldest node is moved to WM. Only the nodes in the WM are considered for loop closure detection, not those on the STM. After a certain period in WM each node is moved to LTM where they are not considered for loop closure detection neither graph optimization. There they are only taken into account when searching for neighbors after a loop closure is detected.

RTABmap tool was developed in C++ language and it is available as a ROS module (http://wiki.ros.org/rtabmap_ros), as a standalone application or as a library. The map building algorithm is completely decoupled from the GUI and other utilities, so it can be used as a library. For instance, it has been ported to Android for use on Tango project from Google. It shows a simple and intuitive graphical user interface which allows the easy generation of 3D maps and continuously provides information about the obtained images, their impact on the map and the reconstruction status. It allows the map generation on several sessions and the fusion of several maps. All the information is stored on a SQLite database for further processing. Several utilities that extend this functionality are available too.

ROBUST 3D VISUAL LOCALIZATION

The proposed system uses a map of the scenario as the baseline, which has to be built before starting the localization. This map is generated with RTABmap tool, which was modified to store on a file the collection of RGBD keyframes and their corresponding 3D locations from where they were taken. In order to speed up the processing, the feature keypoints of each recorded frame are precomputed and also stored on the map file.

The presented localization system works with an input RGB frame and the map. It has three steps as shown if figure 1, that are run iteratively on frames of the input video stream from a moving camera. First, for each new input frame its feature keypoints are computed using SIFT (Lowe, 2004). The second step is to find the most likely keyframe of the map. This second stage consists on a robust matching process which includes an initial kNN 2D matching based on SIFT keypoint similarity. After that, outliers and non-clear matches are rejected using several filters, including epipolar geometric restrictions. All survivor matches have good 2D correspondences and hold the epipolar restrictions. The third step computes a 3D estimation of the camera pose when the input frame was taken. It gets an initial estimation using

Figure 1. Overview of the system stages

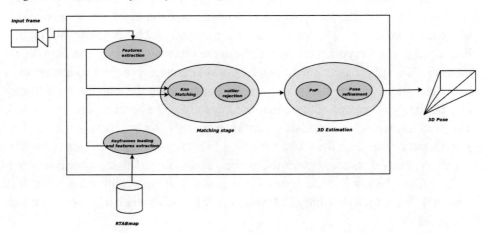

PNP (Lepetit et al, 2009) applied with RANSAC. All the matches included into the RANSAC model are going to be used in the final refinement. Sparse Bundle Adjustment is finally applied in the refinement to get an optimized pose using all the robust matches available at this point.

Keypoints Computation

The first step to include the new camera into the map is computing the keypoints of the input image. SIFT is the main descriptor used for this purpose, but any other descriptor like FAST, ORB, SURF, etc. could be used as well in this stage.

In order to speed up the processing, the feature keypoints of each frame on the baseline map (the RTABmap keyframes) has been also computed during the loading process of the map. All this information is recorded into a file so the descriptors are only being computed during the first time each map is loaded.

Matching

The next step is to decide which keyframe has more similarity with the input image. This similarity is determined by the number of robust matches between the map keyframes and the input image. Each of these matches will be used to compute the position and orientation of the new device so this step is critical in the system. If a wrong keyframe is selected the system will fail, if outliers have been included as good matches the 3D estimation will fail too. This is the reason that several robust methods have been included into this matching stage.

The first restriction is ratio test. Only strong matches will be included as good ones, using the distance between the first matching candidate and the second one as a quality indication. During the matching process, each keypoint from input e image has a set of keypoint candidates from the tentative frame of the map (k-NN matcher). Each of these candidate keypoints has a descriptor so the distance between both descriptors (one on the input frame and the other in the tentative map frame) may be computed to rank all the candidate keypoints. The best keypoint is selected. The ratio test restriction consists on considering only the best keypoint when it is significantly better than the second candidate, that is, only when its clearly the best match. When the distance between the two best candidates is small, no one is selected.

The figure2 shows an example of indecision while matching a keypoint. It is preferable to exclude possible good than include bad ones when it is not clear which one to select.

Up to this point, all the matching process has been performed using only 2D information. No more information has been included so each keypoint has been matched independently. In order to remove more outliers from these successful ratio test keypoints, the geometric information based on epipolar restrictions (Hartley & Zisserman, 2003) is included and applied to the set of keypoints as a whole unit

First, this epipolar restriction is computed by a fundamental matrix estimation. All the survivor keypoints from the ratio test filter are used to compute a fundamental matrix with RANSAC in order to get a good estimation. For each keypoint from one image, its corresponding epipolar line is computed on the second image using the estimated fundamental matrix. If the epipolar line is close enough to its best candidate, the match is labeled as good. On the contrary, if the distance is large the

Figure 2. Matching indecision

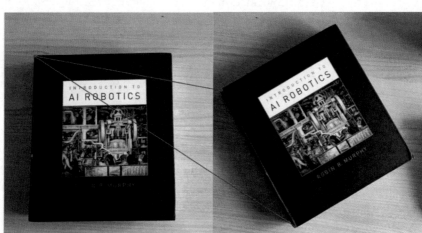

match is discarded. Using this additional restriction, all the keypoints that do not fit into a camera model will be removed.

A second way to apply the related epipolar geometry restriction during the matching stage was also developed. The process here is exactly the same as the explained above but using a homography restriction instead of a fundamental matrix estimation. Depending on the nature of the environment one works better than the other.

3D Estimation

Finally, the closest keyframe is determined as the map keyframe with most robust matches with the input image. Many information is available at this point: the closest keyframe from the baseline map, the position is this closest keyframe and the feature matches between the input image and that keyframe. As the pose of the keyframe is known, the pose the new camera can be estimated using its pose and the robust matches between them.

The system is based on RGBD maps, so combining the pose of the sensor with the depth information we can compute the correspondence between each 2D pixel points to its 3d world point. Given the figure2, where Ik is the kth keypoint of the input image, and pij is its best candidate on the keyframe i, 3d world coordinates to 2D pixel projection can be computed on the input frame as follows: as Pwj projects on Pij and Ik has a robust match with Pij, we can assume that PWj projects on Ik. Using this assumption PnP algorithm is used to initially estimate the pose of the input frame.

Once the pose estimation has been computed all the points that do not fit into this estimated camera model (those points with a high reprojection error) will be ignored. This is the final outlier filtering. At this point we have a set of points that fit into an estimated camera model but not all of them were used to compute the initial 3D estimation as RANSAC computes the "best" model using a subset of the input. In order to adjust the final pose of the camera with all the available information a Bundle Adjustment (BA) optimization (Lourakis & Argyros, 2009). is included in the algorithm. BA uses a Levenberg-Marquardt implementation to minimize the projection error of the whole system given exactly the information available so far, 3D points and their 2D image projections.

EXPERIMENTS

The developed 3D localization system has been experimentally validated in four scenarios. They are spaces of different sizes and cluttered with more or less textured stuff: The RoboticsLab, two office rooms at Rey Juan Carlos University, and a standard room at home. A map of each one was created using the standard RTABmap tool and a Kinect sensor, delivering the maps shown in Figures 3 and 4 (as 3D points collections). The maps are not perfect, as some walls are not orthogonal, but good enough for localization purposes.

The map of the RoboticsLab and the map of an Office are shown here as representative examples. They contain a collection of 274 and 295 RGB-D images (both color and depth) respectively with their corresponding estimated poses. The Office2 map contains 213 images and the Home room map 140.

In order to measure the accuracy of the proposed localization system those maps have been taken as ground truth. For each scenario, there is a loop on every frame of the map, which contains N frames. At each iteration the i-th frame is taken off and a map with the other N-1 frames is built. Such frame is then considered as the input frame and its pose is estimated with the proposed system using that N-1 map. That estimation is compared to its true location, already stored in the N map. Measuring N errors this way the accuracy statistics can be computed, including mean value of the spatial error and percentage of valid or invalid estimations.

The reprojection error is also computed as the difference (in pixels) between (a) the projections of the matched feature points from its true 3D location (available in the map) into the input frame (when the camera placed in the estimated pose) and (b) the pixels on that input frame where those matched feature points were already detected. In case of reprojection error being greater than 100 pixels the estimation is considered invalid.

Figure 3. RTABmap on environment 1

Figure 4. RTABmap on environment 2

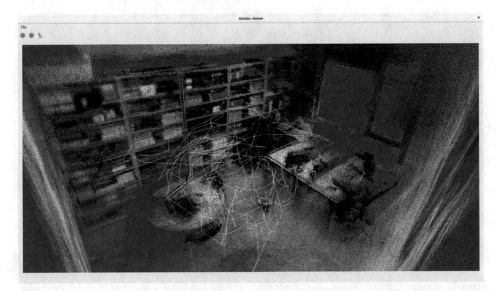

The localization system provides 3D estimations with very low reprojection error. In the table 1 the results of using several outlier rejection mechanisms are compared showing the percentage of valid estimations achieved and the percentage of estimations with low reprojection error within the valid ones.

In addition, a study of the effect of several filters in the outlier rejection, inside matching stage, on the quality of 3D localization estimation has been carried out. Good matches are essential for achieving good 3D pose estimations. The best filter combination is applying both the ratio test and the homography matrix requirements to the candidate matches.

In the right side of the Figures 5,6,7,8 an example of input RGB frame is shown four times. In the left side of the same figures the corresponding most similar image

Table 1. Reprojection error comparison

	%valid estimations				% Reprojection error < 5 pixels			
	Lab	**Home**	**Office**	**Office2**	**Lab**	**Home**	**Office**	**Office2**
Without outlier rejection	6.57	9.29	20.68	14.08	6	0	5	18
Ratio test	77.37	65.71	63.39	53.05	2	2	63	5
Ratio test & Fundamental Matrix	89.42	84.29	83.39	70.90	35	38	39	38
Ratio test & Homograpy Matrix	82.48	77.86	70.17	54.93	85	88	82	78

Figure 5. All matches

Figure 6. Matches filtered with ratio distance filter

Figure 7. Matches filtered with ratio distance filter and fundamental matrix restriction

Figure 8. Matches filtered with ratio distance filter and homografy restrictions

on the map is also shown. It is computed as the one with more successful number of matched feature points with the input frame. The computed matchings are displayed as orange lines across both images. In figure 4, when no outlier rejection at all is used. In figure 5 when using ratio test as outlier rejection. In figure 6 using both ratio test and fundamental matrix filter. In figure 7 using both ratio test and homography matrix filter.

It can be seen that when using no outlier rejection, the system chooses a wrong frame as the most similar one. In figure 6 many matchings are clearly erroneous. In figure 7 the number of false matches is reduced and in figure 7 all the matchings seem to be right. That is the best base to do a good 3D localization estimation.

Another relevant conclusion drawn from the experiments is that the map quality, in terms of density of keyframes in the space and texture in the objects affect the accuracy of the localization algorithm. The higher density of the keyframes the more accurate the 3D estimation is. But the density of keyframes depends on the map building algorithm and on the texture of the stuff in the scenario.

CONCLUSION

We have designed and developed a robust method to localize in 3D a new camera inside a known map, which was previously built with the well-known RTABmap tool. The method is based on feature matching using only RGB information, PnP registration and optimization. The robustness of the method relies on the combination of different restrictions to filter the raw matches and reject outliers. First, the ratio test measuring the quality of the matchings and comparing the best two candidates. Only when their qualities are quite different the best one is accepted. Second, epipolar restrictions, which are expressed through the fundamental matrix or through an homography matrix.

The proposed system has been implemented and experimentally validated in four environments. All the code of the system is open source and it is available in GitHub. The experiments show that the algorithm provides accurate results, with more than 80% estimations with reprojection errors below 5 pixels. In addition, the effect of three outlier rejection filters in the matching stage on the quality of the 3D estimations has been measured. The best filter combination is applying both the ratio test and the homography matrix restrictions to the candidate matches. It reduces the number of accepted matchings but their quality is high and so the final 3D camera estimation computed from them is more reliable.

As future lines, one way to improve the current system is to use more than a single keyframe during the 3D pose estimation stage. The idea is to select the n keyframes most similar to the input image, use their 2D matchings and optimize the 2D pixel projections from more than a single image to extract the 3D estimation. Introducing this enhancement will improve the accuracy of the initial PnP estimation. It will also improve the Bundle Adjustment optimization as more than one single view is going to be used to optimize the final system.

In addition, we are also working on speeding up the algorithm in order to keep real time operation even on low end computers like those onboard drones.

REFERENCES

Bay, H., Ess, A., Tuytelaars, T., & Van Gool, L. (2008, June). Speeded-up robust features (surf). *Computer Vision and Image Understanding*, *110*(3), 346–359. doi:10.1016/j.cviu.2007.09.014

Davison, A. J. (2003). Real-time simultaneous localisation and mapping with a single camera. In *Proceedings of the ninth ieee international conference on computer vision* (vol. 2, pp. 1403). Washington, DC: IEEE Computer Society. doi:10.1109/ICCV.2003.1238654

Davison, A. J., Reid, I. D., Molton, N. D., & Stasse, O. (2007, June). Monoslam: Real-time single camera slam. *IEEE Transactions on Pattern Analysis and Machine Intelligence*, *29*(6), 1052–1067. doi:10.1109/TPAMI.2007.1049 PMID:17431302

Dellaert, F., Burgard, W., Fox, D., & Thrun, S. (1999). Using the CONDENSATION algorithm for robust, vision-based mobile robot localization. In *Proceedings. 1999 IEEE computer society conference on computer vision and pattern recognition (cat. no pr00149)* (Vol. 2, pp. 588–594). Fort Collins, CO: IEEE Comput. Soc. doi:10.1109/CVPR.1999.784976

Dorian, G.-L., & Juan, D. T. (2012). Bags of binary words for fast place recognition in image sequences. IEEE Transactions on Robotics.

Engel, J., Koltun, V., & Cremers, D. (2016). *Direct sparse odometry.* CoRR.

Engel, J., Schops, T., & Cremers, D. (2014, September). *LSD-SLAM: Large Scale Direct Monocular SLAM.* In European conference on computer vision, Zurich, Switzerland.

Fischler, M. A., & Bolles, R. C. (1981, June). Random sample consensus: A paradigm for model fitting with applications to image analysis and automated cartography. *Communications of the ACM, 24*(6), 381–395. doi:10.1145/358669.358692

Forster, C., Pizzoli, M., & Scaramuzza, D. (2014). SVO: Fast semi-direct monocular visual odometry. IEEE international conference on robotics and automation (icra). doi:10.1109/ICRA.2014.6906584

Hartley, R., & Zisserman, A. (2003). *Multiple view geometry in computer vision* (2nd ed.). New York: Cambridge University Press.

Klein, G., & Murray, D. (2007). Parallel tracking and mapping for small ar workspaces. In *Proceedings of the 2007 6th IEEE and ACM international symposium on mixed and augmented reality* (pp. 1–10). Washington, DC: IEEE Computer Society.

Küng, O., Strecha, C., Beyeler, A., Zufferey, J.-C., Floreano, D., Fua, P., & Gervaix, F. (2011). The accuracy of automatic photogrammetric techniques on ultra-light uav imagery. ISPRS -. *The International Archives of the Photogrammetry, Remote Sensing and Spatial Information Sciences, 38*(C22), 125–130.

Labbe, M., & Michaud, F. (2011). Memory management for real-time appearance-based loop closure detection. In *IROS* (pp. 1271–1276). IEEE. doi:10.1109/IROS.2011.6094602

Labbe, M., & Michaud, F. (2014). Online global loop closure detection for large scale multi-session graph-based SLAM. *2014 IEEE/RSJ international conference on intelligent robots and systems,* 2661–2666. doi:10.1109/IROS.2014.6942926

Lepetit, V., Moreno-Noguer, F., & Fua, P. (2009, February). Epnp: An accurate o(n) solution to the pnp problem. *International Journal of Computer Vision*, *81*(2), 155–166.

Lourakis, M. I. A., & Argyros, A. A. (2009, March). Sba: a software package for generic sparse bundle adjustment. *ACM Trans. Math. Softw.*, *36*(1), 2:1–2:30.

Lowe, D. G. (2004, November). Distinctive image features from scale-invariant keypoints. *International Journal of Computer Vision*, *60*(2), 91–110. doi:10.1023/B:VISI.0000029664.99615.94

Lu, F., & Milios, E. (1997, October). Globally consistent range scan alignment for environment mapping. *Autonomous Robots*, *4*(4), 333–349. doi:10.1023/A:1008854305733

McCann, S. (2005). *3d reconstruction from multiple images*. Academic Press.

Mur-Artal, R., Montiel, J. M. M., & Tardos, J. D. (2015). *Orb-slam: a versatile and accurate monocular slam system*. CoRR, abs/1502.00956.

Newcombe, R. A., & Davison, A. J. (2010). Live dense reconstruction with a single moving camera. IEEE conference on computer vision and pattern recognition. doi:10.1109/CVPR.2010.5539794

Newcombe, R. A., Lovegrove, S. J., & Davison, A. J. (2011). Dtam: dense tracking and mapping in real-time. In *Proceedings of the 2011 international conference on computer vision* (pp. 2320–2327). Washington, DC: IEEE Computer Society. doi:10.1109/ICCV.2011.6126513

Rosten, E., & Drummond, T. (2006). Machine learning for high-speed corner detection. In *Proceedings of the 9th European conference on computer vision* (pp. 430–443). Springer-Verlag. doi:10.1007/11744023_34

Rublee, E., Rabaud, V., Konolige, K., & Bradski, G. (2011). Orb: an efficient alternative to sift or surf. In *Proceedings of the 2011 international conference on computer vision* (pp. 2564–2571). Washington, DC: IEEE Computer Society. doi:10.1109/ICCV.2011.6126544

Sivic, J., & Zisserman, A. (2003, October). Video Google: A text retrieval approach to object matching in videos. *Proceedings of the international conference on computer vision*, 2, 1470–1477. doi:10.1109/ICCV.2003.1238663

Strasdat, H., Davison, A. J., Montiel, J. M. M., & Konolige, K. (2011). Double window optimisation for constant time visual slam. In *Proceedings of the 2011 international conference on computer vision* (pp. 2352–2359). Washington, DC: IEEE Computer Society. doi:10.1109/ICCV.2011.6126517

Strasdat, H., Montiel, J. M. M., & Davison, A. J. (2012, February). Editors choice article: visual slam: why filter? *Image and Vision Computing*, *30*(2), 65–77. doi:10.1016/j.imavis.2012.02.009

Thrun, S., Fox, D., Burgard, W., & Dellaert, F. (2001). Robust Monte Carlo localization for mobile robots. *Artificial Intelligence*, *128*(1-2), 99–141. doi:10.1016/S0004-3702(01)00069-8

Thrun, S., & Montemerlo, M. (2006, May). The graph slam algorithm with applications to large-scale mapping of urban structures. *The International Journal of Robotics Research*, *25*(5-6), 403–429. doi:10.1177/0278364906065387

Chapter 2
Object Recognition Pipeline:
Grasping in Domestic Environments

John Alejandro Castro Vargas
University of Alicante, Spain

Alberto Garcia Garcia
University of Alicante, Spain

Sergiu Oprea
University of Alicante, Spain

Sergio Orts Escolano
University of Alicante, Spain

Jose Garcia Rodriguez
University of Alicante, Spain

ABSTRACT

Object grasping in domestic environments using social robots has an enormous potential to help dependent people with a certain degree of disability. In this chapter, the authors make use of the well-known Pepper social robot to carry out such task. They provide an integrated solution using ROS to recognize and grasp simple objects. That system was deployed on an accelerator platform (Jetson TX1) to be able to perform object recognition in real time using RGB-D sensors attached to the robot. By using the system, the authors prove that the Pepper robot shows a great potential for such domestic assistance tasks.

DOI: 10.4018/978-1-5225-5628-2.ch002

INTRODUCTION

Nowadays, social assistant robots have become a way of improving people's quality of life in modern societies by performing domestic tasks. Life expectancy is in continuous growth, causing an increase in the average age of the population. For this reason, the assistance of elderly people becomes a priority for developed countries, which consider social robot assistance as a good initiative for helping dependent persons. This technological approach provides an alternative to the use of qualified human personnel, reducing economic costs in the long term.

A social assistance robot could perform different tasks such as object detection (identify a particular object from the scene), object grasping (with the purpose of bringing objects to the user), interaction with the user by means of gesture and speech recognition, and programmed actions like home cleaning. However, it is very common to design different robots for each particular task instead of integrating all tasks in the same one. Therefore, we consider that a robot equipped with arms and hands would be capable of performing both recognition and grasping tasks. Following this idea, in this project we will perform object recognition alongside grasping tasks in unstructured environments. To that end, we will leverage a humanoid robot such as Pepper designed for social assistance.

Manipulating an object without knowing its position and pose is not straightforward and implies the use of techniques from different areas. On the one hand, an object recognition process is needed in order to detect the objects in the scene. That system must provide information about object positions and orientations. This problem has been addressed in several works, mainly using RGB cameras alongside depth information in order to obtain a partial reconstruction of the environment which can be used to recognize objects. On the other hand, once positions and orientations are known, the hands and arms of the robot have to be moved with the purpose of grabbing the target object. This process is not straightforward since many problems regarding both the object (different texture, size, weight, or shape) and the variation of robot arms and hands degrees of freedom must be solved.

BACKGROUND

Object recognition is the process by which objects are detected in images, obtaining information related to their position and orientation in the scene (Garcia-Garcia et al., 2016). There are several approaches for this purpose but we will emphasize those ones which are based on local features since they are more robust in unstructured environments with occlusions. These techniques extract representative local features from both the scene and the models and then allowing identify those model objects by matching the extracted features.

The classical pipeline for object recognition based on local features is three-staged (Guo et al., 2014). First, several keypoints are detected in order to extract representative information from the scene. This will improve the computational cost of the pipeline by processing and discarding ambiguous regions that do not provide important information. Next, the neighborhoods of those keypoints are described for the training or matching stage by encoding them into descriptors (Bronstein et al., 2010). Finally, correspondences between descriptors from the scene and the model objects are obtained. This last stage of the recognition pipeline can be further divided into three steps (Guo et al., 2014): (1) matching or correspondence search, frequently using techniques like Nearest Neighbor (NN) to match the descriptors, (2) hypothesis generation, obtaining a transformation from the object model to the possibly detected object in the scene, and (3) verification, to determine if the obtained transformation is valid for the model and the hypothesis.

In the literature, grasping methods are classified into two categories (Bohg et al., 2014): analytical and empirical. In the analytical approaches, physical formulations are applied in order to synthesize grasp points (Bicchi and Kumar, 2000). Otherwise, in the case of empirical solutions, mathematical and physical models are used allowing the system to learn from simulations or a real robot (Kamon et al., 1996).

This work is focused on empirical approaches in order to automatically obtain grasp points by using 3D registered object models. A grasp point is normally parametrized by the point on which the center of the tool should be aligned with the object, the vector describing the orientation (3D angles) of the tool to be approached to the grasp point, the orientation of the robot wrist, and an initial configuration of the fingers.

Grasping methods can be evaluated and tested by using several simulation tools such as Graspit! (Miller and Allen, 2004) and OpenRave (Diankov and Kuffner, 2008) among others.

Of the broad set containing different ways of holding a particular object, methods for synthesizing grasp points aim to choose a good subset of possible grips. Those grasping methods can be classified according to the amount of information regarding the object to be grasped (Bohg et al., 2014): *known objects* (a complete model of the object is available), *familiar objects* (grasping points are estimated by using information of similar known objects), and *unknown objects* (focused on estimating the object geometry in order to calculate grasping points).

This work is focused on known objects, applying heuristic models to the information provided by a 3D sensor. Therefore, we will be focused on synthesizing grasping points for known objects. That synthesis goes through a process of experience generation and it can be performed in several different ways: Using 3D object models. Simple geometric shapes such as spheres, cylinders, or cones are usually approximated to the 3D model of the object. Based on those shapes, contact points (Miller and Allen, 2004) are calculated. Another possible approximation is obtaining a bounding box of the object and then estimate normals of approximation on its surface (Diankov, 2010); Learning from human-made grasping examples (Ekvall and Kragic, 2007); Trial and error learning. Instead of using the gripping set as fixed positions, these techniques try to refine the grip by trial and error. In this case, reinforcement learning is applied to improve the initial estimation (Kroemer et al., 2010).

GRASPING SYSTEM

The grasping system consists of two parts: a module for object recognition and pose estimation and another for grasp points synthesis and arm control.

Object Recognition and Pose Estimation

The object recognition pipeline we choose for our robotic platform was the one presented by Garcia-Garcia *et al.* (Garcia-Garcia et al., 2016). This base implementation was chosen due to the fact that it was able to run in near real time to recognize objects in 3D. In our work, the pipeline has been implemented using ROS to publish pose information to topics which then will be used by the grasping process.

The pipeline is able recognize objects in cluttered and occluded scenes and perform accurate pose estimation. The process is divided into six main stages: keypoint extraction, descriptor extraction, feature matching, correspondence grouping, instance alignment and hypothesis verification. We can see a diagram of this process in figure1.

Figure 1. Object recognition pipeline (Garcia-Garcia et al., 2017)

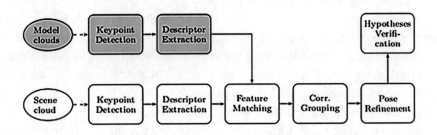

Uniform Sampling is used in the first step to detect keypoints because of its simplicity and speed. After that, SHOT (Signatures of Histograms of Orientations) (Tombari et al., 2010) descriptors are used to describe the neighborhood of each keypoint.

The matching process consists of finding the nearest neighbor to a certain descriptor in terms of Euclidean distance between them. This process is carried out by using an approximate and parallelized neighbor search using FLANN. As a result, several correspondences are obtained although not all of them are ensured to correspond with the actual object in the scene. A grouping step with *Geometric Consistency Grouping* is applied to generate object hypotheses by enforcing certain geometric constraints to clusters of correspondences.

After that, the transformations obtained with *Geometric Consistency Grouping* (GCG) are used to get a coarse estimation of the position and orientation of each object instance. Those estimations are refined using the *Iterative Closest Point* (ICP) algorithm.

In the end, various hypotheses are generated. However, some of them could be false positives which need to be filtered. In this sense, *Global Hypothesis Verification* (Aldoma et al., 2012) (GHV) is used to verify all model hypotheses simultaneously and filter out those which do not fit the scene points properly.

Model Processing

Object models are loaded into two vectors. One of them contains point positions and colors (XYZRGB) and the other one contains normals that have been estimated in an offline process. This data is processed in three steps: preprocessing, keypoint detection, and descriptor extraction.

We can perform two actions during the preprocessing step. It is possible to apply a downsampling process with voxel grids to increase efficiency. In addition, we can compute the cloud resolution, i.e., the average distance between each cloud point and its nearest neighbor. This number is useful to get a reference to make the pipeline invariant to distance up to a certain degree. This way, any other parameter for the rest of the pipeline can be expressed as a factor of the cloud resolution instead of hardcoding them which would make them unable to generalize well to various models.

In the next steps, keypoints and descriptors are extracted using *Uniform Sampling* and SHOT respectively. It is important to notice that keypoints and descriptors are calculated only one time at the beginning of the pipeline process and stored for later use, thus saving computational resources for the online execution. Other parameters are loaded and stored at the beginning to use them in future processes. These parameters are: the radius used in keypoint extraction step, the radius used in the descriptor extraction step, a radius for the local reference frame, the cluster size to use in the grouping step, a threshold to validate the cluster and a threshold applied in the hypotheses verification step. These parameters will be use with the corresponding model in the step where they are needed.

Scene Processing, Matching and Verification

Scenes are processed in the same way as the models; however, the whole pipeline has to be executed online for them. The pipeline considers applying certain preprocessing steps such as bilateral filtering, downsampling, plane removal and scene simplification with *Organized Multi Plane Segmentation* (OMPS) and *Organized Connected Components Segmentation* (OCCS), and also compute the cloud resolution.

Next, keypoints and descriptors are calculated with uniform sampling and SHOT too. These descriptors are matched with the precomputed ones from the object models. In the end, the pose is estimated by clustering the matched correspondences with GCG and refining the results with ICP plus the final hypothesis verification step.

Grasping

As we stated before, we are interested in checking the possibility of using the Pepper robot in grasping tasks. To that end, a method to automatically generate grasping points has been used.

Specifically, we used the method proposed by Diankov (Diankov, 2010) which is implemented in the OpenRave (Diankov and Kuffner, 2008) toolkit. That method estimates normals above model surfaces from a simple geometric shape as a bounding-box or a sphere. Those normals are then used to approach the end-effector in simulation and check if the grasp is satisfactory.

We have used the URDF (*Unified Robot Description Format*) file available in ROS repositories and the *collada_urdf* package to get a compatible file for OpenRave. The file we get is in DAE format, which needs to be configured with another XML file to specify the available end-effectors of the robot, the approach orientation of the hand, and the closing orientation of the fingers.

It is important to remark that the Pepper's hand (figure2) contains five fingers which are powered by only one actuator. When the hand is opened, the joints between phalanges have a maximum angle of 50 degrees (figure3). When the hand is closed, this angle is reduced to zero degrees. This hand architecture poses some problems with the OpenRave algorithm. During training, the hand closes each finger one by one with one increment. When a collision is detected, the joint stops the movement and moves to another joint. At this point, the algorithm stops because Pepper's hand only has one actuator that moves every finger, but in the real robot we have a margin to continue closing the hand. To simulate this effect, we have added additional joints in the robot hand inside the configuration file. The joints that we have added imitate the phalanges movement of the fingers. To that end, we specified the features of each joint and added the joints in the manipulator definition.

Figure 2. Pepper's hand fingers
Source: Official Pepper website documentation

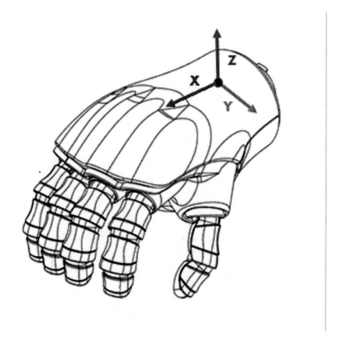

Figure 3. Closing angles of Pepper's fingers
Source: Official Pepper website documentation

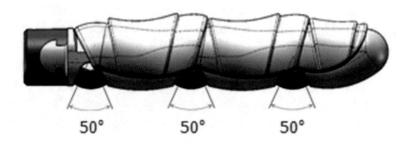

EXPERIMENTS

In this work, we have used various software tools and hardware that enabled us to tackle both recognition and grasping problems.

The software tools and hardware that have been used in this work are constrained by the Pepper robotic platform. Pepper is a humanoid robot designed by the company Aldebaran Robotics. The robot is capable of interacting with the environment and identify emotions on people around the robot. Its equipment and functionalities make it a perfect tool for working and create interaction in environments with people that require some guidance (supermarket, bank, museum, etcetera). The robot can receive voice commands through four microphones located in the head, it has two RGB cameras, a Kinect-based sensor and three tactile sensors.

The development of the system required an intensive use of robot arms and visual sensors, such as the RGB-D camera on its forehead. In order to orchestrate that flow of information we used ROS. ROS (Robot Operating System) is an open source framework used for software development in robotics. It is designed to work as a distributed system, allowing the possibility of distributing the functionalities of the robot to different nodes and at the same time these nodes on different machines. ROS has a set of libraries and tools that abstract its functionalities from the hardware at the same time that it implements controllers for compatible devices. Among its variety of tools and utilities it includes: visualizers, message passing protocol and a simulator. We will make use of the MoveIt! tool integrated inside ROS repository to control arms movement by sending messages across different nodes.

Information obtained from the camera was used by an object recognition pipeline with the main purpose of identifying objects in the scene. In order to speedup the execution of the whole pipeline, we took advantage of CUDA and massive parallel processors like the GPU from the Jetson TX1 (Garcia-Garcia et al., 2017). The Jetson TX1 is a development module built by NVIDIA that enables GPU application development on mobile platforms. Its reduced dimensions and power consumption turn this embedded hardware into an ideal platform for developing mobile robotics solutions.

Additionally, we want to evaluate Pepper's capabilities to perform tasks that require object handling. For this purpose, there are several options: GraspIt!, OpenGrasp and OpenRAVE. We have used OpenRAVE given its powerful simulator and its available tools for computing inverse kinematics and interaction points. Openrave (Open Robotics Automation Virtual Environment) provides a set of utilities to develop motion planning algorithms. Among its applications we have the possibility to generate datasets by selecting points oriented to grasping tasks and to accelerate the calculations for the inverse kinematics with IKfast. By using IKFast, it is possible to accelerate the inverse kinematics calculations to five microseconds, automatically generating, in C++ language, optimal equations for robotic structures of different complexities.

Object Recognition

The object recognition system was tested using the multi-sensor 3D object dataset which provides pose information by Garcia-Garcia *et al.* (Garcia-Garcia et al., 2017). In this section, we shown an example trying to recognize one object model that can be easily grabbed by the Pepper: a foam dice.

Pipeline parameters have been tuned for each model to achieve maximum performance. In this case, *Uniform Sampling* has been configured to obtain more keypoints from the dice model than from the scene in order to obtain many descriptors along the model's borders but keep computational cost at bay at the same time. Figure 4 and figure 5 shows the keypoint detection results.

Figure 4. Keypoints detected on the dice object model

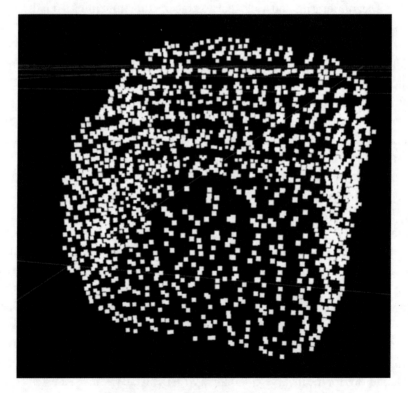

Figure 5. Keypoints detected on a scene where the very same dice appears

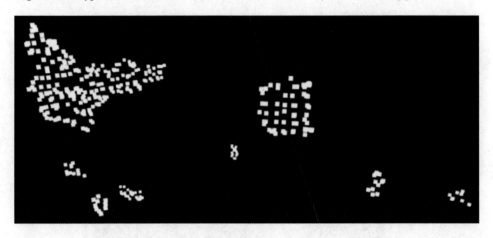

Grasping

We performed experiments with two objects to test the ability of the robot to grasp simple shapes: a sphere and a cylinder.

The sphere size was selected according to the robot's hand constraint. An XML file was defined with the OpenRave format to generate a sphere with a radius of 2.5 cm and placed it on top of a 3D table model. Next, the script was configured to generate grasping points by targeting the sphere we created using a spherical model to estimate normals on the object.

At the end of the training, 1476 grasping points were obtained and we tested its operation by means of a simulation.

The first step is to obtain the valid grasping points from the position of the robot (Figure 6) to reach the target. Subsequently, we obtain a point of attachment from the attainable set of grasp points obtained. Next, we prepare the hand to move it to the target position (Figure 7) and move the arm to the gripping position (Figure 8). Finally, to grasp the object, the robot arm should approach a normal direction to the object before closing the fingers. However, since the robot arm consists of five degrees of freedom, linear motion cannot be performed.

In the case of the cylinder, the dimensions chosen to fit the hand were 15.5 cm in height and 1.75 cm in radius. The model used to estimate the normals of approximation was also a sphere.

Figure 6. Initial position

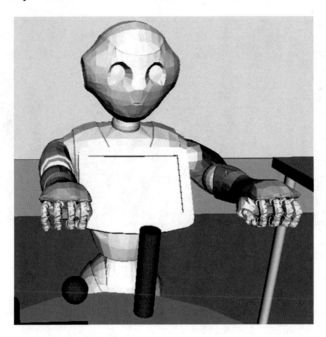

Figure 7. Preshape position

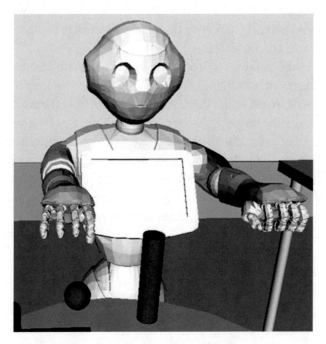

Figure 8. Target position

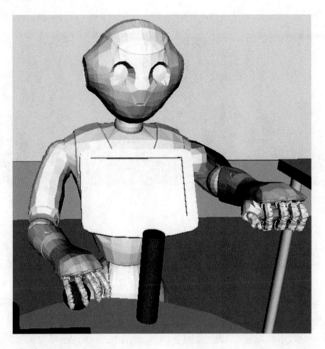

From the training step we got 279 grasping points. However, we did not get enough points to grab the object, even though they have complied with the imposed force-closure restriction (see figure 9).

CONCLUSION

In this work, an object recognition and grasping system has been developed, integrated and deployed on the Pepper social robot as first step towards a domestic robot assistant.

The recognition system has been successfully implemented and accelerated on Jetson TX1 platform which can be easily attached to the robot. From an architectural standpoint, it has been implemented as a ROS node that can be easily used with RGB-D cameras, including the camera of the Pepper robot. Using that node, we were able to obtain object poses in real time. This node can be reused in many robotic tasks, in our case as a first phase of pose estimation for grasping.

Furthermore, a brief analysis of the robot's ability to perform grasping tasks has been carried out. OpenRave was used as a tool for automatic generation of grasping

Figure 9. The subset of grasp points generated with OpenRave to grasp a cylinder with pepper can be observed

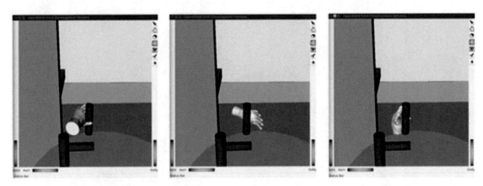

points with custom joint definitions for the Pepper's hand. In this regard, we can conclude that the whole system works reasonably well for simple objects of an appropriate size for the robot's hand. However, the robot itself has many limitations regarding the degrees of freedom, the size, and the shapes of the hands and the arms which impose many constraints to object positions, poses, sizes, and shapes.

Following on this work, we plan to check alternatives for obtaining grasping points by using 5DOF arms or approaching the hand to the object by using an inverse kinematic solver that ignores the orientation of the end-effector-link. Another possible addition could be to accelerate the rest of the object recognition pipeline stages obtaining in this way, a fully accelerated 3D object recognition pipeline.

ACKNOWLEDGMENT

This work has been funded by the Spanish Government TIN2016-76515-R grant for the COMBAHO project, supported with Feder funds; and the University of Alicante project GRE16-19.

REFERENCES

Aldoma, A., Tombari, F., Di Stefano, L., & Vincze, M. (2012). A global hypotheses verification method for 3d object recognition. *Computer Vision–ECCV, 2012*, 511–524.

Bicchi, A., & Kumar, V. (2000). Robotic grasping and contact: A review. In *Robotics and Automation, 2000. Proceedings. ICRA'00. IEEE International Conference on* (vol. 1, pp. 348–353). IEEE. doi:10.1109/ROBOT.2000.844081

Bohg, J., Morales, A., Asfour, T., & Kragic, D. (2014). Data-driven grasp synthesisa survey. *IEEE Transactions on Robotics*, *30*(2), 289–309. doi:10.1109/TRO.2013.2289018

Bronstein, A., Bronstein, M., & Ovsjanikov, M. (2010). 3d features, surface descriptors, and object descriptors. *3D Imaging, Analysis, and Applications*.

Diankov, R. (2010). *Automated Construction of Robotic Manipulation Programs* (PhD thesis). Carnegie Mellon University, Robotics Institute.

Diankov, R., & Kuffner, J. (2008). *Openrave: A planning architecture for autonomous robotics*. Robotics Institute, Pittsburgh, PA, Tech. Rep. CMU-RI-TR-08-34, 79

Ekvall, S., & Kragic, D. (2007). Learning and evaluation of the approach vector for automatic grasp generation and planning. In *Robotics and Automation, 2007 IEEE International Conference on* (pp. 4715–4720). IEEE. doi:10.1109/ROBOT.2007.364205

Garcia-Garcia, A., Orts-Escolano, S., Garcia-Rodriguez, J., & Cazorla, M. (2016). Interactive 3d object recognition pipeline on mobile gpgpu computing platforms using low-cost rgb-d sensors. *Journal of Real-Time Image Processing*, 1–20.

Garcia-Garcia, A., Orts-Escolano, S., Oprea, S., Garcia-Rodriguez, J., Azorin-Lopez, J., Saval-Calvo, M., & Cazorla, M. (2017). Multi-sensor 3d object dataset for object recognition with full pose estimation. *Neural Computing & Applications*, *28*(5), 941–952. doi:10.1007/s00521-016-2224-9

Guo, Y., Bennamoun, M., Sohel, F., Lu, M., & Wan, J. (2014). 3d object recognition in cluttered scenes with local surface features: A survey. *IEEE Transactions on Pattern Analysis and Machine Intelligence*, *36*(11), 2270–2287. doi:10.1109/TPAMI.2014.2316828 PMID:26353066

Kamon, I., Flash, T., & Edelman, S. (1996). Learning to grasp using visual information. In *Robotics and Automation, 1996. Proceedings., 1996 IEEE International Conference on* (vol. 3, pp. 2470–2476). IEEE. doi:10.1109/ROBOT.1996.506534

Kroemer, O., Detry, R., Piater, J., & Peters, J. (2010). Combining active learning and reactive control for robot grasping. *Robotics and Autonomous Systems*, *58*(9), 1105–1116. doi:10.1016/j.robot.2010.06.001

Miller, A. T., & Allen, P. K. (2004). Graspit! a versatile simulator for robotic grasping. *IEEE Robotics & Automation Magazine*, *11*(4), 110–122. doi:10.1109/MRA.2004.1371616

Tombari, F., Salti, S., & Di Stefano, L. (2010). Unique signatures of histograms for local surface description. In *European Conference on Computer Vision* (pp. 356–369). Springer. doi:10.1007/978-3-642-15558-1_26

ADDITIONAL READING

Asada, H. (1979). *Studies on prehension and handling by robot hands with elastic fingers*. University of Kyoto.

Catalano, M. G., Grioli, G., Serio, A., Farnioli, E., Piazza, C., & Bicchi, A. (2012). Adaptive synergies for a humanoid robot hand. In *Humanoid Robots (Humanoids), 2012 12th IEEE-RAS International Conference on*, pages 7–14. IEEE. doi:10.1109/HUMANOIDS.2012.6651492

Fanello, S. R., Pattacini, U., Gori, I., Tikhanoff, V., Randazzo, M., Roncone, A., . . . Metta, G. (2014). 3d stereo estimation and fully automated learning of eye-hand coordination in humanoid robots. In *Humanoid Robots (Humanoids), 2014 14th IEEE-RAS International Conference on*, pages 1028–1035. IEEE.

Flandin, G., Chaumette, F., & Marchand, E. (2000). Eye-in-hand/eye-to-hand cooperation for visual servoing. In *Robotics and Automation, 2000. Proceedings. ICRA'00. IEEE International Conference on*, volume 3, pages 2741–2746. IEEE.

Frome, A., Huber, D., Kolluri, R., Bülow, T., & Malik, J. (2004). Recognizing Objects in Range Data Using Regional Point Descriptors, pages 224–237. Springer Berlin Heidelberg, Berlin, Heidelberg. doi:10.1007/978-3-540-24672-5_18

Ho, H. T., & Gibbins, D. (2008). Multi-scale feature extraction for 3d surface registration using local shape variation. In *Image and Vision Computing New Zealand, 2008. IVCNZ 2008. 23rd International Conference*, pages 1–6. IEEE.

Mian, A., Bennamoun, M., & Owens, R. (2010). On the repeatability and quality of keypoints for local feature-based 3d object retrieval from cluttered scenes. *International Journal of Computer Vision*, *89*(2), 348–361. doi:10.1007/s11263-009-0296-z

Miller, A. T., Knoop, S., Christensen, H. I., & Allen, P. K. (2003). Automatic grasp planning using shape primitives. In *Robotics and Automation, 2003. Proceedings. ICRA'03. IEEE International Conference on*, volume 2, pages 1824–1829. IEEE. doi:10.1109/ROBOT.2003.1241860

Nguyen, V.-D. (1988). Constructing force-closure grasps. *The International Journal of Robotics Research*, 7(3), 3–16. doi:10.1177/027836498800700301

Trevor, A. J., Gedikli, S., Rusu, R. B., & Christensen, H. I. (2013). *Efficient organized point cloud segmentation with connected components. Semantic Perception Mapping and Exploration*. SPME.

KEY TERMS AND DEFINITIONS

Descriptor: They are algorithms that allow describing areas from characteristic points. They allow comparisons of different characteristics obtained to estimate a similarity.

Grasp: Action to catch something.

Humanoid: It is a structure that looks similar to a human.

Keypoint: It is a local and significant point in a surface area.

Pipeline: Referring to a system that does many actions to get a result.

Pose: It is the information that describes the position and orientation in the space of an object.

Sampling: It is the selection of representative elements of a group that allow the description or study of the whole.

Chapter 3
Towards Intelligent Human Behavior Detection for Video Surveillance

Swati Nigam
SP Memorial Institute of Technology, India

Rajiv Singh
Banasthali University, India

A. K. Misra
SP Memorial Institute of Technology, India

ABSTRACT

Computer vision techniques are capable of detecting human behavior from video sequences. Several state-of-the-art techniques have been proposed for human behavior detection and analysis. However, a collective framework is always required for intelligent human behavior analysis. Therefore, in this chapter, the authors provide a comprehensive understanding towards human behavior detection approaches. The framework of this chapter is based on human detection, human tracking, and human activity recognition, as these are the basic steps of human behavior detection process. The authors provide a detailed discussion over the human behavior detection framework and discuss the feature-descriptor-based approach. Furthermore, they have provided qualitative and quantitative analysis for the detection framework and demonstrate the results for human detection, human tracking, and human activity recognition.

DOI: 10.4018/978-1-5225-5628-2.ch003

INTRODUCTION

Human behavior detection is the process of recognizing human body movements and actions. Extensive efforts have been made for intelligent human behavior detection; still it is a challenging area in computer vision research (Forsyth and Ponce, 2011; Sonka et al., 2014). Due to the emergence of interactive multimedia systems, intelligent video surveillance has become popular in applications such as security, smart homes, clinical applications, biometric applications, human robot interaction, entertainment and education (Porikli et al., 2013; Chang et al., 2014; Zhang et al., 2015; Huang et al., 2014; Hanna and Hoyos, 2017; Yumak et al., 2014; Thompson et al., 2016). This wide range of applications shows that human behavior detection is a significant area of research in computer vision particularly for intelligent video surveillance systems.

A lot of organizations, whether they are private or government, pay attention to visual surveillance systems for security point of view. There are many surveillance systems employed in various places like airports, train stations, shopping malls, as well as private residential areas. For a video surveillance system, analysis and understanding of human behavior are the most important features. Many such schemes have been proposed in the meanwhile (Choujaa and Dulay, 2008; Kuryloski et al., 2009; Luo et al., 2007; Collins et al., 2000; Zajdel et al., 2007). Human behavior analysis systems provide a real-time performance and sufficiently high accuracy for the automatic surveillance systems. Simple and fast surveillance systems have been employed for the analysis of abnormal human behavior like sudden stopping, disappearing from a scene, climbing on a wall and falling. The automatic 3D human behavior monitoring systems have more potential for many other types of behaviors too. There are two types of surveillance systems. First type of systems record video events for later analysis whereas second type of systems simultaneously detect and analyze those events for faster reaction. The security systems have also much importance in security control in homely environment. Incorporating artificial intelligence with surveillance, smart surveillance systems obtain particular information about structure and appearance of people and produce much correct result. Furthermore, they are able to discriminate between normal and suspicious events.

Significance of intelligent video surveillance systems is increasing for many reasons. The most important reason is that these systems minimize human factors which reduce the performance to detect security breaches. For example, with human operators there exist several limitations on the number of scenes monitored simultaneously. Moreover, the human operator's concentration may drop suddenly. These limitations caused by human intervention have been overcome by the intelligent video surveillance systems. However, the 9/11 terrorist attacks in USA and 26/11 terrorist attacks in Mumbai, India have indicated the necessity for improvement in existing systems for automatic monitoring of suspicious human behavior. Therefore, an intelligent human behavior analysis and understanding is required that can detect and track humans and identify their normal and abnormal behavior.

The most common devices used for human behavior detection are sensors and cameras. According to position of sensors and cameras, behavior detection systems can be termed as sensor based systems and vision based systems (Gonzàlez et al., 2012). However, vision based systems are quite popular because they provide more important cues for behavior detection. From a review's point of view, many researchers have presented their reviews on human behavior detection. Based on these reviews, the human behavior detection approaches can be divided into two categories: model based and model free. In model based approaches (Wang & Mori, 2011; Lan et al., 2012; Cheng et al., 2014), a prior shape model is constructed for behavior detection. These 2D and 3D explicit shape models are used to recognize human subjects and their behaviors. Model free approaches (Vrigkas et al., 2014; Määttä et al., 2010; Matikainen et al., 2011; Souvenir et al., 2008) overcome the drawbacks of model based approaches. In the model-free approaches, features are extracted from videos for behavior detection. These features are low-level visual features from the region of interest.

An intelligent human behavior detection framework includes human object detection and tracking followed by activity recognition. Since, the framework includes three consecutive modules; therefore, it is important to reduce computational complexity and provide solution of human motion analysis. For this purpose a number of feature descriptors have been used like histogram of oriented gradients (HOG), local binary patterns (LBP) and its variants, moment, moment invariants, scale invariant feature transform (SIFT) etc. Deep learning models learn a pool of features from low level to high level and automate the extraction process of such features (LeCun et al., 2015). Since, the overall accuracy of human behavior analysis system depends on accuracy of the feature descriptors. Hence, feature extraction process should be robust and represent the key characteristics of human objects. In next section, we provide a brief review of several feature descriptors and their variants used for human behavior detection.

FEATURE DESCRIPTORS FOR BEHAVIOR DETECTION

A good feature descriptor is always needed as it represents important characteristics of an image. In recent years, computationally efficient local feature descriptors with good discriminating capabilities have been developed (Zhang & Lu, 2004; Zhang & Tan, 2002). This development led to a significant progress in applying feature descriptors to various vision problems.

For human behavior detection, several feature descriptors based approaches have been developed. The existing approaches for invariant human detection assume two types of feature descriptors for shape recognition: boundary-based and region-based. Fourier descriptor (Zhao & Belkasim, 2012) is an example of a boundary based feature descriptor widely used in literature for multiresolution analysis. The region based feature descriptor approaches are primarily based on moments (Flusser et al., 2009) and their invariants (Hu, 1962). Moment based descriptors have been extensively used as the global feature of an image for behavior detection (Nigam & Khare, 2016; Liao & Pawlak, 1996). They provide efficient local descriptors for image analysis. Main advantage of moment based descriptors is their ability to provide invariant measures of simple and complex shapes (Kotoulas & Andreadis, 2005; Chaumette, 2004). Moment features deal with the digitized, quantized and often noisy version of an image. Several moments based detection techniques for real objects can be found in (Guo & Zhao, 2008; Nigam et al., 2013; Mercimek et al., 2005). Motivated by moment and their invariants, Affine invariant moments (Suk & Flusser, 2003), Zernike moments (Chen et al., 2012) and Legendre moments (Dai et al., 2914) have also been proposed for invariant detection against different linear transformations.

Local binary pattern (LBP) is a region based local feature descriptor used in different applications (Pietikäinen et al., 2011). The original LBP descriptor and its several variants have already been used for behavior detection methods (Nguyen et al., 2013; Ko et al., 2013; Boudissa et al., 2013; Geismann & Knoll, 2010; Shen et al., 2013; Zhou et al., 2012). The most attractive advantages of LBP are its invariance against monotonic gray scale changes and providing multiresolution analysis for better analysis of different space scales (Pietikäinen et al., 2011). It also provides orientation information in an image (Ciocca et al., 2015). Few approaches based on other features also do exist, e.g. a histogram of oriented gradients (HOG) based method was presented in (Dalal & Triggs, 2005) that provided unambiguous representation of human objects in real scene. Methods to speed up this algorithm were proposed in (Zhu et al., 2006; Pang et al., 2011). Several other features have also been proposed in (Liu et al., 2013; Bosch et al., 2007; Skibbe et al., 2012; Nigam et al., 2013; Yussiff et al., 2014).

In comparison to hand-crafted features, deep learning techniques have several advantages such as (i) less effort required (ii) less domain knowledge required (iii) provide a general description of different modalities (iv) automatically learn semantic features. Deep learning models can be applied in four ways (i) Convolutional Neural Networks based (Szegedy et al., 2015), Restricted Boltzmann Machine based (Ngiam et al., 2011), Autoencoder based (Rifai et al., 2011) and Sparse coding based (Gao et al., 2010). They have been successfully applied on several vision problems such as object detection (Huang et al., 2007; Lee et al., 2009a; Angelova et al., 2015), natural language processing (Collobert & Weston, 2008), classification (Lee et al., 2009b), tracking (Vu, Q. D., & Chung, S. T., 2017; Park et al., 2016; Xu, 2017) and activity recognition (Neverova, 2016; Dobhal, 2015). However, deep learned features are treated as mid-level features (Zhang, 2016).

Figure 1 shows a general architecture of feature based human behavior detection methodology and Figure 2 shows architecture of deep learning based human behavior detection methodology. The narrow discriminating line can be understood from Figures 1-2. We know that deep learning model handles the problem of seeking hierarchical representation, hence Figure 2 depicts a layer wise unsupervised learning pool for initialization of each layer. It extracts multiple level of features simultaneously. The low level, mid-level and high-level features may be pixel, edge, texton, parts or objects. The multiple layers in feature learning may be convolutional layer, non-linear layer and pooling (LeCun et al., 2015; Zhang, 2016).

Since feature descriptors play a crucial role in traditional behavior detection as well as in deep learning based behavior detection, therefore here we give a brief overview of feature descriptors used in literature. These are local binary patterns (LBP), moment, moment invariants and several other descriptors.

Local Binary Pattern (LBP)

The local binary pattern (LBP) was first proposed for texture classification and has been successfully applied over different computer vision problems (Pietikäinen et al., 2011). The LBP features are powerful illumination invariant feature descriptor. LBP feature is represented by the relative gray values of eight connected regions as shown in Figure 3.

Figure 1. General human behavior detection system

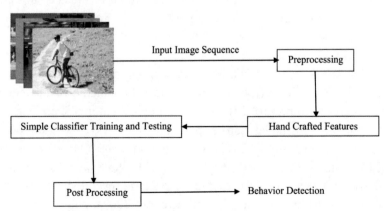

Figure 2. Deep learning based human behavior detection system

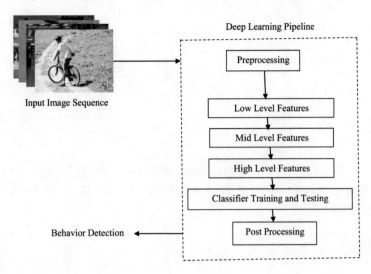

Figure 3. The local binary patterns of center pixel in 8 connected region

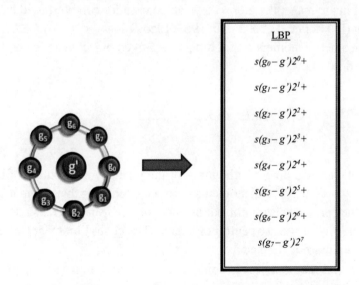

For computation of LBP, let us take an image *Im(x,y)* and *g'* represent the gray value of a pixel at location *(x, y)*, i.e. *g' = Im(x, y)*. Also, let g_l represent a gray level of any sample point in an equispaced circular neighborhood where *Pi* is the number of sample points within radius *Ra*. Then the general local binary pattern operator $LBP_{Pi,Ra}$ can be obtained as follows

$$LBP_{Pi,Ra}(x,y) = \sum_{l=0}^{Pi-1} s(g_l - g')2^l \tag{1}$$

where $s(g)$ is defined as

$$s(g) = \begin{Bmatrix} 1, g \geq 0 \\ 0, g < 0 \end{Bmatrix} \tag{2}$$

The histogram of the $LBP_{Pi,Ra}$ values calculated over its neighborhood can be used for shape representation of an object and proved to be robust against changes in illumination.

Moment

The theory of moments provides an interesting and useful alternative for representing shape of objects in an image. Moments are quantitative measure of the shape of an object in an image; therefore, they can be used for contour based human object detection (Flusser et al., 2009; Hu, 1962; Liao & Pawlak, 1996).

The geometric moment $m_{\alpha\beta}$ of order $\alpha + \beta$ of an object in an image *Im(x, y)* can be defined as follows:

$$m_{\alpha\beta} = \sum_{\alpha=0}^{M-1}\sum_{\beta=0}^{N-1} (x)^\alpha . (y)^\beta \, \text{Im}(x,y) \, \alpha, \beta = 0,1,2,3....... \tag{3}$$

The geometric moment is the mean of the intensity distribution of pixels in an image. However, the central moments are more interesting than geometric moments because they provide clear information about object's shape. Translation invariance can be achieved if we use central moments. The central moment (moment) of an object in an image is defined as

The central moment $\mu_{\alpha\beta}$ is computed from translation of $m_{\alpha\beta}$ by an amount $(-\bar{x}, -\bar{y})$ as

$$\mu_{\alpha\beta} = \sum_{\alpha=0}^{M-1}\sum_{\beta=0}^{N-1} (x - \bar{x})^\alpha . (y - \bar{y})^\beta \, \text{Im}(x,y) \tag{4}$$

where $\bar{x} \triangleq \dfrac{m_{1,0}}{m_{0,0}}$ and $\bar{y} \triangleq \dfrac{m_{0,1}}{m_{0,0}}$ \hfill (5)

The normalized central moment $\eta_{\alpha,\beta}$ is obtained as

$$\eta_{\alpha,\beta} = \frac{\mu_{\alpha,\beta}}{(\mu_{0,0})^\gamma}, \text{ where } \gamma = [(\alpha + \beta) / 2] + 1 \tag{6}$$

i.e. the first central moment is exactly zero. The second central moment is the variance which uses a divisor of n instead of n-1, where n is the sample size.

Moments of lower orders such as from order 0 to order 4 represent some general quantities. For example, zero order moment m_{00} represents the mass of the image. First order moments m_{10}/m_{00} and m_{01}/m_{00} represent the center of gravity or the centroid of the image. The second order moment m_{20} and m_{02} represent the distribution of mass of the image with respect to the coordinate axes and also called the moment of inertia. The functions of second order moments, $\sqrt{m_{20}/m_{00}}$ and $\sqrt{m_{02}/m_{00}}$ are called the radius of gyration. If an image is represented in the form of a probability density function such that $m_{00} = 1$, then the values m_{10} and m_{01} represent the mean of the image. When the mean is zero, m_{20}, m_{02} and m_{11} represent the variances of horizontal projection, variances of vertical projections and covariance respectively. In this way, the second order moments represent the orientation of the image and can be used to calculate oriented features of objects to provide invariant detection.

Moment Invariants

Moment invariants are scalar quantities used to characterize and represent significant features of an object. The seven moment invariants are defined in terms of normalized central moment $\eta_{\alpha,\beta}$ of order 2 and 3 (Flusser et al., 2009; Hu, 1962; Liao & Pawlak, 1996). Central moments of order 2 are $\eta_{1,1}$, $\eta_{2,0}$, and $\eta_{0,2}$; and central moments of order 3 are $\eta_{1,2}$, $\eta_{2,1}$, $\eta_{3,0}$ and $\eta_{0,3}$. The seven moment invariants are

$$MomInv_1 = \left(\eta_{20} + \eta_{02}\right)$$

$$MomInv_2 = \left(\eta_{20} - \eta_{02}\right)^2 + \left(4\,\eta_{11}\right)^2$$

$$MomInv_3 = \left(\eta_{30} - 3\eta_{12}\right)^2 + \left(3\eta_{21} - \eta_{03}\right)^2$$

$$MomInv_4 = \left(\eta_{30} + \eta_{12}\right)^2 + \left(\eta_{21} + \eta_{03}\right)^2 \tag{7}$$

$$MomInv_5 = \left(\eta_{30} - 3\eta_{12}\right)\left(\eta_{30} + \eta_{12}\right)\left[\left(\eta_{30} + \eta_{12}\right)^2 - 3\left(\eta_{21} + \eta_{03}\right)^2\right] +$$

$$3\left(\eta_{21} - \eta_{03}\right)\left(\eta_{21} + \eta_{03}\right)\left[3\left(\eta_{30} + \eta_{12}\right)^2 - \left(\eta_{21} + \eta_{03}\right)^2\right]$$

$$MomInv_6 = \left(\eta_{20} + \eta_{02}\right)\left[\left(\eta_{30} + \eta_{12}\right)^2 - \left(\eta_{21} + \eta_{03}\right)^2\right] + 4\,\eta_{11}\left(\eta_{30} + \eta_{12}\right)^2\left(\eta_{21} + \eta_{03}\right)^2$$

$$MomInv_7 = \left(3\eta_{21} - \eta_{03}\right)\left(\eta_{30} + \eta_{12}\right)\left[\left(\eta_{30} + \eta_{12}\right)^2 - 3\left(\eta_{21} + \eta_{03}\right)^2\right] - \left(\eta_{30} - 3\eta_{12}\right)\left(\eta_{21} + \eta_{03}\right)$$

$$\left[3\left(\eta_{30} + \eta_{12}\right)^2 - \left(\eta_{21} + \eta_{03}\right)^2\right]$$

These 7 moment invariants are significant in behavior detection (Nigam & Khare, 2016) since they are invariant against rotation, translation and scaling transformations shown in Figure 4.

Histogram of Oriented Gradients (HOG)

Histogram of oriented gradients (HOG) was first developed for object detection. It counts number of occurrences of gradient orientation in local patch of an image which is used as features. The gradient information is useful for finding values near edges and corners (Dalal & Triggs, 2005; Zhu et al., 2006; Pang et al., 2011).

The HOG descriptor is computed over an image of $m \times 2m$ pixels. The HOG vector is computed using x and y direction derivatives by applying following filters

(-1 0 1) and (-1 0 1)^T

The x-derivative is useful for finding information in horizontal direction and y-derivative is useful for finding information in vertical direction. Change in derivative magnitude indicate intensity variation and it doesn't change if region of interest is smooth. It helps to discard insignificant information such as constant colored background.

Figure 4. Rotation, scaling and translation transformation of Lena image

At every pixel, the gradient has a magnitude V_{mag} and a direction V_{dir} which is determined using the following formula

$$V_{mag} = \sqrt{V_x^2 + V_y^2} \quad V_{dir} = Tan^{-1}\frac{V_y}{V_x}$$

where V_x is *x*-direction derivative and V_y is *y*-direction derivative. Image is divided in 8×8 blocks and gradient value is calculated for each block. The 8×8 block size is significant as 8×8 mask in a 64×128 image is sufficient enough to retrieve useful information.

Histogram normalized is done using a 16×16 block. Normalizing a vector removes the scale. A 16×16 block has 4 histograms which can be merged together to form a 36×1 element vector. The window is then moved by 8 pixels and a normalized 36×1 vector is calculated over this window in a recursive manner. To calculate the final feature vector for whole image, the 36×1 vectors are merged together to form one large vector. The HOG feature of an image is visualized by plotting the 9×1 normalized histograms in the 8×8 cells (see Figure 5). We can notice that dominant direction of the histogram captures the shape of the face.

Hough Transform

The Hough Transform is used to detect lines using following parametric representation of a straight line:

rho = x cos(theta) + y sin(theta)

The variable *rho* is distance of line from the origin along a vector perpendicular to line. Variable *theta* is the angle of perpendicular projection from origin to the line measured in degrees clockwise from the positive *x*-axis. The range of theta is $-90° \leq theta \leq 90°$. The angle of line is $theta + 90°$ which is measured clockwise with respect to the positive *x*-axis. A general representation of Hough transform is shown in Figure 6.

Hough transform is a parameter space whose rows and columns represent *rho* and *theta*, respectively. Its elements correspond to accumulator cells where each cell is initialized to zero. For each foreground-background point, rho is calculated for every *theta*. After that cell is incremented by 1 and a recursive procedure is followed. Finally, a value Q in $hough(row, column)$ means Q points lie in the *xy* plane on the line $theta(column)$ and $rho(row)$. Now, the Hough transform matrix is *n (rho)* $\times$ *n (theta)*. A graphical representation of Hough transform is shown in Figures 7-8.

Figure 5. HOG vectors for a sample image

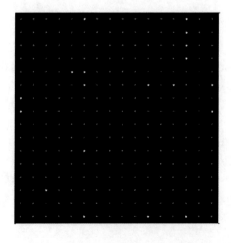

Figure 6. Hough transform domain of a point

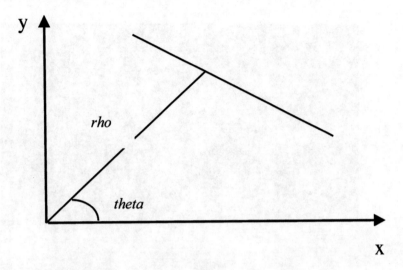

Figure 7. Hough transform of sample image

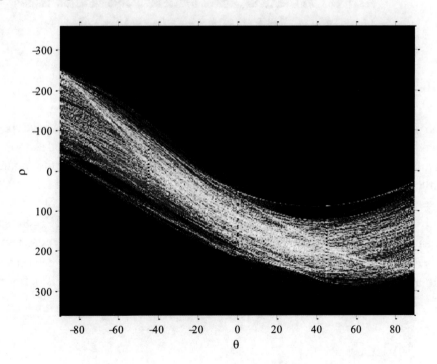

Figure 8. Limited Theta range Hough transform of sample image

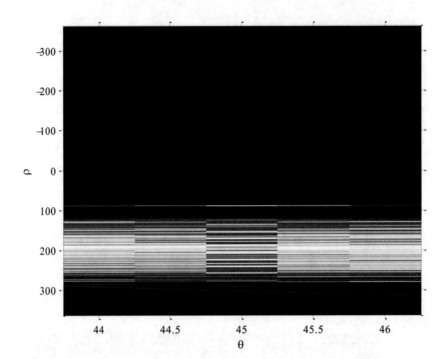

Principal Component Analysis (PCA)

The principal component analysis (PCA) feature reduction algorithms have special speed advantage in increasing behavior detection process. It can be used as a tool for finding the best projection directions that represent the original data on the condition of the least mean-square (Bro & Smilde, 2014; Bengio et al., 2013). It selects a few deserving portions of the feature vector in the following way.

Let number of classes in training set is C and each class i ($i = 1,2,.....,C$) comprises of a number of face images M. These images are $F_{i1}, F_{i2}, ..., F_{iM}$ where each image F is a $m \times n$ size 2D array of intensity values and each image can be converted into a vector of $m \times n$ pixels. If training set of $N = C \times M$ images is defined by $X_k = \left[F_{i1}, F_{i2}, ..., F_{ij} \right]$, then the covariance matrix is defined as

$$\Phi = \frac{1}{N} \sum_{k=1}^{N} XX^T \tag{8}$$

where $X = \left[F_{i1} - \bar{F}, F_{i2} - \bar{F}, ..., F_{ij} - \bar{F} \right]$ and $\bar{F} = \sum_{i=1}^{C} \sum_{j=1}^{M} F_{ij}$ is mean of training set. The eigenvalues and eigenvectors are then calculated from the covariance matrix. Let $P = (p_1, p_2, ..., p_r)$ $(r < N)$ are the r normalized eigenvectors corresponding to r largest eigenvalues. Each of the r eigenvectors is called an eigenface. Now, each face image of the training set is projected into the eigenfaces space to obtain its corresponding eigenface based features Y_s, which is defined as

$$Y_s = P^T A_k, \quad k = 1, 2, ..., N \tag{9}$$

where A_k is the mean subtracted image of X_k. For an image of size 256×256 pixels, we get a multiscale LBP feature vector of size 1×3584 pixels. This large size of feature vector is reduced into a smaller feature vector of size 64×2 pixels using PCA.

HUMAN BEHAVIOR DETECTION FRAMEWORK

The semantic analysis of human behavior can be performed at several levels of understandings such as human detection, activity analysis and interaction analysis (Borges et al., 2013; Gonzàlez et al., 2012). However, there are trade-offs between achieving detailed information about human behavior at different levels with the efficiency and robustness of the algorithm. Therefore, research studies have focused on behavior understanding at one level depending on specific application (Wiliem et al., 2012; Tran et al., 2012). Here, we focus on human behavior understanding with the help of human detection, human object tracking and human activity recognition for video surveillance purpose. It should be mentioned that an effective video surveillance system needs to be human behavior centric and should take into consideration information about human objects interacting in a holistic manner (Vishwakarma & Agrawal, 2013; Loy, 2010).

In particular, this would form a core building block of intelligent surveillance systems. Therefore, analysis and understanding of human behavior in video sequences must be dealt with better accuracy and requires a complete framework. This framework could be understood from Figure 9 where this task is divided into following three key steps:

- **Human Detection:** Detection of human objects in a given scenario.
- **Human Tracking:** Tracking of human object in frame to frame.

Figure 9. A general framework for human behavior detection

- **Activity Recognition:** Analysis of human behavior by understanding their motion patterns.

HUMAN DETECTION

Human detection is the foundation of human behavior based surveillance application. It can be defined as labelling the human objects in images or videos which have been modelled before. To facilitate automatic human detection good features and flexible classifiers are needed. Many approaches have been developed for human detection. Most of the methods rely on local shape features. The following challenges should be considered while implementing human detection methods (i) changing number of humans, (ii) wide range of human pose, (iii) variations in appearance, (iv) cluttered background, and (v) variations in the illumination, etc.

Therefore, an invariant approach against these challenges, is often required. Moreover, degree of computational efficiency should be considered for accurate detection results. Hence, the first need is to find a robust feature set that allows human objects to be distinguished clearly, even for multiple humans, gray scale variations and different space scales. They also reduce computational time in detection and are able to detect humans even in low resolution images. This is mainly achieved by segmentation (Jacob et al., 2017) of human objects. Although several other detection methods can also be used for human detection such as audio sensing, face detection, blob detection, motion detection, etc., but there exist various reasons so that better detection techniques are always needed such as

- Human detection methods based on facial features may fail if a person is not present in frontal view camera position.
- Human detection methods based on motion features may fail if a person is not doing significant movement.
- Human detection methods based on blob features may fail if a non-human object appears in the scene. The blob detection method may give false alarm for this non-human object.
- Human detection methods based on audio sensing may fail if a person is not making any type of sound.

For this reason, a variety of methods have been developed in literature for human detection. Most of those methods are based on following general algorithm, given in Table 1.

Several quantitative evaluation parameters exist for evaluation of different human behavior detection methods based on above algorithm. These parameters are Precision, Recall, False Positive Rate (FPR), Negative Accuracy (NegAccuracy), Accuracy, F-measure, Time, Receiver Operating Characteristic (ROC) curve and Standard Error of Measurement (SEM). These parameters are computed with the aid of four measures, namely True Positive (TP), True Negative (TN), False Positive (FP) and False Negative (FN). The 9 evaluation parameters are defined as follows:

Precision

The percentage detection rate, termed as precision, is computed using following equation

$$Precision = \frac{TP}{TP + FP} \times 100 \qquad (10)$$

Table 1. A general framework for human detection

• *Human object representation in real scenes*
• *Preprocessing of images*
o *Normalization of image size.*
o *Normalization of color space.*
• *Feature vector calculation*
• *Classification of feature data*

Recall

Detection rate is computed as the percentage recall of different methods equation given below

$$Recall = \frac{TP}{TP + FN} \times 100 \qquad (11)$$

FPR

The percentage False Positive Rate (FPR) of different methods is computed as follows

$$FPR = \frac{FP}{TN + FP} \times 100 \qquad (12)$$

NegAccuracy

Detection rate in terms of negative accuracy is accuracy of the method for negative test images. It is computed as percentage of total number of true detections for negative test images and can be computed using following equation

$$NegAccuracy = \frac{TN}{TN + FP} \times 100 \qquad (13)$$

Accuracy

Accuracy is the percentage average detection rate of the method for positive and negative test images. It is computed using equation given below

$$Accuracy = \frac{TP + TN}{TP + TN + FP + FN} \times 100 \qquad (14)$$

F-Measure

F-measure is calculated in terms of the harmonic mean of precision and recall, and can be computed with the help of following equation

$$F - measure = 2 \cdot \frac{precision \cdot recall}{precision + recall} \tag{15}$$

Time

The time parameter is computed in terms of computation time elapsed in seconds to run different methods for each dataset.

Receiver Operating Characteristic (ROC) Curve

The Receiver Operating Characteristic (ROC) curve is a graphical representation that shows the performance of the classifier based method. To draw an ROC curve, the quantity FPR is plotted on x axis and quantity Recall is plotted on y axis.

Standard Error of Measurement (SEM)

Standard error of measurement (SEM) is the standard deviation of the sample-mean's estimate of mean of a sequence. It can be calculated using following equation

$$SEM = \frac{SD}{\sqrt{N}} \tag{16}$$

where SEM = standard error of measurement, SD = standard deviation of the samples and N = size of the samples.

For better performance the parameters Precision, Recall, NegAccuracy, Accuracy and F-measure should have a higher value, whereas parameters FPR and time should have a lower value.

Several benchmark datasets exist for human detection. Few of them are INRIA person dataset (Dalal & Triggs 2005), Caltech Pedestrian Detection Benchmark Dataset (Dollar et al. 2012), Penn-Fudan Database for Pedestrian Detection and Segmentation (Wang et al. 2007), Daimler Pedestrian Segmentation Benchmark Dataset (Flohr & Gavrila 2013) and dataset created in (Nigam & Khare 2015). Among these datasets, INRIA dataset is the most widely used dataset for its complexity and variety of images. It contains 2521 positive images and 1686 negative images. Most of the images in this dataset are of size 96×160. This dataset contains objects of different spatial resolutions and varying appearances. Images in this dataset exist in different resolution of space scale. These images are differently illuminated, and appearance varies rapidly within-class. Few sample images of the INRIA dataset are shown in Figure 10.

Figure 10. Samples of INRIA Pedestrian Dataset (Dalal & Triggs 2005)

In Figure 11, we provide quantitative evaluation results in terms of Precision, Recall, FPR, NegAccuracy, Accuracy, F-measure and time of local binary feature descriptor (Pietikäinen et al., 2011) based method for benchmark INRIA person dataset. Performance of the LBP method (Pietikäinen et al., 2011) has been found effective under different spatial resolutions and gray scale changes and provides better human detection for single as well as for multiple humans. The reason for better performance of this method over other features based methods is that it provides invariance against gray scales and multiresolution analysis of different space scales.

The detected human object is tracked in consecutive video frames. Hence, next step of behavior detection is human object tracking.

HUMAN OBJECT TRACKING

Human object tracking in video sequences is the second key step in the formation of a human behavior analysis and understanding system. Human object tracking is a process of locating a moving human object (or multiple human objects) over time using a single camera or multiple cameras. In order to perform object tracking in video sequences, an algorithm analyzes sequential video frames and outputs the movement of target between the frames. Its objective is to associate target objects in consecutive video frames. Tracking of moving human object is a complicated task due to several reasons such as object's shape and size may vary from frame to frame, object may be occluded by other object(s), presence of noise and blur in video, luminance and intensity changes, object's abrupt motion, real time scene analysis requirements.

Figure 11. Detection results of LBP feature (Pietikäinen et al. 2011) over INRIA dataset

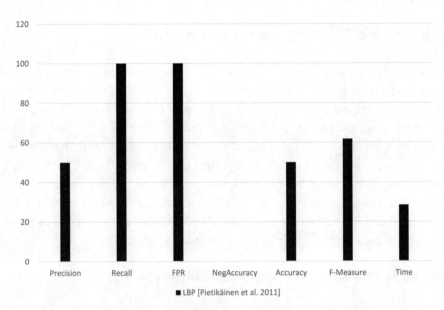

To deal with above challenges, several tracking systems have been developed that can be categorized as non-vision based tracking systems, vision based tracking systems with markers, vision based tracking systems without markers and robot guided tracking systems. These four type of tracking systems are briefly discussed here one by one.

Non-Vision Based Tracking Systems

The non-vision based tracking is very initial approach in the field of tracking. It takes advantage of human body movements. The non-vision based systems are implemented by attaching sensors to different part of the human body. These sensors retrieve information about different human movements. The sensors are generally categorized as mechanical, inertia, acoustic, radio or microwave and magnetic sensors. For example, as part of inertia sensors, accelerometer sensors convert the inputting signal of linear acceleration or angular acceleration or a combination of both into an output signal. There are three common types of accelerometer sensors. The piezo-electric sensors exploit the piezoelectric effect which naturally occur when quartz crystal is used to produce an electric charge between two terminals. The piezo-resistive sensors measure the resistance of a fine wire which is mechanically deformed by a massive body. The variable capacitive sensors compute the change in capacitance which is proportional to acceleration or deceleration.

Vision Based Tracking Systems With Markers

Vision based tracking systems using markers overcome the limitations of non-vision based tracking methods. They resolve above problem upto some extent and seem more suitable for tracking. These techniques use cameras in association with ordinary sensors and place some markers on the body to track different human body movements. Since human skeleton is a highly articulated structure therefore twists and rotations make the movement fully three dimensional. Hence each body part continuously moves in and out of occlusion from the view of the cameras. It results in inconsistent and unreliable tracking of the human body. As a good solution to this problem, vision based tracking systems with markers have attracted the attention of researchers and scientists of different science and engineering fields.

Vision Based Tracking Systems Without Markers

The vision based tracking systems with markers are restrictive to some extent due to the presence of markers. The Vision based tracking systems without markers overcome this drawback. They are a less restrictive motion capture technique. The markerless approaches are only concerned about boundaries or features on human bodies hence capable of overcoming the mutual occlusion problem. This is an active and promising approach. This approach is very widely used and found to be most appropriate for tracking of objects.

Robot-Guided Tracking Systems

The Robot guided tracking systems have become very popular because they provide capabilities for human robot interaction. This provides assistance to humans in various situations. Most of these systems can operate in both indoor as well as outdoor environments. These systems include sensor technologies to distinguish the static activities (like standing, sitting, lying etc.) from dynamic activities (like walking, cycling etc). Robot guided tracking is directly linked to both the robot watching a user and showing the user that it is doing so. In this type of tracking a user would exert some pressure in the sense of surveillance and that a verbal cue from the robot in conjunction with the tracking function could effectively influence human decision-making. Also robot can get the object position information through processing image captured by cameras to achieve the visual task. For robot guided tracking systems, it is the main task to recognize and track object correctly and quickly, get the position, pose, and velocity of object and pass the information to robot. These intelligent service robots depend on effective utilization of available sensors to retrieve information for decision making, planning, and also for interaction with humans.

All these four type of tracking systems operate on algorithm as shown in Table 2.

For evaluation of above general algorithm, following four objective measures are used for quantitative determination of tracking performance.

Centroids

The x and y direction values of actual centroids and x and y direction values of centroids computed by different methods are primary evaluation parameters. For better performance of a method, centroids computed by the method should vary in the same way as the actual centroid. It means, movement of computed centroid should be similar to the movement of actual centroid.

Euclidean Distance (EuDis)

The Euclidean distance between the centroid of tracked object bounding box and actual centroid is computed as follows:

$$EuDis = \sqrt{(x_A - x_c)^2 + (y_A - y_c)^2} \tag{17}$$

where (x_A, y_A) is the actual centroid value and (x_c, y_c) is computed centroid value.

Bhattacharyya Distance (BhDis)

The Bhattacharyya distance is used as a separability measure for tracked object region and actual object region. For two classes of actual and computed values, it is given by

$$BhDis = \frac{1}{8}(mean_c - mean_a)^T \left[\frac{cov_a + cov_c}{2}\right]^{-1}(mean_c - mean_a) + \frac{1}{2}\ln\frac{\left|(cov_a + cov_c)/2\right|}{\left|cov_a\right|^{1/2}\left|cov_c\right|^{1/2}} \tag{18}$$

Table 2. A general framework for human object tracking

• *Input sequence of video frames*   • *Locating a moving object*   • *Associate target object*   • *Predicting movement of target in consecutive video frames*

where $mean_a$ = mean vector for actual object region, $mean_c$ = mean vector for computed object region, cov_a = covariance matrix for actual object region and cov_c = covariance matrix for computed object region.

Mean Square Error (MSE)

Mean square error (MSE) is defined between the parameters of tracked object bounding box and the actual object over all frames in a video as

$$MSE = \frac{1}{N}\sum_{i=1}^{N}[(x_{i1}^A - x_{i1}^C)^2 + (y_{i1}^A - y_{i1}^C)^2] \tag{19}$$

where (x_{i1}^A, y_{i1}^A) are actual centroids, (x_{i1}^C, y_{i1}^C) are computed centroids and N is total no of frames in a video.

For implementing a tracking algorithm, several challenging datasets are available such as PETS 2000, PETS 2001, PETS 2002 (http://www.cvg.reading.ac.uk/slides/pets.html). Several authors randomly selected various videos from internet for evaluation of their tracking performance. Here, we discuss motion of a player in the Soccer video. This video consists of a total of 329 frames of size 352×288 pixels. In Figure 12, we present visual results of representative video frames for frame number 1 to 320 with difference of 40 frames for method based on Corrected Background Weighted Histogram (CBWH) (Ning et al. 2012) feature descriptor based method.

From Figure 12, one can easily observe that this video sequence contains multiple human objects. From frame no 1 to 40, the target object is well covered within the bounding box by the proposed method. In frame 120 other object comes in the area of bounding box partially. But one can observe that bounding box captures the target object up to frame 200 accurately. Again, in frames 240 and 280, another object crosses the target object and comes fully within the area of the bounding box. But due to this, not much track loss occurs, and the target object is covered by the bounding box in frame 320. The background condition in this video is not simple and camera moves a little, however it does not affect the prediction of the object. Even for small size of objects in this video, the given method does not lose its track. This tracking can be applied to different target objects which makes it suitable for tracking of distinct target objects up to some extent. Therefore, from Soccer video sequence it is clear that, the CBWH method (Ning et al., 2012) tracks the target object correctly even if another object occludes the target object partially or fully. Background conditions and object size do not influence the tracking accuracy.

We have quantitatively evaluated Corrected Background Weighted Histogram (CBWH) (Ning et al., 2012) and Joint Color Texture Histogram (JCTH) (Ning et al.,

Figure 12. Tracking of Soccer video for frame no 1 to 240 in steps of 20 frames by CBWH feature descriptor based method (Ning et al., 2012)

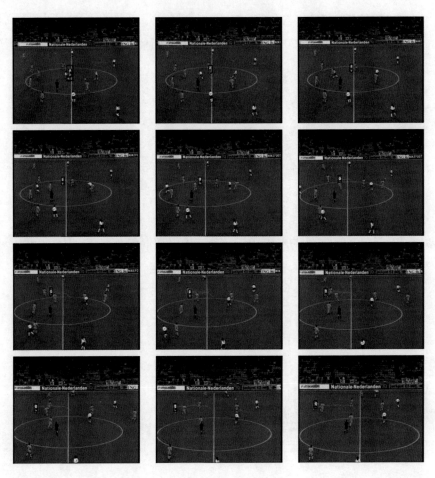

2009) feature descriptor based methods in terms of centroid in x-direction, centroid in y-direction, Euclidean distance, Bhattacharyya distance in Figures 13-14. Mean Square Error is shown in Table 3. From Figures 13-14 and Table 3, it is clear that CBWH and JCTH features provide promising results.

Table 3. Mean square error of different methods

Method	MSE
Method CBWH (Ning et al. 2012)	395.2773
Method JCTH (Ning et al. 2009)	549.5349

Figure 13. Centroids of object using features CBWH (Ning et al. 2012) and JCTH (Ning et al. 2009)

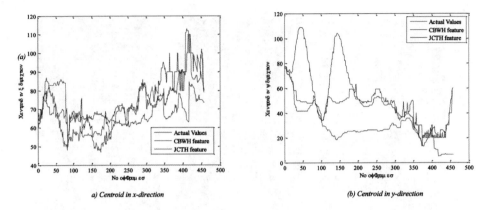

a) Centroid in x-direction

(b) Centroid in y-direction

Figure 14. Distances calculated for CBWH feature (Ning et al. 2012) and JCTH feature (Ning et al., 2009)

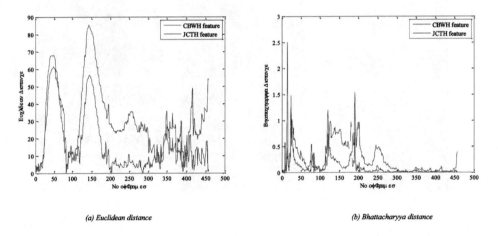

(a) Euclidean distance

(b) Bhattacharyya distance

The detected and tracked object is analyzed for its action patterns. Hence, third key step of behavior detection is activity recognition.

ACTIVITY RECOGNITION

In human activity recognition, human behavior is modelled as a stochastic sequence of activities. In simple terms, activity recognition is matching a time-varying feature data with a group of labeled reference and identifying typical behavior. These activities are described by a holistic feature vector comprising of a set of local motion descriptors. After that a pattern classifier is used for recognition of different activities which should be flexible enough to discriminate activities of different classes. Activity recognition is achieved through probabilistic search of the image feature database representing previously seen activities. But this is a difficult problem due to several challenges. Robustness against environment variations, actor's movement variations, various activities and insufficient amount of training videos are a few of them. To handle these challenges following general algorithm for human activity recognition is given in Table 4.

In addition to evaluation parameters described for human detection, Confusion matrix is the most widely used parameter for evaluation of above activity recognition algorithm.

Confusion Matrix

A confusion matrix is a representation of performance values in tabular form. It shows all true value for a particular given instance.

For implementing activity recognition algorithm, several benchmark activity recognition datasets exist that are KTH (Schuldt et al., 2004), Weizmann (Gorelick et al., 2007), CASIA (Wang et al., 2007), IXMAS (Weinland et al., 2006), Collective (Choi et al., 2009), Muhavi (Singh et al., 2010), UCF-Sports (Rodriguez et al., 2008), Hollywood (Laptev et al., 2008), Hollywood 2 (Marszalek et al. 2009), MSR Action (https://www.microsoft.com/en-us/download/details.aspx?id=52315), MSR Action 2 (Cao et al., 2010), etc. Background subtraction is an important step in activity recognition. It segments moving foreground object from its background as shown in Figure 15.

Among aforementioned activity datasets, INRIA Xmas Motion Acquisition Sequences (IXMAS) activity recognition dataset (Weinland et al., 2006) is one of the most challenging datasets due to its multi-view nature. In this dataset, 13 daily-live activities have been included. These activities are performed by 11 actors and each activity is performed 3 times by every actor. These activities are nothing, check watch, cross arms, scratch head, sit down, get up, turn around, walk, wave, punch, kick, point, pick up, throw (overhead), and throw (from bottom up). The actors choose

Table 4. A general framework for human activity recognition

• *Input video*
• *Preprocessing*
• *Background subtraction*
• *Feature extraction*
• *Multiclass classification*

Figure 15. Results of background subtraction (a and c) Original images (b and d) corresponding background subtracted images

(a) Frame 15	*(b) Frame 15*	*(c) Frame 25*	*(d) Frame 25*

freely position and orientation. 5 calibrated cameras have been used for this purpose that are cam 1, cam 2, cam 3, cam 4 and cam 5. The frame rate is 23 frames per second and frame size is 390×291. We selected 3 activities among them which are kick, punch and turnaround from 5 cameras and hence a total of 15 activities. 45 frames have been chosen from each video. We demonstrate visual results of center symmetric local binary pattern (CSLBP) (Nguyen et al., 2013) feature descriptor based method for IXMAS dataset in Figure 16.

Figure 16 clearly shows the accuracy of the CSLBP method for human activity recognition at multiple views. Although, the human subjects are performing different activities which are kick, punch and turn around, even then the recognition results are very proper. These activities have been performed with the help of 5 cameras placed at different viewing angles and activities have been captured simultaneously with these cameras. These visual results show that the obtained results are accurate and the CSLBP method provide proper recognition results for this set of videos.

Now, quantitative results are shown for IXMAS dataset in Table 5. Diagonal values indicate the recognition rate which is high for the method. We renamed activities as follows for the sake of space in confusion matrix. Kick: cam 1 as A1, Kick: cam 2 as A2, Kick: cam 3 as A3, Kick: cam 4 as A4, Kick: cam 5 as A5, Punch: cam 1 as B1, Punch: cam 2 as B2, Punch: cam 3 as B3, Punch: cam 4 as B4, Punch: cam 5 as B5, Turn around: cam 1 as C1, Turn around: cam 2 as C2, Turn around: cam 3 as C3, Turn around: cam 4 as C4 and Turn around: cam 5 as C5. Quantitative comparison of the CSLBP method with moment based method (Flusser et al., 2009) and moment invariants based method (Hu, 1962) is shown in Table 6 which proves the superiority of the CSLBP method.

We can extend human behavior detection work with deep learning techniques by using hierarchy of different features and making a pool of several layers of features. This pool of features will provide automatic feature processing and robust classification resulting in better detection rate of human behavior.

Figure 16. Visual recognition results of the CSLBP method (Nguyen et al., 2013) over IXMAS dataset (Weinland et al., 2006)

Table 5. Confusion matrix for CSLBP feature (Nguyen et al., 2013) based method

Activities	A1	A2	A3	A4	A5	B1	B2	B3	B4	B5	C1	C2	C3	C4	C5
A1	1.00	0	0	0	0	0	0	0	0	0	0	0	0	0	0
A2	0.05	0.95	0	0	0	0	0	0	0	0	0	0	0	0	0
A3	0.02	0.05	0.93	0	0	0	0	0	0	0	0	0	0	0	0
A4	0.02	0	0.03	0.95	0	0	0	0	0	0	0	0	0	0	0
A5	0	0	0	0	1.00	0	0	0	0	0	0	0	0	0	0
B1	0.07	0.08	0	0.03	0	0.82	0	0	0	0	0	0	0	0	0
B2	0.03	0.08	0.06	0	0	0.31	0.52	0	0	0	0	0	0	0	0
B3	0	0.05	0.10	0	0	0.03	0.07	0.75	0	0	0	0	0	0	0
B4	0.02	0.02	0	0.07	0	0.03	0	0	0.86	0	0	0	0	0	0
B5	0	0	0	0	0	0	0	0	0	1.00	0	0	0	0	0
C1	0.02	0	0	0.06	0	0.07	0.02	0	0.05	0	0.78	0	0	0	0
C2	0.02	0	0.08	0.03	0	0.03	0.03	0.03	0	0	0.12	0.66	0	0	0
C3	0.05	0.07	0.03	0	0	0.07	0.05	0.05	0	0	0	0	0.68	0	0
C4	0.02	0	0	0	0	0.03	0	0	0.16	0	0.03	0.10	0	0.66	0
C5	0	0	0	0	0	0	0	0	0	0	0	0	0	0	1.00

Table 6. Recognition results over the IXMAS dataset (Weinland et al. 2006)

Method	Accuracy (%)
Mom (Flusser et al. 2009)	6.7
Inv Mom (Hu 1962)	11.2
CSLBP (Nguyen et al. 2013)	83.7

CONCLUSION

The main objective of the present chapter is to provide a framework for analysis and understanding of human behavior for vision applications. The overall framework has been divided into three steps: human detection, human object tracking and human activity recognition. This chapter has provided a detailed discussion of the human behavior detection framework and discussed human detection, human object tracking and human activity recognition problems separately. The qualitative as well as quantitative results have been discussed for the feature descriptors based method. We have used local binary patterns and their invariants for analyzing the human detection framework. The quantitative results clearly demonstrated the usefulness of feature descriptors for the proposed framework. Moreover, the properties of feature descriptors and their variants have a lot of scope in behavior analysis. However, this work can be extended for deep learning models as well. A few possible areas of work where behavior analysis framework can be explored are discussed in the following section.

FUTURE RESEARCH DIRECTIONS

Real Time Human Motion Recognition

The human motions, actions and activities create a large amount of database. So it takes a lot of time for searching this database. Therefore, keeping the searching time shorter will be a major improvement for recognition algorithms. Also, more improved motion compression techniques will provide better performance. In addition, which recognition algorithm will be more effective for a particular environment, this approach has not been well explored also. The algorithms for the recognition of a variety of human motions including walking, running, bending or dancing need to be explored. A large number of possible feature combination is required for these techniques, therefore efficient methods for feature selection or feature induction are necessary. More complex human motion recognition systems based on the ideas described here may be constructed using advanced tools.

Intelligent Robot Systems

The methods for allowing a robot to provide help for a task being carried out in a neighborhood which include one or more non-human objects each having associated object positions, still needs to be developed. The techniques which include detection of changes in object locations within the neighborhood and estimating a task required for the comparison of change in the human position with stored data, is the topic of future research. The stored video data stream which includes change of human locations associated with previously observed sequences and providing robotic help for this type of situation to obtain the required task, further needs to be explored. The implementation of world knowledge and the development of global representations while preserving the power of reactive execution and responses to the changes of surrounding neighborhood is the subject of future research.

Intention Recognition

The recognition of intention of a subject is difficult for weak model based approaches presented so far. Also, the approaches are not completely automated. They require significant manual effort to review the runs and classify them and much of the effort was application-specific therefore future research could more readily make this learning process highly automated by using clustering algorithms to group similar types of runs. Moreover, it is important to select the most indicative environmental variables for observation and a suitable level of behavioral abstraction. Automating the selection of these variables is the subject of future research. Furthermore, the operational environment needs to be properly instrumented to gather the training data required and it must do so in real-time. Finally, the entity's behavior needs to exhibit all modes during training while exhibiting minimal unforeseen or inconsistent modes during operation.

ACKNOWLEDGMENT

This work is supported by Science and Engineering Research Board, Department of Science and Technology, Government of India under grant no. PDF/2016/003644.

REFERENCES

Angelova, A., Krizhevsky, A., Vanhoucke, V., Ogale, A. S., & Ferguson, D. (2015, September). *Real-Time Pedestrian Detection with Deep Network Cascades* (Vol. 2). BMVC. doi:10.5244/C.29.32

Bengio, Y., Courville, A., & Vincent, P. (2013). Representation learning: A review and new perspectives. *IEEE Transactions on Pattern Analysis and Machine Intelligence*, *35*(8), 1798–1828. doi:10.1109/TPAMI.2013.50 PMID:23787338

Borges, P. V. K., Conci, N., & Cavallaro, A. (2013). Video-based human behavior understanding: A survey. *IEEE Transactions on Circuits and Systems for Video Technology*, *23*(11), 1993–2008. doi:10.1109/TCSVT.2013.2270402

Bosch, A., Zisserman, A., & Munoz, X. (2007, July). Representing shape with a spatial pyramid kernel. In *Proceedings of the 6th ACM international conference on Image and video retrieval* (pp. 401-408). ACM. doi:10.1145/1282280.1282340

Boudissa, A., Tan, J. K., Kim, H., Shinomiya, T., & Ishikawa, S. (2013). A novel pedestrian detector on low-resolution images: Gradient LBP using patterns of oriented edges. *IEICE Transactions on Information and Systems*, *96*(12), 2882–2887. doi:10.1587/transinf.E96.D.2882

Bro, R., & Smilde, A. K. (2014). Principal component analysis. *Analytical Methods*, *6*(9), 2812–2831. doi:10.1039/C3AY41907J

Cao, L., Liu, Z., & Huang, T. S. (2010, June). Cross-dataset action detection. In Computer vision and pattern recognition (CVPR), 2010 IEEE conference on (pp. 1998-2005). IEEE. doi:10.1109/CVPR.2010.5539875

Chang, H., Lee, H. D., & Overill, R. (2014). Human-centric security service and its application in smart space. *Security and Communication Networks, 7*(10), 1439–1440.

Chaumette, F. (2004). Image moments: A general and useful set of features for visual servoing. *IEEE Transactions on Robotics, 20*(4), 713–723. doi:10.1109/TRO.2004.829463

Chen, B. J., Shu, H. Z., Zhang, H., Chen, G., Toumoulin, C., Dillenseger, J. L., & Luo, L. M. (2012). Quaternion Zernike moments and their invariants for color image analysis and object recognition. *Signal Processing, 92*(2), 308–318. doi:10.1016/j.sigpro.2011.07.018

Cheng, Z., Qin, L., Huang, Q., Yan, S., & Tian, Q. (2014). Recognizing human group action by layered model with multiple cues. *Neurocomputing, 136*, 124–135. doi:10.1016/j.neucom.2014.01.019

Choi, W., Shahid, K., & Savarese, S. (2009, September). What are they doing?: Collective activity classification using spatio-temporal relationship among people. In *Computer Vision Workshops (ICCV Workshops), 2009 IEEE 12th International Conference on* (pp. 1282-1289). IEEE.

Choujaa, D., & Dulay, N. (2008, December). Tracme: Temporal activity recognition using mobile phone data. In *Embedded and Ubiquitous Computing, 2008. EUC'08. IEEE/IFIP International Conference on* (Vol. 1, pp. 119-126). IEEE.

Ciocca, G., Cusano, C., & Schettini, R. (2015). Image orientation detection using LBP-based features and logistic regression. *Multimedia Tools and Applications, 74*(9), 3013–3034. doi:10.1007/s11042-013-1766-4

Collins, R. T., Lipton, A. J., Kanade, T., Fujiyoshi, H., Duggins, D., Tsin, Y., ... & Wixson, L. (2000). A system for video surveillance and monitoring. *VSAM final report*, 1-68.

Collobert, R., & Weston, J. (2008, July). A unified architecture for natural language processing: Deep neural networks with multitask learning. In *Proceedings of the 25th international conference on Machine learning* (pp. 160-167). ACM. doi:10.1145/1390156.1390177

Dai, X., Zhang, H., Liu, T., Shu, H., & Luo, L. (2014). Legendre moment invariants to blur and affine transformation and their use in image recognition. *Pattern Analysis & Applications*, *17*(2), 311–326. doi:10.1007/s10044-012-0273-y

Dalal, N., & Triggs, B. (2005, June). Histograms of oriented gradients for human detection. In *Computer Vision and Pattern Recognition, 2005. CVPR 2005. IEEE Computer Society Conference on* (Vol. 1, pp. 886-893). IEEE. doi:10.1109/CVPR.2005.177

Dobhal, T., Shitole, V., Thomas, G., & Navada, G. (2015). Human activity recognition using binary motion image and deep learning. *Procedia Computer Science*, *58*, 178–185. doi:10.1016/j.procs.2015.08.050

Dollar, P., Wojek, C., Schiele, B., & Perona, P. (2012). Pedestrian detection: An evaluation of the state of the art. *IEEE Transactions on Pattern Analysis and Machine Intelligence*, *34*(4), 743–761. doi:10.1109/TPAMI.2011.155 PMID:21808091

Flohr, F., & Gavrila, D. (2013). PedCut: an iterative framework for pedestrian segmentation combining shape models and multiple data cues. BMVC. doi:10.5244/C.27.66

Flusser, J., Zitova, B., & Suk, T. (2009). *Moments and moment invariants in pattern recognition*. John Wiley & Sons. doi:10.1002/9780470684757

Forsyth, D., & Ponce, J. (2011). *Computer vision: a modern approach*. Upper Saddle River, NJ: Prentice Hall.

Gao, S., Tsang, I. W. H., Chia, L. T., & Zhao, P. (2010, June). Local features are not lonely–Laplacian sparse coding for image classification. In *Computer Vision and Pattern Recognition (CVPR), 2010 IEEE Conference on* (pp. 3555-3561). IEEE. doi:10.1109/CVPR.2010.5539943

Geismann, P., & Knoll, A. (2010). Speeding up HOG and LBP features for pedestrian detection by multiresolution techniques. *Advances in Visual Computing*, 243-252.

Gonzàlez, J., Moeslund, T. B., & Wang, L. (2012). Semantic Understanding of Human Behaviors in Image Sequences: From video-surveillance to video-hermeneutics. *Computer Vision and Image Understanding*, *116*(3), 305–306. doi:10.1016/j.cviu.2012.01.001

Gonzàlez, J., Moeslund, T. B., & Wang, L. (2012). Semantic Understanding of Human Behaviors in Image Sequences: From video-surveillance to video-hermeneutics. *Computer Vision and Image Understanding*, *116*(3), 305–306. doi:10.1016/j.cviu.2012.01.001

Gorelick, L., Blank, M., Shechtman, E., Irani, M., & Basri, R. (2007). Actions as space-time shapes. *IEEE Transactions on Pattern Analysis and Machine Intelligence*, *29*(12), 2247–2253. doi:10.1109/TPAMI.2007.70711 PMID:17934233

Guo, L. J., & Zhao, J. Y. (2008, December). Specific human detection from surveillance video based on color invariant moments. In *Intelligent Information Technology Application, 2008. IITA'08. Second International Symposium on* (Vol. 2, pp. 331-335). IEEE. doi:10.1109/IITA.2008.326

Hanna, K. J., & Hoyos, H. T. (2017). *U.S. Patent Application No. 15/477,633*. Retrieved from https://www.microsoft.com/en-us/download/details.aspx?id=52315

Hu, M. K. (1962). Visual pattern recognition by moment invariants. *I.R.E. Transactions on Information Theory*, *8*(2), 179–187. doi:10.1109/TIT.1962.1057692

Huang, F. J., Boureau, Y. L., & LeCun, Y. (2007, June). Unsupervised learning of invariant feature hierarchies with applications to object recognition. In *Computer Vision and Pattern Recognition, 2007. CVPR'07. IEEE Conference on* (pp. 1-8). IEEE.

Huang, Z., Bao, Y., Dong, W., Lu, X., & Duan, H. (2014). Online treatment compliance checking for clinical pathways. *Journal of Medical Systems*, *38*(10), 123. doi:10.1007/s10916-014-0123-0 PMID:25149871

Jacob, G. M., & Das, S. (2017). Moving Object Segmentation for Jittery Videos, by Clustering of Stabilized Latent Trajectories. *Image and Vision Computing*, *64*, 10–22. doi:10.1016/j.imavis.2017.05.002

Ko, B. C., Kim, D. Y., Jung, J. H., & Nam, J. Y. (2013). Three-level cascade of random forests for rapid human detection. *Optical Engineering (Redondo Beach, Calif.)*, *52*(2), 027204–027204. doi:10.1117/1.OE.52.2.027204

Kotoulas, L., & Andreadis, I. (2005, October). Image analysis using moments. *5th Int. Conf. on Technology and Automation*, 360364.

Kuryloski, P., Giani, A., Giannantonio, R., Gilani, K., Gravina, R., Seppa, V. P., . . . Yang, A. Y. (2009, June). DexterNet: An open platform for heterogeneous body sensor networks and its applications. In *Wearable and Implantable Body Sensor Networks, 2009. BSN 2009. Sixth International Workshop on* (pp. 92-97). IEEE.

Lan, T., Wang, Y., Yang, W., Robinovitch, S. N., & Mori, G. (2012). Discriminative latent models for recognizing contextual group activities. *IEEE Transactions on Pattern Analysis and Machine Intelligence*, *34*(8), 1549–1562. doi:10.1109/TPAMI.2011.228 PMID:22144516

Laptev, I., Marszalek, M., Schmid, C., & Rozenfeld, B. (2008, June). Learning realistic human actions from movies. In *Computer Vision and Pattern Recognition, 2008. CVPR 2008. IEEE Conference on* (pp. 1-8). IEEE. doi:10.1109/CVPR.2008.4587756

LeCun, Y., Bengio, Y., & Hinton, G. (2015). Deep learning. *Nature, 521*(7553), 436–444. doi:10.1038/nature14539 PMID:26017442

Lee, H., Grosse, R., Ranganath, R., & Ng, A. Y. (2009a, June). Convolutional deep belief networks for scalable unsupervised learning of hierarchical representations. In *Proceedings of the 26th annual international conference on machine learning* (pp. 609-616). ACM. doi:10.1145/1553374.1553453

Lee, H., Pham, P., Largman, Y., & Ng, A. Y. (2009b). Unsupervised feature learning for audio classification using convolutional deep belief networks. Advances in neural information processing systems, 1096-1104.

Liao, S. X., & Pawlak, M. (1996). On image analysis by moments. *IEEE Transactions on Pattern Analysis and Machine Intelligence, 18*(3), 254–266. doi:10.1109/34.485554

Liu, H., Xu, T., Wang, X., & Qian, Y. (2013, January). Related HOG Features for Human Detection Using Cascaded Adaboost and SVM Classifiers. MMM, (2), 345-355. doi:10.1007/978-3-642-35728-2_33

Loy, C. C. (2010). *Activity understanding and unusual event detection in surveillance videos* (Doctoral dissertation). Queen Mary University of London.

Luo, R. C., Chou, Y. T., Liao, C. T., Lai, C. C., & Tsai, A. C. (2007, November). NCCU security warrior: An intelligent security robot system. In *Industrial Electronics Society, 2007. IECON 2007. 33rd Annual Conference of the IEEE* (pp. 2960-2965). IEEE.

Määttä, T., Härmä, A., & Aghajan, H. (2010, August). On efficient use of multi-view data for activity recognition. In *Proceedings of the Fourth ACM/IEEE International Conference on Distributed Smart Cameras* (pp. 158-165). ACM. doi:10.1145/1865987.1866012

Marszalek, M., Laptev, I., & Schmid, C. (2009, June). Actions in context. In *Computer Vision and Pattern Recognition, 2009. CVPR 2009. IEEE Conference on* (pp. 2929-2936). IEEE. doi:10.1109/CVPR.2009.5206557

Matikainen, P., Pillai, P., Mummert, L., Sukthankar, R., & Hebert, M. (2011, March). Prop-free pointing detection in dynamic cluttered environments. In *Automatic Face & Gesture Recognition and Workshops (FG 2011), 2011 IEEE International Conference on* (pp. 374-381). IEEE. doi:10.1109/FG.2011.5771428

Mercimek, M., Gulez, K., & Mumcu, T. V. (2005). Real object recognition using moment invariants. *Sadhana*, *30*(6), 765–775. doi:10.1007/BF02716709

Neverova, N. (2016). *Deep learning for human motion analysis* (Doctoral dissertation). INSA Lyon.

Ngiam, J., Chen, Z., Koh, P. W., & Ng, A. Y. (2011). Learning deep energy models. *Proceedings of the 28th International Conference on Machine Learning (ICML-11)*, 1105-1112.

Nguyen, D. T., Ogunbona, P. O., & Li, W. (2013). A novel shape-based non-redundant local binary pattern descriptor for object detection. *Pattern Recognition*, *46*(5), 1485–1500. doi:10.1016/j.patcog.2012.10.024

Nigam, S., & Khare, A. (2015). Multiresolution approach for multiple human detection using moments and local binary patterns. *Multimedia Tools and Applications*, *74*(17), 7037–7062. doi:10.1007/s11042-014-1951-0

Nigam, S., & Khare, A. (2016). Integration of moment invariants and uniform local binary patterns for human activity recognition in video sequences. *Multimedia Tools and Applications*, *75*(24), 17303–17332. doi:10.1007/s11042-015-3000-z

Nigam, S., Deb, K., & Khare, A. (2013, May). Moment invariants based object recognition for different pose and appearances in real scenes. In *Informatics, Electronics & Vision (ICIEV), 2013 International Conference on* (pp. 1-5). IEEE. doi:10.1109/ICIEV.2013.6572697

Nigam, S., Khare, M., Srivastava, R. K., & Khare, A. (2013, April). An effective local feature descriptor for object detection in real scenes. In *Information & Communication Technologies (ICT), 2013 IEEE Conference on* (pp. 244-248). IEEE. doi:10.1109/CICT.2013.6558098

Ning, J., Zhang, L., Zhang, D., & Wu, C. (2009). Robust object tracking using joint color-texture histogram. *International Journal of Pattern Recognition and Artificial Intelligence*, *23*(07), 1245–1263. doi:10.1142/S0218001409007624

Ning, J., Zhang, L., Zhang, D., & Wu, C. (2012). Robust mean-shift tracking with corrected background-weighted histogram. *IET Computer Vision*, *6*(1), 62–69. doi:10.1049/iet-cvi.2009.0075

Pang, Y., Yuan, Y., Li, X., & Pan, J. (2011). Efficient HOG human detection. *Signal Processing*, *91*(4), 773–781. doi:10.1016/j.sigpro.2010.08.010

Park, Y., Moon, S., & Suh, I. H. (2016). *Tracking Human-like Natural Motion Using Deep Recurrent Neural Networks.* arXiv preprint arXiv:1604.04528

Pietikäinen, M., Hadid, A., Zhao, G., & Ahonen, T. (2011). *Computer vision using local binary patterns* (Vol. 40). Springer. doi:10.1007/978-0-85729-748-8

Porikli, F., Bremond, F., Dockstader, S. L., Ferryman, J., Hoogs, A., Lovell, B. C., ... Venetianer, P. L. (2013). Video surveillance: Past, present, and now the future (DSP Forum). *IEEE Signal Processing Magazine, 30*(3), 190–198. doi:10.1109/MSP.2013.2241312

Rifai, S., Vincent, P., Muller, X., Glorot, X., & Bengio, Y. (2011). Contractive auto-encoders: Explicit invariance during feature extraction. *Proceedings of the 28th international conference on machine learning (ICML-11)*, 833-840.

Rodriguez, M. D., Ahmed, J., & Shah, M. (2008, June). Action mach a spatio-temporal maximum average correlation height filter for action recognition. In *Computer Vision and Pattern Recognition, 2008. CVPR 2008. IEEE Conference on* (pp. 1-8). IEEE. doi:10.1109/CVPR.2008.4587727

Schuldt, C., Laptev, I., & Caputo, B. (2004, August). Recognizing human actions: a local SVM approach. In *Pattern Recognition, 2004. ICPR 2004. Proceedings of the 17th International Conference on* (*Vol. 3*, pp. 32-36). IEEE. doi:10.1109/ICPR.2004.1334462

Shen, J., Yang, W., & Sun, C. (2013). Real-time human detection based on gentle MILBoost with variable granularity HOG-CSLBP. *Neural Computing & Applications, 23*(7-8), 1937–1948. doi:10.1007/s00521-012-1153-5

Singh, S., Velastin, S. A., & Ragheb, H. (2010, August). Muhavi: A multicamera human action video dataset for the evaluation of action recognition methods. In *Advanced Video and Signal Based Surveillance (AVSS), 2010 Seventh IEEE International Conference on* (pp. 48-55). IEEE. doi:10.1109/AVSS.2010.63

Skibbe, H., Reisert, M., Schmidt, T., Brox, T., Ronneberger, O., & Burkhardt, H. (2012). Fast rotation invariant 3D feature computation utilizing efficient local neighborhood operators. *IEEE Transactions on Pattern Analysis and Machine Intelligence, 34*(8), 1563–1575. doi:10.1109/TPAMI.2011.263 PMID:22201055

Sonka, M., Hlavac, V., & Boyle, R. (2014). *Image processing, analysis, and machine vision*. Cengage Learning.

Souvenir, R., & Babbs, J. (2008, June). Learning the viewpoint manifold for action recognition. In *Computer Vision and Pattern Recognition, 2008. CVPR 2008. IEEE Conference on* (pp. 1-7). IEEE. doi:10.1109/CVPR.2008.4587552

Suk, T., & Flusser, J. (2003). Combined blur and affine moment invariants and their use in pattern recognition. *Pattern Recognition, 36*(12), 2895–2907. doi:10.1016/S0031-3203(03)00187-0

Szegedy, C., Liu, W., Jia, Y., Sermanet, P., Reed, S., Anguelov, D., ... Rabinovich, A. (2015). Going deeper with convolutions. *Proceedings of the IEEE conference on computer vision and pattern recognition*, 1-9.

Thompson, M. A., Scott, I. R., Shah, P. L., Ohnstad, T. W., & Weldon, K. A. (2016). *U.S. Patent No. 9,269,215*. Washington, DC: U.S. Patent and Trademark Office.

Tran, C., Doshi, A., & Trivedi, M. M. (2012). Modeling and prediction of driver behavior by foot gesture analysis. *Computer Vision and Image Understanding, 116*(3), 435–445. doi:10.1016/j.cviu.2011.09.008

Vishwakarma, S., & Agrawal, A. (2013). A survey on activity recognition and behavior understanding in video surveillance. *The Visual Computer, 29*(10), 983–1009. doi:10.1007/s00371-012-0752-6

Vrigkas, M., Karavasilis, V., Nikou, C., & Kakadiaris, I. A. (2014). Matching mixtures of curves for human action recognition. *Computer Vision and Image Understanding, 119*, 27–40. doi:10.1016/j.cviu.2013.11.007

Vu, Q. D., & Chung, S. T. (2017, May). Real-time robust human tracking based on Lucas-Kanade optical flow and deep detection for embedded surveillance. In *Information and Communication Technology for Embedded Systems (IC-ICTES), 2017 8th International Conference of* (pp. 1-6). IEEE.

Wang, L., Shi, J., Song, G., & Shen, I. F. (2007, November). Object detection combining recognition and segmentation. In *Asian conference on computer vision* (pp. 189-199). Springer.

Wang, Y., & Mori, G. (2011). Hidden part models for human action recognition: Probabilistic versus max margin. *IEEE Transactions on Pattern Analysis and Machine Intelligence, 33*(7), 1310–1323. doi:10.1109/TPAMI.2010.214 PMID:21135448

Wang, Y., Huang, K., & Tan, T. (2007, June). Human activity recognition based on R transform. In *Computer Vision and Pattern Recognition, 2007. CVPR'07. IEEE Conference on* (pp. 1-8). IEEE. doi:10.1109/CVPR.2007.383505

Weinland, D., Ronfard, R., & Boyer, E. (2006). Free viewpoint action recognition using motion history volumes. *Computer Vision and Image Understanding, 104*(2), 249–257. doi:10.1016/j.cviu.2006.07.013

Wiliem, A., Madasu, V., Boles, W., & Yarlagadda, P. (2012). A suspicious behaviour detection using a context space model for smart surveillance systems. *Computer Vision and Image Understanding, 116*(2), 194–209. doi:10.1016/j.cviu.2011.10.001

Xu, Q. (2017). *3D Body Tracking using Deep Learning*. Academic Press.

Yumak, Z., Ren, J., Thalmann, N. M., & Yuan, J. (2014). Modelling multi-party interactions among virtual characters, robots, and humans. *Presence (Cambridge, Mass.), 23*(2), 172–190. doi:10.1162/PRES_a_00179

Yussiff, A. L., Yong, S. P., & Baharudin, B. B. (2014). Detecting people using histogram of oriented gradients: a step towards abnormal human activity detection. In *Advances in Computer Science and its Applications* (pp. 1145–1150). Berlin: Springer. doi:10.1007/978-3-642-41674-3_159

Zajdel, W., Krijnders, J. D., Andringa, T., & Gavrila, D. M. (2007, September). CASSANDRA: audio-video sensor fusion for aggression detection. In *Advanced Video and Signal Based Surveillance, 2007. AVSS 2007. IEEE Conference on* (pp. 200-205). IEEE. doi:10.1109/AVSS.2007.4425310

Zhang, C. (2016). *Human Activity Analysis using Multi-modalities and Deep Learning* (Doctoral dissertation). The City College of New York.

Zhang, D., & Lu, G. (2004). Review of shape representation and description techniques. *Pattern Recognition, 37*(1), 1–19. doi:10.1016/j.patcog.2003.07.008

Zhang, J., & Tan, T. (2002). Brief review of invariant texture analysis methods. *Pattern Recognition, 35*(3), 735–747. doi:10.1016/S0031-3203(01)00074-7

Zhang, J., Shan, Y., & Huang, K. (2015). ISEE Smart Home (ISH): Smart video analysis for home security. *Neurocomputing, 149*, 752–766. doi:10.1016/j.neucom.2014.08.002

Zhao, Y., & Belkasim, S. (2012). Multiresolution Fourier descriptors for multiresolution shape analysis. *IEEE Signal Processing Letters, 19*(10), 692–695. doi:10.1109/LSP.2012.2210040

Zhou, S., Liu, Q., Guo, J., & Jiang, Y. (2012). ROI-HOG and LBP based human detection via shape part-templates matching. In Neural Information Processing (pp. 109-115). Springer Berlin/Heidelberg. doi:10.1007/978-3-642-34500-5_14

Zhu, Q., Yeh, M. C., Cheng, K. T., & Avidan, S. (2006). Fast human detection using a cascade of histograms of oriented gradients. In *Computer Vision and Pattern Recognition, 2006 IEEE Computer Society Conference on* (Vol. 2, pp. 1491-1498). IEEE.

KEY TERMS AND DEFINITIONS

Datasets: A large collection of images or videos indicating a specific task.

Feature Descriptors: $m \times n$ dimensional matrices indicating particular values for particular objects.

Human Behavior Detection: Analysis and understanding of human behavior and predicting their motion patterns from videos.

Multiview: An incident captured with more than one camera placed at different location and different camera angles.

Quantitative Parameters: Parameters used to describe performance of a particular method. They are generally used for comparison of different methods.

Video Frames: A video is composed of a sequence of consecutive images. These images are called video frames.

Video Surveillance: Monitoring of a specific area though close circuit television cameras (CCTV).

Vision Systems: Systems that employ vision devices in their environment such as sensors or cameras.

Chapter 4
A Survey of 3D Rigid Registration Methods for RGB–D Cameras

Vicente Morell-Gimenez
University of Alicante, Spain

Jose Garcia-Rodriguez
University of Alicante, Spain

Marcelo Saval-Calvo
University of Alicante, Spain

Miguel Cazorla
University of Alicante, Spain

Victor Villena-Martinez
University of Alicante, Spain

Sergio Orts-Escolano
University of Alicante, Spain

Jorge Azorin-Lopez
University of Alicante, Spain

Andres Fuster-Guillo
University of Alicante, Spain

ABSTRACT

Registration of multiple 3D data sets is a fundamental problem in many areas. Many researches and applications are using low-cost RGB-D sensors for 3D data acquisition. In general terms, the registration problem tries to find a transformation between two coordinate systems that better aligns the point sets. In order to review and describe the state-of-the-art of the rigid registration approaches, the authors decided to classify methods in coarse and fine. Due to the high variety of methods, they have made a study of the registration techniques, which could use RGB-D sensors in static scenarios. This chapter covers most of the expected aspects to consider when a registration technique has to be used with RGB-D sensors. Moreover, in order to establish a taxonomy of the different methods, the authors have classified those using different characteristics. As a result, they present a classification that aims to be a guide to help the researchers or practitioners to select a method based on the requirements of a specific registration problem.

DOI: 10.4018/978-1-5225-5628-2.ch004

INTRODUCTION

Registration of multiple 3D data sets is a fundamental problem in many areas as computer vision, medical imaging (Yang et al., 2013), object reconstruction (Pottmann et al., 2002), mobile robotics (Tamas and Goron, 2012), augmented reality (Duan et al., 2009), etcetera. Many researches and applications in this area are using low-cost RGB-D sensors for 3D data acquisition.

In general terms, the registration problem tries to find a transformation between two coordinate systems that better aligns the point sets. This problem is aimed in the case of computer vision by finding (commonly using iterative techniques) the transformation that minimizes the distance between two data sets with an overlapped region. Related to this problem, RGB-D low-cost cameras (e.g. Microsoft Kinect, Primesense Carmine...) provide both depth and color data simultaneously with a good frame rate, which fit many requirements in a wide range of applications. Several reviews related to the registration problem can be found in the literature. In (Zitová and Flusser, 2003) a complete color image registration survey is presented. Tam et al. (Tam et al., 2013) made a survey of registration methods for rigid and non-rigid point clouds and meshes. In (Rusinkiewicz and Levoy, 2001) a comparison among different ICP (Iterative Closest Point) methods is presented while in (Pomerleau et al., 2013) it is proposed a similar study but with real-world data sets.

In this paper, we are focused on a review and classification of the state-of-the-art in rigid registration methods for RGB-D sensors. Therefore, our main contributions are:

- A study of the most used approaches to register data obtained from RGB-D sensors
- A classification and presentation of the different proposals based on a set of different characteristics.

Different techniques can be used to estimate the 3D information from the real world: 3D lasers, stereo cameras, time-of-flight cameras, RGB-D cameras, etcetera. Each kind of sensor has some advantages for a specific purpose. However, many of them are used in a wide range of problems. Some 3D laser systems do not provide color information, so algorithms, which need visual features, are not suitable. Other 3D lasers systems provide color (using different approaches to incorporate color to the depth information), but their cost is prohibitive. Stereo cameras suffer from the lack of textures: image areas without texture do not provide depth information. The visual information of time-of-flight cameras, like SR4000, is infrared. It is affected by natural light and, normally, is noisy. In our previous work (Cazorla et al., 2010) we made some experiments using the SIFT visual feature method (Lowe, 2004) with this kind of cameras. As the SR4000 camera provides noisy images, the repeatability of the SIFT feature was low. RGB-D low-cost sensors (we will refer Kinect as a RGB-D sensor), provide both color and depth information with about 15 frames/second, using structured light. They are composed of three sensors: an IR (infrared) projector, an IR CMOS camera and a RGB camera. The IR sensor provides the depth information. The IR projector sends out a fixed pattern of bright and dark speckles. Using structured light techniques, depth is calculated by triangulation against a known pattern from the projector. The pattern is memorized at a known depth and then for each pixel, a correlation between this known pattern and current pattern is done, providing the current depth at that pixel. The Kinect camera has a resolution of 640 x 480 (307,200 pixels) and works in a range between 1 and 8 meters approximately. A detailed analysis of the accuracy and resolution of this camera can be found in (Khoshelham and Elberink, 2012) and (Lee et al., 2012). Other cameras based on the same RGB-D sensor are Primesense Carmine1 and Asus Xtion2.

Regarding to the registration problem, it can be addressed in two ways. First, searching the solution in the correspondence space. In this case, the problem is comprised of two related sub-problems: correspondence selection and motion (or transformation) estimation. In the former, candidate correspondences between data sets are chosen, while in the latter, transformation minimizing the distances between corresponding points are estimated. In this category lie the feature-based methods, which works with visual or 3D features. Since global properties of objects are vulnerable to occlusions and clutter in the scene (Hetzel et al., 2001), local invariant features are used for this purpose. Moreover, local features can be used with non-rigid objects in scenarios, i.e. articulated or deformable objects. With the features of both data sets, the correspondences are calculated. RANSAC (Random Sample Consensus) (Fischler and Bolles, 1981) paradigm is one of the most used methods to reject wrong matches. It is faster than other methods and allows a proper registration in presence of noisy matched features. However, it depends on the ratio between inliers and outliers. If there are many more outliers than inliers and the number of inliers is low, the probability of finding the best solution is low. Furthermore, if the number of matched features is low, there is a high probability to obtain a small number of inliers.

The second way consists in searching the solution in the transformation space. An objective function is defined (for example, the distance between two datasets) and a search using different transformations to find the transformation that minimizes the objective function is performed. ICP (Chen and Medioni, 1991; Besl and McKay, 1992) is a well-known algorithm included in this second category, based on closest distances. It uses all the points in the scene and needs an initial alignment to register the scene. ICP is extremely slow compared to RANSAC. There exist several variants of it that are faster calculated by reducing the amount of points or accelerating the distance calculation.

In order to review and describe the state-of-the-art of the rigid registration approaches, we decided to classify the methods in coarse methods, which estimates an initial transformation with a more relaxed accuracy, and fine methods, which accurately find the best alignment. This classification is used in (Campbell and Flynn, 2001; Salvi et al., 2007) but many others can be found in the literature, such as dense/sparse, intrinsic/extrinsic, etc. Despite this classification, most of the registration approaches use a hybrid method to firstly coarse register using only a subset of the data and, next, to refine the result using the whole set.

In order to establish a taxonomy of the different methods, we have classified those using different characteristics. The result is a classification table (Table 1) that has a first level according to the application, registration type, data used as input and other characteristics, which subdivides in the second level in a more detailed description. The aim of this classification is to help the reader to select a method based on the requirements of a specific registration problem.

Due to the high variety of methods, we have made a study of the registration methods, which use RGB-D sensors in static scenarios. This study pretends to cover most of the expected aspects to consider when a registration has to be used with RGB-D sensors.

The remainder of this paper is organized as follows; Section 2 presents the registration problem. Then, coarse methods are presented in Section 3 and fine methods in Section 4. Next, summary table with a visual organization of the methods previously detailed, together with a discussion, are presented in Section 5. Finally, the conclusions are drawn in section 6.

REGISTRATION PROBLEM

Figure 1 shows an example of a scene registration process. On the left, we show the two point clouds provided by the Kinect camera each one in its own reference system. As both point clouds are taken from different viewpoints, the displacement creates the effect of objects repeated. On the right, we show both point clouds registered (aligned) together with the reference data (green point set) and the registered one (red points).

As we stated before, registration problem can be afforded by two approaches. But they both share a common definition: Registration problem is the process of transforming different sets of data into the same coordinate system. This means, to find the transformation needed to align one new dataset S to a reference dataset M. In this survey, we focused on the registration of static scenarios, so the transformation needed to align two different views of the scene is the same for all points. Formally, the transformation T (comprised of a rotation and a translation) that minimizes the

Figure 1. Left, two non-aligned point clouds; right, both point clouds aligned using green points as the reference set and red the registered one

distance between the transformed points $S = \{s\}$ and the points $M = \{m\}$ is obtained minimizing:

$$T^* = \arg \min_{T \in V} \sum_{s \in S} \sum_{m \in M} \left\| m - T(s) \right\| \tag{1}$$

where m is the point that matches with the point s, $1 \bullet 1$ is the distance measure between points, usually euclidean distance, and $V = \{T\}$ is the set of all the possible transformations. There are several approaches to solve the registration problem but all of them can be fitted in a general scheme (Figure 1). The main steps of a registration process are:

- The coarse registration step refers to an initial and non-accurate registration. Commonly, this is the first step of the whole system and uses a subset of all the points in each point cloud.
- The fine registration step is commonly applied when more accurate results are needed. Usually, it needs a previous coarse registration. However, a previous alignment is not necessary if point clouds are initially close enough, e.g. when the difference between two point cloud consecutive acquisitions is small (in particular, small movements using high frame rates).

These two main steps can be preceded by a pre-processing step in which a filtering of raw data or a segmentation of specific parts of the scene can be applied. Furthermore, a post-processing step is usually considered for performing surface reconstruction after registration. Regarding the registration process, most approaches follow a similar workflow (Figure 3):

Figure 2. General scheme of registration process

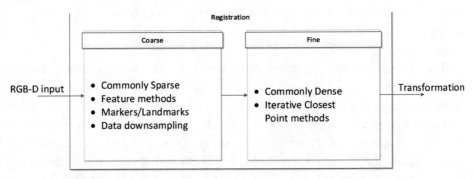

- Subset matching. Here, the goal is to find the best matching between a subset of points in S and a subset of points in M. In feature-based algorithms, descriptors associated to the features are compared to match the subsets. In ICP, on the other hand, just a point as a subset, the closest point, is used.
- Matching evaluation. Once the matches are found, some of them could be wrong so it is necessary to reject them. In feature-based methods, a Random RANSAC technique is a common way to evaluate the matches. However, in ICP-based methods, different techniques of rejection based on the information about the matches are used. For example, keeping only those matches whose distances are below a threshold, which is computed using the standard deviation.
- Finding the transformation. Different techniques can be used, but one of the most used is the Procrustes analysis with Single Value Decomposition.

There exist different ways to apply the registration according the data sets used to be aligned. In a pairwise registration, two subsets of S and M are aligned separately, where both could be point clouds, or one a point set and the other a whole scene (either all previously registered points or a surface). Whereas, multi-view registration, maps a group of data sets all together.

Despite the general registration problem could be clear as aligning different views in a common coordinate system, requirements of a specific problem determine the registration variants. For example, registration of 3D data can be used in many applications. However, some methods are more focused in certain applications as other methods are more adequate to fulfill temporal constraints.

Regarding the application area, we distinguish two main problems: scene and object registration. The former is generally included as a step in the Simultaneous Location and Mapping (SLAM) problem. SLAM (Dissanayake et al., 2001; Endres et al., 2012; Chang et al., 2013; Shen et al., 2013) uses large data sets of a scene and register all of them into a common coordinate system. Moreover, this technique generally makes use of post-processing steps for rectifications in order to reduce the incremental error produced by the cumulative error in each iteration of the system registration.

The second problem regarding application is the object registration. Here, the amount of data involved in each data set is much shorter than the previous one. Moreover, objects are commonly more detailed, having the registration methods problems to determine subtle features instead of noise. A critical aspect in objects registration is the resolution of the depth sensors. The depth resolution expresses the minimum difference in depth that the camera is able to distinguish and is determined by the number of bits dedicated to sample the distances. For example, Microsoft Kinect has 11 bits, where only 10 are used, so 210 (1024) levels of depth can be sampled. Another important issue is that the depth is estimated using a sliding window, so if the object has very thin parts, the window could be larger than the object and estimate a wrong distance as using the mean of all values in this region.

Regarding time performance, coarse registration methods could be faster than fine methods since they use features from the scene reducing the amount of data to be registered. However, they need additional time to calculate features and to match them. Generally speaking, generic algorithms that were conceived to be used with different 3D sensors (stereo, laser, etc.), e.g. ICP for fine registration and RANSAC for coarse registration, have not been developed considering temporal constraints. Despite the ICP has several variants, including the use of a kd-tree to accelerate the search of the closest pair of points, or reducing the number of noise by rejecting wrong data, it is still a slow algorithm. Furthermore, RANSAC is also time consuming in those cases where the number of tested random samples is too large, and then several iterations of the algorithm have to be executed. However, implementations able to work in real-time (15-30 fps) can be found in the literature for both methods (Rusinkiewicz and Levoy, 2001; Raguram et al., 2008). Specific methods designed for RGB-D cameras, including ICP for refinement, as KinectFusion (Izadi et al., 2011b), Dense Visual Odometry (Steinbrucker et al., 2011) and RGBDemo (Kramer et al., 2012) were developed to work with cameras that provide about 30 fps such as the Microsoft Kinect. Therefore, variants of registration methods can be used to work at video frame rates.

COARSE METHODS

In contrast to the methods based on the calculation of distances between pairs of points, the coarse methods do not use all available data, but downsample the data. Feature based methods are commonly used, which try to reduce the amount of

Figure 3. Workflow of registration: a subset matching (a) step is represented by two point-sets S (red points) and M (blue points). The green lines are the matches found. The second image, represents the matching evaluation (b), the black hyphened lines show wrong matches to reject. Finally, the transformation is calculated and applied: the two datasets are coarsely registered (c) and finely aligned (d).

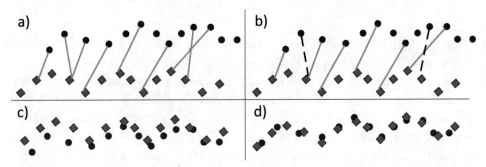

points from both sets (model and scene) using a given detection and description feature method to represent the input data. A feature has a position and a descriptor (the information around the position is described). Features can come from image (visual features) or directly from 3D data (3D features). Irrespective of the kind of feature used, the steps of the registration methods are: feature detection/description, feature matching and transformation model estimation. These steps are shown in Figure 4 and a 2D example is shown in Figure 5.

The feature detection step tries to detect salient and distinctive parts of an object (shapes, closed regions, contours, lines, line intersections, etc.) in the data sets using a feature detection method, and then represent the detected part as a set of values normally called feature descriptor. This step can be directly applied to the 3D data or to the 2D image (when using RGB-D cameras) and then assigning their 3D information. Thus, the number of elements is reduced extremely (from $340,000$ to less than $1,000$ in the case of a Kinect camera).

There are several feature detectors and descriptors that work with 2D data. One of the most used is the SIFT (Scale Invariant Features Transforms) (Lowe, 2004) which provides both feature detection and description.

The SURF feature (Bay et al., 2008) is similar but faster than SIFT. For a deep study of different visual features see (Gil et al., 2010). There are some approaches which use 2D features over the depth images provided by the RGB-D sensors like the NARF (Normal Aligned Radial Feature) (Steder et al., 2010) which is used in systems like (Nowicki and Skrzypczyski, 2013).

Only a few general purpose pure 3D feature detectors/descriptors has been presented. Some extensions of the well-known 2D Harris detector are proposed in

Figure 4. Basic scheme of the feature registration model

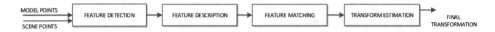

(Gomb, 2009). A pure 3D descriptor is presented in (Rusu et al., 2009). It is called Fast Point Feature Histograms (FPFH) and it is based on a histogram of the differences of angles between the normal of the neighbor points of the source point. Johnson proposes a representation of a 3D surface for matching (Johnson and Hebert, 1997). A planar patches feature extraction process is applied to the raw 3D data in order to obtain a complexity reduction in (Viejo and Cazorla, 2008, 2014). Zeisl et al. use geometric constraints from normals to achieve 3D registration of indoor datasets

(Zeisl et al., 2013). Feature matching methods are commonly based on the Euclidean distance between the feature descriptors.

There are other methods using visual features that allow to directly obtain the registration in the matching process. For example, in (Wu et al., 2008), a new visual feature is presented and used for 3D scene alignment. Other work (Koser and Koch, 2007) uses depth and texture from the visual data to build a visual feature which is invariant in planar surfaces. In (Bauer et al., 2011), surface features are used, concretely histograms of oriented gradients extension (MeshHOG) and rotation-invariant fast features (RIFF) in order to detect the initial position of the patient in radiation therapy.

Figure 5. 2D Feature based registration example: two different point-sets represented (red points and blue diamonds) at their initial position in a); b) Good feature matches are shown as green lines, while bad correspondences are showed using black hyphened lines; c) Final feature registration.

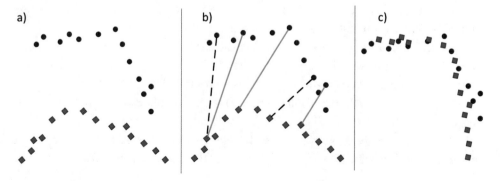

The most used method for finding the transformation between correspondences is based on the RANSAC algorithm (Fischler and Bolles, 1981) since the matching step usually yields a lot of outliers. It is an iterative method that estimates the parameters of a mathematical model from a set of observed data which contains outliers. In our case, we look for a 3D transformation (our model) which best explains the data (matches between 3D features). At each iteration of the algorithm, a subset of data elements (matches) is randomly selected. These elements are considered as inliers. A model (3D transformation) is fitted to those elements. Remaining data are then tested against the fitted model and included as inliers if its error is below a given threshold. If the estimated model is reasonably good (its error is low enough and it has enough matches), it is considered as a good solution. This process is repeated a number of times and then, the best solution is returned.

Other registration methods are based on Genetic Algorithms (GA) as in (Brunnstrom et al., 1996). Using these strategies, the problem of registration is dealt as a search/optimization problem. The final transformation is generated using a genetic algorithm, getting some information of pairs to estimate the best transformation of all the transformation generated by the GA.

Stückler and Behnke (Stückler and Behnke, 2012) use a multi-resolution surfel (surface element) representation of the RGB-D images. This approach uses shape descriptors of the surfels similar to (Rusu et al., 2009) and color histograms in a CIE-Lab space. It uses these feature descriptors and the spatial properties of the multi-resolution octree to get the surfels correspondences. The method iterates to get the estimated transformation in a similar way than ICP.

FINE METHODS

Fine registration methods are commonly used to refine a nearly close registration. In contrast to coarse methods, fine methods usually use all the available information in order to get the correct transformation between data sets. They usually follow an iterative method to incrementally refine the estimated registration due to the amount of data used. Nowadays, one of the most used methods is the Iterative Closest Points (Chen and Medioni, 1991; Besl and McKay, 1992) and its variants. Warping Image methods were used in the past to register (Lucas and Kanade, 1981) colored stereo images. Color is used to constraint the search of the closest points in (Druon et al., 2006). Recently, Kerl et al. presented a 3D colored variation of the method in order to register consecutive RGB-D images (Kerl et al., 2013).

Iterative Closest Point and Variations

Some of the 2D/3D registration methods use the distance information between the matched points to calculate the global transformation which best explains the change of the position of two data sets. In this kind of methods, the registration solves two problems iteratively, (a) finding the correspondence (or matching) between points and (b) estimating the transformation which best explains the correspondences. The most used of these methods is the Iterative Closest Point (ICP) which was introduced in (Chen and Medioni, 1991; Besl and McKay, 1992). The structure of the ICP method is shown in Figure 6.

One of the data sets is the model and the other one is called the scene. The ICP starts with a given initial transformation, and then continues iterating into two consecutive steps. First, scene points are processed using the current transformation. After that, the correspondence pairs are calculated using the scene and model points. At the end of each iteration and using the correspondence pair information, the transformation that best explained the correspondences is calculated. Base scheme of the ICP normally gets a local optimum solution for the registration, depending on the initial transformation given to the ICP method. This is the basic structure of the ICP, from which a lot of variations have emerged which seek to change or improve any of the steps of the classical ICP. Figure 7 shows a 2D example of the Iterative Closest Point algorithm.

The initial ICP (Chen and Medioni, 1991) uses all of the points of the scene and model sets, matching the points with the least Euclidean distance. There are several methods that try to improve this time-consuming step. For example, (Turk and Levoy, 1994) uses a uniform sub-sampling method to reduce the amount of points of the data sets. Another approach is the random selection of points (Masuda et al., 1996), which quickly reduces the number of points, at the risk of losing some parts of the structure of the data sets. The method proposed by Weik (Weik, 1997) uses additional information to find the correspondences, like point color or intensity changes. Other methods use a kd-tree or a closest-point cache system (Simon, 1996) in order to speed up the search process. Other works like (Godin et al., 1994) weights the correspondence pairs with respect to their distance, giving less weight to pairs with higher distance or also depending on the difference between the normal of

Figure 6. Basic scheme of the Iterative Closest Point algorithm

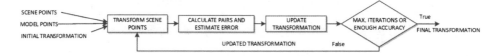

Figure 7. Iterative Closest Point 2D example: two different point-sets represented (red points and blue diamonds) at their initial position in a); b-e) Different iterations of the ICP with the closest points correspondences showed as green lines. f) Final ICP registration.

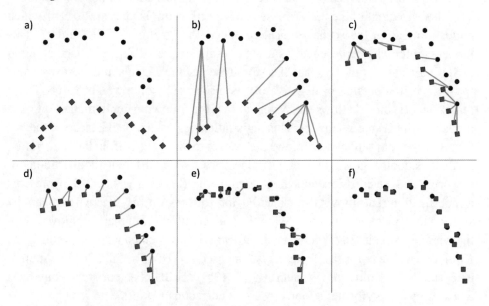

the points. Another criterion for weighting the matching step is to assign different weights with respect to the noise model of the sensors. For example, if it is known that the camera produces more noisy data to distant points, give them less weight than the closest points to the camera. Another approach (Pulli, 1999) proposes rejecting a percentage of the worst matches, according to some criterion, usually distance from the points. Other variants, as (Masuda et al., 1996), reject the pairs whose distance is higher than a multiple of the standard deviation of the distances. Some papers, like (Zinsser et al., 2003), propose a collection of variations of the classical ICP in order to make it more robust and efficient.

Iterative Closest methods are also used in current systems. The method proposed by Zhang et al. (Zhang et al., 2011) searches multiple nearest points, then discard the correspondences with larger distance than a computed threshold and only takes the correspondences that are bi-unique (i.e. only uses a correspondence if its model point has only one correspondence with the scene points).

Henry et al. (Henry et al., 2010) present a hybrid approach of ICP and visual features. This modification of the original ICP makes use of SIFT visual features (Lowe, 2004) and RANSAC (Fischler and Bolles, 1981) to get an initial guess transformation and then applies the ICP iterations but instead of just getting the estimation that reduces the nearest neighbor distance of the points; it also uses the distances between the selected visual features using a parameter to weight both distances. This weighted system allows the ICP to align the two data sets using both the color of the visual features and the geometric information of the point cloud.

Other variations of the ICP are based on KinectFusion (Izadi et al., 2011b), which builds a model of the scene while it computes the positions of the camera. This model is internally represented as a volumetric Truncated Signed Distance Field (TSDF). Each point in the space has stored the distance against the closest surface (positive if it is outside or negative if it is inside) and some weight value. These representation model allows the system to fuse the following depth images into one model, getting a smooth model. This registration against a model instead of the last frame images or point clouds allows the system to avoid the drift in the registration and gets smooth maps and camera trajectories. Some different modifications of the original KinectFusion appeared. Kintinuous (Whelan et al., 2012) presents a modification that allows the KinectFusion to work on bigger environments by shifting the model volume and saving the triangulation mesh that is removed from the working volume. In (Whelan et al., 2013a), they presented an integration of the Kintinous with a color fast feature system based on (Huang et al., 2011). Another extension of the Kintinous (Whelan et al., 2013b) uses SURF features and constructs a pose graph to perform the loop closure to correct camera trajectories.

Warping Image Methods

Warping Image methods are based on the photo-consistency of the image pixels. Lucas-Kanade (Lucas and Kanade, 1981) presented an image registration method that uses the spatial intensity gradient at each point to modify the current esti- mated transformation and uses a Newton-Raphson iteration method to converge to better transformations. Following the same idea, Koch (Koch, 1993) used this approach to efficiently estimate the transformation of a textured model onto an image. This method is based on minimizing the photometric error between the observed and the synthesized image, where this synthesized image is generated by a 3D trans- formation of the 3D projected pixels of the image and then projecting again the transformed 3D points to a 2D image. Comport et al. (Comport et al., 2007) used this approach to estimate the camera position over consecutive stereo images due to the slightly movement of the camera. This approach has been adapted to RGB-D sensors in (Steinbrucker et al., 2011) and (Audras et al., 2011) where they show good registration results and camera position estimations using Kinect images. Figure 8 shows the registration process of the approach presented in (Audras et al., 2011). Recently, Kerl et al. (Kerl et al., 2013) presented a refined approach of their Dense Visual Odometry (DVO) method where they use a weight system of residuals images (differences of the image's gradients) in order to gain robustness against noise and large residual values.

DISCUSSION

The registration methods could be classified according to different characteristics (see Table 1). In this survey, we have decided to initially categorize the methods (Registration type) in coarse, which estimates an initial transformation with a more relaxed accuracy, and fine methods, which accurately find the best alignment. As we can see in Table 1, most of the registration approaches (57%) use a fine registration. They assume that the different data sets are close registered so only a fine registration is needed like the ones based on the Kinect fusion (Chang et al., 2013; Izadi et al., 2011b; Whelan et al., 2012, 2013a). This is the case of the incremental real-time registration methods which only need a few iterations to align the data. However, some of them (20%) (Endres et al., 2012; Chang et al., 2013; Shen et al., 2013; Kramer et al., 2012; Nowicki and Skrzypczyski, 2013; Whelan et al., 2013b) use a hybrid method to firstly coarse register using only a subset of the data and, next, to refine the result using the whole set.

Related to the Registration type, the methods are based on the ICP, Features or Warping. ICP and its variants are the most used methods to fine register a dataset. They search the solution in the transformation space defining an objective function and use different transformations to find the transformation that minimizes the objective function. In general, they use all the points in the scene and needs an initial alignment to register the scene. Features and Warping methods search the solution in the correspondence space. The feature-based methods work with visual or 3D features. Generally, local invariant features are used due to global properties of objects are vulnerable to occlusions and clutter in the scene. Feature based methods try to reduce the amount of points from both sets (model and scene) using a given detection and description feature method to represent the input data. With the features of both data sets, the correspondences are mainly calculated using RANSAC (Fischler and Bolles, 1981). Finally, Warping methods are based on the photo-consistency of the image pixels. It is a fine method that was used in the past to register (Lucas and Kanade, 1981) colored stereo images. Color is used to constraint the search of the closest points in (Druon et al., 2006). Recently, in (Kerl et al., 2013) a 3D colored variation of the method in order to register consecutive RGB-D images. The Warping and ICP methods assume that the different data sets are close registered so only a fine registration is needed (Steinbrucker et al., 2011; Lucas and Kanade, 1981; Kerl et al., 2013; Koch, 1993; Comport et al., 2007; Audras et al., 2011). Despite some exceptions like Genetic Algorithms (Brunnstrom et al., 1996) or warping image methods, most of the current methods (68%) use or a coarse method which uses features (27%) or a variation of the Iterative Closest Point (41%) method. Moreover, a combination of both (Features and ICP) is presented in the 16% of the analyzed methods (Endres et al., 2012; Chang et al., 2013; Shen et al., 2013; Kramer et al., 2012; Nowicki and Skrzypczyski, 2013; Whelan et al., 2013b).

Regarding the application that uses the registration method, it is important to distinguish methods that are more focused in scene or objet reconstruction. Scene reconstruction is included as a previous stage of the Simultaneous Location and Mapping (SLAM) (Whelan et al., 2013a; Huang et al., 2011; Whelan et al., 2013b; Koch, 1993) problem. The methods have to deal with large datasets and they often include post-processing steps for rectifications in order to reduce the incremental error produced by the cumulative error occurred in the registration of the different views of the scene. Since the scene reconstruction uses large datasets, 80% of the methods provide a coarse registration and 70% of the methods use visual features. However, 11 of 16 methods use also the ICP to reconstruct the scene.

The accuracy is the main requirement that the methods aimed to object registration have to fulfill. The datasets are shorter than those used for the scene reconstruction due to the size of the region of interest (centimeters versus meters). However, a more detailed reconstruction is needed. Hence, methods have to deal with noisy data (i.e. signal to noise ratio is lower in this case). About 90% of the studied methods use a fine registration to reconstruct objects because they need high accuracy, being 90% of them related to an ICP variant and just the 10% of them use features extracted from objects (Hetzel et al., 2001; Bauer et al., 2011; Chane et al., 2013; Saval-Calvo et al., 2013). In objects, the use of external markers or the use of a known environment is a well-studied problem. RGBDemo (Shen et al., 2013), which has been specifically developed for object reconstruction using RGB-D sensors, uses color markers (ARToolKit markers) to make an initial coarse registration. Once the initial alignment is done, an ICP and then a subsampling process return the final result. As known environment, Lin and Subbarao (Chane et al., 2013) uses a turntable with a known angle between views to estimate manually the transformation. Finally, few methods (22%) are able to deal with object and scene reconstruction due to the requirements.

Another characteristic of the methods that is much related to the registration type and the application is the data used as an input for the registration. The most used input for all methods is the dense data (48%), using about 31% of the analyzed methods a sparse input. Few methods (20) are able to deal with both input data. Sparse registration methods use only a subset of the dataset with few data, only few key points to calculate the correspondences, whereas a dense input attempts to find correspondences among the whole data set. Hence, a sparse registration is most related to a coarse registration. About 72% of the works share a sparse input with

Table 1. Classification of registration methods

Method	Registration Type		Method Based On			Application		Data Used		Other Features	
	Coarse	Fine	ICP	Features	Warping	Objects/ Surfaces	Scenes	Sparse	Dense	Sequence Management	Landmarks
(Hetzel et al., 2001)	x			x		x	x	x			
(Chen and Medioni, 1991)		x	x			x	x		x		
(Besl and McKay, 1992)		x	x			x	x		x		
(Dissanayake et al., 2001)	x			x			x	x			x
(Endres et al., 2012)	x	x	x	x			x	x	x	x	
(Chang et al., 2013)	x	x	x	x		x	x	x	x	x	
(Shen et al., 2013)	x	x	x	x		x	x	x	x	x	
(Steinbrucker et al., 2011)		x			x		x		x	x	
(Kramer et al., 2012)		x	x	x		x			x	x		x
(Nowicki and Skrzypczyski, 2013)	x	x	x	x		x	x	x	x		
(Viejo and Cazorla, 2008, 2014)	x			x			x	x			
(Zeisl et al., 2013)	x			x			x	x			
(Wu et al., 2008)	x			x			x	x			
(Bauer et al., 2011)	x			x		x		x			
(Stückler and Behnke, 2012)	x			x			x	x			
(Lucas and Kanade, 1981)	x	x			x		x	x			
(Druon et al., 2006)	x		x				x	x			
(Kerl et al., 2013)	x				x		x	x			
(Turk and Levoy, 1994)	x	x	x			x			x		
(Masuda et al., 1996)		x	x			x			x		
(Weik, 1997)		x	x			x		x			
(Simon, 1996)		x	x			x			x		

continued on following page

Table 1. Continued

Method	Registration Type		Method Based On			Application		Data Used		Other Features	
	Coarse	Fine	ICP	Features	Warping	Objects/ Surfaces	Scenes	Sparse	Dense	Sequence Management	Landmarks
(Godin et al., 1994)		x	x			x			x		
(Pulli, 1999)	x	x	x			x			x		
(Zinsser et al., 2003)		x	x			x			x		
(Zhang et al., 2011)		x	x			x			x		
(Whelan et al., 2012)		x	x				x		x		
(Whelan et al., 2013a)		x	x				x		x		
(Huang et al., 2011)		x		x			x	x		x	
(Whelan et al., 2013b)		x	x				x	x	x	x	
(Koch, 1993)		x			x		x	x	x		
(Comport et al., 2007)		x			x		x	x	x		
(Audras et al., 2011)		x			x		x	x	x		
(Izadi et al., 2011a)		x	x			x	x		x		
(Chane et al., 2013)		x		x		x			x	x	x
(Newcombe et al., 2011)		x	x			x	x		x	x	
(Saval-Calvo et al., 2013)		x	x			x		x	x	x	

a coarse registration. Only 5 of 24 methods use the whole data to provide a coarse registration. However, 50% of the methods that uses a subset of keypoints can provide a fine registration. Hence, it is feasible to use just a subset of the data to provide high accuracy in the registration. According to the relationship with the application, more than 70% of the techniques have a sparse input (72%) to reconstruct a scene, being also more than 70% the methods that use dense information to reconstruct an object. On the other hand, if the aim is to reconstruct a scene, 58% use dense input data as 50% to do the same with an object for a sparse input. In conclusion, the methods that use sparse input are more adequate for scenes and dense inputs for objects.

Sequence management is a characteristic of the methods that considers the order of the captured views in the scene. All works that take into account the sequence are fine registration methods in contrast to only 3 methods that provide also coarse

Figure 8. Example of a Warping Image method: the error image and the weight image is used to estimate the transformation of the next iteration; the new image is simulated (warped RGB image) and compared again with the reference one; the process is repeated until convergence and the transformation is provided.

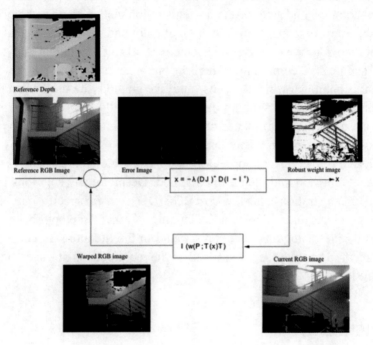

registration (Endres et al., 2012; Chang et al., 2013; Shen et al., 2013). The methods could be irrespectively based on ICP (40%), Feature (58%) and Warping (33%).

According to the application, this management is more typical in scene reconstruction (75%) than in objects (50%). Moreover, is close related to dense input data representing the 75% of the works in opposite to sparse data (50%).

Finally, special landmarks or markers are used to help in the registration, localization or reconstruction task (Dissanayake et al., 2001; Kramer et al., 2012; Chane et al., 2013) due to their special needs of accuracy or the allowed resources. Very few methods use this characteristic (8%) to reconstruct objects or scenes. The most noticeable relation is with feature based registration. The 3 methods that make use of landmarks are feature-based methods.

CONCLUSION

In this paper, we have first made a description of different registration methods using RGB-D sensors, dividing them in coarse and fine methods. We have analyzed and classified common and state-of-the-art registration methods and techniques which are suitable to work using the information of color and depth images that this kind of sensors provide. We can conclude some general rules from our study: methods that use features are commonly to register big areas or surfaces where the initial alignment is unknown while the dense and fine methods are used when the initial alignment is close to the solution because they usually fall in local minima's. In order to speed up the performance of the methods, most methods try to perform a coarse-to-fine registration where less information is used at firsts steps and then the results are refined using more information using hierarchical schemes or using first a coarse method and then a fine method. Despite many solutions have been proposed for registration using low-cost RGB-D sensors for specific purposes, there are many problems that still remain challenging. A general method able to deal with objects or scenes using any data is not found in the literature. In consequence, a specific method has to be selected based on the requirements of a specific problem of registration.

REFERENCES

Audras, C., Comport, A. I., Meilland, M., & Rives, P. 2011. Real-time dense RGBD localisation and mapping. In *Australian Conference on Robotics and Automation*. Monash University.

Bauer, S., Wasza, J., Haase, S., Marosi, N., & Hornegger, J. (2011). Multi-modal surface registration for markerless initial patient setup in radiation therapy using Microsoft's Kinect sensor. *Computer Vision Workshops (ICCV Workshops), 2011 IEEE International Conference on*, 1175–1181.

Bay, H., Ess, A., Tuytelaars, T., & Gool, L. V. (2008). Speeded-Up Robust Features (SURF). *Computer Vision and Image Understanding, 110*(3), 346–359. doi:10.1016/j. cviu.2007.09.014

Besl, P. J., & McKay, N. D. (1992). A method for registration of 3-D shapes. *IEEE Transactions on Pattern Analysis and Machine Intelligence, 14*(2), 239–256. doi:10.1109/34.121791

Brunnstrom, K., Eklundh, J., & Uhlin, T. (1996). Active Fixation for Scene Exploration. *International Journal of Computer Vision*, *17*(2). doi:10.1007/BF00058749

Campbell, R. J., & Flynn, P. J. (2001). A survey of free-form object representation and recognition techniques. *Computer Vision and Image Understanding*, *81*(2), 166–210. doi:10.1006/cviu.2000.0889

Cazorla, M., Viejo, D., & Pomares, C. (2010). Study of the SR4000 camera. In *Workshop of Physical Agents*. Red de Agentes Físicos.

Chane, C. S., Schütze, R., Boochs, F., & Marzani, F. S. (2013). Registration of 3D and Multispectral Data for the Study of Cultural Heritage Surfaces. *Sensors (Basel)*, *13*(1), 1004–1020. doi:10.3390/s130101004 PMID:23322103

Chang, P., Shen, J., & Cheung, S.-C. (2013). A Robust RGB-D SLAM System for 3D Environment with Planar Surfacess. *Proc. of the IEEE International Conference on Image Processing*.

Chen, Y., & Medioni, G. (1991). Object modeling by registration of multiple range images. *Proceedings IEEE International Conference on Robotics and Automation*, 2724-2729. doi:10.1109/ROBOT.1991.132043

Comport, A. I., Malis, E., & Rives, P. (2007). Accurate Quadrifocal Tracking for Robust 3D Visual Odometry. *Robotics and Automation, 2007 IEEE International Conference on*, 40–45.

Dissanayake, M., Newman, P., Clark, S., Durrant-Whyte, H. F., & Csorba, M. (2001). A solution to the simultaneous localization and map building (SLAM) problem. Robotics and Automation. *IEEE Transactions on*, *17*(3), 229–241.

Druon, S., Aldon, M.-J., & Crosnier, A. (2006). Color Constrained ICP for Registration of Large Unstructured 3D Color Data Sets. *Information Acquisition, 2006 IEEE International Conference on*, 249–255.

Duan, L., Guan, T., & Yang, B. (2009). Registration Combining Wide and Narrow Baseline Feature Tracking Techniques for Markerless AR Systems. *Sensors (Basel)*, *9*(12), 10097–10116. doi:10.3390/s91210097 PMID:22303164

Endres, F., Hess, J., Engelhard, N., Sturm, J., Cremers, D., & Burgard, W. (2012). An Evaluation of the {RGB-D SLAM} System. *Proc. of the IEEE International Conference on Robotics and Automation (ICRA)*. doi:10.1109/ICRA.2012.6225199

Fischler, M. A., & Bolles, R. C. (1981). Random sample consensus: A paradigm for model fitting with applications to image analysis and automated cartography. *Communications of the ACM*, *24*(6), 381–395. doi:10.1145/358669.358692

Gil, A., Mozos, O., Ballesta, M., & Reinoso, O. (2010). A comparative evaluation of interest point detectors and local descriptors for visual SLAM. *Machine Vision and Applications*, *21*(6), 905–920. doi:10.1007/s00138-009-0195-x

Godin, G., Rioux, M., & Baribeau, R. (1994). Three-dimensional registration using range and intensity information. *Proc. SPIE*, 2350, 279-290. doi:10.1117/12.189139

Gomb, P. (2009). Detection of Interest Points on 3D Data: Extending the Harris Operator. In Computer Recognition Systems 3. Springer Berlin Heidelberg.

Henry, P., Krainin, M., Herbst, E., Ren, X., & Fox, D. (2010). Rgbd mapping: Using depth cameras for dense 3d modeling of indoor environments. RGB-D: Advanced Reasoning with Depth Cameras Workshop in conjunction with RSS.

Hetzel, G., Leibe, B., Levi, P., & Schiele, B. (2001). 3D Object Recognition from Range Images using Local Feature Histograms. In *CVPR* (vol. 2, pp. 394–399). IEEE Computer Society. doi:10.1109/CVPR.2001.990988

Huang, A. S., Bachrach, A., Henry, P., Krainin, M., Maturana, D., Fox, D., & Roy, N. (2011). *Visual Odometry and Mapping for Autonomous Flight Using an RGB-D Camera. Int. Symposium on Robotics Research (ISRR)*, Flagstaff, AZ.

Izadi, S., Kim, D., Hilliges, O., Molyneaux, D., Newcombe, R. A., Kohli, P., . . . Fitzgibbon, A. W. (2011a). KinectFusion: Real-time 3D reconstruction and interaction using a moving depth camera. UIST, 559–568.

Izadi, S., Newcombe, R. A., Kim, D., Hilliges, O., Molyneaux, D., Hodges, S., . . . Fitzgibbon, A. W. (2011b). KinectFusion: Real-time dynamic 3D surface reconstruction and interaction. SIGGRAPH Talks, 23:1-23:1.

Johnson, A. E., & Hebert, M. (1997). Surface registration by matching oriented points. *3-D Digital Imaging and Modeling, 1997. Proceedings., International Conference on Recent Advances in*, 121–128.

Kerl, C., Sturm, J., & Cremers, D. (2013). Robust Odometry Estimation for RGB-D Cameras. *Proc. of the IEEE Int. Conf. on Robotics and Automation (ICRA)*.

Khoshelham, K., & Elberink, S. O. (2012). Accuracy and Resolution of Kinect Depth Data for Indoor Mapping Applications. *Sensors (Basel)*, *12*(2), 1437–1454. doi:10.3390/s120201437 PMID:22438718

Koch, R. (1993). *Dynamic 3D Scene Analysis through Synthesis Feedback Control*. Academic Press.

Koser, K., & Koch, R. (2007). Perspectively Invariant Normal Features. *Computer Vision, 2007. ICCV 2007. IEEE 11th International Conference on*, 1–8. doi:10.1109/ICCV.2007.4408837

Kramer, J., Parker, M., Burrus, N., Echtler, F., & Herrera, D. (2012). Object Modeling and Detection. Hacking the Kinect, 173–206. doi:10.1007/978-1-4302-3868-3_9

Lee, H. F., Siddiqui, M. K., Rafibakhsh, N., Gong, J., & Gordon, C. (2012). Analysis of XBOX Kinect Sensor Data for Use on Construction Sites. *Depth Accuracy and Sensor Interference Assessment. Ch.*, *86*, 848–857.

Lowe, D. G. (2004). Distinctive Image Features from Scale-Invariant Keypoints. *International Journal of Computer Vision*, *60*(2), 91–110. doi:10.1023/B:VISI.0000029664.99615.94

Lucas, B. D., & Kanade, T. (1981). An Iterative Image Registration Technique with an Application to Stereo Vision. Academic Press.

Masuda, T., Sakaue, K., & Yokoya, N. (1996). Registration and Integration of Multiple Range Images for 3-D Model Construction. *Proceedings of the 1996 International Conference on Pattern Recognition (ICPR '96)*, 879. doi:10.1109/ICPR.1996.546150

Newcombe, R. A., Izadi, S., Hilliges, O., Molyneaux, D., Kim, D., Davison, A. J., . . . Fitzgibbon, A. W. (2011). KinectFusion: Real-time dense surface mapping and tracking. ISMAR, 127–136.

Nowicki, M., & Skrzypczyski, P. (2013). Robust Registration of Kinect Range Data for Sensor Motion Estimation. *Proceedings of the 8th International Conference on Computer Recognition Systems CORES 2013*, 835–844. doi:10.1007/978-3-319-00969-8_82

Pomerleau, F., Colas, F., Siegwart, R., & Magnenat, S. (2013). Comparing ICP variants on real-world data sets. *Autonomous Robots*, *34*(3), 133–148. doi:10.1007/s10514-013-9327-2

Pottmann, H., Leopoldseder, S., & Hofer, M. (2002). Simultaneous registration of multiple views of a 3D object. Intl. Archives of the Photogrammetry, Remote Sensing and Spatial Information Sciences, 34(3A), 265–270.

Pulli, K. (1999). Multiview registration for large data sets. *Proc. Second International Conference on 3-D Digital Imaging and Modeling*, 160–168. doi:10.1109/IM.1999.805346

Raguram, R., Frahm, J.-M., & Pollefeys, M. (2008). A Comparative Analysis of RANSAC Techniques Leading to Adaptive Real-Time Random Sample Consensus. Lecture Notes in Computer Science, 5303, 500–513. doi:10.1007/978-3-540-88688-4_37

Rusinkiewicz, S., & Levoy, M. (2001). Efficient variants of the ICP algorithm. *Proc. Third International Conference on 3-D Digital Imaging and Modeling*, 145–152. doi:10.1109/IM.2001.924423

Rusu, R. B., Blodow, N., & Beetz, M. (2009). Fast Point Feature Histograms (FPFH) for 3D registration. *Robotics and Automation, 2009. ICRA '09. IEEE International Conference on*, 3212–3217.

Salvi, J., Matabosch, C., Fofi, D., & Forest, J. (2007). A review of recent range image registration methods with accuracy evaluation. *Image and Vision Computing*, 25(5), 578–596. doi:10.1016/j.imavis.2006.05.012

Saval-Calvo, M., Azorin-Lopez, J., & Fuster-Guillo, A. (2013). Model-Based Multi-view Registration for RGB-D Sensors. Lecture Notes in Computer Science, 7903, 496–503. doi:10.1007/978-3-642-38682-4_53

Shen, J., Su, P.-C., Cheung, S. S., & Zhao, J. (2013, September). Virtual Mirror Rendering With Stationary RGB-D Cameras and Stored 3-D Background. *Image Processing. IEEE Transactions on*, 22(9), 3433–3448. PMID:23782808

Simon, D. A. (1996). *Fast and accurate shape-based registration* (Ph.D. thesis). Carnegie Mellon University.

Steder, B., Rusu, R. B., Konolige, K., & Burgard, W. (2010). NARF: 3D range image features for object recognition. In: Workshop on Defining and Solving Realistic Perception Problems in Personal Robotics. *IEEE/RSJ Int. Conf. on Intelligent Robots and Systems (IROS)*.

Steinbrucker, F., Sturm, J., & Cremers, D. (2011). Real-time visual odometry from dense RGB-D images. *Computer Vision Workshops (ICCV Workshops), 2011 IEEE International Conference on*, 719–722. doi:10.1109/ICCVW.2011.6130321

Stückler, J., & Behnke, S. (2012). *Model Learning and Real-Time Tracking Using Multi- Resolution Surfel Maps*. AAAI.

Tam, G. K. L., Cheng, Z.-Q., Lai, Y.-K., Langbein, F. C., Liu, Y., Marshall, D., ... Rosin, P. L. (2013). Registration of 3D Point Clouds and Meshes: A Survey from Rigid to Nonrigid. *Visualization and Computer Graphics. IEEE Transactions on*, 19(7), 1199–1217.

Tamas, L., & Goron, L. C. (2012). 3D map building with mobile robots. *Control Automation (MED), 2012 20th Mediterranean Conference on*, 134–139.

Turk, G., & Levoy, M. (1994). Zippered polygon meshes from range images. *Proceedings of the 21st annual conference on Computer graphics and interactive techniques*, 311–318.

Viejo, D., & Cazorla, M. (2008). 3D Model Based Map Building. *International Symposium on Robotics, ISR 2008.*

Viejo, D., & Cazorla, M. (2014). A robust and fast method for 6DoF motion estimation from generalized 3D data. *Autonomous Robots*, *36*(4), 295–308. doi:10.1007/s10514-013-9354-z

Weik, S. (1997). Registration of 3-D partial surface models using luminance and depth information. *3-D Digital Imaging and Modeling, 1997. Proceedings., International Conference on Recent Advances in*, 93–100.

Whelan, T., Johannsson, H., Kaess, M., Leonard, J. J., & McDonald, J. B. (2013a). Robust Real-Time Visual Odometry for Dense {RGB-D} Mapping. IEEE Intl. Conf. on Robotics and Automation, ICRA.

Whelan, T., Kaess, M., Fallon, M. F., Johannsson, H., Leonard, J. J., & McDonald, J. B. (2012). Kintinuous: Spatially Extended {K}inect{F}usion. RSS Workshop on RGB-D: Advanced Reasoning with Depth Cameras, Sydney, Australia.

Whelan, T., Kaess, M., Leonard, J. J., & McDonald, J. B. (2013b). Deformation-based Loop Closure for Large Scale Dense {RGB-D SLAM}. IEEE/RSJ Intl. Conf. on Intelligent Robots and Systems, IROS, Tokyo, Japan.

Wu, C., Clipp, B., Li, X., Frahm, J.-M., & Pollefeys, M. (2008). 3D model matching with Viewpoint-Invariant Patches (VIP). *Computer Vision and Pattern Recognition, 2008. CVPR 2008. IEEE Conference on*, 1–8.

Yang, F., Ding, M., Zhang, X., Wu, Y., & Hu, J. (2013). Two Phase Non-Rigid Multi- Modal Image Registration Using Weber Local Descriptor-Based Similarity Metrics and Normalized Mutual Information. *Sensors (Basel)*, *13*(6), 7599–7617. doi:10.3390/s130607599 PMID:23765270

Zeisl, B., Köser, K., & Pollefeys, M. (2013). Automatic Registration of RGBD Scans via Salient Directions. *Computer Vision, 2013. ICCV 2013. IEEE 16th International Conference on.*

Zhang, L., Choi, S.-I., & Park, S.-Y. (2011). Robust ICP Registration Using Biunique Correspondence. *3D Imaging, Modeling, Processing, Visualization and Trans- mission (3DIMPVT), 2011 International Conference on*, 80–85. doi:10.1109/3DIMPVT.2011.18

Zinsser, T., Schmidt, J., & Niemann, H. (2003). A refined ICP algorithm for robust 3-D correspondence estimation. Image Processing, 2003. *ICIP 2003. Proceedings. 2003 International Conference on, 2.*

Zitová, B., & Flusser, J. (2003). Image registration methods: A survey. *Image and Vision Computing, 21*(11), 977–1000. doi:10.1016/S0262-8856(03)00137-9

Section 2
Image Processing

Chapter 5
Applying Cellular Automata–Based Structures to Hyperspectral Image Processing

Blanca María Priego Torres
Mytech Ingeniera Aplicada Ltd, Spain & University of A Coruña, Spain

Richard J. Duro Fernández
University of A Coruña, Spain

ABSTRACT

This chapter addresses the problem of processing hyperspectral images (HI) and sequences leading to high efficiency implementations. A new methodology based on the application of cellular automata (CA) is presented to solve two different processing tasks, the segmentation and denoising of HI and sequences, respectively. CA structures present potential benefits over traditional approaches since they are computationally efficient and can adapt to the particularities of the task to be solved. However, it is necessary to generate an appropriate rule set for each particular problem, which is usually a difficult task. The generation of the rule sets is handled here following a new methodology based on the application of evolutionary algorithms and using synthetic low-dimensionality images and sequences as training datasets, which results in CA structures that can be used to process HI and sequences successfully, thus avoiding the problem of lack of labeled reference images. Both processing approaches have been tested over real HI providing very competitive results.

DOI: 10.4018/978-1-5225-5628-2.ch005

INTRODUCTION

In hyperspectral images, the spectral information of every pixel is collected in a large number of contiguous discrete spectral bands. The wealth of information provided by the large amount of data produced for a single scene is a great help in solving a variety of processing tasks. However, practical hyperspectral applications typically require these large amounts of data to be processed in (near) real-time. Decreasing the data processing time involves, on the one hand, the design of time-efficient data analysis techniques. On the other hand, it is desirable that these algorithms can be easily processed in a concurrent fashion within hardware such as GPUs

In this respect, Cellular Automata (CA) are some of the most common and simple models of parallel computation. CAs are dynamic systems consisting of a regular spatially distributed grid of cells, each one characterized by its state. The state of every cell is updated in parallel depending on its current state, the state of neighboring cells and a set of transition rules. The crucial point in the use of CAs is to properly determine this set of transition rules, that is, to infer a set of rules that when applied locally to every cell, lead to the desired global behavior of the automata, which is far from being a straightforward task.

Recent works have demonstrated the applicability of CAs to grayscale and RGB (Red, Green and Blue) images when solving processing tasks such as image compression, resizing, skeletonization, erosion/dilation, edge detection, segmentation, forgery detection, content based retrieval and pattern generation (Díaz-Pernil et al. 2014; Dogaru and Dogaru, 2014; Gao and Yang, 2014; Ioannidis et al. 2014; Mardiris and Chatzis, 2014; Minoofam et al. 2014; Rosin and Sun, 2014; Tralic et al. 2014; van Zijl, 2014). However, very little work has been carried out for the application of CAs to processing hyperspectral images (Lee and Bruce, 2010) and, in most cases, the rules are set manually and in an ad-hoc manner.

This chapter describes a methodology for applying CAs to hyperspectral data in order to address different processing tasks. The first one of these tasks is the segmentation of still hyperspectral images, aiming to transform the hyperspectral datacubes into modified versions that are easier to process by, for example, subsequent classification methods. Once this approach has been analyzed and validated, the applicability of CAs to hyperspectral data is pushed to a higher complexity level by introducing the temporal dimension in the processing of sequences of multi-temporal hyperspectral images. In this the case, the cellular automata structures deal with the denoising problem by taking into account the inter-dimensional diversity by jointly processing the spatial, spectral and temporal information of multi-temporal image sequences.

The application of the proposed methodology entails the following advantages:

- The CA structures have the capacity of adapting to what the user desires contemplating the fact that there may be multiple ways of solving the processing task.
- The transition rules are obtained automatically by following a training procedure based on evolutionary algorithms that avoids having to resort to large training or labelled sets of real images. In the evaluation step of the evolutionary algorithm low dimensional reference samples are used, thus simplifying and accelerating the training process.
- The CA structures work with the complete spectral breadth of the images, avoiding projecting the spectral information onto lower dimensional spaces.

The remainder of this chapter is structured as follows. In section II, the CA-based approach for the segmentation of hyperspectral images is introduced. The particular encoding of the CA structures is presented, as well as the strategy followed for the proper selection of the transition rules that determine the segmentation behavior of the CA. Examples of the application of the method over benchmark hyperspectral images are presented and compared to the results obtained using classification algorithms extracted from the literature. Section III presents a novel CA-based filtering method for the denoising of hyperspectral image sequences. The encoding of the rules particularized to this problem and the methodology followed to learn the set of transition rules are described. Furthermore, the proposed method is compared over both simulated and real sequences to several state-of-the-art algorithms. Finally, some concluding remarks are summarized in section IV.

APPLICATION OF CA STRUCTURES TO SEGMENT HYPERSPECTRAL IMAGES

The segmentation or classification of hyperspectral images is perceived as a challenging task mainly due to three problems. Firstly, the segmentation of an image depends on the application and the needs of the user. For instance, a same urban scene can be segmented into regions corresponding to buildings, roads, vegetation, etc. or into more detailed regions such as facades, roofs, defects, travelled ways, sidewalks, etc. Secondly, there is a lack of labelled publicly available hyperspectral datasets, making it difficult to train algorithms to obtain robust and generalizable methods. The last issue is related to the fact that the segmentation and classification of hyperspectral data usually presents very high computing requirements. This is usually addressed by projecting the high dimensional image onto a lower dimension before segmenting in order to minimize the processing and hence the execution times, leading to the problem of possible loss of information.

Aiming to address these segmentation issues, this section presents a cellular automata based segmenter structure called Multi-Gradient based Cellular Automaton (MGCA). The effect of the application of the MGCA structure to a hyperspectral cube is an image "regularization" or segmentation in which pixels that should belong to the same region following a particular type of segmentation turn out to share a very similar spectrum.

The behavior of the MGCA mainly depends on a set of transition rules that are determined through an evolutionary based procedure called ECAS-II. The ECAS-II methodology automatically provides transition rule sets adapted to particular segmentation requirements. Moreover, the training step of the ECAS-II is fed by low dimensional training images, created taking into account the user segmentation requirements.

The remainder of this section is structured as follows. Firstly, the MGCA structure is presented and the ECAS-II methodology is described. Afterwards, experimental results of the proposed algorithm are compared to those found in the literature. For the purpose of presenting a quantitative comparison, a classification step is utilized after the MGCA segmentation.

MGCA

For the application of the MGCA structure, a cell of the CA is placed over each pixel of the hyperspectral image. The cell is in a particular state (s_i), that is initially given by the N-band spectrum of its corresponding pixel. The state space of the MGCA is continuous and corresponds to the positive vector space $\mathbb{R}^N$. During the execution of the MGCA, the state of each cell is iteratively modified making the global result converge towards a segmented image. In order to update the spectrum of each cell every iteration of the CA, one out of a set of M transition rules that controls the automaton behavior must be selected. This selection is performed based on the state of the spectrum of the cell and on the spectra of the $N_{s_{max}} \times N_{s_{max}}$ closest neighboring cells, where $N_{s_{max}}$ is the maximum size considered for the spatial window centered over each cell.

To take into account the spectral information of the neighboring cells, it is necessary to establish a spectral distance measure. The authors have opted for the spectral angle, SA, (normalized between 0 and 1), taking advantage of its independence from the number of spectral components, which allows running the same CA over images of different number of spectral bands. For a cell i, the normalized spectral angle, $\alpha_{i,j}$, with respect to its neighboring cell j is defined as:

$$\alpha_{i,j} = \frac{2}{\pi} \cos^{-1} \left(\frac{\sum s_{ij} s_i}{\sqrt{\sum s_{ij}^2} \sqrt{\sum s_i^2}} \right), \ \alpha_{i,j} \in \left[0, 1\right] \tag{1}$$

where the summation is performed over the components of the state of s_i, i.e., the spectral dimension of a pixel.

As stated earlier, the CA applies a particular transition rule over each cell depending on the information from its neighborhood. More specifically, spatial gradients, are calculated taking into account the pixels contained in three differen $N_S \times N_S$ cell windows, where $N_S = \{3, 5, 7\}$, providing information on the intensity and direction of spectral changes in the image at different resolutions. For each of the $N_S \times N_S$ windows, two bi-dimensional masks, $M_{X_{N_S}}$ and $M_{Y_{N_S}}$, are used to extract the spatial gradients:

$$\boldsymbol{G}_{N_{S_i}} = \left(G_{X_{N_{S_i}}}, G_{Y_{N_{S_i}}} \right), \ N_S = \{3, 5, 7\} \tag{2}$$

$$G_{X_{N_{S_i}}} = \sum_{j=1}^{N_S \cdot N_S} \alpha_{i,j} M_{X_{N_{S_j}}}, \ G_{Y_{N_{S_i}}} = \sum_{j=1}^{N_S \cdot N_S} \alpha_{i,j} M_{Y_{N_{S_j}}} \tag{3}$$

where $M_{X_{N_{S_j}}}$ and $M_{Y_{N_{S_j}}}$ represent the jth elements of the gradient masks $M_{X_{N_S}}$ and $M_{Y_{N_S}}$, and $\boldsymbol{G}_{N_{S_i}}$ denotes the gradient vector located at cell i, calculated considering the neighboring cells in a window of size $N_S \times N_S$.

Each gradient vector can be expressed as a modulus value, $\left| \boldsymbol{G}_{N_{S_i}} \right|$, related to the intensity of the spectral change following the direction given by the angle value, $\phi_{N_{S_i}}$, defined as:

$$\left| \boldsymbol{G}_{N_{S_i}} \right| = \sqrt{G_{X_{N_{S_i}}}^2 + G_{Y_{N_{S_i}}}^2}, \ \phi_{N_{S_i}} = \tan^{-1} \left(\frac{G_{Y_{N_{S_i}}}}{G_{X_{N_{S_i}}}} \right) \tag{4}$$

In terms of the structure of the cellular automaton, the transition rule set that governs its behavior consists of a set of **M** rules, each one of them made up of 6 parameters, the first five corresponding to the condition and the last one to the action:

$$CA = \begin{pmatrix} \left|G_{r3_1}\right| & \left|G_{r5_1}\right| & \left|G_{r7_1}\right| & \phi_{r5_1} & \phi_{r7_1} & \theta_{r_1} \\ \vdots & \vdots & \vdots & \vdots & \vdots & \vdots \\ \left|G_{r3_k}\right| & \left|G_{r5_k}\right| & \left|G_{r7_k}\right| & \phi_{r5_k} & \phi_{r7_k} & \theta_{r_k} \\ \vdots & \vdots & \vdots & \vdots & \vdots & \vdots \\ \left|G_{r3_M}\right| & \left|G_{r5_M}\right| & \left|G_{r7_M}\right| & \phi_{r5_M} & \phi_{r7_M} & \theta_{r_M} \end{pmatrix} \tag{5}$$

Each iteration of the CA, only one of these M rules is applied over each cell. To decide which, the neighborhood information of the pixel $\left(\left|G_{3_i}\right|, \left|G_{5_i}\right|, \left|G_{7_i}\right|, \phi_{3_i}, \phi_{5_i}, \phi_{7_i}\right)$ is compared to the first 5 parameters of each of the M rules $\left(\left|G_{r3_k}\right|, \left|G_{r5_k}\right|, \left|G_{r7_k}\right|, \phi_{r3_k}, \phi_{r5_k}, \phi_{r7_k}\right)$ and the rule that is closest is chosen. Only 5 parameters are used because the representation has been chosen so that the three gradient vectors as a group are independent from rotations and reflections. For this reason, parameter ϕ_{r3_k} is taken as zero and is not included as a parameter of the rule.

The distance between the neighborhood vector and the vectors that represent a rule, which is calculated as the sum of the L^2 norms of the vector differences once the vectors have been rotated and reflected will be denoted as d_{ik}:

$$d_{ik} = \left\|\boldsymbol{G}_{3_i} - \boldsymbol{G}'_{r3_k}\right\| + \left\|\boldsymbol{G}_{5_i} - \boldsymbol{G}'_{r5_k}\right\| + \left\|\boldsymbol{G}_{7_i} - \boldsymbol{G}'_{r7_k}\right\| \tag{6}$$

where $\left\{\boldsymbol{G}_{3_i}, \boldsymbol{G}_{5_i}, \boldsymbol{G}_{7_i}\right\}$ are the gradient vectors of the cell under evaluation and $\left\{\boldsymbol{G}'_{r3_k}, \boldsymbol{G}'_{r5_k}, \boldsymbol{G}'_{r7_k}\right\}$ those of the gradient vectors representing rule k after rotating them an angle ϕ and, if necessary, reflecting them.

Summarizing, the process of selecting a rule consists in calculating the minimum distance d_{ik} for each rule and selecting the rule, s, that provides the lowest value for the distance, $s = \arg\min_{k \in \{1,2,\dots,M\}} d_{ik}$.

The last parameter of the selected rule contains the information required to update the state of cell i. The state of the cell will be modified by performing a weighted average of its state or spectrum and that of some of its neighbors. If the direction given by $\phi + \theta_{rs}$ for a distance of 1 pixel is followed, where ϕ is the rotation angle of the selected rule that was used to calculate the distance d_{is}, and θ_{rs} is the last parameter of rule s, we will be at a point of the image, P_i. The neighboring cells used to modify the spectrum of cell i will be located at a maximum distance of one pixel from P_i .

Thus, the update of the state of cell i, $\boldsymbol{s'}_i$, will be given by the weighted average of the spectrum of those cells and that of i:

$$\boldsymbol{s'}_i = \sum\nolimits_{j=1}^{n} w_{ij} \boldsymbol{s}_{ij} + w_i \boldsymbol{s}_i \tag{7}$$

$$w_{ij} = \frac{f_r(r_j)}{\sum_{j=1}^{n} f_r(r_j) + f_{th}} , \ w_i = \frac{f_{th}}{\sum_{j=1}^{n} f_r(r_j) + f_{th}} \tag{8}$$

$$f_r(r_j) = \begin{cases} f_{th}, & \dfrac{1}{r_j} > f_{th} \\[2ex] \dfrac{1}{r_j}, & \dfrac{1}{r_j} \le f_{th} \end{cases} \tag{9}$$

$\boldsymbol{s'}_i$ is the updated spectrum of cell i; $\boldsymbol{s}_i$ represents the original spectrum of cell i; $\boldsymbol{s}_{ij}$ is the spectrum of cell j which is a neighbor of cell i; n is the number of neighboring cells that will participate in the update of the state of cell i; r_j is the distance between the neighboring cell j and point P_i; w_{ij} is the weight associated to the spectrum of cell j; w_i is the weight associated to the spectrum of cell i; $f_r(r_j)$ is a function that assigns weights as a function of distance r_j.

Following this procedure, the CA is applied iteratively to the whole image producing a new hyperspectral cube every iteration, preventing this way any projection onto lower dimensions. With the appropriate rules, the final hyperspectral cube will be a segmented version of the original, where each region will be represented by a narrow range of spectra.

ECAS-II

To select the rules that will control the behavior of the cellular automata, automatic optimization process in the form of an Evolutionary Algorithm (EA) has been chosen. In particular, for this implementation a Differential Evolution algorithm (DE) (Storn and Price, 1997) has been chosen.

Regarding the encoding of the individuals, in this case, the set of transition rules that make up the CA is encoded as a vector of $6 \cdot M$ floating point values. The values corresponding to $\left|G_{r3_k}\right|$, $\left|G_{r5_k}\right|$ and $\left|G_{r7_k}\right|$ belong to $\left[0, \sqrt{2}\right]$ and those corresponding to ϕ_{r5_k}, ϕ_{r7_k} and θ_{r_k} are in the interval $\left[0, 2\pi\right]$.

The fitness function to be minimized by the DE is defined as the maximum value of two error measurements: intra-region $\left(e_{intra}\right)$ error and inter-region $\left(e_{inter}\right)$ error:

$$e = \max\left(e_{intra}, e_{inter}\right) \tag{10}$$

The intra-region error provides a measure of the homogeneity of the regions in the image, being a region a set of pixels that share the same label in the ground truth associated to the training image. On the other hand, the inter-region error provides a measure of the dissimilarity of the different regions in the segmented image.

Every time the CA is evaluated, it needs to be executed over a training image for a given number of iterations and the result compared to the ground truth. Since the number of publicly available hyperspectral images is very limited, and the labelling of the available hyperspectral images is not entirely reliable, it seems advantageous to use synthetic datasets, thus preventing the validation from always using the same dataset and considering the type of segmentation that is desired with a reliable dataset.

Furthermore, the fact that the application of the ECAS-II algorithm over an image is independent from its dimensionality, due to the use of the Spectral Angle as the distance measure among adjacent cells, can be exploited in order accelerate and simplify the evolutionary process. Using low dimensional images (RGB) in the training image datasets for the evolutionary process, computational complexity may be reduced due to the fact that, as long as the behavior in terms of Spectral Angle is preserved, the resulting CA will be valid for any dimensionality. This is a very powerful concept as, once the CA is evolved in whatever dimensionality, it can be applied to both low (RGB) or high dimensional (HS) images. Figure 1 shows miniatures of a set of synthetic images used to train/evaluate an evolved MGCA.

Application to Real Hyperspectral Images

To be able to compare the results of segmentation algorithms it is usually necessary to label the segmented regions, that is, to provide a complete classification of the image. A multi-stage classification based on the application of the ECAS-II along with a pixel-wise SVM classification method has been used here.

Figure 1. Set of synthetic images used to train/evaluate an evolved MGCA

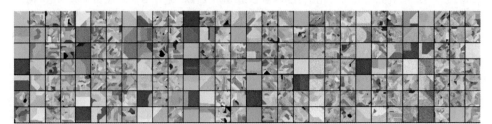

The set of hyperspectral images selected for this experimental section includes the Pavia University scene. It is an image recorded by the ROSIS-03 satellite sensor. It has 115 bands and spatial dimensions of 610 × 340 pixels. The second hyperspectral image was captured by the AVIRIS sensor over Salinas Valley, CA, USA, and is composed of 224 bands with a spatial dimension of 512 × 217 pixels. Finally, the Indiana scene is considered. It was recorded by the AVIRIS sensor over the Indian Pines test site in Northwestern Indiana, with a spatial dimension of 145 × 145 pixels and 200-bands per pixel.

The selected hyperspectral images exhibit different types of scenarios that should be segmented using MGCAs that make use of distinct rule sets. For this reason, three different MGCAs were evolved using as training datasets synthetic RGB images with spectral and spatial characteristics similar to those of the corresponding hyperspectral scenes. The particular parameters for the DE algorithm used to evolve the MGCA structures are shown in Table 1.

Before applying the SVM, the hyperspectral images were normalized with respect to the maximum spectral intensity found in the whole data cube. The specific C and γ parameters used for the SVM algorithm are indicated in Table 2. These have been selected by means of a fivefold cross validation procedure. The number of samples used to train the SVM is homogeneous with respect to the methods extracted from the literature (Tarabalka et al. 2010; Plaza et al. 2009; Lopez-Fandino et al. 2015).

Table 1. Differential Evolution (DE) parameters

Number of parameters:	180 (30 rules × 6 parameters/rule)
NP (Population Size):	100
CR (Crossover):	0.7
F (Mutation):	0.8
Stopping criterion:	Max. number of generations OR Min. cost function
Minimum cost function:	1e-6

Table 2. Class specific accuracies (%) for the raw SVM and the ECAS-II + SVM algorithm applied to the Pavia, Indiana and Salinas Scenes

	N. of Training Samples	N. of Test Samples	Class-specific accuracies (%)	
			ECAS-II + SVM	SVM
PAVIA SCENE (SVM parameters: $C = 256, \; \gamma = 0.5$)				
1: Asphalt	548	6083	**99,34**	89.42
2: Meadows	540	18109	**99,94**	93.12
3: Gravel	392	1707	**98,24**	85.12
4: Tree	524	2540	95,59	**97.63**
5: Metal sheets	265	1080	97,59	**99.16**
6: Base soil	532	4497	**99,53**	92.75
7: Bitumen	375	955	**98,84**	92.04
8: Bricks	514	3168	**99,55**	85.63
9: Shadows	231	716	83,24	**99.44**
INDIANA SCENE (SVM parameters: $C = 512, \; \gamma = 0.5$)				
1: Alfalfa	5	41	**92.17**	55.12
2: Corn-notill	143	1285	**90.25**	78.35
3: Corn-mintill	83	747	**95.69**	65.0
4: Corn	24	213	**96.20**	57.75
5: Grass-pasture	49	434	**96.11**	89.54
6: Grass-trees	73	657	**98.55**	95.46
7: Grass-mowed	3	25	73.57	**73.60**
8: Hay-windrowed	48	430	**99.96**	97.40
9: Oats	2	18	**100**	56.67
10: Soybean-notill	98	874	**87.57**	72.31
11: Soybean-mintill	246	2209	**96.66**	83.29
12: Soybean-clean	60	533	**93.19**	67.58
13: Wheat	21	184	**98.44**	96.41
14: Woods	127	1138	**99.83**	94.85
15: Buildings-Grass	39	347	**97.04**	54.12
16: Stone-Steel-Towers	10	83	**88.60**	87.47
SALINAS SCENE (SVM parameters: $C = 512, \; \gamma = 8$)				
1: Weeds 1	201	1808	**100**	99.47

continued on following page

Table 2. Continued

	N. of Training Samples	N. of Test Samples	Class-specific accuracies (%)	
			ECAS-II + SVM	SVM
2: Weeds 2	373	3353	**99.88**	99.79
3: Fallow	198	1778	**100**	99.58
4: Fallow plow	140	1254	99.12	**99.35**
5: Fallow smooth	268	2410	**99.46**	98.88
6: Stubble	396	3563	99.80	**99.87**
7: Celery	358	3221	**99.78**	99.53
8: Grapes	1128	10143	**96.79**	88.84
9: Soil	621	5582	**99.88**	99.87
10: Corn	328	2950	**98.26**	96.89
11: Lettuce 4wk	107	961	**99.81**	99.15
12: Lettuce 5wk	193	1734	**100**	99.63
13: Lettuce 6wk	92	824	97.97	**99.54**
14: Lettuce 7wk	107	963	96.07	**98.03**
15: Vinyard untrained	727	6541	**93.27**	78.27
16: Vinyard trellis	181	1626	**99.46**	98.71

The SVMs for classifying the Salinas and Indiana Scenes were trained using 10% of the samples for each class.

Figure 2a shows a 2D angular transformation of each original hyperspectral scene where each pixel corresponds to the angle between the spectrum of the pixel and a reference spectrum with all of its bands at the maximum value. Figure 2b represents the 2D angular transformation after applying the MGCA obtained using ECAS-II. The final classification results for the raw SVM and ECAS-II + SVM algorithms are represented in Figures 2c-2f. In Figures 2e-2f, the pixels that were misclassified are indicated using red dots instead of providing the color corresponding to the class they were wrongly assigned to. In the three cases, it can be clearly noticed that by introducing the MCGA stage, the salt and pepper type noise resulting from the misclassified pixels of the pixel-wise SVM classification process is drastically reduced.

The class specific accuracies for the raw pixel-wise SVM and the ECAS-II + SVM algorithms are presented in Table 2. It can be observed that most of the classes experiment an improvement in terms of accuracy. The only worrying result is the accuracy degradation (16.2%) for the shadow class from the Pavia scene by the

Table 3. Accuracy measurements (%) for different algorithms

	$\kappa(\%)$	OA(%)	AA(%)
	PAVIA SCENE		
ECAS-II + SVM (C = 256, γ = 16)	**98.64**	**99.01**	**96.87**
SVM (C = 256, γ = 16)	89.43	92.16	93.00
SVM [Tarabalka et al., 2010] (C = 128, γ = 0.125)	75.86	81.01	88,25
W-RCMG [Tarabalka et al., 2010]	81.30	85.42	91.31
EMP [Plaza et al., 2009]	96.05	97.07	96.79
V-ELM-1 [Lopez-Fandino et al., 2015]	95.00	96.66	95.92
	INDIANA SCENE		
ECAS-II + SVM (C = 512, γ = 0.5)	**94.48**	**95.12**	**93.99**
SVM (C = 512, γ = 0.5)	78.06	80.82	76.56
SVM [Tarabalka et al., 2010] (C = 1024, γ = 2−7)	75.73	78.86	69.66
W-RCMG [Tarabalka et al., 2010]	91.39	92.48	77.26
	SALINAS SCENE		
ECAS-II + SVM (C = 512, γ = 8)	**97.87**	**98.09**	**98.72**
SVM (C = 512, γ = 8)	93.62	94.27	97.21

application of ECAS-II. However, shadows are a controversial class because they do not represent a unique material by themselves, just different materials but with a low intensity spectrum.

For the Indiana scene, the improvement in terms of class-specific accuracies after applying the ECAS-II is clear since 15 out of 16 classes saw an accuracy rise of 18.59%. Finally, 12 classes of the Indiana scene increment their class-specific accuracy by an average of 2.33% while 4 classes see their accuracy decrease by an average of 0.95%.

Finally, in order to quantitatively compare the classification results to other approaches found in the literature, in addition to including a purely spectral algorithm based on a pixel-wise SVM, three reference algorithms have been selected: the extended morphological profile algorithm, EMP, (Plaza et al., 2009); a watershed transformation-based algorithm (Tarabalka et al., 2010), labeled as W-RCMG in Table 3; and the V-ELM-1 implementation of ELM found in (Lopez-Fandino et al. 2015). The comparisons between different methods have been restricted to those with consistency in terms of the number of reference samples used for training the algorithms.

Figure 2. 2D transformation of the original scenes (a) and of the ECAS-II segmented images (b), SVM based classification applied to the original images (c) and to the ECAS- II segmented images (d), SVM based classification applied to the original scenes showing only the labeled areas (red circles mark misclassified pixels) (e) and to the ECAS-II segmented images (f)

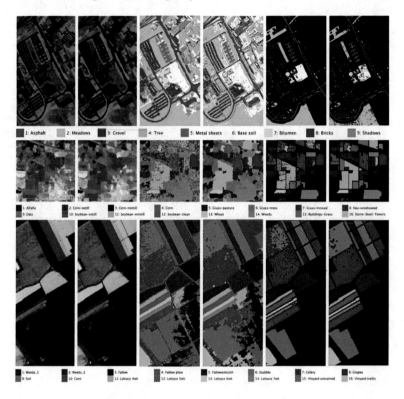

It can be observed that the ECAS-II technique followed by a SVM pixel-wise classification stage is the algorithm that provides the best classification accuracies in the three measures considered.

APPLICATION OF CA STRUCTURES TO DENOISING HYPERSPECTRAL IMAGES SEQUENCES

As an extension of the work developed to segment hyperspectral images by including the temporal dimension, this section presents a strategy for the denoising of hyperspectral image sequences.

The denoising of images is one of the most researched topics within the image processing field in the last two decades. Most of the algorithms that have been developed are focused on processing single images (2-D approaches) (Rudin et al., 1992; Portilla et al., 2003; Buades et al., 2005; Aharon et al., 2006; Luisier and Blu, 2008; Dabov et al., 2006), on denoising video sequences (Dabov et al., 2007; Priego et al., 2013; Maggioni et al., 2013) or still hyperspectral images (Peng et al., 2014; Renard et al., 2008; Liu et al., 2012; Lam et al., 2012; Liao et al., 2015; Salmon et al., 2014). However, while there is an abundant literature on denoising (standard) video sequences or denoising (still) hyperspectral images, there are very limited contributions towards the denoising of whole hyperspectral image sequences. This came about because, until recently, hyperspectral acquisition technology was not mature enough to enable the acquisition of temporal sequences of hyperspectral images.

The method presented here deals with the preprocessing of hyperspectral image sequences as a previous step to other applications such as segmentation or classification tasks. In particular, the method proposed in this section is aimed at noise filtering or denoising of sequences that are significantly corrupted by noise. This problem is very common in some applications, especially when the spectral coverage of the data reaches the thermal domain.

The denoising algorithm is based on the application of a cellular automata structure called 4DCAF (4-dimensional cellular automata based filtering) which iteratively filters each frame of the sequence explicitly taking the temporal, spectral and spatial diversity into account. Also for this task, the transition rules that govern the denoising behavior of the 4DCAF are automatically tuned following an evolutionary process called ECAF (evolutionary method for obtaining cellular automata filters), fed by synthetic hyperspectral image sequences functioning as training datasets. These are created reflecting similar characteristics to those of the real image sequences to be denoised, which makes the methodology able to adapt to hyperspectral image sequences exhibiting different spatial, spectral and temporal features, as well as to different types of noise.

In what follows, the proposed 4DCAF structure is presented, as well as the procedure followed to determine the transition rules of the cellular automata based structures (ECAF). Afterwards, the experimental results obtained from applying the denoising method over both synthetic and real image sequences are presented, including a comparison with algorithms extracted from the state of the art.

4DCAF

In this implementation of the CA to denoise hyperspectral image sequences, a cell of the automaton is placed over each pixel of the image sequence, so that the state of the cell (s_i) is given by an N-band spectrum, taking values for each band in the range $[0,1]$.

The 4DCAF structure is executed K times over a section of the hyperspectral image sequence centered on a temporal hyperspectral frame f, whose cells are gradually modified converging towards a denoised version of it. Once a frame is properly denoised, the 4DCAF is moved to the next frame, performing again the denoising operation.

The crux of the operation of the CAF relies on the criteria which define the updating of the cell state. This updating is based, on one hand, on information on the spectral values of the $N_S \times N_S \times N_T$ closest neighboring cells, where N_S and N_T are the spatial and temporal size of the window in which every cell is centered. On the other hand, it depends on the set of updating/transition rules that control the automaton behavior.

Following the same reasoning as for the MGCA structure, in order to consider the spectral information of the neighboring cells, the selected distance measure is, again, the spectral angle (SA), normalized between 0 and 1 (Eq. 1).

Thus, the local information is extracted based on the gradient vector (G) of the cell, taking into account the pixels contained in an $N_S \times N_S \times N_T$ 3-dimensional window. The gradient measurements will provide information about the strength and direction of intensity changes in each pixel of the image sequence, which will provide relevant information to the 4DCAF for distinguishing between fluctuations among neighboring pixels due to real edges or noise.

In order to calculate the gradient vector, three different 3-dimensional masks are applied to the pixel, obtaining this way three gradient components, $G_{X_{N_{S_i}}}$, $G_{Y_{N_{S_i}}}$ and $G_{T_{N_{T_i}}}$, calculated as:

$$G_{X_{N_{S_i}}} = \sum_{j=1}^{N_S \cdot N_S \cdot N_T} \alpha_{i,j} M_{X_{N_{S_j}}}$$

$$G_{Y_{N_{S_i}}} = \sum_{j=1}^{N_S \cdot N_S \cdot N_T} \alpha_{i,j} M_{Y_{N_{S_j}}}$$

$$G_{T_{N_{T_i}}} = \sum\nolimits_{j=1}^{N_S \cdot N_S \cdot N_T} \alpha_{i,j} M_{T_{N_{T_j}}} \tag{11}$$

where $\alpha_{i,j}$ denotes the normalized spectral angle between a cell i and its neighboring cell j.

The modulus of the spatial projection of the gradient vector ($\rho_P = \sqrt{G_X^2 + G_Y^2}$) and the absolute value of the temporal component (G_T) are taken as the information the 4DCAF needs in order to operate. ρ_P is related to the intensity change in the spatial dimension, whereas G_T is associated with an intensity variation in the temporal dimension within a spatio-temporal $N_S \times N_S \times N_T$ 3-dimensional window. Additionally, a plane perpendicular to the gradient direction is defined based on this gradient vector in order to divide the neighborhood into two parts: a positive and a negative side (Figure 3).

When the CA is applied to a particular cell, the **G** vector is obtained and the positive and negative sides are identified. Based on this separation, a transition rule will decide which pixels on each side are going to participate in the modification of the cell state and how they are going to contribute to this cell state updating process.

Figure 3. (Left) Example of spatio-temporal window when $N_S = 3$ and $N_T = 3$ including the plane defined by the gradient vector; gray colored boxes represent spectral distances between neighboring pixels and the cell which is being evaluated; (right) Gradient vector decomposition

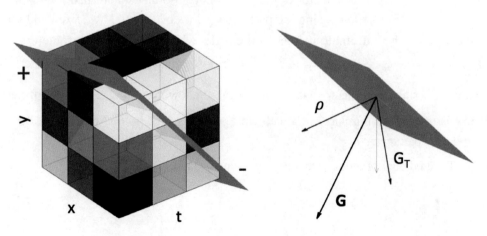

The CA is provided with a set of transition rules which consists of M rules and in every iteration of the CA structure, and for each pixel, one rule is selected to perform the updating. Each rule is made up of five parameters (2 state parameters + 3 updating parameters):

$$CA = \begin{cases} \rho_{rP_1} & G_{rT_1} & S_{rWS_1} & T_{rWS_1} & b_{r_1} \\ \vdots & \vdots & \vdots & \vdots & \vdots \\ \rho_{rP_k} & G_{rT_k} & S_{rWS_k} & T_{rWS_k} & b_{r_k} \\ \vdots & \vdots & \vdots & \vdots & \vdots \\ \rho_{rP_M} & G_{rT_M} & S_{rWS_M} & T_{rWS_M} & b_{r_M} \end{cases} \tag{12}$$

where ρ_{rP_k} and G_{rT_k} are the state parameters (they define which pixels will use this rule) and are related to the spatial and temporal projection of the vector gradient; S_{rWS_k} and T_{rWS_k} denote the spatial and temporal size of the updating window which will define which pixels will be used to calculate the updated state of the current cell; b_{r_k} indicates the contribution of the selected pixels on the positive side and negative side to the updating process. Sub-index r is used here to avoid confusing rule parameters with the values of the gradient vectors extracted from the neighborhood information of a cell.

To decide which rule, out of the rule set, is selected, a comparison between the neighborhood information (ρ_{P_i} and G_{T_i}) and the state parameters of each rule (ρ_{rP_k} and G_{rT_k}) is performed. As mentioned before, ρ_{rP_k} and G_{rT_k}, are obtained from projections of a gradient vector calculated within a 3-dimensional spatio-temporal $N_S \times N_S \times N_T$ window, being the particular values of N_S and N_T fixed and set manually. The automaton selects the rule whose first two parameters ($\{\rho_{rP_1}, G_{rT_1}\}, \{\rho_{rP_2}, G_{rT_2}\}, ..., \{\rho_{rP_M}, G_{rT_M}\}$) are most similar to $\{\rho_{P_i}, G_{T_i}\}$. The selected rule, q, establishes the spatial and temporal window size ($\{S_{rWS_q}, T_{rWS_q}\}$) of the pixels that are taking part in the cell state updating process and the value of the updating parameter b_{r_q}.

The updating process of the new cell state is calculated as:

$$s_{i,t+1} = \overline{p}_{i,t} \cdot b_{r_q} + \overline{n}_{i,t} \cdot (1 - b_{r_q}) \tag{13}$$

where $s_{i,t+1}$ is the new spectrum of cell i and $\bar{p}_{i,t}$ and $\bar{n}_{i,t}$ denote the averaged spectra of all the pixels contained in the positive and negative sides of the spatio-temporal window defined by S_{rWS_q} and T_{rWS_q}.

This procedure is iteratively applied to all the cells of every frame producing, in the end, an updated and denoised hyperspectral image sequence.

ECAF

In a similar way to the case of ECAS-II strategy, to obtain the rules that determine the behavior of the 4DCAF structure in an automatic fashion, an automatic optimization process in the form of an Evolutionary algorithm that encodes the 4DCAF rule set (eq. 12) has been chosen. In this case, the algorithm that was selected to infer the set of transition rules was a Genetic Algorithm (GA). The reason for selecting a Genetic Algorithm instead of a Differential Evolutionary Algorithm was empirical.

Concerning the evaluation of individuals, the fitness of a prospective 4DCAF is determined by running it over a training image sequence and comparing the result to the desired original one. The quality of the denoising obtained after applying the automaton is calculated using the mean squared error (MSE) between the original and denoised sequences:

$$MSE = \frac{1}{X \cdot Y \cdot N \cdot F} \sum_{f=1}^{F} \sum_{b=1}^{N} \sum_{x=1}^{X} \sum_{y=1}^{Y} \left[I(x, y, b, f) - I'(x, y, b, f) \right]^2$$

(14)

where $I(x, y, b, f)$ and $I'(x, y, b, f)$ represent the b-band spectral value of pixel (x, y) in frame f for the original and denoised sequences; X and Y are the spatial dimensions of the image, N is the number of bands and F is the number of frames of the sequences.

Every time a prospective 4DCAF needs to be evaluated, it is run over a training image sequence and the denoising result it obtains is compared to the noise-free image sequence.

Thus, evolving CA-based filtering structures capable of dealing with noise filtering effectively requires providing the evolutionary algorithm with suitable training image sequence datasets. These should reflect the spatial, temporal and spectral properties of the type of the real image sequences to be denoised, as well as particular characteristics of the type of noise tat corrupts those real sequences.

The steps followed for the creation of synthetic single-band and hyperspectral image sequences are: firstly, the creation of the noise-free image sequence (reference sequence). In this step, the ground truth of the first frame of the sequence is created. The ground truths of subsequent frames are a modified version of the first frame by growing or decreasing some selected regions in size. Then, global spectrum vectors are assigned to each area with the same associated label, thus obtaining the noise-free or reference multidimensional image sequence. Secondly, the reference sequence is corrupted with noise. Ideally, a previous study of the real sequence to be denoised is carried out in order to approximate which noise model is affecting the real sequence. Then, the synthetic reference image is noised following the type of noise model that has been determined. Figure 4 displays a single band of a noise-free and noisy synthetic image sequences created as a training image sequence for tuning the 4DCAF method.

Application to Synthetic and Real Hyperspectral Image Sequences

This section is devoted to the presentation of the experimental results obtained from applying the 4DCAF structure to synthetic and real sequences and to its comparison to recent successful methods from the state of the art: K-SVD (Aharon et al., 2006), BM3D (Dabov et al., 2007), BM4D (Maggioni et al., 2013) and DNTDL (Decomposable Nonlocal Tensor Dictionary Learning for MS) (Peng et al., 2014), respectively.

Before the application of the 4DCAF structure to the hyperspectral image sequences, the set of transition rules that define its behavior was evolved using the ECAF evolutionary method, feeding the evaluation step of the genetic algorithm with training datasets created synthetically. The technical specifics of the ECAF procedure and 4DCAF structures used are summarized in table 4.

Figure 4. Selected band from a noise-free and noisy synthetic image sequences created for testing or tuning temporal- denoising methods

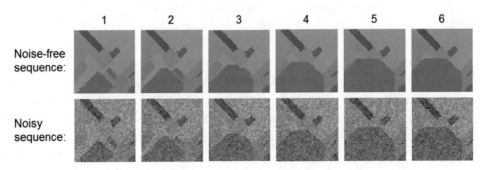

Table 4. Genetic Algorithm (GA) and 4DCAF parameters

(Genetic Algorithm)	
Number of parameters:	75 (15 rules × 5 parameters/rule)
NP (Population Size):	200
Elite count (number of individuals that are guaranteed to survive to the next generation)	0.05 · NP
CR (Fraction of the next generation, other than elite children, that are produced by crossover)	0.8
Ratio (Crossover):	0.7
Stopping criterion:	Max. number of generations
(4DCAF)	
N_S	7
N_T	7

In order to construct each training image sequence for the evaluation step of the GA, a ground truth map sequence was created and each band of the reference sequence was corrupted using the following model:

$$g(x,y,b,t) = f(x,y,b,t) + \left(p_2(b) + p_1(b) \cdot f(x,y,b,t)\right)^{\frac{1}{2}} \cdot u(x,y,b,t) \quad (15)$$

where g denotes the spectral value being noised, f is the corresponding signal value without noise; u is a zero-mean random variable with standard deviation 1; and p_2 and p_1 are the offset and the slope of the linear regression fit when representing the variance (σ) versus the averaged intensity value (μ) for each spectral band b of the sequence.

Thus, before corrupting the training dataset employed in the ECAF method, it will be necessary to estimate the noise model (p_1 and p_2 parameters of the linear regression fit) of the hyperspectral image sequence to be denoised. As mentioned before, the analysis of the type of noise model that affects a sequence has been carried out by representing the variance (σ) versus the averaged intensity value (μ) for each spectral band of the sequence (Figure 5).

Once the 4DCAF structure was evolved, a quantitative validation of the 4DCAF method was performed using synthetic hyperspectral image sequences. These synthetic image sequences created for validation purposes were noised following the same estimated noise model (Figure 5) exhibited by the real test image (Figure 7).

Figure 5. Noise variance vs. intensity signal value graph for the 1006.59 nm (a), 1079.92 nm (b) and 1156.58 nm (c) bands of the real hyperspectral image shown in Figure 7

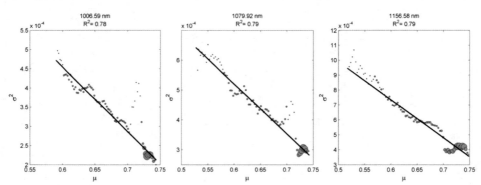

The creation process of this synthetic image differs from the training dataset in the selection of the spectral signatures for creating the noise-free hyperspectral image sequence. The spectral signatures (composed of 129 bands) have been extracted from the real sequence to be denoised. The reference image sequence has been corrupted following the same procedure as indicated for the construction of the training hyperspectral image sequence dataset.

Regarding the evaluation of the performances of the algorithms, four quantitative picture quality indices (PQI) were calculated, including peak signal-to-noise ratio (PSNR), structure similarity (SSIM) (Wang et al., 2004b), feature similarity (FSIM) (Zhang et al., 2011) and spectral angle mapper (SAM).

The 4DCAF structure was applied directly to the synthetic sequence, while in the case of the other methods, before the application of fw-bw-KSVD, fw-bw-BM3D, fw-DNTDL and fw-BM4D, the hyperspectral sequence was transformed using a variance-stabilizing transformation (VTS).

Quantitative and visual results are shown in Table 5 and Figure 6, respectively. The picture quality indices demonstrate that the proposed method is able to efficiently operate over noisy hyperspectral image sequences, consistently providing values for the indices that are much better than those given by the other methods. On the other hand, the spectral bands from a selected frame of the sequence represented in Figure 6 show that 4DCAF reduces the noise and preserves small structures and edges sharp.

Once the proposed method was validated over synthetic sequences, the algorithm was applied to a real hyperspectral image sequence of a dispersion of a chemical plume acquired by a LWIR sensor. The sequence consists of 25 frames, each one containing 129 spectral bands in the [853,1.280] nm range. For this sequence, since

Table 5. PQI comparison of the proposed 4DCAF, fw-bw-KSVD, fw-bw-BM3D, fw-DNTDL and fw-BM4D applied to a synthetic image sequence corrupted by signal dependent noise

Method	*PSNR*	*SSIM*	FSIM	SAM
fw-bw-KSVD (Aharon et al., 2006)	41.36	0.972	0.932	0.010
fw-bw-BM3D (Dabov et al., 2007)	42.85	0.976	0.924	0.009
fw-DNTDL (Peng et al., 2014)	44.99	0.983	0.971	0.006
fw-BM4D (Maggioni et al., 2013)	44.01	0.984	0.958	0.010
4DCAF	**49.62**	**0.993**	**0.982**	**0.003**

Figure 6. Original, noisy and denoised images of a selected frame from a synthetic hyperspectral image sequence. Only ten bands (out of 129) are shown.

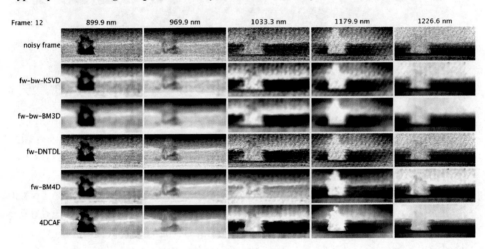

a noise-free version of it is not available, a first evaluation of the denoising has to be performed visually. Figure 7 demonstrates that the 4DCAF method produces the most satisfactory result: the background appears more homogeneous and the shape of the plume looks sharper than in the case of the other methods.

CONCLUSION

Two processing strategies based on cellular automata have been designed and implemented for the processing of still and sequences of hyperspectral images.

Figure 7. Noisy and denoised images of a selected frame from a real hyperspectral image sequence representing a chemical plume; only five bands (out of 129) are shown

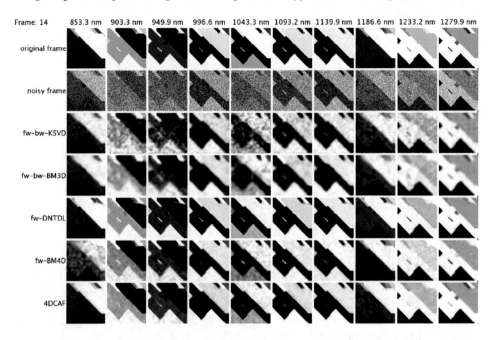

The first processing strategy consists in a segmentation approach based on a CA structure called Multi-Gradient based Cellular Automata (MGCA), whose behavior depends on a predefined set of transition rules. The effect of applying the MGCA over a multi-dimensional image is to gradually modify the spectra of pixels belonging to the same region until a spectral homogenization is achieved. In order to adjust the transition rules that direct the behavior of the CA, a methodology called ECAS-II based on evolutionary algorithms, has been designed. Through ECAS-II, the appropriate transition rules for MGCAs are generated using low dimensional synthetic training images created from the parameterization of certain characteristics of the real images to be processed.

The proposed segmentation method addresses some issues related to the processing of multi-dimensional images. It solves the problem of projecting spectral information onto lower dimensionalities by jointly processing the spatial and spectral information through algorithms based on cellular automata (CA). Furthermore, the intrinsic structure of CAs can be easily implemented over high speed GPU based platforms, significantly increasing their suitability for real time applications. On the other hand, the segmentation behavior of the CA structure can be adjusted following an evolutionary procedure through the use of synthetically created images that solves the problem of the lack of appropriately labeled reference images for training the algorithm.

The performance of the MGCA segmenters evolved using the ECAS-II methodology has been tested in terms of accuracy metrics after the inclusion of the segmentation step in a multistage SVM-based classification approach (ECAS-II + SVM). The proposed method improves the raw SVM-based classification accuracy results when it is applied to benchmark hyperspectral images. Additionally, the algorithm has been compared to state-of-the-art classification methods applied to benchmark images showing that the ECAS-II + SVM algorithm outperforms the state of the art methods in all cases.

The second processing strategy deals with the denoising of hyperspectral image sequences through the design and application of a CA-based filtering approach called 4DCAF. In the application of the 4DCAF filter, the spectrum of each pixel is modified so that after a number of iterations, every frame of the image sequence converges to a denoised version of it. The transition rules that solve the denoising problem adapted to a particular type of noisy sequence are adjusted by an evolutionary-based methodology denoted as ECAF. The evaluation step of the evolutionary algorithm is fed by synthetic image sequences created on-line that exhibit the same type of noise as the real sequences to be denoised. This solves the problem of the shortage of real sequences for training algorithms.

The performances of the evolved 4DCAF structures have been compared to state-of-the-art denoising methods by applying them to synthetic hyperspectral and real hyperspectral image sequences whose spectral coverage reaches the infrared domain. The quantitative results of applying the denoising methods to synthetic image sequences show that the proposed method outperforms in terms of PSNR, SSIM, FSIM and SAM the filtering strategies that are considered state of the art, especially when the signal to noise ratio is very low.

ACKNOWLEDGMENT

This work has been funded by the Ministerio de Economía y Competitividad (MINECO) of Spain and European Regional Development (FEDER) funds under grant TIN2015-63646-C5-1-R, as well as by the Xunta de Galicia under grants ED431C 2017/12 and ED341D R2016/012 (redTEIC network). This work was also partially funded by the Ministry of Economy, Industry and Competitiveness of the Government of Spain, through the Torres Quevedo programme under grant PTQ-16-08226.

REFERENCES

Aharon, M., Elad, M., & Bruckstein, A. (2006). K-SVD: An algorithm for designing overcomplete dictionaries for sparse representation. *IEEE Transactions on Signal Processing*, *54*(11), 4311–4322. doi:10.1109/TSP.2006.881199

Buades, A., Coll, B., & Morel, J. M. (2005, June). A non-local algorithm for image denoising. In *Computer Vision and Pattern Recognition, 2005. CVPR 2005. IEEE Computer Society Conference on* (Vol. 2, pp. 60-65). IEEE. doi:10.1109/CVPR.2005.38

Dabov, K., Foi, A., Katkovnik, V., & Egiazarian, K. (2006, January). Image denoising with block-matching and 3 D filtering. *Proceedings of the Society for Photo-Instrumentation Engineers*, *6064*(30), 606414–606414. doi:10.1117/12.643267

Dabov, K., Foi, A., Katkovnik, V., & Egiazarian, K. (2007). Video denoising by sparse 3D transform-domain collaborative filtering. In *European Signal Processing Conference* (*Vol. 149*). Tampere, Finland: Academic Press.

Díaz-Pernil, D., Peña-Cantillana, F., & Gutiérrez-Naranjo, M. A. (2014). Skeletonizing Digital Images with Cellular Automata. In P. Rosin, A. Adamatzky, & X. Sun (Eds.), *Cellular Automata in Image Processing and Geometry. Emergence, Complexity and Computation* (Vol. 10). Cham: Springer.

Dogaru, R., & Dogaru, I. (2014). Cellular Automata for Efficient Image and Video Compression. In Cellular Automata in Image Processing and Geometry (pp. 1-23). Springer International Publishing. doi:10.1007/978-3-319-06431-4_1

Gao, Y., & Yang, J. (2014). The Application of Cellular Automaton in Medical Semiautomatic Segmentation. In P. Rosin, A. Adamatzky, & X. Sun (Eds.), *Cellular Automata in Image Processing and Geometry. Emergence, Complexity and Computation* (Vol. 10). Cham: Springer. doi:10.1007/978-3-319-06431-4_9

Ioannidis, K., Sirakoulis, G. C., & Andreadis, I. (2014). Cellular Automata for Image Resizing. In P. Rosin, A. Adamatzky, & X. Sun (Eds.), *Cellular Automata in Image Processing and Geometry. Emergence, Complexity and Computation* (Vol. 10). Cham: Springer.

Lam, A., Sato, I., & Sato, Y. (2012, November). Denoising hyperspectral images using spectral domain statistics. In *Pattern Recognition (ICPR), 2012 21st International Conference on* (pp. 477-480). IEEE.

Lee, M. A., & Bruce, L. M. (2010, July). Applying cellular automata to hyperspectral edge detection. In *Geoscience and Remote Sensing Symposium (IGARSS), 2010 IEEE International* (pp. 2202-2205). IEEE. doi:10.1109/IGARSS.2010.5652717

Liao, C. S., Choi, J. H., Zhang, D., Chan, S. H., & Cheng, J. X. (2015). Denoising stimulated Raman spectroscopic images by total variation minimization. *The Journal of Physical Chemistry C, 119*(33), 19397–19403. doi:10.1021/acs.jpcc.5b06980 PMID:26955400

Liu, X., Bourennane, S., & Fossati, C. (2012). Denoising of hyperspectral images using the PARAFAC model and statistical performance analysis. *IEEE Transactions on Geoscience and Remote Sensing, 50*(10), 3717–3724. doi:10.1109/TGRS.2012.2187063

López-Fandiño, J., Quesada-Barriuso, P., Heras, D. B., & Argüello, F. (2015). Efficient ELM-based techniques for the classification of hyperspectral remote sensing images on commodity GPUs. *IEEE Journal of Selected Topics in Applied Earth Observations and Remote Sensing, 8*(6), 2884–2893. doi:10.1109/JSTARS.2014.2384133

Luisier, F., & Blu, T. (2008). SURE-LET multichannel image denoising: Interscale orthonormal wavelet thresholding. *IEEE Transactions on Image Processing, 17*(4), 482–492. doi:10.1109/TIP.2008.919370 PMID:18390357

Maggioni, M., Katkovnik, V., Egiazarian, K., & Foi, A. (2013). Nonlocal transform-domain filter for volumetric data denoising and reconstruction. *IEEE Transactions on Image Processing, 22*(1), 119–133. doi:10.1109/TIP.2012.2210725 PMID:22868570

Mardiris, V., & Chatzis, V. (2014). Image Processing Algorithms Implementation Using Quantum Cellular Automata. In P. Rosin, A. Adamatzky, & X. Sun (Eds.), *Cellular Automata in Image Processing and Geometry. Emergence, Complexity and Computation* (Vol. 10). Cham: Springer. doi:10.1007/978-3-319-06431-4_4

Minoofam, S. A. H., Dehshibi, M. M., Bastanfard, A., & Shanbehzadeh, J. (2014). Pattern Formation Using Cellular Automata and L-Systems: A Case Study in Producing Islamic Patterns. In P. Rosin, A. Adamatzky, & X. Sun (Eds.), *Cellular Automata in Image Processing and Geometry. Emergence, Complexity and Computation* (Vol. 10). Cham: Springer. doi:10.1007/978-3-319-06431-4_12

Peng, Y., Meng, D., Xu, Z., Gao, C., Yang, Y., & Zhang, B. (2014). Decomposable nonlocal tensor dictionary learning for multispectral image denoising. In *Proceedings of the IEEE Conference on Computer Vision and Pattern Recognition* (pp. 2949-2956). IEEE. doi:10.1109/CVPR.2014.377

Plaza, J., Plaza, A. J., & Barra, C. (2009). Multi-channel morphological profiles for classification of hyperspectral images using support vector machines. *Sensors (Basel)*, *9*(1), 196–218. doi:10.3390/s90100196 PMID:22389595

Portilla, J., Strela, V., Wainwright, M. J., & Simoncelli, E. P. (2003). Image denoising using scale mixtures of Gaussians in the wavelet domain. *IEEE Transactions on Image Processing*, *12*(11), 1338–1351. doi:10.1109/TIP.2003.818640 PMID:18244692

Priego, B., Veganzones, M. A., Chanussot, J., Amiot, C., Prieto, A., & Duro, R. (2013, September). Spatio-temporal cellular automata-based filtering for image sequence denoising: Application to fluoroscopic sequences. In *Image Processing (ICIP), 2013 20th IEEE International Conference on* (pp. 548-552). IEEE.

Renard, N., Bourennane, S., & Blanc-Talon, J. (2008). Denoising and dimensionality reduction using multilinear tools for hyperspectral images. *IEEE Geoscience and Remote Sensing Letters*, *5*(2), 138–142. doi:10.1109/LGRS.2008.915736

Rosin, P. L., & Sun, X. (2014). Edge Detection Using Cellular Automata. In P. Rosin, A. Adamatzky, & X. Sun (Eds.), *Cellular Automata in Image Processing and Geometry. Emergence, Complexity and Computation* (Vol. 10). Cham: Springer.

Rudin, L. I., Osher, S., & Fatemi, E. (1992). Nonlinear total variation based noise removal algorithms. *Physica D. Nonlinear Phenomena*, *60*(1-4), 259–268. doi:10.1016/0167-2789(92)90242-F

Salmon, J., Harmany, Z., Deledalle, C. A., & Willett, R. (2014). Poisson noise reduction with non-local PCA. *Journal of Mathematical Imaging and Vision*, *48*(2), 279–294. doi:10.1007/s10851-013-0435-6

Storn, R., & Price, K. (1997). Differential evolution–a simple and efficient heuristic for global optimization over continuous spaces. *Journal of Global Optimization*, *11*(4), 341–359. doi:10.1023/A:1008202821328

Tarabalka, Y., Chanussot, J., & Benediktsson, J. A. (2010). Segmentation and classification of hyperspectral images using watershed transformation. *Pattern Recognition*, *43*(7), 2367–2379. doi:10.1016/j.patcog.2010.01.016

Tralic, D., Rosin, P. L., Sun, X., & Grgic, S. (2014). Copy-Move Forgery Detection Using Cellular Automata. In P. Rosin, A. Adamatzky, & X. Sun (Eds.), *Cellular Automata in Image Processing and Geometry. Emergence, Complexity and Computation* (Vol. 10). Cham: Springer.

van Zijl, L. (2014). Content-Based Image Retrieval with Cellular Automata. In P. Rosin, A. Adamatzky, & X. Sun (Eds.), *Cellular Automata in Image Processing and Geometry. Emergence, Complexity and Computation* (Vol. 10). Cham: Springer.

Wang, H. M., Guo, S. D., & Yu, D. H. (2004). A New CA Method for Image Processing Based on Morphology and Coordinate Logic. *Application Research of Computers, 1*, 81.

Zhang, L., Zhang, L., Mou, X., & Zhang, D. (2011). FSIM: A feature similarity index for image quality assessment. *IEEE Transactions on Image Processing, 20*(8), 2378–2386. doi:10.1109/TIP.2011.2109730 PMID:21292594

Chapter 6

Role of Clustering Techniques in Effective Image Segmentation

Bhavneet Kaur
Chandigarh University, India

Meenakshi Sharma
Chandigarh University, India

ABSTRACT

Image segmentation is gauged as an essential stage of representation in image processing. This process segregates a digitized image into various categorized sections. An additional advantage of distinguishing dissimilar objects can be represented within this state of the art. Numerous image segmentation techniques have been proposed by various researchers, which maintained a smooth and easy timely evaluation. In this chapter, an introduction to image processing along with segmentation techniques, computer vision fundamentals, and its applied applications that will be of worth to the image processing and computer vision research communities has been deeply studied. It aims to interpret the role of various clustering-based image segmentation techniques specifically. Use of the proposed chapter if made in real time can project better outcomes in object detection and recognition, which can then later be applied in numerous applications and devices like in robots, automation, medical equipment, etc. for safety, advancement, and betterment of society.

DOI: 10.4018/978-1-5225-5628-2.ch006

INTRODUCTION

The major highlighting view of vision is its inference issues. For instance, one have few measurements, and desires to determine its root cause using a mode. There are numerous vital features that differentiate vision from multiple other inferences glitches; mainly, to identify the object items from the data through which an effective decision making can be conducted. For example, it is quite challenging to identify whether a pixel lies on the dalmation (See Figure 1) just by observing at the pixel. The solution to this issue can be resolved by working over the selection of "interesting" sections. Obtaining this sections is recognized as Segmentation.

Image segmentation is indispensable yet precarious component in image analysis, pattern recognition, low level vision and now optimally contribute in robotics. Besides, being one of the problematic and challenging chores in the field, it evaluates the outcome`s quality for image analysis. Intuitively, image segmenting is termed as a procedure of image segregation into multiple segments such that each segment is homogenous while not unified to any two contiguous segments. A supplementary requisition with image segmentation would be segments correspondence to real identical regions those belongs to objects in the respective scene.

The broadly accepted formal image division is defined as follows:

If $H_p(o)$ is considered as a homogeneousness predicate defined on coupled group pixels, then segmentation is defined as a division of set S into multiple associated regions $\{R_1, R_2, ..., R_n\}$ such that

$$\bigcup_{x=1}^{n} R_x \text{ With } R_x \cap R_y = \Phi, \; \forall x \neq y \tag{1}$$

The $H_p(R_i)$ is uniform predicate that is true for all regions R_i and $H_p(R_x \cup R_y)$ is false when x! = y and regions R_x and R_y are neighbors.

Moreover, it should be significant to make in consideration that image segmentation problematic issues are one of the psychological perceptions and thus does not exposed to pure analytical solution. This might be the reason behind the proposition of numerous segmentation techniques in the state-of-the-art principally versed on monochrome segmentation and very less survey has been reported over color image segmentation.

By the time passed the attention towards the color image segmentation is attaining due to one of the reasons discussed below:

- **Reliability:** Information provided by the color images is far more reliable in comparison to grayscale images.

- **Computational Power:** The computational power of computers has increased hastily in recent years, even for color image processing.
- **Database Management:** Image database handling, which mainly formed by color images.
- **Advance Capabilities:** There has been an enhancement in sensing proficiencies all intelligent machines.

Numerous image segmentation techniques such as graph based, threshold based, clustering based, morphological based, neural network based and many more are proposed. Each of these technique carries its own pros and cons, therefore the selection of particular technique directly depends on needs from one's own perspective. Out of these the most effective and optimized technique is clustering based image segmentation. In this chapter, a detailed discussion of various segmentation methods are deeply discussed together with a detail study of several clustering algorithms along with recent updates in the field.

A collective representation of the ideas has been made in this chapter. These methods work over diverse categories of data set: several are envisioned for images, several are envisioned for video series and several to be applied to tokens. (Note: Tokens- it is basically a point that designates the presence of interesting arrangement, such as a dot or edge point (See Figure 1)). Although they all appears to be diversified, there exists a strong similarity among them. Each method tries to attain a compact representation of its respective data sets using various similarity model.

When one attempts to compute the belongingness between the components, it is depicted as Clustering. A wide collection of literature has been reported for clustering; generally, it can be categorized into two ways:

- **Partitioning:** The process of whittling up the large data set into smaller sections according to the notion of association among the data inside the set is known as partitioning. Here the decomposition is made into the fragments that are "good" as per the requirement. For instance, we:
  - Fragment an image into sub sections having coherent texture and color inside them.
  - Fragment a video sequence into shots.
  - Fragment a video sequence into motion globules, compress of coherent color, texture and motion regions.
- **Grouping:** The process merging the diverse data items into something meaningful as per the requirement is known as grouping. If an image component belonging to same object that often parted is described as occlusion. For instance:

- ○   Collection of tokens, obtaining an interesting item (As collection of spots in Figure 1).
- ○   Collaboration of similar tokens.

At variance with others, a contribution has been made in the state of the art by proposing numerous algorithms those have resolved a few issues to an extend even then with the execution of whom multiple problems has been identified over which great focus is soon required:

1.   Challenging chore in selection of k while implementing k-mean clustering, due to the huge amount of noisy elements in the data.
2.   The identification of inappropriate shapes formation of the cluster.
3.   Computationally expensiveness while the execution of clustering based segmentation.
4.   The sensitivity in segmentation performance is identified for cluster centers and numbers.
5.   Non-suitability for high-dimensional features for majority of segmentation techniques.

APPLICATIONS: BOUNDARY SUBSTRATION AND SHOT BOUNDARY SUBSTRACTION

Basic segmentation algorithms are quite helpful in substantial applications. Basic algorithms compute great outcomes when one can easily depicts the "valuable"

Figure 1. Essential vision components forming into expressive information from dalmation image on shadowed background (Marr, 1982)

decompositions from it. The most significant cases of the state-of-the-art are background subtraction and shot boundary detection.

Boundary Subtraction

There are many applications where background objects are very stable. For instance, parts identification on conveyor belt or calculating the number of cars in overhead vision of road. In such applications helpful segmentation can be performed by subtracting an estimated appearance of the background from an image and searching for larger values in outcomes. The major concern is computation of good background estimation. Taking a picture can be considered as a poor example for the respective case because its background varieties as per the time. Like road might became shinier on the rainy day in comparison to a dry day.

In contrast to it is a concept of moving average. Moving average, majorly estimate the background pixels value. In this approach, an estimation is made to the value of selected background pixel as an average of preceding values. Usually, pixel values in past must be weighted as zero and smoothly increase accordingly. Technically, moving average must focus the variation in background, i.e. on the rapid weather change few image pixels must have non-zero weights, and else non-zero weights should escalate slowly. The algorithm of the background subtraction has been discussed in Algorithm 1.

Shot Boundary Detection

Lengthy video sequences are generally composed of shots. Shots are squatter subsequences that when combined depicts the same length objects. Shots are usually the outcomes of editing practice. Seldom there is any record having a fall between the shots boundaries. Technically, each shot in the video can be represented with key frame. This can be helpful in searching and encapsulating the videos and their content for browsing or set a video for user.

Algorithm 1. Background subtraction algorithm

Begin
    Define $B^{E(0)}$ // $B^{E(0)}$ is Background Estimate
    At each Ψ // Ψ depicts the frame
        Update $B^{E(0)}$ by,
        $B^{E(n-1)} = \dfrac{W_\alpha \Psi + \Sigma_i W_\beta B^{(n-1)}}{W_\gamma}$ // W_α, W_β and W_γ are various weight choices
        Subtract $B^{E(n-1)}$ from Ψ,
        Report each pixel value, having respective difference magnitude greater than pre-defined threshold.
End

The practice of automatically computing the boundaries of the shots is described as shot boundary detection. It must identify unlike frames from the videos in comparison to the previous frames. Test of significance must be take into consideration of the fact that both objects and background can variate around the view field in a given shot. Basically, action over the distance has been taken in this test; shot boundary will be declared only if the computed distance is larger than a threshold.

Several standard techniques for figuring out the distance are discussed below:

- Frame differencing algorithms considers the pixel by pixel difference between the two frames from the sequence, later summation the square of the computed differences. These algorithms lacks in popularity because of been slower in speed. Secondly, because they tends to identify various shots on shaking of the camera.
- Histogram based algorithms evaluate color histogram for every frame and calculate the distance between the same. A difference in color histograms are considered as a sensible measure to use, as it is insensitive to spatial arrangement of color in frame. For instance, a small jitters by camera will not cause any effect on the histogram.
- Block comparison algorithms equate frames by decomposing them into grid boxes, and later compare them. Basically, the challenges with color histogram can be avoided. For instance, the vanishing of black colored object from top edge is equivalent to appearing it on screen from bottom left corner.
- Edge differencing algorithms calculate edge maps for each frame, later made a comparison between them. Here, the comparison is done by adding the total number of potential edges in following frame. If potential edges are present, then it is treated as a shot boundary. A distance can be easily computed by transforming the corresponding edge count.

There are numerous ad hoc approaches, but are sufficient to resolve the challenges at hands.

Algorithm 2. Shot boundary detection algorithm using interframe differences

```
Begin
    For each frame F in a video
        Compute a Distance D between F and previous frame
            If D > threshold
            Classify frame as Shot Boundary
    End
```

SEGMENTATION TECHNIQUES

By the time passed numerous image segmenting techniques have been recognized by researchers and scientists. Basically the image segmentation techniques can be classified as:

1. Threshold based segmentation
2. Region based segmentation
   a. Seeded Region Growing
   b. Unseeded Region Growing
   c. Region merging and splitting
3. Edge based segmentation
4. Clustering based segmentation
5. Bayesian based segmentation
6. Classification based segmentation

Threshold Based Segmentation

The conducive technique to differentiate foreground region of an image from its background is thresholding. The procedure is to use intensity histogram and compute the intensity value which is known as threshold value. Basically, this technique segment the image as per its threshold value and thus is considered as a fast and computationally effective method. It has been observed that the threshold based image segmentation is intensity heterogeneous and sensitive to noise.

Thresholding implementation can be categorized into two: locally or globally. The selection of brightness threshold value to segment the input image into respective object and background is termed as a global thresholding. It generally computes a binary image from the given image. If the selected pixel falls under predefined threshold range, are considered as object pixels with value "1" else are made background pixel with value "0".

$$I\,(a,\,b) = \begin{cases} 1, & G\left(a,b\right) \geq T_{hold} \\ 0, & Otherwise \end{cases} \tag{2}$$

Here T_{hold}, is the predefined threshold value.

The threshold value can be computed either by automatic threshold selection method or by an interactive way. Basically, a global threshold segments an image into multiple objects and background respectively, but an object can poses various characteristic grey value. Thus, multiple threshold values are required in such situation, which can be applied over various areas of the image. Therefore, threshold value for individual region is termed as local threshold and the respective process is termed as multilevel thresholding; which identify various objects from the image separately.

Let us consider an image consisting of two different objects, then identification of two thresholds $\propto_{Thold}$, β_{Thold} such that

$$
\left.
\begin{array}{ll}
\propto_{Thold} \leq G\left(a,b\right) \leq \beta_{Thold,} & for\,one\,object \\
G\left(a,b\right) \geq \beta_{Thold}, & for\ \ the\,other\,object \\
G\left(a,b\right) \leq \propto_{Thold,} & for\,the\,background
\end{array}
\right\} \quad (3)
$$

Figure 2(a) depicts the threshold histogram of an image consist of one light object and shaded background, and Figure 2(b) depicts the threshold histogram of an image consist of two different light objects and obscure background.

Region Based Segmentation

Region based segmentation is an approach of constructing a region either by associating or dissociating the neighboring pixels. The approach follow the principle of homogeneity. A comparison is made between each pixel of an image with its neighboring pixel for similarity check. If the outcome of the comparison is positive then that respective pixel is inserted to the region.

If Φ represents the region of an image, then segmentation to decompose it into n disjoint regions Φ_1, Φ_2,...., Φ_n such that

Figure 2. (a) Threshold for image with one object; (b) Threshold for image with two objects

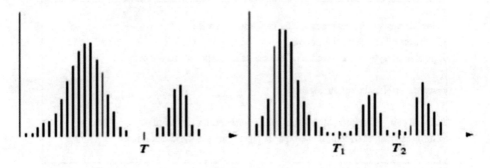

$$\cup \Phi_i = \Phi, \qquad \Phi_i \cap \Phi_j = \emptyset, \qquad \qquad if \, i \neq j$$
$$Prop\left(\Phi_i\right) = True, \qquad \qquad \qquad where \, i = 1,2,3,\ldots,n$$
$$Prop\left(\Phi_i \cup \Phi_j\right) = False, \qquad \qquad where \, i = 1,2,3,\ldots,n$$

$$(4)$$

Here Prop (Φ_i) is demarcated in terms of feature values over region Φ.

Region based segmentation is divided into two parts: Region Growing and Region Splitting

Seed Region Growing (SRG)

Seed Region Growing is an approach projected by R. Adam, for computing the connected segments of an image which consist of similar intensities of pixels. Here, initially a seed point is defined, and respective seed points connected nodes having alike intensity are selected and added to growing regions (See Figure 3). Note: The selection of an appropriate seed is very crucial step in this approach. This process is continued till no more pixel is left to add in respective region.

Unseeded Seed Region Growing (UsRG)

Unseeded Region Growing is pixel similarity within an individual region measuring method. It is completely automatic, flexible and non-dependable over tuning parameters.

Algorithm 3. Seed Region Growing (SRG) algorithm

```
Begin
Select the seed pixel from the image for image segmentation.
Choose the criteria for region growth.
If pixel is 8-neighbor connected to at least one of the respective region pixel
{
Insert the pixel in the current region
}
Label all designed regions, after testing all image pixels for allocation.
Perform merging of regions, if two separate regions assigns the identical label.
End
```

Figure 3. Seeded Region Growing

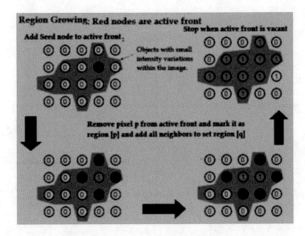

Algorithm 4. Unseeded Region Growing (UsRG)

Begin
Initialize Segmentation with Region Φ_1 consist of individual pixel and results in Φ_1, Φ_2, ...,
Φ_n
regions on completion.
Difference measure of test pixels together with mean value of statistics is made under
consideration for pixel allocation.
If the value computed from difference < predefined threshold
{
Allocate the pixel to specific region Φ_i,
}
Else
Allocate the pixel to other region Φ_j,
Repeat the steps for all the image pixels
End

Region Splitting and Merging (U$_s$RG)

Unlike region growing, region splitting donot follow the concept of seed point. This
method was proposed by B. Penetal. Basically it is two step technique where first
splitting is made, later merging is considered. The most common example of region
splitting is Quad tree method (See Figure 4).

Figure 4. Region splitting and merge method

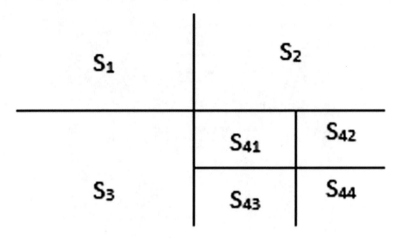

Algorithm 5. Region splitting and merge method algorithm

```
Begin
Let Φ depicts the entire image region and Pd by any predicate
If Pd(Φ) == FALSE
{
Split image into quadrants
If (Pd is FALSE for any Subquadrant)
{
Subdivide that quadrant into sub-quadrant
}
}
Merge Region Φj and Φk (j != k; j=1 till n, k=1 till n)
If Pd(Φj U Φk) == TRUE
End
```

Edge Based Segmentation

This is a principle of intensity variation among the pixels based approach. The identification of boundaries or pixels between regions is edge detection. The rapid transition in intensities values cause the formation of different regions. Because of which boundaries are created and its respective identification is termed as Edge Detection. Edges are originated by applying masks over the image. Edges of the inputted image are identified by gradient or zero crossing approach. Edge set for an image is determined by the convolution between mask and the image. Technically, edge detection operators are first derivative operator and second derivative operator. Gradient for first derivative operator is

$$\nabla a = G\big[a\left(m,n\right)\big] = \begin{bmatrix} \dfrac{\partial a}{\partial m} \\ \dfrac{\partial a}{\partial n} \end{bmatrix}.$$

(5)

Here, direction of gradient is $\theta = \tan^{-1}\left[\dfrac{\partial n}{\partial m}\right]$ .where θ is measured with respect to x- axis. Operators used in such categories are Robert`s operator, Prewitt operator, Sobel`s operator etc. Second order derivative operator works on zero crossing detection, gradient for this operator is

$$\nabla^2 = \frac{\partial^2 a}{\partial m^2} + \frac{\partial^2 a}{\partial n^2}$$

(6)

Here, $\dfrac{\partial^2 a}{\partial m^2}$.= a (m, n+1) – 2 a (m, n) + a (m, n-1)

$\dfrac{\partial^2 a}{\partial n^2}$ = a (m+1, n) – 2 a (m, n) + a (m-1, n)

Operators used here are laplacian of Gaussian and canny edge operator.

Clustering Based Segmentation

Clustering is basically considered as an unsupervised segmentation method. Here image is classified into various clusters, where cluster count directly depends on algorithm or on user definition. Thus, this technique do not contain any training stages, rather made self-training based on available data. Pixel grouping is based on self-adoptive criterion that later leads to clustering. The vital element for effective segmentation performance are value initialization, therefore, a serious care has to be taken care off.

Bayesian Based Segmentation

It is basically a classification technique which works by evaluating the probability in image for model construction. Based on this probability the class assignment utilization of image can be made. Approaches like Markov Random Field (MRF), Expectation Maximization (EM) are various Bayesian Method approaches.

Classification Based Segmentation

Here image feature space is partitioned through known data labels. Based on functions defined in feature space, the further partition is carried out. Classification technique can be both supervised and unsupervised.

IMAGE SEGMENTATION BASED ON CLUSTERING PIXELS

Clustering is a method of collecting a data points denoted as clusters that carries a same characteristics. The clustering criteria directly relies on the requirements of the application. Belongingness between the cluster pixels might be because of their alike color, texture or many more characteristics.

Simple Clustering Techniques

Clustering can be naturally classified into two categories: agglomerative clustering and divisive clustering. In agglomerative clustering, every individual data item is considered as a cluster, which on merging create a good clustering. In Divisive Clustering, a complete data set is considered as a cluster, which later the segmentation is into the good clustering (See Figure 5).

Two major concerns about clustering:

- *What is good inter-cluster distance?* Agglomerative clustering practices an inter-cluster space to fuse adjoining cluster; divisive clustering practices the

Algorithm 6. Clustering by merging (agglomerative clustering)

```
Begin
Create every node a discrete cluster
Till the satisfactory clustering is reached
Amalgamate the two smallest inter-cluster element clusters
End
```

Algorithm 7. Clustering by Splitting (Divisive Clustering)

```
Begin
Create a singly cluster consisting of all the elements
Till the satisfactory clustering is reached
Perform cluster fragmentation over the components holding large inter-cluster space
End
```

splitting of coherent clusters. Even with the presence of the distance between the data points, no inter-cluster distance exists. Normally, a choice is made for a distance that is appropriate for a data set. For instance, one can make a choice in selection of space between the nearest elements as the inter-cluster distance; this is technically termed as single-link clustering. Computation of the maximum distance between the two elements is another choice, which is termed as complete-link clustering. Lastly, average of the distance between the clusters elements that yield to the rounded clusters can be used, which is statistically termed as average clustering.

- *What is the present cluster count?* The computation of cluster count would be a challenging chore if there is no model process that cause in generation of the clusters. The discussed algorithm here can successfully generate a hierarchy of the clusters; which can displayed in the form of dendrogram. Dendrogram is a representation of the hierarchical structure of the clusters that exhibits the inter-cluster distances. Basically, a suitable choice of the cluster can be performed using dendrogram.

Figure 5. Left: represents the data set; right: represents the dendrogram that has been obtained by the agglomerative clustering using single link clustering; on selection of a specific values of distance, a horizontal line at that distance will fragmented into clusters; this depicts the possibility to guess the cluster count and its goodness

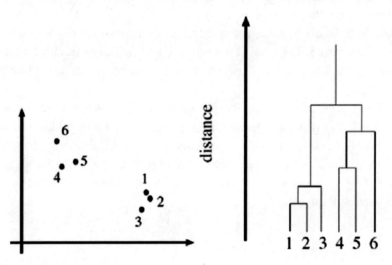

Clustering Algorithm

A greedy interactions with the present clusters are used by the various simple clustering approaches for generating acceptable representation. For instance, the best available merge is repeatedly performed in agglomerative clustering. Nevertheless, approaches are not concern about the objective function that the respective approach is endeavoring to optimize. Substitute to it, approach can note an objective function that articulates its goodness, and then attempts to design an algorithm for obtaining the best possible representation.

Here we will discuss the various clustering techniques. Clustering can be defined as a division of data into few unsets, in such a way that each subset data carries few common properties with each other.

K-Mean Algorithm

Begin with the random selection of cluster midpoints along with alternately iterate these stages. Continuity of the procedure will leads the convergence to local minimum of the objective function; but does not guaranteed the convergence to global minimum of the objective function. Moreover, no guarantee is ensured for the production of k clusters, till a modification in allocation phase is made to confirm that each cluster consists of few non-zero points. Such an algorithm is termed as K-means.

Basically, K- means clustering technique to divide a dataset into various k amount of groups. Each cluster is defined by its members along with cluster centroid. Centroid is basically a point where distance sum from all objects in particular cluster is minimized. Thus, K-means can also be titled as an iterative algorithm as it diminishes the distance sum between individual object and its respective centroid, over all clusters.

Unlike its pros, the k-mean algorithm attains few cons too. It has been studied that the quality of final segmentation outcome of the k-mean algorithm directly depends on the initial selection of the clusters centroid. Secondly, fragments are not combined and can dispersed very extensively as presented in Figure 7 and Figure 8. This issue can be resolved by reducing the pixels coordinates as features as presented in Figure 8.

Algorithm 8. K-Means clustering algorithm

Begin
    Assume I be an image of $\alpha*\beta$ resolution and N_c be the number of clusters.
    Let $X(\alpha, \beta)$ be the input image pixels. Δ be cluster centers.
    Thus k-means clustering is:
        Initialization of C counted clusters together with each cluster`s center.
        Calculate Euclidean distance D using discussed relations:
    $D = \| X(\alpha, \beta) - c_k \|$
        Here $X(\alpha, \beta)$ represents the pixel X at $(\alpha, \beta)^{th}$ location of the image. And c_k represents the center for k^{th}
cluster.
    Based on D, all the pixels are assigned to the nearest center.
    New center position is now recalculated from:

$$Ck = \frac{1}{Nc} \cdot \sum_{\beta \,\epsilon\, \alpha} \sum_{\alpha \,\epsilon\, \alpha} X(\alpha, \beta).$$

    Repeat the process till the respective tolerance value.
End

Figure 6. (a) Represents an image of vegetables, which will be segmented using k-means algorithm to produce the resultant images. (b) A segmentation outcome obtained using intensity information; (c) a segmentation outcome obtained using color information.

    (a)   (b)   (c)

In 1967, K mean was introduced by James MacQueen. In the time frame of 1967 to 1998, all the research chores were related to modifications and improvements of K-Means clustering. Some scholars generated the step stones in the state-of-the-art. Alsabti et al. worked over effective pattern making in k-d tree clustering for optimal finding of the patterns. Tapas et al. discussed the implement of Lloyd`s K-mean clustering which was popularly termed as filtering algorithm. Later Modha et al. developed a structure for integrating multiple feature spaces in K-mean clustering algorithm. V.H.Duong et al. proposed an algorithm that aims in reduction of execution time of K-means. This algorithm may be affected by the noise points as the choosing

Figure 7. First image represent all the segments composed together, with a mean value at the location of original image value. Rest of Figure represents the four segments. (NOTE: this algorithm might lead to the formation of segments that are not associated together). For the given image, few segments are closely associated with objects and one segment could represent various objects (such as peppers); rest are worthless. The deficiency of texture measure leads to a very serious challenge, as various segments are resulting from the slide of cabbage.

Figure 8. A histogram encountered while fragmenting Figure 6 into hierarchy of Figure 7 through divisive clustering algorithm

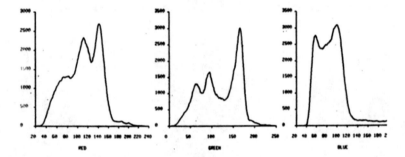

of random critical points can produce instable clusters. This limitation was resolved by the M.Li et al. using the systematic selection of the values such as cluster count and initial centroids. This systematic selection reduced the noise points count, but cause in more computation time. Tian et al. proposed a novel parallel K-means clustering algorithm and discussed the superior initial centers technique which aims at the reduction of actions count while grouping. Later A.Kane et al. proposed an automatic finding of the clusters count from the dataset. This proposed method was density-independent which was effectively applicable for clustering methods such as Expectation-maximization. Vast quantity of work has been attempted over the state-of-the-art to overcome the drawbacks. Haiyang Li et al. worked on the dependency of the algorithm over a count of initial clusters; by developing a hybrid method. The proposed method is a collaboration of Dynamic Particle Swarm Optimization (DPSO) and k-means.

Later, a hybrid method based on DSPO and flower pollination was developed by R. Jensi et al. the aim was to avoid k-means algorithm trapping in the local optimum algorithm. S.B. Belhaouari et al. attempt an effort over optimization method of k-means. The input image is reshaped into vector through localization later to which twice implementation of optimized k-means algorithm was made with an aim to cluster image pixels into a single class. Later in the years, S. Khanmohammadi et al. introduced an innovative and enhanced k-means clustering algorithm by the name OKM (overlapping k-means) algorithm. More advancement was made with the introduction of a new hybrid method known as k-harmonic means and overlapping k-means algorithm (KHM-OKM). Basically, productivity of KHM is used for initialization of the cluster center in OKM algorithm.

Fuzzy C-Mean Algorithm

FCM algorithm is a data clustering method which segments similar data to different homogenous groups. Therefore, it might be possible for a pixel value to belong in more than one cluster. However, each image pixel attains a value known as 'membership value' for each cluster, which basically defines the degree of share of that particular point in each cluster. Thus, a membership matrix is data matrix which contains the membership value of each pixel for all clusters. It achieves segmentation through fuzzy pixel classification accordingly that pixels are to be there in multiple classes with membership degree of 0 and 1.

Let us consider a finite set of N number of data D= $\{D_1, D_2, D_3, ..., D_N\}$. Here, fuzzy c-mean algorithm segments the dataset D into multiple groups based on some specific conditions. It is an objective function minimization based iterative process. The objective function can defined as:

$$\Psi_m = \sum_{\alpha=1}^{N}\sum_{\beta=1}^{C}\varphi_{\alpha\beta}^m \cdot \| d_\alpha - C_\beta \|^2 \tag{7}$$

Degree of fuzziness in clusters are computed through fuzzification parameter m. $\varphi_{\alpha\beta}$ .depicts the degree of d_α in cluster β, d_α represents the αth data points and C represents β^{th} center of cluster. Minimizing the cost function while changing the membership degree value of each data is the major goal of each iteration.

Huge amount of work has been completed in fuzzy based clustering. Thus few stepping stoned contributions are discussed here; Brar S. Gurusewak et al. used fuzzy algorithm over the dataset of process control. Mean square error was considered as an effective parameter for performing the comparisons. Later the field was

Algorithm 9. Fuzzy c-mean algorithm

Begin
   Initialize Total Cluster count and MFM membership function Matrix) φ
   Compute the each cluster center:

$$C_\beta = \frac{\sum_{\beta=1}^{N} \varphi_{\alpha\beta}^{m} \, d\alpha}{\sum_{\beta=1}^{N} \varphi_{\alpha\beta}^{m}} \, .$$

Compute the Error or Cost Function
If (Error or Cost Function) < Threshold Value
{
Cluster the data
}
Else
{
Update MFM (φ)

$$\varphi_{\alpha\beta} = \frac{1}{\sum_{k=1}^{C} \left[\dfrac{D_{\alpha\beta}}{D_{k\beta}} \right]^{\frac{2}{m-1}}} \, . \text{ continue}$$

}
End

expanded and data clustering applications of fuzzy logic, artificial neural network was developed and published in multiple well established journals worldwide by numerous scholars, scientists and engineers. With more advancement Janvesivu M et. al developed an intelligent kiln control system. Here, the neural network model was used in collaboration with advanced fuzzy logics based high-level controllers and linguistic equation approach. Kuo-Lung et al. proposed new validity partition coefficient and an exponential separation index with an aim of performing effective fuzzy clustering in noisy environment. By the time passed S Kalyani et al., worked over a fuzzy C- mean logical algorithm proposed for security assessment and power systems. The execution of which obtained the remarkable results. Later with the improvement in the field Gustafson-Kessel fuzzy clustering based algorithm for sensor fault detection in water treatment has been proposed by Skrjanc I. Numerous tests were conducted those results in acceptable outcomes. In latest evolution, development of the hybrid algorithm based on K-cell mean algorithm, Adaptive Swarm Optimization and ant colony optimization have been initiated by Taher Niknam et al.; with an aim to resolve the various nonlinear partitioning clustering algorithm.

Li Ma et al. developed a new amalgam method of AFSA (Artificial Fish Swam Algorithm) with FCM. The work resolved the issues of initial clusters dependency, attaining of optimal solutions and sensitivity to noise distribution in FCM algorithm.

Improvement in the state-of-the-art was made with attempting an optimization in parameters. Yogita et al. proposed an enhanced FCM algorithm by analyzing multiple FCM functions and modifying standard fuzzy objective function, fuzzy membership function and cluster center. Later, a development was made by E.A. Zanaty et al. with an introduction of kernelized fuzzy c-cluster based cluster count method. The use of GRBF (Gaussian Radian Basis Function Basis Function Classifier) with Euclidean Distance in FCM was made for effective outcomes from the simulations. The improvement in Fuzzy c-mean was encouraged by Yong-Xian et al. with the use of quantum GA. Attempt was made with the collaboration of bits encoding together with real number techniques to encode chromosomes in GA. As a results the attained chromosomes are refurbished through quantum rotating gates and mutated through quantum hadamard gate.

Subtractive Algorithm

One of the most highly used clustering technique is subtractive clustering. It is surrounding data points density based method which aims to compute the optimal data point from defining a cluster centroid. Thus, subtractive clustering can be reflected as an enlargement of Mountain method. This is so because, the exponential increase in computational complexity with the increase in data dimension is the only limitation of mountain method which has been resolved by subtractive clustering.

Algorithm 10. Subtractive clustering

Begin
    Consider n data points:
    $N = \{n_1, n_2, n_3, \ldots, n_n\}$.
    Here every element is treated as a potential cluster center.
    Potential of each element n_n is defined as:

$$\phi_n = \sum_{\alpha=1}^{n} e^{\frac{-4|n_n - n_1|^2}{r_a^2}}.$$

Here r_a is hyper sphere cluster radius in respective area. It must be a non-positive constant that defines the radius of the neighborhoods. |*| depicts the Euclidean distance. Thus, potential of data points measure can be considered as distance function measure to all various data points.

    After computing all the elements, one with the maximum ability is declared as an initial cluster midpoint. Thus, elements nearby to initial cluster midpoint will prominently diminish potential, thus chances of it's to being next cluster center reduced highly. After revise potential computation of each data points, the element having highest ability will be nominated as the next cluster midpoint. The process will continue till generation of sufficient cluster count are not accomplished.

    Technically, the outperformance of the cluster are highly depended over the values of hyperspace cluster radius and hyperspace penalty radius.
End

G. Bilgin et al. proposed a new subtractive clustering technique that worked over similarity segmentation and OC-SVM validation concept. Later Mariam El-Tarabily et al. developed a PSO based subtractive clustering technique. Basically, the subtractive clustering was used in computation of the cluster count and centroid evaluation, whose outcomes were made as in input data in PSO technique. Advancement with the collaboration of fuzzy c- mean was attempted by A.H. Rabgkkuti. Unlike, M. Tarabily computed the cluster centroid using fussy c-mean with an aim to find the membership function.

Expectation and Maximization

Expectation and Maximization (EM) is an density based segmentation technique that aims to compute the maximum likelihood estimation of data set parameters. The EM technique is a two-step process. Initializing from expectation process, the evaluation of probability function $F(\tau_k / \varphi_{\alpha,\beta})$. Where, $F(\tau_k / \varphi_{\alpha,\beta})$ outlines the each pixel $\varphi_{\alpha,\beta}$ probability into a respective cluster τ_k. Followed by maximization process, it evaluates the maximum estimations of the parameters. The two outcomes are used for expectation process till the evaluated outcomes does not converges.

Algorithm 11. Expectation and maximization

Begin
   Given training set T and Model M (T; Z)
   Here Z depicts the latent variable,
   We have,

$$L(\Phi) = \sum_{j=1}^{n} \log M(\text{T}; \Phi)$$

$$= \sum_{j=1}^{n} \log \sum M(\text{T}, \text{z}; \Phi)$$

Here, the likelihood can be depicted from T, Z and Φ.
Note, since Z is unknown latent variable, even though approximation values are considered.
These approximation values can be mathematically formulated as:
E Step, for each j:
   $Q_j(Z^{(j)}) := M(Z^{(j)} \mid T^{(j)}; \Phi)$
M Step, for all Z:

$$\Phi := \arg\max \sum\sum Q_j\left(Z^{(j)}\right) \log \frac{M(Z^{(j)} \mid T^{(j)}; \Phi)}{Q_j\left(Z^{(j)}\right)}.$$

Here, Q_j is posterior distribution of Z (j) `s for given T (j) `s.
End

Theoretically, EM Algorithm is demarcated as a K-Means algorithm variant where membership of any respective cluster point is not complete and can be functional.

Great attempts were made by Chad Carson et al. over EM technique. A spatially constrained EM algorithm which can iteratively maximize a data likelihood lower bound by A. Diplaros et al. Later, A. Mahjoun et al. developed an adaptive distance based EM Algorithm. They conceptually demarcated a new approach that defines the new distance which thus permit to compute new variant of the EM method.

DBSCAN

DBSCAN is a pixel values density based clustering algorithm. The priori initialization of the parameters such as E_{ps} and MP_{ts} are the basic requirement. MP_{ts} depicts the minimum neighborhood points and E_{ps} depicts the neighborhood radius. In DBSCAN method, pixel can be declared as a border pixel if any non-core pixel is reachable from any core pixel, else it will be declared as outlier pixel. DBSCAN attempts clustering in a sequential manner.

Hierarchical Clustering

Hierarchical clustering generates a hierarchical tree based on the similarities between the vectors, termed as dendrogram. Basically, its execution is concepts of agglomerative clustering based. Here, algorithm amalgamates the two closest clusters and modernizes the distances to the latest designed clusters; the process is repeated till the only single cluster left consisting of all the vectors. Commonly, for distance updations, the ways are single, complete or average linkages.

The procedure avoid dealing with the segmentation of the system but deals with an arrangement of the nested divisions, where each partition consist of n-1 clusters in comparison to the previous one. To acquire a partition with n clusters, the process must get stopped at n-1 steps before it ends. According to observation each linkage lead to different partitions, therefore, the kind of linkage used must be selected as per the type of data over which clustering has to be performed. For example, complete and average linkages are capable of building a compressed clusters, whereas single linkage inclines to form complex shaped cluster but is more likely to be affected by spurious data.

Self-Organizing Map

Self-organizing map (SOM) is a clustering approach that maps a multi-dimensional dataset onto two-dimensional surface. Basically, this surface is an ordered explanation of the probability distribution of the genes available in the input dataset. The two major purposes of SOM are: visualization and cluster analysis. NOTE: visualization has always been a challenging matter for high-dimensional.

This approach can be used to identify various groups and relations within the data by projecting the data onto 2-D image that can clearly identify the similarity regions. Usually, 2-D grid is used in higher dimensional grid, but in case of clustering preference is always given to 1-D grid. Such clustering is quite effective in visualization of the data, as it facilitates through its low dimensionality and exposes a huge volume of useful evidence on data.

Graph Theoretical Approach

Clustering has always faced a challenging task in cutting of graphs into good segments. Technically, every data element is linked with a weighted graph`s vertex. Graphs in which some weights are associated over each edge is termed as weighted graphs. NOTE: Weights are always large between edge elements carries a similarity and small in vice-a-versa scenario. On the basis of this concept an attempt is made to cut the graph into several connected components, carrying a large interior weights that later corresponds to the clusters by cutting the edges.

Weighted graphs are normally represented by a square matrix as depicted in Figure 17. Each vertex here consists of rows and columns. The xth, y^{th} elements of the matrix depicts the edge weight from vertex x and vertex y.

Figure 9. Top left, an image represents an undirected weighted graph; on top right, a weight matrix that has been associated with that respective graph; lighter pixels depict the larger values; on bottom, shows a cut of the graph that decomposed the graph into two tightly linked components; with this cut, a graph`s matrix is decomposed into two main blocks on the diagonal

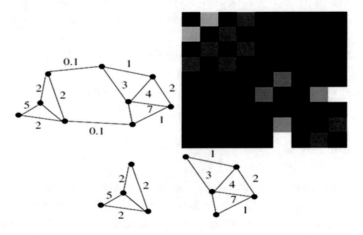

In graph theoretic clustering approach, method picks each element from the collection that is supposed to be clustered, and associate it with a vertex on a graph. Now edge is formation is made from each element to other and associate a weight with it. An edge cutting will now be performed in the graph for the formation of a good set of connected components. For instance, Figure 9 represents a collection of a well disjointed points and undirected weighted graph that obtains from a respective similarity measure.

ANALYSIS OF VARIOUS SEGMENTATION METHODS

Various segmenting methods have been proposed in the literature each of which carries pros and cons. Therefore, a comparative analysis of the various image segmentation approaches has been made in Table 1 based on its advantages and disadvantages.

*NP_k - No need of prior knowledge; *I_{Exp}- Computational Inexpensive; *F_nS- Fast and Simple for implementation; *RT_a- Can be applied in real time applications; *HN_s- High Noise Sensitive; *CS_T- Selection of threshold is crucial; * NS_k- Neglects the spatial information of an image; F_{lx}- Flexibility; * F_{io}- Flow from inner point to outer; *A_{ccy}- Accracy; *S_{ns}- Noisy Seed Selection; DS_c- Selection of Stop criteria is Difficult; *S_{re}-Second order differential is reliable; *CR_{eg}- work well for image having good contrast between regions; *BD_c- boundaries determined are discontinuous; SO_s- Single operator doesn`t suits; *RF_b- Reduces False blobs; *ENs- Eliminates noisy spots; *H_r - Homogeneous Regions; *C_f –Computationally Faster; * C_{Exp} – Computationally expensive; * S_{nsv} - Sensitive; * NG_c - Does not work for non-globular clusters; *B_{tr}- Better than previous approaches.

Comparative study of proposed methods based on various standard parameters such as: spatial information, speed, computation complexity, automaticity, multiple object detection, accuracy, region continuity is made. The detailed analytical discussion is done Table 2.

Table 1. Advantages and disadvantages of various image segmentation methods

Methods	Advantages			Disadvantages		
Threshold Based Methods	NP_k	I_{Exp}	F_nS	RT_a	HN_s	CS_T	NS_k
Region Based Methods	F_{lx}	F_{io}	A_{ccy}	N_{ap}	I_{Exp}	S_{ns}	DS_c
Discontinuity Based Methods	S_{re}	CR_{eg}	N_{ap}	N_{ap}	BD_c	SO_s	N_{ap}
Cluster Based Method	RF_b	ENs	H_r	C_f	C_{Exp}	S_{nsv}	NG_c
Fuzzy C- Means	B_{tr}	C_{ver}	N_{ap}	N_{ap}	HN_s	C_{Exp}	N_{ap}

Table 2. Parametric analysis of various proposed segmentation methods

Parameters	THM	RBM	DBM	CBM	FCM
Spatial Information	I_{gn}	C_{nsd}	I_{gn}	C_{nsd}	C_{nsd}
Speed	F_{st}	S_{lw}	F_{st}	F_{st}	M_{od}
Computation Complexity	L_{s}	R_{pd}	M_{od}	R_{pd}	M_{od}
Automaticity	S_{em}	S_{em}	I_{ntrv}	A_{utc}	A_{utc}
Multiple Object Detection	P_{or}	F_{r}	P_{or}	F_{r}	F_{r}
Accuracy	M_{od}	F_{n}	M_{od}	M_{od}	M_{od}
Region Continuity	R_{sble}	G_{d}	R_{sble}	R_{sble}	G_{d}
Noise Resistance	L_{s}	L_{s}	L_{s}	M_{od}	M_{od}

*THM- Threshold Based Method; *RBM- Region Based Method; *DBM-Discontinuity Based Method; *CBM- Cluster Based Method; *FCM- Fuzzy C-Means Method; *I_{gn}-Ignored; *C_{nsd}- Considered; *R_{sble}- Reasonable; *G_{d}- Good; *F_{st}- Fast; *S_{lw}- Slow; *M_{od}- Moderate; *L_{s}- Less; *R_{pd}-Rapid; *S_{em}- Semiauto; *I_{ntrv}- Interactive; *A_{utc}- Automatic; *P_{or}- Poor; *F_{r}-Fair; *F_{n}- Fine

COMPARATIVE ANALYSIS OF VARIOUS CLUSTERING TECHNIQUES

There are various algorithm those are categorized under the heading of clustering. Thus, it became very essential to effectively analyze the difference between these algorithm which may later to the selection of optimized technique and will lead to best outcomes.

Here comparisons of various clustering algorithms based on performance by memory usage and computational time. The algorithm made under consideration for

Table 3. Equations of maximum memory usage in respective clustering approaches

Algorithms	Memory Usage	E-i	E-ii	E-iii
K_M	$4m + 8K(2D+1) + 72$	8151	8711	12182
F_CM	$4K (6m + 4D + 3) + 114$	96199	768815	100230
H_C	$16m^2 + 40m + 56$	64087955	64087955	64087955
S_O_M	$8KD + 132$	160	350	2178
E_M	$4K(10m +12D +7) +$ $8D(m + 2D + 2) +214$	192555	1314290	2484748

the study are K-mean algorithm (K_M), Fuzzy C-Mean (F_C_M), Self-organizing Maps (S_O_M) with 1-D grid with the Euclidian distance metric and Hierarchical with the Euclidian distance metric.

Each experiment in this study was defined by cluster model together with the parameters such as:

- Dimensions Count (D): $D = 2^n$, here n falls from 1 to 7.
- Total Points Count (P): 50, 100, 200, 500, 1K, 2K, 5K.
- Cluster Count (C): $C = 2^n$, here n falls from 1 to 5.
- Variance between each cluster (σ^2): 0.1, 0.25, 0.5, 1, 2.5, 5.

A memory outcomes summary is represented in Table 3. The comparison of run times for respective experiments and corresponding outcomes of cluster count, dimension count and total points count used in every experimentation are conversed in Table 4.

CHALLENGES OF CLUSTERING TECHNIQUE AND FUTURE SCOPE

Clustering algorithm carries a very significant role in image segmentation. Although it carries a lot of pros but numerous challenges issues are encountered from the

Table 4. Average run time of experiments (in milliseconds)

Variance (σ^2)	KM	FCM	HC	SOM	EM
E-1: C = 2, D = 2, P = 2K					
0.25	0.0	0.0	4360.0	20.0	0.0
1	0.0	20.0	4260.0	0.0	140.0
5	0.0	80.0	4160.0	0.0	540.0
E-2: C = 16, D = 2, P = 2K					
0.25	16.0	184.0	5920.0	8.0	592.0
1	16.0	840.0	6440.0	0.0	936.0
5	24.0	944.0	6904.0	0.0	1216.0
E-3: C = 16, D = 128, P = 2K					
0.25	142.0	114.0	8057.0	114.0	742.0
1	142.0	171.0	8057.0	114.0	5457.0
5	142.0	171.0	8057.0	142.0	4828.0

deep study of the various clustering techniques. The major challenging problems of clustering techniques are those needed to be resolved for effective outcomes are discussed below:

1. **Outliers:** The variation in results has been observed, with the presence of outliers in data. That means, no stable outcomes on simulated executions of the same data. Outliers are such dataset's objects those does not result in the formation of the clustering. The increment in sum of square error within the clusters can be caused by the outliers. They can be eliminated using preprocessing techniques.

2. **Number of Clusters:** Estimating the cluster count in advance is a very challenging chore. Although advance determining of the cluster count is very beneficial. It has been observed that cluster count are assigned as per number of classes in the dataset.

3. **Empty Clusters:** On non-assignment of the points, the empty clusters may occur. It is basically an issue of traditional k- mean clustering algorithm.

4. **Non Globular Shapes and Sizes:** As per the study, if clusters varies in size, densities and non-globular shapes, the outcomes are not considered as optimal. Therefore, issue of convex shaped clusters are always there.

5. **Distance Evaluation:** Several distance calculations of each data point from all the centroids in each iteration is a great angle to work on.

6. **Centroid Dependency:** The dependency of final cluster over the selection of initial centroids must be improved.

7. **Noise Sensitivity and Heterogeneity:** It has been observed that the image segmentation is intensity heterogeneous and sensitive to noise.

8. **Role of Pixel Counts:** The generation of pixels count while looking for the best cluster division or amalgamation is major challenge to be resolved.

9. **Impact Over Average Space:** When two clusters consisting of large pixels count. The computation of the average space between the cluster elements is expensive; alternative to it includes the space between center of gravity.

10. **Lack of Optimized Merging:** Technically there is a merging of those clusters who shares the boundaries; and avoidance in merging of widely separated cluster regions has been identified. Thus, it would be helpful to amalgamate the regions merely by image scanning and integrate the pairs whose distance falls below the predefined threshold, besides searching for the adjoining pair.

11. **Prior Initialization:** On the basis of the study made, it has been identified that nearly all methods require a prior user initialization, which automatically becomes a major limitation of clustering techniques.

Quite a bit of efforts have been made in acquiring an optimal image segmentation. It has come to a long way from manual division to automated segmentation via numerous methodologies. Meaningful objects can be identified by the variation in color depth beyond threshold value. In certain case boundary between the regions are evaluated by intensity differences across the edges and neighboring pixels with a region. Even then, so far attempts are not able to obtain an optimal image segmentation in all cases, specifically with the variation in threshold values, colors and other features. Although it is safe to draw a conclusion that a very accurate and optimal image segmentation world be exceptionally be difficult to acquire in imaginable future, past and present and current efforts seems to be appropriate and similar should be continued to acquire more accuracy. Even then we suggest to keep the provision of segmentation based on color, texture, shape or locations so accuracy of segmentation can be optimally achieved to an extent.

CONCLUSION

In mainframe visualization, image segmentation is termed as a process of partitioning an image into multiple sections. The goal of segmentation is to depict an image that can lead to more essential, relevant and easy examination. It is a tool which is widely used in applications such as object detection, object tracking, object based coding, and image retrieval and much more. Numerous image segmentation techniques have been proposed by various researchers, which maintained a smooth and easy timely evaluation. In this chapter an attempt has been made to present a big image while ignoring that detail. It is a single level platform for understanding the role of various clustering based image segmentation techniques. Both pros and cons are discussed for each method. On the basis of the study made, it has been identified that nearly all methods require a prior user initialization, which automatically becomes a major limitation of clustering techniques. Thus, there is a need of a careful and an appropriate decision making while selecting a method based on the availability of data and user desires. Such a useful yet challenging limitations are discussing in detailed that need to be resolved soon for better results. Lastly, recent updates in the clustering technique have been covered for better visualization of the field.

REFERENCES

Alsabti, K., Ranka, S., & Singh, V. (1997). *An Efficient K-Means Clustering Algorithm*. Electrical Engineering and Computer Science.

Aneja, D., & Rawat, T. K. (2013). Fuzzy Clustering Algorithms for Effective Medical Image Segmentation. *International Journal of Intelligent Systems and Applications, 5*(11), 55–61. doi:10.5815/ijisa.2013.11.06

Bataineh, K. M., Najia, M., & Saqera, M. (2011). A Comparison Study between Various Fuzzy Clustering Algorithms. *Jordan Journal of Mechanical and Industrial Engineering, 5*(4), 335–343.

Bilgin, G., Ertürk, S., & Yildirim, T. (2011). Segmentation of Hyperspectral Images via Subtractive Clustering and Cluster Validation Using One-Class Support Vector Machines. *IEEE Transactions on Geoscience and Remote Sensing, 49*(8), 2936–2944. doi:10.1109/TGRS.2011.2113186

Brar, G. S. (2007). An Efficient Data Clustering Algorithm Using Fuzzy Logic For Control Of A Multi Compressor System. *IETECH Journal of Electrical Analysis, 1*(2), 130–136.

Carson, C., Belongie, S., Greenspan, H., & Malik, J. (2002). Blobworld: Image Segmentation Using Expectation Maximisation and Its Application to Image Querying. *IEEE Transactions on Pattern Analysis and Machine Intelligence, 24*(8), 1026–1038. doi:10.1109/TPAMI.2002.1023800

Chen, Qin, & Jia. (2008). *A Weighted Mean Substractive Clustering Algorithm.* Academic Press.

Corona, C., & Llanes-santiago, O. (2018). An Approach to Fault Diagnosis Using Fuzzy Clustering. Conference of the European Society for Fuzzy Logic and Technology, 641. doi:10.1007/978-3-319-66830-7

Dalton, L., Ballarin, V., & Brun, M. (2009). Clustering Algorithms: On Learning, Validation, Performance, and Applications to Genomics. *Current Genomics, 10*(6), 430–445. doi:10.2174/138920209789177601 PMID:20190957

Dave, R. N. (1993). Robust Fuzzy Clustering Algorithms. *IEEE International Conference on Fuzzy Systems,* 1281–86. doi:10.1109/FUZZY.1993.327577

Dhanachandra, N., & Chanu, Y. J. (2017). A Survey on Image Segmentation Methods Using Clustering Techniques. *European Journal of Engineering Research and Science, 2*(1), 15–20. doi:10.24018/ejers.2017.2.1.237

Dhanachandra, N., Manglem, K., & Chanu, Y. J. (2015). Image Segmentation Using K -Means Clustering Algorithm and Subtractive Clustering Algorithm. *Procedia Computer Science, 54,* 764–771. doi:10.1016/j.procs.2015.06.090

Diplaros, Vlassis, & Gevers. (2007). A Spatially Constrained Generative Model and an EM Algorithm for Image Segmentation. *IEEE Transactions on Neural Networks*, *18*(3), 798–808. doi:10.1109/TNN.2007.891190

Do, C. B., & Batzoglou, S. (2008). What Is the Expectation Maximization Algorithm? *Nature Biotechnology*, *26*(8), 897–899. doi:10.1038/nbt1406 PMID:18688245

Dougherty, Barrera, Brun, Kim, Cesar, Chen, … Trent. (2002). Inference from Clustering with Application to Gene-Expression Microarrays. *Journal of Computational Biology*, *9*(1), 105–26. doi:10.1089/10665270252833217

Dubey & Mushrif. (2016). FCM Clustering Algorithms for Segmentation of Brain MR Images. *Advances in Fuzzy Systems*, *2016*(2013), 1–15.

Duraiswamy, K., & Valli Mayil, V. (2008). Similarity Matrix Based Session Clustering by Sequence Alignment Using Dynamic Programming. *Computer and Information Science*, *1*(3), 66–72. doi:10.5539/cis.v1n3p66

Gonzalez, R., & Woods, R. (2002). *Digital Image Processing*. Prentice Hall. doi:10.1016/0734-189X(90)90171-Q

Hou, J., Gao, H., & Li, X. (2016). DSets-DBSCAN : A Parameter-Free Clustering Algorithm. *IEEE Transactions on Image Processing*, *25*(7), 3182–3193. doi:10.1109/TIP.2016.2559803 PMID:28113183

Jarek, S. (1994). Seeded Region Growing. *IEEE Transactions on Pattern Analysis and Machine Intelligence*, *16*(6), 641–647. doi:10.1109/34.295913

Jiji, G. (2015). Hybrid Data Clustering Approach Using K-Means And Flower Pollination Algorithm. *Advanced Computational Intelligence: An International Journal*, *2*(2), 15–25.

Kanungo, T., Mount, D. M., Netanyahu, N. S., Piatko, C. D., Silverman, R., & Wu, A. Y. (2002). An Efficient K-Means Clustering Algorithm: Analysis and Implementation. *IEEE Transactions on Pattern Analysis and Machine Intelligence*, *24*(7), 881–892. doi:10.1109/TPAMI.2002.1017616

Kaur, P. (2011). *Kernelized Type-2 Fuzzy C-Means Clustering Algorithm in Segmentation of Noisy Medical Images*. IEEE. doi:10.1109/RAICS.2011.6069361

Khan, M. (2013). Image Segmentation Methods: A Comparative Study. *International Journal of Soft Computing and Engineering*, *3*(4), 84–92. doi:10.1117/1.2762250

Khanmohammadi, S., Adibeig, N., & Shanehbandy, S. (2017). An Improved Overlapping K-Means Clustering Method for Medical Applications. *Expert Systems with Applications*, *67*, 12–18. doi:10.1016/j.eswa.2016.09.025

Kushwah, A. (2017). A Review: An Optimized Technique For Image Segmentation. *International Journal of Advanced Research in Computer Science*, *8*(5), 1375–1380.

Lee, Bullmore, & Frangou. (2010). Quantitative Evaluation of Simulated Functional Brain Networks in Graph Theoretical Analysis. *Deep-Sea Research Part II*, 1–32. doi:10.1016/j.dsr2.2010.12.006

Li, He, & Wen. (2015). Dynamic Particle Swarm Optimization and K-Means Clustering Algorithm for Image Segmentation. *Optik - International Journal for Light and Electron Optics*, *126*(24), 4817–22. doi:.10.1016/j.ijleo.2015.09.127

Li, J., & Lewis, H. W. (2016). Fuzzy Clustering Algorithms — Review of the Applications. *2016 IEEE International Conference on Smart Cloud (SmartCloud)*, 282–88. doi:10.1109/SmartCloud.2016.14

Li, M., Suohai, F., & Runzhu, F. (2016). A Hybrid Method for Image Segmentation Based on Artificial Fish Swarm Algorithm and Fuzzy -Means Clustering. *A Hybrid for Image Segmentation Based on Artificial Fish Swarm Algorithm and Fuzzy-Means Clustering*, 1–13. http://www.emis.de/journals/HOA/CMMM/Volume4_2/459642. abs.html

Lukac, P., Hudec, R., Benco, M., Kamencay, P., Dubcova, Z., & Zachariasova, M. (2011). Simple Comparison of Image Segmentation Algorithms Based on Evaluation Criterion. *Proceedings of 21st International Conference, Radioelektronika 2011*, *1*, 233–36. doi:10.1109/RADIOELEK.2011.5936406

Mahjoub & Kalti. (2011). Image Segmentation by EM Algorithm Based on Adaptive Distance. *International Journal of Advanced Computer Science and Applications*, 19–25.

Maintz, T. (2005). *Segmentation*. Digital and Medical Image Processing. Retrieved from http://www.cs.uu.nl/docs/vakken/ibv/reader/chapter10.pdf

Masood, S., Sharif, M., Masood, A., Yasmin, M., & Raza, M. (2015). A Survey on Medical Image Segmentation. *Current Medical Imaging Reviews*, *11*(1), 3–14. doi:10.2174/1573405611011150423103441

Matko, D. (2002). Direct Fuzzy Model-Reference Adaptive Control. *International Journal of Intelligent Systems*, *17*, 943–963. doi:10.1002/int.10054

Mendel, J. M., John, R. I., Liu, F., Mendel, J. M., John, R. I., & Liu, F. (2006). Interval Type-2 Fuzzy Logic Systems Made Simple. *IEEE Transactions on Fuzzy Systems*, *14*(6), 808–821. doi:10.1109/TFUZZ.2006.879986

Morse, B. S. (2000). Lecture 18: Segmentation (Region Based). Brigham Young University.

Naik, D., & Shah, P. (1993). A Review on Image Segmentation Techniques. *Pattern Recognition*, *26*(9), 1277–1294. doi:10.1016/0031-3203(93)90135-J

Otsu, N. (1979). A Threshold Selection Method from Gray-Level Histograms. *IEEE Transactions on Systems, Man, and Cybernetics*, *20*(1), 62–66. doi:10.1109/TSMC.1979.4310076

Peng, B., Zhang, L., & Zhang, D. (2012). A Survey of Graph Theoretical Approaches to Image Segmentation. *Pattern Recognition*, *46*(3), 1020–1038. doi:10.1016/j.patcog.2012.09.015

Prasantha, H. S. (2010). Medical Image Segmentation. *Medical Image Segmentation*, *2*(4), 1209–1218. doi:10.1201/9781420090413-c10

Rangkuti, A. H., Rasjid, Z. E., Imaduddin, M., Chandra, A. S., & Chancra, D. (2015). Face Skin Disease Recognation Using Fuzzy Subtractive Clustering Algorithm. *Journal of Theoretical and Applied Information Technology*, *73*(1), 174–182.

Ravi, S., & Khan, A. M. (2012). Operators Used In Edge Detection Computation : A Case Study. *International International Journal of Applied Engineering Research*, *7*(11), 7–12.

Rutakemwa, M. M. (2013). A PSO-Based Substractive Data Clustering Algorithm. *International Journal of Research in Computer Science*, *3*(1), 19–25. doi:10.7815/ijorcs.31.2013.057

Sandhya, H. (2017). A Survey on Clustering Algorithms Used to Perform Image Segmentation. *International Journal of Advance Research Ideas and Innovations in Technology*, *3*(1), 655–661.

Senthilkumaran, N., & Rajesh, R. (2009). Edge Detection Techniques for Image Segmentation–a Survey of Soft Computing Approaches. *International Journal of Recent Trends in Engineering and Technology*, *1*(2), 250–254. doi:10.1109/ARTCom.2009.219

Sharma, P., & Suji, J. (1993). A Review on Image Segmentation with Its Clustering Techniques. *Pattern Recognition*, *26*(9), 1277–1294. doi:10.1016/0031-3203(93)90135-J

Sjoerds, Z., Stufflebeam, S. M., Veltman, D. J., Van den Brink, W., Penninx, B. W. J. H., & Douw, L. (2017). Loss of Brain Graph Network Efficiency in Alcohol Dependence. *Addiction Biology*, 22(2), 523–534. doi:10.1111/adb.12346 PMID:26692359

Tatiraju, Suman, & Mehta. (2008). Image Segmentation Using K-Means Clustering, EM and Normalized Cuts. *Department of EECS*. Retrieved from http://ares.utcluj. ro/psi/tsg/proiect/Tema4/image_segmentation_using_k-means_clustering.pdf

Wang, H., & Dong, Y. (2008). An Improved Image Segmentation Algorithm Based on Otsu Method. In *Proceedings of SPIE*, 6625, 1–8. doi:10.1117/12.790781

Wang, J., Delabie, J., Aasheim, H., Smeland, E., & Myklebost, O. (2002). Clustering of the SOM Easily Reveals Distinct Gene Expression Patterns: Results of a Reanalysis of Lymphoma Study. *BMC Bioinformatics*, 3(1), 36. doi:10.1186/1471-2105-3-36 PMID:12445336

Yang, M.-S., & Nataliani, Y. (2017). Robust-Learning Fuzzy c-Means Clustering Algorithm with Unknown Number of Clusters. *Pattern Recognition*, 71, 45–59. doi:10.1016/j.patcog.2017.05.017

Yang, Y., & Huang, S. (2007). Image Segmentation By Fuzzy C-Means Clustering Algorithm With a Noval Penalty Term. *Computer Information*, 26, 17–31.

Yanp, M.-S., & Wu, K.-L. (2003). A Novel Fuzzy Clustering Algorithm. *IEEE International Conference in Robotucs and Automation*, 647–52.

Zafar, M. H., & Ilyas, M. (2015). A Clustering Based Study of Classification Algorithms. *International Journal of Database Theory and Applications*, 8(1), 11–22. doi:10.14257/ijdta.2015.8.1.02

Zanaty, E. A. (2012). Determining the Number of Clusters for Kernelized Fuzzy C-Means Algorithms for Automatic Medical Image Segmentation. *Egyptian Informatics Journal*, 13(1), 39–58. doi:10.1016/j.eij.2012.01.004

Section 3
Recognition Systems

Chapter 7
Bag of Visual Words Based on Co-HOG Features for Word Spotting in Handwritten Documents

Thontadari C.
Kuvempu University, India

Prabhakar C. J.
Kuvempu University, India

ABSTRACT

In this chapter, the authors present a segmentation-based word spotting method for handwritten documents using bag of visual words (BoVW) framework based on co-occurrence histograms of oriented gradients (Co-HOG) features. The Co-HOG descriptor captures the word image shape information and encodes the local spatial information by counting the co-occurrence of gradient orientation of neighbor pixel pairs. The handwritten document images are segmented into words and each word image is represented by a vector that contains the frequency of visual words appeared in the image. In order to include spatial information to the BoVW framework, the authors adopted spatial pyramid matching (SPM) method. The proposed method is evaluated using precision and recall metrics through experimentation conducted on popular datasets such as GW and IAM. The performance analysis confirmed that the method outperforms existing word spotting techniques.

DOI: 10.4018/978-1-5225-5628-2.ch007

INTRODUCTION

Document Image Analysis (DIA) is one of the active research areas, which attracts research community due to its complexity and the increasing requirement for accessing the content of digitized contents. Optical Character Recognition (OCR) has been investigated for a few decades with huge achievement, which helps to automate the human process. The automatic recognition by traditional OCR system is suitable for modern high quality printed documents with simple layouts and known fonts. The poor quality printed text and handwritten text is not feasible by traditional OCR system. Processing of these documents through the OCR system requires high computation cost because of complexity involved in understanding the page layout of documents, irregular writing styles, faded ink, stained paper and other undesirable factors. In order to overcome these problems, the DIA community has developed a technique called word spotting. Word spotting technique is a moderately new alternative for character recognition and retrieval in both printed and handwritten documents.

Word spotting can b e defined as the pattern recognition task aimed at locating and retrieving a particular word from a document image collection without explicitly transcribing the whole corpus. The word spotting approaches do not require the recognition of every letter of the query word or the target word and thus are capable of similar word retrieval in the presence of small distortions. Generally, a typical word spotting system consists of three main modules: preprocessing, features extraction and feature matching. Among them, features extraction is one of the most important factors for achieving high retrieval performance, because features with strong discriminative information can be well classified even using simplest classifier. The literature survey reveals that Histogram of Oriented Gradients (HOG) descriptor is widely used in several recognition applications because of its discriminating ability compared to other existing feature descriptors. The HOG feature descriptor is developed by Dalal et al. (2005) for human detection using Support Vector Machine (SVM) classifier. The HOG has been successfully applied in many research fields such as word spotting task (Rodrıguez 2008; Terasawa et al., 2009), body parts detection (Corvee et al., 2010), face recognition (Deniz et al., 2011; Shu et al., 2011), character recognition (Newell et al., 2011), text/non-text classification problem (Minetto et al., 2013) and vehicle detection in traffic video (Arrospide et al., 2013).

Rodriguez, J. A. et al. (2008) have proposed local gradient histogram features for word spotting in unconstrained handwritten documents. A sliding window moves from left to right over a word image. At each position, the window is subdivided into cells, and in each cell, a histogram of orientations is accumulated. Slit style HOG features for handwritten document image word spotting is proposed by Terasawa et al. (2009). Newell et al. (2011) have extended the HOG descriptor to include features at multiple scales for character recognition. Saidani et al. (2015) have proposed a novel approach for Arabic and Latin script identification based on Histogram of Oriented Gradients feature descriptors. HOG is first applied at word level based on writing orientation analysis. Then, they are extended to word image partitions to capture fine and discriminating details. The unsupervised segmentation-free HOG based word spotting method was proposed by Almazan, et al. (2014). Documents are represented by a grid of HOG descriptors, and a sliding-window approach is used to locate the document regions that are most similar to the query.

The appearance and shape of the local object in an image is represented through distribution of the local intensity gradient orientation and edge direction without requiring equivalent gradient and edge positions (Carcagnì et al., 2015). This orientation analysis is robust to lighting changes since the histogram provides translational invariance. The HOG feature descriptor summarizes the distribution of measurements within the image regions. When extracting HOG features, the orientations of gradients are usually quantized into histogram bins and each bin has an orientation range. A histogram of oriented gradients falling into each bin is computed and then normalized to overcome the illumination variation. The orientation of gradients from all blocks are then concatenated together to form a feature descriptor of the whole image.

HOG feature descriptor captures orientation of only isolated pixels, whereas spatial information of neighboring pixels is ignored. Co-HOG descriptor (Watanabe et al., 2009) is an extension of the original HOG descriptor that captures the spatial information of neighboring pixels. Instead of counting the occurrence of the gradient orientation of a single pixel, gradient orientations of two or more neighboring pixels are considered. For each pixel in an image block, the gradient orientations of the pixel pair formed by its neighbor and itself are examined. Co-HOG is a dominant descriptor widely used in object detection due to its accurately representing significant characteristics of the object structure. At the same time, it is more efficient compared with HOG and therefore more suitable for real-time applications such pedestrian detection (Watanabe et al.,2009), object detection (Ren et al., 2010), face recognition (Do, 2012) and detection of vehicles in traffic video sequence (Arunkumar et al., 2016). Recently, DIA community has successfully applied Co-HOG feature in several application such as character recognition in natural scenes (Su et al., 2014), scene text recognition (Tian et al., 2013) and multilingual scene character recognition (Tian et al., 2015).

In the previous work (Thontadari et al., 2016), we proposed segmentation based word spotting using Co-HOG feature extracted in scale space representation. In order to extract holistic shape of word image at coarse level (multiscale) using Co-HOG descriptor, initially, we derive multi scale images using Gaussian convolution operation at $\sigma = 0$, $\sigma = 1$, and $\sigma = 2$ employed on original image. Further, the

Co-HOG descriptor is extracted from all three scale image, and finally concatenated to form a scale space Co-HOG descriptor which yields scale space representation of a word image. Thus, the dimension of the Scale space Co-HOG feature vector of a word image is $34704 \times 3 = 104112$. When we represent the word image in multi scale environment, the dimension of the feature vector is increased which is a negative impact on the computational cost when matching by the DTW algorithm. In order to overcome the drawback of scale space Co-HOG approach, in this chapter, we propose segmentation-based word spotting technique using a Bag of Visual Words powered by Co-HOG features aimed to reduce the dimension of feature vector.

In order to include spatial distribution of visual words information to the BoVW framework, we adopted Spatial Pyramid Matching (SPM) method, which recaptures spatial distribution of visual words information by creating a spatial pyramid bins. The rest of the article is organized as follows. In Section 2, we provide related work on word spotting. In Section 3, description of HOG and Co-HOG descriptors are presented. This is followed by proposed handwritten word spotting approach. The experimental results are reported and discussed in section 5 and finally, the conclusion is drawn.

RELATED WORK

Word spotting algorithms intend to reduce tedious and time overwhelming manual annotation applied to the pictorial representation of input document words. The literature survey reveals that a lot of techniques have been developed to spot the words in handwritten and printed documents. Word profile features-based technique is the first technique developed by Manmatha, R. et al. (1996, 2003) for word spotting in handwritten documents. Word spotting algorithms for handwritten documents are broadly classified into two categories (Manmatha et al., 2003) such as pixel-based and features-based matching algorithms. In pixel-based matching, the similarity between the two images are measured in the pixel domain using various metrics such as Euclidean distance, XOR difference, Scott and Longuet-Higgins distance, Hausdorff distance or a sum of the squared differences. On the other hand, in feature-based matching, images compared with representative features extracted from the images. Similarity measures such as Dynamic Time Warping (DTW) and point correspondence are defined on the feature domain. The prominent learning algorithms for handwritten word spotting are Hidden Markov Models (HMM) (Fischer et al., 2010; Chan et al., 2006; Rodriguez 2008) and Neural networks (Wollmer. et al., 2009; Fernandez et al., 2007) which were used to a large extent of research for word spotting in handwritten documents.

Depending on the query format, feature-based word spotting algorithms are further classified into two categories: query by example (QBE) and query by string (QBS). In QBE (Manmatha et al., 1996; Rothfeder, et al., 2003; Terasawa et al., 2009), the user manually locates a word instance in the document image and uses it as a template for locating the other instances. An advantage of this approach is that the template images are rather easy to obtain, even if the underlying language and its alphabet are unknown. These methods work well only for documents of a specific style such as imaging condition, font or handwriting style, etc. The QBS (Rodriguez et al., 2008; Frinken et al., 2010) is more convenient for the users to enter the query by keyboard and is flexible for spotting words of arbitrary style. By this method, the character or word model needs to be trained with a large number of samples.

Rath et al. (2003) proposed an algorithm for matching handwritten words in noisy historical documents. The segmented word images are preprocessed to create 1-dimensional features, which are used to train the probabilistic classifier, which is then used to estimate similarity between word images. Rothfeder et al. (2003) presented an algorithm to draw correspondences between points of interest in two word images and utilizes these correspondences to measure the similarities between the images. Srihari et al. (2005) indexed documents using global word image features such as stroke width and slant. Word gaps are used to measure the similarities among the spotted words and a set of prototypes from known writers. Srihari et al. (2006) developed a word spotting system that retrieves the candidate words from the documents and ranks them based on global word shape features. Rath et al. (2007) proposed an approach which involves grouping word images into clusters of similar words by using both K-means and agglomerative clustering techniques. They construct an index automatically that links words to the locations of occurrence which helps to spot the words easily.

Rodriguez-Serrano (2010) proposed an unsupervised handwritten word spotting using semi-continuous hidden Markov model to separate the word model parameters into a codebook of shapes and a set of word-specific parameters. Kesidis et al. (2011) extracted pixel density of zones and projection profile features and computes the Euclidean distance between word images, and refines the search procedure by user feedback. A template free word spotting method for handwritten documents was described by Frinken et al. (2011) which is derived from the neural network based system. The word spotting is done using a modification of the Connectionist Temporal Classification (CTC) token passing algorithm in conjunction with a recurrent neural network. Khurshid et al. (2012) represent a word image as a sequence of sub-patterns, each sub-pattern as a sequence of feature vectors, and calculate a segmentation-driven edit (SDE) distance between words. Rodríguez-Serrano et al. (2012) proposed a model-based similarity between vector sequences of handwritten word images with semi-continuous Gaussian mixture HMMs. Kessentini et al. (2013)

proposed a novel system for segmentation free and lexicon free word spotting and regular expression detection in handwritten documents using filler model which allows to accelerate the decoding process. Huang et al. (2013) proposed contextual word model for keyword spotting in off-line Chinese handwritten documents by combining a character classifier and the geometric context as well as linguistic context. They conducted experiments on handwriting database CASIA-HWDB demonstrate the effectiveness of the proposed method and justify the benefits of geometric and linguistic contexts. Coherent learning segmentation based Arabic handwritten word spotting system proposed by Khayyat et al. (2014) which can adapt to the nature of Arabic handwriting and the system recognizes Pieces of Arabic Words (PAWs).

Wshah et al. (2014) proposed a statistical script independent line based word spotting framework for offline handwritten documents based on Hidden Markov Models. The candidate keywords are pruned in a two-stage spotting framework using the character-based and lexicon- based background models. They evaluated proposed approach on a mixed corpus of the public dataset such as IAM for English, AMA for Arabic and LAW for Devanagari. An efficient segmentation free word spotting method for the historical document is proposed by Rusinol et al. (2015). They used patch-based framework of the BoVW model powered by SIFT descriptors. By projecting the patch descriptors to a topic space with the latent semantic analysis technique and compressing the descriptors with the product quantization method efficiently index the document information both in terms of memory and time. Based on inkball character models, Howe (2015) proposed a word spotting method using synthetic models composed of individual characters. Line-level keyword spotting method proposed by Toselli et al. (2016) on the basis of frame-level word posterior probabilities of a full-fledged handwritten text recognizer based on hidden Markov models and N-gram language models.

Histogram of Oriented Gradients (HOG)

Figure 1 shows extraction of HOG features for a word image. In order to extract HOG feature, initially gradient orientation θ of every pixel is calculated using Equation (1).

$$\theta = arctan\left(\frac{I_y}{I_x}\right) \tag{1}$$

where, $arctan\left(\,\right)$ returns the inverse tangent of the elements in degrees. I_y and I_x are vertical and horizontal gradient respectively calculated by Gaussian filter. Then,

Figure 1. Procedure for HOG calculation

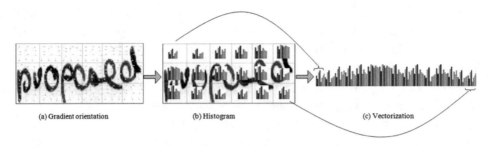

(a) Gradient orientation   (b) Histogram   (c) Vectorization

histogram of each orientation in a small rectangular region is calculated. The orientation of pixels is quantized to n bins and a histogram of orientation is calculated at each bin as follows:

$$H\left(i\right) = \sum_{x,y \in I,\ R_o(x,y)=i} R_g\left(x,y\right) \ ,\ i = 1,2,\dots,n. \tag{2}$$

Where R_g and R_o is magnitude and orientation of gradient at $\left(x,y\right)$ respectively. Finally, HOG feature descriptor is constructed by concatenating the histogram $H\left(i\right)$ for all small regions..

Co-Occurrence of Histogram of Oriented Gradients (Co-HOG)

Co-HOG feature is robust against deformation and illumination variation because it is gradient based histogram feature descriptor. Co-HOG capture spatial information by counting frequency of co-occurrence of oriented gradients between pixel pairs. For each pixel in an image block, the gradient orientations of the pixel pair formed by its neighbor and itself are examined. Since, the pair of gradient orientations has more lexis than single one because single gradient orientation has only eight verities (Figure 2(a)) and in a pair of them has many more than single orientation as shown in Figure 2(b).

In order to extract Co-HOG features from an image, firstly, gradient orientations at every pixel are calculated using Equation (1). In particular, gradient image R of I is computed as $R = \left\{R_g, R_o\right\}$ where R_g and R_o being respectively magnitude and orientation of the gradient. For each pixel in an image, the gradient orientations of the pixel pair formed with its neighbor, and itself are examined. The relative

Figure 2. Lexis of gradient orientation: (a) single gradient orientation (b) a pair of gradient orientation (Courtesy: Watanabe et al. 2009)

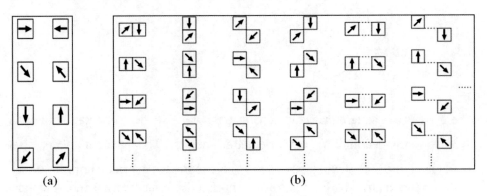

(a)   (b)

locations are reflected by the offset between two pixels as shown in Figure 3(a). The pixel at the center is the pixel under study and the neighboring ones are pixels with different offsets. Each neighboring pixel forms an orientation pair with the center pixel and accordingly votes to the co-occurrence matrix as illustrated in Figure 3(b).

We compute co-occurrence matrix K over an image I of size $N \times M$ at an offset (x, y) as follows:

Figure 3. Extraction of Co-HOG features: (a) offset used in Co-HOG, (b) Co-occurrence matrix for the given offset (Courtesy: Tian et al. 2016)

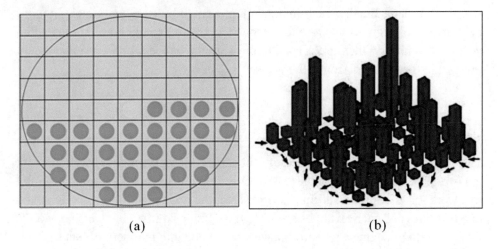

(a)   (b)

$$K_{x,y}(i,j) = \sum_{p=1}^{N} \sum_{q=1}^{M} \begin{cases} 1 & \text{If } I(p,q) = i \text{ and } I(p+x,q+y) = j \\ \\ 0 & \text{otherwise} \end{cases}$$

$$(3)$$

where, $K_{x,y}$ is a square matrix of dimension 8×8. Gradient orientation interval $[0, 360^0]$ is divided into $N_{bin} = 8$ orientations per 45^0. The maximum offset is set to 4 as in Figure 3(a), it will give rise to 31 co-occurrence matrices. For zero offset, co-occurrence matrix size is 1×8 (only eight effective values) because non-diagonal components are zero and the co-occurrence matrix size for other offsets is 8×8. One such co-occurrence matrix is shown in Figure 3(b).

Bag of Visual Words (BoVW) Framework

The Bag of Visual Words (Fei-Fei, et al., 2007) is an extension of Bag of Words (Csurka et al., 2004) to the container of digitized document images. The BoVW framework consists of three main steps: in the first step, a certain number of image local interest points are extracted from the image. These keypoints are significant image points having rich of information content. In the second step, feature descriptors are extracted from these keypoints, and these feature descriptors are clustered. Each cluster corresponds to a visual word that is a description of the features shared by the descriptors belongs to that cluster. The cluster set can be interpreted as a visual word vocabulary. Finally, each image is represented by a vector, which contains occurrences of each visual word that appears in the image. Based on these feature vectors, a similarity measure is used to measure the likeness between given query image and the set of images in the dataset.

PROPOSED METHOD

The proposed method is composed of four stages: (i) segmentation of a document into words (ii) computation of the Co-HOG descriptor (iii) codebook generation and (iv) word instances retrieval. In the first stage, the document image is segmented into text lines and each text lines are segmented into primitive segments i.e. words. In second stage, segmented word images are divided into number of blocks. Then, Co-HOG features are computed from each block. In third stage, codebook is used to quantize them into visual words. The codebook is obtained by clustering the descriptor feature space into k-different clusters by using the k-means algorithm. Then, visual words are obtained by simply assigning each Co-HOG descriptor to the nearest visual word of the codebook. Finally, each word image is represented by a vector that contains the frequency of visual words appeared in the image. The feature descriptor of each segmented word images consists of frequency of visual words and does not take into account the spatial distribution of the visual words within the word image. In order to include spatial distribution information to the BoVW framework, we adopted spatial pyramid matching method (Lazebnik et al. 2006). In the word retrieval phase, for a given query image, we construct the visual word vector. Then, Nearest Neighbor Search is used to match the visual word vector of the query word image and the visual word vectors presented in the codebook. Finally, based on the ranking list, retrieved word images are presented.

Segmentation of Handwritten Documents

The handwritten documents are unconstrained and therefore contain different writing styles, artifacts and other types of noise. The handwritten document images are denoised and segmented into individual text lines using directional local profile

Figure 4. BoVW framework for handwritten word images (a) Segmented word images from the handwritten documents (b) Extraction of Co-HOG feature descriptors (c) clustering of Co-HOG descriptors using k-means clustering (d) vocabulary of visual words

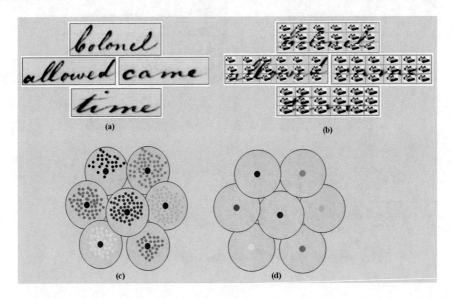

technique (Shi et al., 2009) and then words are segmented using adjacent connected components technique (Papavassiliou et al., 2010). The sample results of denoised and segmented word images are shown in Figure 5.

Extraction of Co-HOG Features

The handwritten word image is having more local variation within the class when compared to the variation between classes because of variation in the writing style of writers. Hence, in order to capture distinct local shape information within the class, we divide the word image into a number of blocks of Equal size. The advantages of dividing an image into blocks are that the feature descriptor can express local and global shapes in detail and decreases the space computation complexities for feature extraction, and to utilize the distinct location relate information from each block.

In order to extract Co-HOG features, we divide an image into $Block_h \times Block_w$ non overlapping blocks and co-occurrence matrices are computed for each block using Equation.3 presented in section 3.2. The Figure 6(b) shows word image which is divided into non-overlapping blocks and corresponding co-occurrence matrices. The computed co-occurrence matrix from each block is represented using Co-HOG

Figure 5. Sample results of segmented words. (a) Original image (b) corresponding horizontal profile feature (c) segmented text lines and (d) segmented word images

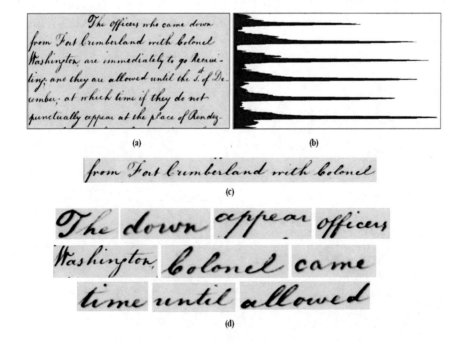

172

histogram is called as Co-HOG descriptor. The co-occurrence matrix expresses the distribution of gradient orientations at a given offset over a grid and combinations of neighbor gradient orientations can express shapes in detail.

Codebook Generation

The single codebook is the house of all possible visual words that correspond to spotting the word image in handwritten document images. Generally, the codebook must hold the following constraints, the codebook should be small, that guarantees to minimum computational rate through minimum dimensionality, redundant visual words minimization, and provide high discrimination performance.

In order to generate codebook, the computed Co-HOG descriptors from each block of word image are clustered by k-means clustering algorithm. The Co-HOG descriptors computed from each block is allotted to a cluster through minimum

Figure 6. Illustration of Co-HOG feature descriptor extraction process: (a) Sample word image (b) Word image divided into 3x6 blocks and corresponding co-occurrence matrices of each block

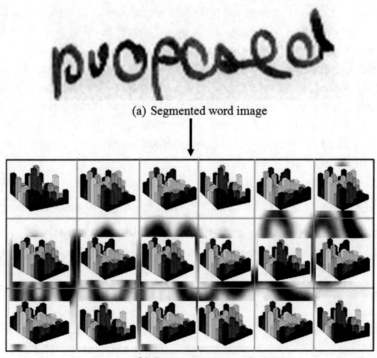

(a) Segmented word image

(b) Co-occurrence matrices

distance from the center of the corresponding cluster. These clusters are treated as visual words. The number of visual words characterizes the dimension of a codebook. Finally, word image is formally represented as visual word vector with the help of frequency of occurrences of the visual words in the codebook. Therefore, the dimension of visual word vector of word image is same as the number of visual words present in the codebook. For example, consider a codebook of dimension 5 (five visual words) and a word image consists of 18 Co-HOG descriptor, then the visual word vector of word image is constructed as follows: 5 Co-HOG descriptors are lies in the first visual word, 4 descriptors for second visual word, 6 descriptors for the third visual word, 2 descriptors for the fourth visual word and 1 Co-HOG descriptors for fifth visual word. Then, the visual word vector of a word image is [5, 4, 6, 2, 1].

Spatial Pyramid Matching

When we represent word image using visual word vector, it does not consider their spatial location. Hence, visual word vector suffers from spatial distribution information. In word spotting, spatial distribution information is essential because it helps to determine a location exclusively with visual information when the different location can be perceived as the same. This is the drawback of BoVW framework for representing a word image using visual word vector. In order to add spatial distribution information of visual words into the unstructured BoVW framework, we adopted Spatial Pyramid Matching (SPM) technique (Lazebnik et al. 2006). This technique takes into account the visual word distribution over the image by creating a pyramid of spatial bins. This spatial pyramid representation sacrifices the geometric invariance properties of bags of features. It more than compensates for this loss with increased discriminative power derived from the global spatial information. Therefore, the spatial pyramid method significantly outperforms BoVW on handwritten word spotting tasks.

The spatial pyramid is constructed by splitting the word image I into $I_x \times I_y$ spatial bins, where I_x and I_y represents the number of partitions along horizontally X and vertically Y directions, respectively. After splitting the word image into $I_x \times I_y$ spatial bins, we compute descriptor of each spatial bin using codebook, which consists of frequency of visual words present within the spatial bin. Finally, the resultant descriptor of the I is obtained by concatenating all the descriptor of each spatial bin.

In our experiments, we split the word image into two levels of spatial pyramids. In the first level, $I_x = I_y = 1$ and i.e. word image is considered and in the second level, $I_x = 1$ and $I_y = 2$ i.e. right and left parts of the word image (Figure 7). Therefore, three spatial bins such as whole word, left and right part of the word images are obtained from two level representation of spatial pyramid. With this configuration we aim to capture information about the right and left parts of the word. Since the frequency of visual words computed from each spatial bin is minimum when considering at higher levels of the pyramid, because of the spatial bins are smaller and visual words contribution is weighted according to the spatial coverage. Finally, descriptor of word image is represented by concatenating all the three spatial bins and is described by

$$f_I = \left[f_I^w, f_I^l, f_I^r \right] \tag{4}$$

Where, f_I^w, f_I^l, f_I^r represents descriptor corresponds to the whole, left and right spatial bins of the word image. Therefore, dimension D_I of each word image is calculated by using Equation. (5). This spatial distribution information increases the performance of our method.

$$D_I = \sum_{l=1}^{L} I_x^l \times I_y^l \tag{5}$$

where, L is number of levels and l is corresponding pyramid level.

Word Image Retrieval

In order to retrieve the word images similar to query word, we compute the similarity between visual word vector of the query word image and visual word vector of word images present in the dataset. We obtain matches through a Nearest Neighbor Search

Figure 7. The second level SPM configuration of our approach

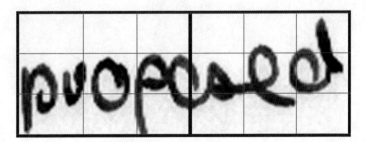

(NNS) approach using Euclidean distance between a training samples and query image descriptor by considering appropriate threshold T.

$$NNS = \sqrt{\sum_{i=1}^{n} \left(d_j\left(i\right) - q\left(i\right) \right)^2} \quad < T \tag{6}$$

where, n is the dimension of visual word vector, d_j and q are visual word vectors of jth training sample and query word image respectively.

EXPERIMENTAL RESULTS

For evaluating the proposed word spotting algorithm, two datasets are used such as George Washington (GW) dataset (Lavrenko et al., 2004) and the IAM off-line dataset (Marti et al., 2002). Figure 8 shows sample document images of GW and IAM dataset. In order to evaluate the performance of our approach, we conducted the experiments and results are evaluated based on popular metrics such as *Precision (P)*, *Recall (R)* and f-*measure*. Precision gives the percentage of true positives as compared to the total number of word images retrieved by the approach. Recall gives the percentage of true positives as compared to the total number of true positives in the dataset and f-measure is the weighted harmonic mean of precision and recall, which can be used to calculate the accuracy of the approach. For a given query word image, we evaluate, *True Positives (TP)*, *False Positives (FP)*, and *False Negative (FN)*. Based on these values, we calculate *Precision* and *Recall* values.

$$P = \frac{|\{relavant \text{ instances }\}| \quad \cap \quad |\{retrieved \text{ instances }\}|}{|\{retrieved \text{ instances }\}|} \tag{7}$$

$$R = \frac{|\{relavant \text{ instances }\}| \quad \cap \quad |\{retrieved \text{ instances }\}|}{|\{relavant \text{ instances }\}|} \tag{8}$$

$$f - measure\left(f\right) = 2\frac{P.R}{P+R}, \tag{9}$$

Figure 8. Samples handwritten document images from (a) GW dataset (b) IAM dataset

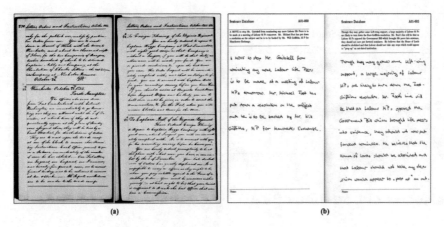

where, *TP* is the number of relevant word instances correctly retrieved, *FP* is the number of word images retrieved as other than query image and *FN* is the number of relevant word instances does not retrieve from the dataset.

We employed five-fold cross-validation method to validate our approach, each dataset is partitioned into five complementary subsets i.e. four subsets are used for training and remaining one subset is used as validation (test) set. The cross-validation process is repeated five times, with each subset used exactly once for validation. To estimate the overall evaluation results of our approach, we compute the mean Average Precision (mAP) of the five validation results. The mean Average Precision (mAP) provides a single value measure of precision for all the query word images.

Parameter Selection

One of the important factors to achieve the highest accuracy is an optimal number of blocks of an image. Hence, in order to find an optimal number of blocks, we conducted the experiments using GW and IAM dataset for a different number of blocks such as $1 \times 2\left(2blocks\right)$, $2 \times 4\left(8blocks\right)$, $3 \times 6\left(18blocks\right)$ and $4 \times 8\left(32blocks\right)$. The mean Average Precision (*mAP*) obtained on two datasets using our approach for a different number blocks is presented in Table 1. It is observed that when the word image is divided into $3 \times 6blocks\left(18blocks\right)$, the accuracy of our approach is significantly better than other number of blocks. Hence, in all the experiments, we divide the word image into $3 \times 6blocks\left(18blocks\right)$ and co-occurrence matrices are extracted from each block.

Table 1. mean Average Precision (mAP) of our approach for different number of blocks

Number of blocks	mAP(%)	
	For GW dataset	*For IAM dataset*
1 × 2 (2 blocks)	95.02	94.12
2 × 4 (8 blocks)	97.72	95.31
3 × 6 (18 blocks)	**99.57**	**97.48**
4 × 8 (32 blocks)	98.14	96.62

Selection of Codebook Size

The size of the codebook is pre-defined and selection of the optimal size of a codebook is one of the important factors in achieving highest accuracy. Predicting the desirable clusters and optimal codebook size is non-straightforward and it is dataset-dependent. Hence, in order to find an optimal size for each dataset, we conducted the experiments using GW and IAM datasets by varying codebook size. In all the experiments, the optimal number of blocks for each dataset is used. The mAP obtained on two datasets using our approach for a different codebook size is presented in Table 1.

We can see from the Figure 9, the evolution of the mAP for varying codebook size from 2^5 to 2^{13} visual words for the two datasets. The system tends to perform better with large codebook size in terms of accuracy. The increase in performance as the optimal number of blocks and codebook size grows due to the perceptual aliasing. From the Table 2 and Figure 5, it is observed that, for GW dataset, the performance of our approach is significantly better when a size of the codebook is set to 1024. Similarly, for IAM dataset, the performance of our approach yields good accuracy when a size of the codebook is set to 4096. Hence, in all the experiments, we used codebook size is 1024 and 4096 for GW and IAM dataset respectively.

Experiments for GW Dataset

The GW dataset includes 20 pages of letters written by George Washington and his associates in the year 1755. The most important challenge for word spotting using this dataset is to deal with a small amount of training data, because this dataset consists of twenty pages. The optimal number of blocks for this dataset is 3 × 6 and codebook size is 1024.

From this dataset, we have taken segmented 1680 non-stop word instances of 42 different classes of words from all the 20 pages of scanned handwritten documents.

Figure 9. mAP of our approach for varying codebook size for two datasets

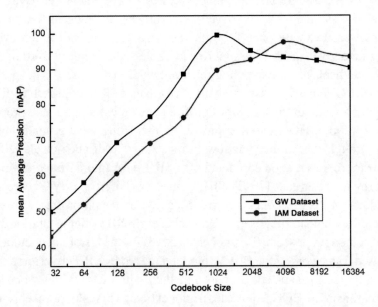

Table 2. Performance evaluation of our approach for varying codebook size

Codebook Size	(mAP %)	
	GW Dataset	IAM Dataset
32	50.23	43.21
64	58.36	52.29
128	69.47	60.83
256	76.73	69.24
512	88.64	76.49
1024	**99.57**	89.68
2048	95.21	92.64
4096	93.37	**97.58**
8192	92.42	95.21
16384	90.36	93.49

Each class of words may occur at least two times per document ($42\,classes \times 2\,instances \times 20\,pages = 1680$). While performing five-fold cross-validation, we partitioned the dataset into five disjoint subsets and each subset consists of 336 word images (from each class of words we have considered 8 word instances). In the training stage, 1344 word instances are used and remaining 336 word images are used for testing. Hence, for every experiment, we have 336 word images as test samples. The cross-validation process is repeated five times, with each subset used exactly once for validation. Table 3 shows the retrieved word instances for a given query. The first row in Table 3 shows query word images and each column displays corresponding retrieved word instances.

We used a GW dataset to compare the performance of our approach with existing word spotting methods such as word profile features based approach proposed by Rath et al. (2007), HOG based approach by extracting local gradient histogram features through the sliding window proposed by Rodriguez et al. (2008) and Fisher vector representation computed over SIFT descriptors from the word image proposed by Almazan et al. (2013). SIFT descriptors based on BoVW representation with Hidden Markov Models in a patch-based segmentation-free framework in handwritten documents proposed by Rothacker et al.(2013). Segmentation free word spotting method proposed by Rusinol et al.(2015) for the historical document using patch-based framework of the BoVW model powered by SIFT descriptors. We also compared the performance of proposed method with our previous work for word spotting based on Co-HOG feature descriptor extracted in scale space representation (Thontadari et al, 2016) and Co-HOG alone (Thontadari et al, 2017). The existing methods are implemented and five-fold cross-validation method is used to validate based on mean average precision (mAP). Table 4 shows the comparison results of our approach with existing methods. It is observed that, compared to existing methods, our approach yields the highest accuracy of 99.57%.

Table 3. Some query words and their retrieval results of our approach for GW dataset.

Orders	Captain	Company	Alexandria
Orders	Captain	Company	Alexandria
Order	Captain	Company	Alexandria
orders	Captain	Company	Alexandria
Ordered	Captain	Company	Alexandria
Orders	Captain	Company	Alexandria
Order	Captain	Company	Alexandria
Ordered	Captains	Companies	Alexandria

Table 4. Results comparison of our approach with existing methods for GW dataset

Method	Features	Segmentation	mAP (%)
Rath T.M. et al. (2007)	Word profile	Word	73.71
Rodriguez J.A et al. (2008)	Histogram of oriented gradients	Word	71.70
Almazan J. et al. (2013)	SIFT descriptors	Word	85.63
Rothacker et al. (2013)	SIFT descriptors	None	61.10
Rusinol et al. (2015)	SIFT descriptors	None	61.35
Thontadari et al. (2017)	Co-occurrence of oriented gradients histogram	Word	91.03
Thontadari et al. (2016)	Scale space Co-occurrence of oriented gradients histogram	Word	98.76
Our approach	BoVW Co-occurrence of oriented gradients histogram	Word	99.57

Experiments for IAM Dataset

IAM off-line dataset consists of 1539 pages of handwritten modern English text from the Lancaster–Oslo/Bergen Corpus (LOB) (Johansson, S. et al. 1978), written by 657 writers. From the IAM dataset, we have considered 2070 segmented non-stop word images of 46 different classes i.e., each class of word image has 45 instances of different writing styles among all pages. For five-fold cross-validation process, each subset consists of 414 word images (from each class of words we have taken 9 word images). In the training stage, 1656 word images are used and remaining 414 word images are used for testing. The cross-validation process is repeated five times, with each subset used exactly once for validation. Table 5 shows the experimental results of our approach for the IAM dataset. The first row shows query word and corresponding retrieved word instances of a given query word are shown. The results show the robustness of our approach for different kinds of words with variation in writing style.

We compared the performance of our approach with existing word spotting methods using IAM dataset. The existing word spotting methods considered for comparison are (a) HOG based approach by extracting local gradient histogram features through the sliding window proposed by Rodrıguez et al. (2008) and (b) word profile based approach proposed by Rath et al. (2007). SIFT descriptor based method proposed by Almazan et al. (2014) using Fisher vector representation computed over extracted densely from the word image. We also compared the proposed approach with previous work Thontadari et al., (2016 and 2017). We implemented existing methods and validated using five-fold cross-validation method. To estimate the

Table 5. Some query words and their retrieval results of our approach for IAM dataset

overall evaluation results, we have taken the mean average precision (mAP). Table 6 presents results comparison of our approach with existing methods based on mAP. From the experimental results, it is notified that our approach outperforms existing methods for IAM dataset.

Based on the experimental results obtained on IAM and GW dataset, we can conclude that our approach efficiently retrieves the handwritten words which are having non uniform illumination, suffering from the noise and written by different writers. The highest accuracy of our approach is due to many factors and one of the important factors is Co-HOG descriptor which captures the characters shape information more precisely and encodes the local spatial information by counting the frequency of co-occurrence of gradient orientation of neighboring pixel pairs. Moreover, Co-HOG descriptor is more robust and discriminative, because it captures the occurrence of edge characteristics of text strokes by exhaustively considering

Table 6. Results comparison of our approach with existing methods for IAM dataset

Method	Features	Segmentation	mAP (%)
Rath et al. (2007)	Word profile	Word	73.71
Rodriguez et al. (2008)	Histogram of oriented gradients	Word	71.70
Almazan et al. (2014)	SIFT descriptors	None	72.16
Thontadari et al. (2017)	Co-occurrence of oriented gradients histogram	Word	88.41
Thontadari et al. (2016)	Scale space Co-occurrence of oriented gradients histogram	Word	96.53
Our approach	BoVW Co-occurrence of oriented gradients histogram	Word	97.58

every block within a word image, which captures the local variations within the class. Another important factor for highest accuracy is the construction visual words using Co-HOG descriptor. In addition, the experiment results demonstrate that the performance of the approach is improved when the spatial information incorporated into BoVW framework through Spatial Pyramid Matching technique. A benefit of using BoVW representation is that, word retrieval can be effectively carried out because word image is retrieved by computing the histogram of visual word frequencies, and returning the word image, with the closest histogram. Therefore, word images can be retrieved with no delay. It is identified through evaluation of experimental results on IAM and GW dataset that our approach outperforms existing HOG and SIFT based word spotting methods.

CONCLUSION

In this chapter, we proposed a word spotting method for handwritten documents using Bag of Visual Words framework based on Co-HOG features. The Co-HOG features are robust to illumination variation and invariance to local geometric transformation compared to HOG features. The proposed method combines the construction of Bag of Visual Words using Co-HOG descriptor and the later spatial distribution information of visual words is added to BoVW framework by using the spatial pyramid matching technique. This spatial pyramid representation sacrifices the geometric invariance properties of bags of features and it compensates for this loss with increased discriminative power derived from the global spatial information. The experimental results obtained using two publicly available datasets such as IAM and GW dataset demonstrate that our approach achieves consistently highest accuracy compared to existing word spotting methods for handwritten documents.

REFERENCES

Almazan, J., Gordo, A., Fornés, A., & Valveny, E. (2013). Handwritten word spotting with corrected attributes. *Proceedings of the IEEE International Conference on Computer Vision*, 1017-1024.

Almazan, J., Gordo, A., Fornés, A., & Valveny, E. (2014). Segmentation-free word spotting with exemplar svms. *Pattern Recognition, 47*(12), 3967–3978. doi:10.1016/j.patcog.2014.06.005

Arrospide, J., Salgado, L., & Marinas, J. (2013). HOG-like gradient-based descriptor for visual vehicle detection. *Intelligent Vehicles Symposium (IV)*, 223-228.

Bay, H., Ess, A., Tuytelaars, T., & Van Gool, L. (2008). Speeded-up robust features (SURF). *Computer Vision and Image Understanding, 110*(3), 346–359. doi:10.1016/j. cviu.2007.09.014

Bay, H., Tuytelaars, T., & Van Gool, L. (2006). Surf: Speeded up robust features. In *European conference on computer vision*, Springer Berlin Heidelberg.

Carcagnì, P., Del Coco, M., Leo, M., & Distante, C. (2015). Facial expression recognition and histograms of oriented gradients: A comprehensive study. *SpringerPlus, 4*(1), 645. doi:10.1186/s40064-015-1427-3 PMID:26543779

Chan, J., Ziftci, C., & Forsyth, D. (2006). Searching off-line arabic documents. *Computer Vision and Pattern Recognition, 2*, 1455-1462. doi:10.1109/ CVPR.2006.269

Corvee, E., & Bremond, F. (2010, August). Body parts detection for people tracking using trees of histogram of oriented gradient descriptors. *Advanced Video and Signal Based Surveillance, Seventh IEEE International Conference*, 469-475. doi:10.1109/ AVSS.2010.51

Dalal, N., & Triggs, B. (2005, June). Histograms of oriented gradients for human detection. *Computer Vision and Pattern Recognition, 1*, 886-893. doi:10.1109/ CVPR.2005.177

Deniz, O., Bueno, G., Salido, J., & De la Torre, F. (2011). Face recognition using histograms of oriented gradients. *Pattern Recognition Letters, 32*(12), 1598–1603. doi:10.1016/j.patrec.2011.01.004

Do, T. T., & Kijak, E. (2012). Face recognition using co-occurrence histograms of oriented gradients. *Acoustics, Speech and Signal Processing (ICASSP), IEEE International Conference on,* 1301-1304. doi:10.1109/ICASSP.2012.6288128

Fernandez, S., Graves, A., & Schmidhuber, J. (2007). An application of recurrent neural networks to discriminative keyword spotting. *Artificial Neural Networks,* 220–229.

Fischer, A., Keller, A., Frinken, V., & Bunke, H. (2010). HMM-based word spotting in handwritten documents using subword models. *Pattern recognition (icpr), International conference*, 3416-3419. doi:10.1109/ICPR.2010.834

Frinken, V., Fischer, A., & Bunke, H. (2010). A novel word spotting algorithm using bidirectional long short-term memory neural networks. Artificial Neural Networks in Pattern Recognition, 185-196. doi:10.1007/978-3-642-12159-3_17

Frinken, V., Fischer, A., Manmatha, R., & Bunke, H. (2011). A novel word spotting method based on recurrent neural networks. *Pattern Analysis and Machine Intelligence. IEEE Transactions on*, *34*(2), 211–224.

Huang, L., Yin, F., Chen, Q. H., & Liu, C. L. (2013). Keyword spotting in unconstrained handwritten Chinese documents using contextual word model. *Image and Vision Computing*, *31*(12), 958–968. doi:10.1016/j.imavis.2013.10.003

Jain, R., & Doermann, D. (2012). Logo retrieval in document images. *Document analysis systems (das), 10th iapr international workshop on*, 135-139. doi:10.1109/DAS.2012.54

Kessentini, Y., Chatelain, C., & Paquet, T. (2013). Word spotting and regular expression detection in handwritten documents. *International Conference on Document Analysis and Recognition (ICDAR)*, 516-520. doi:10.1109/ICDAR.2013.109

Khayyat, M., Lam, L., & Suen, C. Y. (2014). Learning-based word spotting system for Arabic handwritten documents. *Pattern Recognition*, *47*(3), 1021–1030. doi:10.1016/j.patcog.2013.08.014

Lavrenko, V., Rath, T. M., & Manmatha, R. (2004). Holistic word recognition for handwritten historical documents. *Document Image Analysis for Libraries, 2004. Proceedings. First International Workshop on*, 278-287. doi:10.1109/DIAL.2004.1263256

Lowe, D. G. (2004). Distinctive image features from scale-invariant keypoints. *International Journal of Computer Vision*, *60*(2), 91–110. doi:10.1023/B:VISI.0000029664.99615.94

Manmatha, R., Han, C., & Riseman, E. M. (1996). Word spotting: A new approach to indexing handwriting. *Computer Vision and Pattern Recognition,* 631-637. doi:10.1109/CVPR.1996.517139

Manmatha, R., & Rath, T. (2003). Indexing of handwritten historical documents-recent progress. *Proceedings 2003 Symposium on Document Image Understanding Technology*, 77-86.

Marti, U. V., & Bunke, H. (2002). The IAM-database: An English sentence database for offline handwriting recognition. *International Journal on Document Analysis and Recognition*, *5*(1), 39–46. doi:10.1007/s100320200071

Minetto, R., Thome, N., Cord, M., Leite, N. J., & Stolfi, J. (2013). T-HOG: An effective gradient-based descriptor for single line text regions. *Pattern Recognition*, *46*(3), 1078–1090. doi:10.1016/j.patcog.2012.10.009

Newell, A. J., & Griffin, L. D. (2011). Multiscale histogram of oriented gradient descriptors for robust character recognition. *Document Analysis and Recognition, International Conference on*, 1085-1089. doi:10.1109/ICDAR.2011.219

Papavassiliou, V., Stafylakis, T., Katsouros, V., & Carayannis, G. (2010). Handwritten document image segmentation into text lines and words. *Pattern Recognition*, *43*(1), 369–377. doi:10.1016/j.patcog.2009.05.007

Rath, T. M., Lavrenko, V., & Manmatha, R. (2003). *Retrieving historical manuscripts using shape*. Massachusetts Univ Amherst Center For Intelligent Information Retrieval. doi:10.21236/ADA477875

Rath, T. M., Lavrenko, V., & Manmatha, R. (2003). *A statistical approach to retrieving historical manuscript images without recognition* (No. CIIR-MM-42). Space and Naval Warfare Systems Center.

Rath, T. M., & Manmatha, R. (2007). Word spotting for historical documents. *International Journal on Document Analysis and Recognition*, *9*(2-4), 139–152. doi:10.1007/s10032-006-0027-8

Ren, H., Heng, C. K., Zheng, W., Liang, L., & Chen, X. (2010). Fast object detection using boosted co-occurrence histograms of oriented gradients. *Image Processing (ICIP), 17th IEEE International Conference*, 2705-2708. doi:10.1109/ICIP.2010.5651963

Rodriguez, J. A., & Perronnin, F. (2008). Local gradient histogram features for word spotting in unconstrained handwritten documents. *International Conference on Frontiers in Handwriting Recognition*, 7-12.

Rodriguez-Serrano, J. A., Perronnin, F., Sánchez, G., & Lladós, J. (2010). Unsupervised writer adaptation of whole-word HMMs with application to word-spotting. *Pattern Recognition Letters*, *31*(8), 742–749. doi:10.1016/j.patrec.2010.01.007

Rothacker, L., Rusinol, M., & Fink, G. A. (2013). Bag-of-features HMMs for segmentation-free word spotting in handwritten documents. *Document Analysis and Recognition (ICDAR), 12th International Conference IEEE*, 1305-1309. doi:10.1109/ICDAR.2013.264

Rothfeder, J. L., Feng, S., & Rath, T. M. (2003). Using corner feature correspondences to rank word images by similarity. *Computer Vision and Pattern Recognition Workshop*, 3, 30-30. doi:10.1109/CVPRW.2003.10021

Rusinol, M., Aldavert, D., Toledo, R., & Llados, J. (2011). Browsing heterogeneous document collections by a segmentation-free word spotting method. *Document Analysis and Recognition (ICDAR), International Conference*, 63-67. doi:10.1109/ICDAR.2011.22

Rusinol, M., Aldavert, D., Toledo, R., & Llados, J. (2015). Efficient segmentation-free keyword spotting in historical document collections. *Pattern Recognition*, *48*(2), 545–555. doi:10.1016/j.patcog.2014.08.021

Saidani, A., Kacem Echi, A., & Belaid, A. (2015). Arabic/Latin and Machine-printed/Handwritten Word Discrimination using HOG-based Shape Descriptor. *ELCVIA: electronic letters on computer vision and image analysis*, 0001-23.

Schroth, G., Hilsenbeck, S., Huitl, R., Schweiger, F., & Steinbach, E. (2011). Exploiting text-related features for content-based image retrieval. *Multimedia (ISM), IEEE International Symposium*, 77-84.

Shekhar, R., & Jawahar, C. V. (2012). Word image retrieval using bag of visual words. *Document Analysis Systems (DAS), 2012 10th IAPR International Workshop*, 297-301. doi:10.1109/DAS.2012.96

Shu, C., Ding, X., & Fang, C. (2011). Histogram of the oriented gradient for face recognition. *Tsinghua Science and Technology*, *16*(2), 216–224. doi:10.1016/S1007-0214(11)70032-3

Sivic, J., & Zisserman, A. (2003). Video google: A text retrieval approach to object matching in videos. ICCV, 2(1470), 1470-1477. doi:10.1109/ICCV.2003.1238663

Smith, D. J., & Harvey, R. W. (2011). Document Retrieval Using SIFT Image Features. *J. UCS*, *17*(1), 3–15.

Srihari, S. N., Huang, C., & Srinivasan, H. (2005). Search engine for handwritten documents. *Proceedings of the Society for Photo-Instrumentation Engineers*, *5676*, 66–75. doi:10.1117/12.585883

Srihari, S. N., Srinivasan, H., Babu, P., & Bhole, C. (2005). Handwritten arabic word spotting using the cedarabic document analysis system. *Proc. Symposium on Document Image Understanding Technology*, 123-132.

Srihari, S. N., Srinivasan, H., Haung, C., & Shetty, S. (2006). Spotting words in Latin, Devanagari and Arabic scripts. *Vivek: Indian Journal of Artificial Intelligence, 16*(3), 2–9.

Su, B., Lu, S., Tian, S., Lim, J. H., & Tan, C. L. (2014). Character recognition in natural scenes using convolutional co-occurrence hog. *22nd International Conference on Pattern Recognition*, 2926-2931. doi:10.1109/ICPR.2014.504

Terasawa, K., & Tanaka, Y. (2009). Slit style HOG feature for document image word spotting. *Document Analysis and Recognition, 10th International Conference*, 116-120.

Thontadari, C., & Prabhakar, C. J. (2016). Scale Space Co-Occurrence HOG Features for Word Spotting in Handwritten Document Images. *International Journal of Computer Vision and Image Processing, 6*(2), 71–86. doi:10.4018/IJCVIP.2016070105

Thontadari, C., & Prabhakar, C. J. (2017). Segmentation Based Word Spotting Method for Handwritten Documents. *International Journals of Advanced Research in Computer Science and Software Engineering., 7*(6), 35–40. doi:10.23956/ijarcsse/V7I6/0127

Tian, S., Bhattacharya, U., Lu, S., Su, B., Wang, Q., Wei, X., & Tan, C. L. (2015). Multilingual scene character recognition with co-occurrence of histogram of oriented gradients. *Pattern Recognition, 51*, 125–134. doi:10.1016/j.patcog.2015.07.009

Tian, S., Lu, S., Su, B., & Tan, C. L. (2013). Scene text recognition using co-occurrence of histogram of oriented gradients. *Document Analysis and Recognition, 12th International Conference on*, 912-916. doi:10.1109/ICDAR.2013.186

Wang, J., Yang, J., Yu, K., Lv, F., Huang, T., & Gong, Y. (2010). Locality-constrained linear coding for image classification. *Computer Vision and Pattern Recognition (CVPR), 2010 IEEE Conference*, 3360-3367.

Watanabe, T., Ito, S., & Yokoi, K. (2009). Co-occurrence histograms of oriented gradients for pedestrian detection. In *Advances in Image and Video Technology* (pp. 37–47). Springer Berlin Heidelberg. doi:10.1007/978-3-540-92957-4_4

Wollmer, M., Eyben, F., Keshet, J., Graves, A., Schuller, B., & Rigoll, G. (2009). Robust discriminative keyword spotting for emotionally colored spontaneous speech using bidirectional LSTM networks. *Acoustics, Speech and Signal Processing, IEEE International Conference*, 3949-3952. doi:10.1109/ICASSP.2009.4960492

Wshah, S., Kumar, G., & Govindaraju, V. (2014). Statistical script independent word spotting in offline handwritten documents. *Pattern Recognition, 47*(3), 1039–1050. doi:10.1016/j.patcog.2013.09.019

Yalniz, I. Z., & Manmatha, R. (2012). An efficient framework for searching text in noisy document images. *Document Analysis Systems (DAS), 10th IAPR International Workshop*, 48-52. doi:10.1109/DAS.2012.18

Chapter 8
Novel Techniques in Skin and Face Detection in Color Images

Mohammadreza Hajiarbabi
University of Kansas, USA

Arvin Agah
University of Kansas, USA

ABSTRACT

Human skin detection and face detection are important and challenging problems in computer vision. The use of color information has increased in recent years due to the lower processing time of face detection compared to black and white images. A number of techniques for skin detection are discussed. Experiments have been performed utilizing deep learning with a variety of color spaces, showing that deep learning produces better results compared to methods such as rule-based, Gaussian model, and feed forward neural network on skin detection. A challenging problem in skin detection is that there are numerous objects with colors similar to that of the human skin. A texture segmentation method has been designed to distinguish between the human skin and objects with similar colors to that of human skin. Once the skin is detected, image is divided into several skin components and the process of detecting the face is limited to these components—increasing the speed of the face detection. In addition, a method for eye and lip detection is proposed using information from different color spaces.

DOI: 10.4018/978-1-5225-5628-2.ch008

INTRODUCTION

Human skin detection is an active area of research in computer vision. Skin detection has numerous applications, such as face detection (Das et *al.*, 2015; Gondaliya et *al.*, 2015; Hajiarbabi & Agah, 2014; Hajiarbabi & Agah, 2015), identifying and filtering nude pictures on the internet (Fleck et *al.*, 1996), and so on. Skin detection is challenging due to several factors, such as the similarity between human skin color and other entities like color of sand, walls, etc. (Alshehri, 2012), differences of illumination between images, images being taken by different cameras with different lenses, the ranges of human skin colors due to ethnicity, and others. Skin color is an indication of various characteristics such as race, health, age, etc. (Fink et *al.*, 2006). In video images, skin color can be used to show the existence of humans in media (Elgammal et *al.*, 2009). There are several color spaces that can be used for skin detection, and among them RGB, YCbCr, and HSV are more common (Singh et *al.*, 2003). The color spaces can be used individually, or the information of the color spaces can be combined (Hajiarbabi & Agah, 2014).

Face detection is an important step not only in face recognition systems, but also in many other computer vision systems, such as video surveillance (Grace, J., Reshmi, K., 2015), human-computer interaction (HCI) (Khedekar, P. et *al.*, 2016), and face image retrieval systems. Face detection is the initial step in any of such systems. The main challenges in face detection are face pose and scale, face orientation, facial expression, ethnicity and skin color. Other challenges such as occlusion, complex backgrounds, inconsistent illumination conditions, and quality of the image further complicate face detection in images. The problem with most of the popular face detection methods is that they are based on a window that is moved over the image. This process can be time-consuming. In this book chapter, a methodology is described that locates faces based on the human skin color. This process is significantly faster.

Deep learning methods are a type of neural network, which have been designed to work properly when the number of hidden layers in a neural network is increased. In ordinary neural networks when the number of hidden layers increases, the back propagation algorithm often fails to train the network well. Deep learning techniques introduced advanced methods for training a neural network with multiple hidden layers. Because of having several parameters such as the number of nodes in the hidden layer, the random initial weights, etc., the neural network is very flexible, unlike other methods used for skin detection. To the authors knowledge deep learning has not been used for skin detection.

One of the issues in skin detection is that the color of several objects like the color of sand, soil, etc. are quite similar to human skin color, which can cause even a well-designed classifier not to be able to distinguish between such similar pixels.

What makes the objects with similar colors to human skin be different from the real human skin is the texture of the objects. A method for distinguishing between human skin texture and other textures is proposed in this book chapter.

After detecting the human skin components, a face can be detected by using template-matching algorithm. Another method for detecting the faces can be detecting the place of the eyes and lip in the image and detecting the face based on the placement of the eyes and lip in the image. A technique for detecting eyes and lip using the information based on their colors, is proposed in this book chapter.

This book chapter is organized into six sections. In Section 2, previous methods in skin detection and face detection are reviewed. In Section 3, skin detection techniques using neural network and deep learning are presented. The texture segmentation method is proposed in Section 4. In section 5, face detection methods are presented. Section 6 concludes the book chapter.

BACKGROUND AND RELATED WORK

Different methods have been used for detecting human skin in images. Among them, Gaussian, rule-based, and neural networks are some of the more popular approaches.

The Gaussian model (Wu & Ai, 2008) uses the YCbCr color space. The density function for Gaussian variable is used to make a decision of whether or not a pixel belongs to human skin. The parameters of the density function are calculated using training images. If the probability is more than a given threshold then that pixel is considered as human skin. The density function for Gaussian variable $X = \left(Cb\, Cr \right)^T \in R^2$ is calculated as:

$$f\left(Cb \;\; Cr \right) = \frac{1}{2\pi \left| C \right|^{1/2}} \, exp\left\{ -\frac{1}{2}\left(X - \mu \right)^T C^{-1} \left(X - \mu \right) \right\}$$

where $X = \begin{pmatrix} Cb \\ Cr \end{pmatrix}$, $\mu = \begin{pmatrix} \mu_{Cb} \\ \mu_{Cr} \end{pmatrix}$, $C = \begin{pmatrix} C_{CbCb} & C_{CbCr} \\ C_{CrCb} & C_{CrCr} \end{pmatrix}$, and the parameters are:

$$\mu_{skin} = \begin{pmatrix} 112.1987 \\ 151.3993 \end{pmatrix}, \; C_{skin} = \begin{pmatrix} 89.3255 & 32.2867 \\ 32.2867 & 252.9336 \end{pmatrix}$$

Chen et al. (2008) used conditional probability density function and Bayesian classification in order to define some rules for detecting human skin. RGB was used as color space. The rules are:

$$r\left(i\right) > \alpha \quad , \; \beta_1 < \left(r\left(i\right) - g\left(i\right)\right) < \beta_2 \quad , \quad \gamma_1 < \left(r\left(i\right) - b\left(i\right)\right) < \gamma_2$$

$$\sigma_1 < \left(g\left(i\right) - b\left(i\right)\right) < \sigma_2$$

where

$$\alpha = 100 \; , \; \beta_1 = 10 \; , \; \beta_2 = 70 \; , \; \gamma_1 = 24 \; , \; \gamma_2 = 112 \; , \; \sigma_1 = 0 \; and \, \sigma_2 = 70$$

Kovac et al. (Kovac, J., Peer, P. and Solina. F., 2003) introduced two sets of rules one for indoor images and one for images taken in daylight illumination. Kovac also used RGB as color space. The rules are as follow:
For indoor images:

$$R > 95 \quad , G > 40 \quad , B > 20 \quad , \; \max\left\{R,G,B\right\} - \min\left\{R,G,B\right\} > 15 \; ,$$

$$\left|R - G\right| > 15 \quad , \quad R > G \quad , \quad R > B$$

For images taken in daylight illumination:

$$R > 220 \quad , G > 210 \quad , B > 170 \quad , \left|R - G\right| \leq 15 \quad , \quad R > B \quad , \quad G > B$$

Kong et al. (2007) introduced rules, which utilized two different color spaces of HSV and normalized RGB. RGB color space contains the information of illumination. HSV and normalized RGB both reduce the effects of illumination. The rules are:

$$0.4 \leq r \leq 0.6 \quad , \quad 0.22 \leq g \leq 0.33 \; , \; r > g > \frac{1-r}{2} \quad ,$$

$$0 \leq H \leq 0.2 \quad , \; 0.3 \leq S \leq 0.7 \quad , \quad 0.22 \leq V \leq 0.8$$

Neural network has been used in skin color detection in a number of research projects. Dukim *et al.* (2010) used YCbCr as the color space with a Multi-Layer Perceptron (MLP) neural network. Two types of combining strategies were used, and several combining rules were applied. A coarse to fine search method was used to find the number of neurons in the hidden layer. The combination of Cb/Cr and Cr features produced the best result. Brancati *et al.* (2016) introduced a methodology based on the correlation rules between different color spaces.

Seow *et al.* (2003) used a three-layered neural network and the RGB as the color space. Then the skin regions were extracted from the planes and were interpolated in order to get an optimum decision boundary and the positive skin samples for the skin classifier. Yang *et al.* (2010) used YCbCr color space with a back propagation neural network. The luminance Y was sorted in ascending order, and the Y values were divided into some intervals. The covariance and the mean of Cb and Cr of each interval were calculated and used to train the back propagation neural network. Al-Mohair *et al.* (2012) introduced another method using neural network. Zuo *et al.* (2017) proposed using convolutional and recurrent neural networks for human skin detection.

Face detection can be accomplished using color images or gray-scale images. Two popular methods in face detection are by (Rowley *et al.*, 1998) and (Viola & Jones, 2001) methods.

Rowley *et al.* (1998) used neural networks and it detects upright frontal faces in gray-scale images. For detecting faces a 20*20 window is used which moves pixel by pixel on the image. The extracted sub image is then applied to a receptive field neural network in order to decide if the sub image contains a face. The image is subsampled several times in order to find faces with sizes less than 20*20.

Viola & Jones (2001) trained a strong classifier using Adaboost algorithm. Three types of Haar features were used in order to extract features from the images. In two-rectangle feature, the feature value is the subtraction between the sums of the pixels within two regions. In three-rectangle feature, the feature value is the sum within two outside rectangles subtracted from the inside rectangle. In four-rectangle feature, the feature value is the difference between diagonals of the rectangle. These numbers were used to train the classifier. The integral image method were used that allowed the features to be computed very fast (Viola & Jones, 2001). In their proposed method similar to the Rowley method, a window is moved over the image, and the features are applied on the sub image.

Another approach that increased the speed of Viola-Jones face detection method was constructing a cascade of classifiers (Viola & Jones, 2001). In the first classifier, some of the features are applied on the sub image, if the classifier decides that this sub image does not contain a face then that sub image is rejected and the search for face will not continue. If the answer is yes, then it goes to second classifier and other features are applied on the sub image. This process will continue until the last classifier, if the sub image passes all the classifiers then it means that there is a face in the sub image.

A number of methods have been proposed and used for eyes and lip detection. Peng *et al.* (2005) detect eyes using feature-based method on gray intensity face without spectacles. In (Rajpathak *et al.,* 2009) morphological and color image processing have been used to detect the eyes based on the fact that eye regions in an image are characterized by low illumination with high density edges. Sidbe *et al.* (2006) employ some constraints based on the anthropological characteristics of human eyes in order to detect eyes. In (Soetedjo, 2011) a three step method—composed of eye localization, white color thresholding, and ellipse fitting—has been used for eye detection. Information from Entropy has been reported by (Hassaballah *et al.,* 2011); and eyes and mouth detection using the Viola-Jones method has been demonstrated in (Khan *et al.,* 2013).

A variety of methods have been used for lip detection. For instance, Chin *et al.* (2009) used watershed segmentation; Kalbkhani & Amirani (2012) employed statistical methods based on local information, and Chiang *et al.* (2003) utilized a simple quadratic polynomial model for detecting skin and lips.

SKIN DETECTION

Neural network is a strong and effective tool in artificial intelligence and machine learning, therefore, it was used in order to distinguish between what is face skin pixel and what is a non-face skin pixel. Information from more than one color space was used instead of using just the information from one color space; the reason was that each color space has different characteristics that could be used to increase the detection rate. Around 100,000 pixels for face and 200,000 for non-face pixels were chosen from images which were selected from the Web (Hajiarbabi & Agah, 2014). As non-skin images is a huge category, images were chosen from different categories, especially those that are very similar to human skin color.

For the implementation, the MLP neural networks were used. Several entities can be used as the input of the neural network, namely, RGB, HSV, and YCbCr. Based on similarity between the pixels, the pixels were divided into two categories, around 50% of samples were used for training and the rest for validation. Different numbers of neurons were examined in the hidden layer (Hajiarbabi & Agah, 2014). The color spaces used included RGB, CbCr (eliminating Y because it contains illumination information), and HS (eliminating V because it contains illumination information). Also a combination of the different color space, which was named CbCrRGBHS by the authors, was used as the input.

Another method that was used is the boosting method. Different boosting methods, AND, OR and VOTING were used. The outputs of the three different neural networks (RGB, CbCr and HSV) were used. If the output shows that the pixel belongs to human skin, it is considered as 1 and otherwise as 0 (Hajiarbabi & Agah, 2014).

Several different neural networks were trained and tested on the UCD database and VT-AAST (Abdallah *et al.*, 2007a; Abdallah *et al.*, 2007b), using MATLAB (developed by MathWorks) for implementation. The UCD database contains 94 images from different races. The images vary from one person in the image to multiple people. VT-AAST database contains 286 images, which offers a wide range of difference in illumination and race. Both databases also contain the images after cropping the face skin.

The experimental results are reported as precision, recall, specificity and accuracy. Precision or positive predictive value (PPV):

$$PPV = TP \Big/ \left(TP + FP\right)$$

Sensitivity or true positive rate (TPR) equivalent with hit rate, recall:

$$TPR = TP \Big/ P = TP \Big/ \left(TP + FN\right)$$

Specificity (SPC) or true negative rate:

$$SPC = TN \Big/ N = TN \Big/ \left(FP + TN\right)$$

Accuracy (ACC):

$$ACC = \left(TP + TN\right) \Big/ \left(P + N\right)$$

In the skin detection experiments, P is the number of the skin pixels; and N is the number of the non-skin pixels. TP is the number of the skin pixels correctly classified as skin pixels. TN is the number of the non-skin pixels correctly classified as non-skin pixels. FP is the number of the non-skin pixels incorrectly classified as skin pixels. FN is the number of the skin pixels incorrectly classified as non-skin pixels.

In the first experiment, a neural network using the HSV color space were trained, in order to test the effect of the illumination on the detection rate. In HSV color space the V components contains the illumination effect. The results for HS and HSV on UCD database are listed in Table 1. The accuracy of using HS as input is higher than HSV, and the Recall has decreased by about 30%, which is high. Therefore, removing the V component produced better results.

In another experiment the CbCr Component of the YCbCr, HS component of the HSV and RGB were chosen as the input of the neural network. The Y and V components were excluded because they contain the illumination information that have negative effect on the skin detection rate.

The results for CbCr, HS and RGB on UCD database are listed in Table 2. The CbCr experiments have better accuracy rate compared to HS and RGB. The HS experiment detects more skin pixels correctly than other color spaces.

In another experiment, the boosting method was used in order to improve the performance of the neural networks. AND, OR and VOTING were applied among the three outputs of neural networks trained with CbCr, HS and RGB. The results on UCD database are shown in Table 3. The AND operation has the highest precision and specificity compared to the other two methods but much lower recall. This means that many of skin pixels are considered as non-skin pixels. In case of recall, the OR method detects much more skin pixels correctly comparing to other two methods, but also more non-skin pixels detecting as skin pixel. The voting method has the highest accuracy among these three methods.

The boosting which was used was not acceptable because whenever the precision is high,then the recall is low, and vice versa. It was decided to combine the information from different color spaces because each color space has its own characteristics. The

Table 1. Accuracy results for HS and HSV on UCD database

	Precision	Recall	Specificity	Accuracy
HS	56.66%	63.06%	83.37%	78.17%
HSV	58.72%	35.28%	91.45%	77.05%

Table 2. Accuracy results for CbCr, HS and RGB on UCD database

	Precision	Recall	Specificity	Accuracy
CbCr	67.55%	46.23%	92.34%	**80.52%**
HS	56.66%	**63.06%**	83.37%	78.17%
RGB	**81.06%**	26.45%	**97.87%**	79.56%

Table 3. Accuracy results for AND, OR and VOTING on UCD database

	Precision	Recall	Specificity	Accuracy
AND	**78.40%**	21.45%	**97.96%**	78.35%
OR	55.62%	**70.36%**	80.65%	78.01%
VOTING	73.34%	39.53%	95.05%	**80.82%**

combination of RGB, YCbCr and HSV was called CbCrRGBHS. The CbCrRGBHS vector was generated and yielded the results on the UCD database in Table 4. This shows an improvement, compared to the previous methods.

Figure 1 shows the Receiver Operating Characteristic (ROC) graph for CbCrRGBHS vector with two nodes in the output for the validation set. The results for CbCrRGBHS vector on UCD database are listed in Table 5. The results show that in cases of accuracy and recall some improvement is observed; however, the precision has decreased.

Table 6 shows the result of other methods discussed compared to authors' best results on using the UCD database. Comparing the other methods with the results from the CbCrRGBHS vector shows that the result is better in precision, specificity and accuracy. The authors' method accepts much less non-skin pixels as skin comparing to other methods.

It should be noted that there is a tradeoff between precision and recall. If the goal is to have high recall (detecting more skin pixels correctly), then it is highly possible to detect many non-skin pixels as human skin which will reduce the precision, and vice versa. Table 3 shows illustrates this concept, where the AND and VOTING methods have high precision but low recall, whereas the OR method has high recall, while having low precision. The Gaussian, Chen, Kovac, and Kong methods were implemented based on the related papers.

In addition, the designed neural network was applied to the VT-AAST database using CbCrRGBHS as the input. Table 7 shows the results of the new method compared with other methods on VT-AAST database. The authors' results are better in terms of precision and accuracy; and they are comparable in recall and specificity, relative to the best results.

Table 4. Accuracy results for CbCrRGBHS on UCD database

	Precision	Recall	Specificity	Accuracy
CbCrRGBHS	77.73%	51.35%	95.92%	81.93%

Figure 1. ROC graph for CbCrRGBHS on validation samples

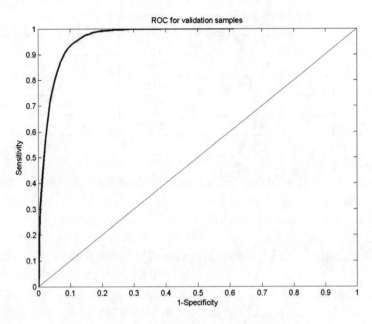

Table 5. Accuracy results for CbCrRGBHS on UCD database

	Precision	Recall	Specificity	Accuracy
CbCrRGBHS	71.30%	60.25%	93.43%	82.36%

Table 6. Accuracy results for other methods on UCD database

	Precision	Recall	Specificity	Accuracy
Gaussian	54.96%	66.82%	81.12%	77.46%
Chen	63.75%	51.13%	89.98%	80.02%
Kovac	62.51%	**69.09%**	85.71%	81.45%
Kong	37.47%	14.58%	91.61%	71.87%
CbCrRGBHS	**71.30%**	60.25%	**93.43%**	**82.36%**

In order to improve the results, two operations were performed on the output image from the neural network. The first operation was using the filling method, in which the holes in the components are filled. This method is useful and can cause an increase in recall, because the output image from the neural network may have

Table 7. Accuracy results for other methods on VT-AAST database

	Precision	Recall	Specificity	Accuracy
Gaussian	30.00%	60.37%	79.84%	77.40%
Chen	31.62%	54.59%	83.10%	79.53%
Kovac	31.81%	**65.02%**	80.05%	78.17%
Kong	45.97%	29.51%	95.03%	86.83%
CbCrRGBHS	**54.26%**	59.07%	**93.36%**	**88.56%**

some undetected part inside the face or other parts of the body components, which can be recovered by using this method.

The other operation is the opening method, which is applying erosion followed by dialation method. Erosion is a morphological operation in image processing. A small disk (called structuring element) is defined which will be moved on the image. The center of the structuring element is placed on each pixel of the binary image which has the one value. If all the image pixels that are covered by the structuring element are 1, then that pixel (which is covered by the center of the structuring element) is considered 1. It is otherwise 0 in the final image. In the dilation process, similar to erosion, the center of the structuring element is placed on the image (pixels which are 1). Now any 0 pixel which is covered by the structuring element pixels is changed to 1 in the final image.

The structuring element, which was used in our experiments, was 3 by 3. This size produced better results than the other structuring elements. Table 8 and Table 9 show the result after applying filling and opening methods. The modified method is referred to as CbCrRGBHS+. The results show that recall has increased. In addition, there are small increases in precision and accuracy.

In order to increase the system's performance, a number of boosting techniques were applied to the network. The idea was similar to the Rowley method, which was used in face detection method (Rowley *et al.*, 1998), and in this work, it is used for skin detection.

In the first set of experiments, several images were gathered that did not contain human skin. These images were analyzed using the neural network. The pixels which were considered as human skin were collected and added to the training pixels. The process was repeated two times. By using this method, some new pixels were found and added to the non-skin pixels. In addition, as mentioned before, some of the pixels were common between the human skin color and non-skin color. After using this method, additional common pixels were found.

The 10-fold cross validation technique was employed for training the neural network. Table 10 and Table 11 show the primary results and the results after using

Table 8. Accuracy results for CbCrRGBHS+ on UCD database

	Precision	Recall	Specificity	Accuracy
CbCrRGBHS	71.30%	60.25%	93.43%	82.36%
CbCrRGBHS+	73.43%	65.54%	93.08%	83.45%

Table 9. Accuracy results for CbCrRGBHS+ on VT-AAST database

	Precision	Recall	Specificity	Accuracy
CbCrRGBHS	54.26%	59.07%	93.36%	88.56%
CbCrRGBHS+	54.77%	62.61%	93.07%	88.76%

bootstrapping method on UCD and VT-AAST databases. CbCrRGBHSI shows the results after applying the bootstrapping method for the first time and CbCrRGBHSII shows the results after applying the bootstrapping method for the second time.

As shown in Tables 10 and 11, the results were improved by using the bootstrapping method. The results can improve further if the number of bootstrapping is increased (Hajiarbabi & Agah, 2015). Using the samples from the last phase, five different neural networks were trained using different initial weights, different random sets of skin and non-skin pixels, and different permutations of the pixels that were presented to the network. Although the networks had close detection and error rates, the resulting errors were different from one another. A combination of the networks, using AND operation, OR operation, and the voting method were used. The results are shown in Table 12 and Table 13 for the UCD and VT-AAST databases.

Table 14 and Table 15 show the results after applying filling the holes and the opening methods.

Table 16 shows the comparison between different methods with CbCrRGBHS and VOTE method on UCD database and Table 17 shows the same result on VT-AAST database.

Table 10. Accuracy results for CbCrRGBHS on UCD database using 10 fold cross validation

	Precision	Recall	Specificity	Accuracy
CbCrRGBHS	63.19%	55.55%	88.85%	80.31%
CbCrRGBHS I	64.90%	**58.04%**	89.18%	81.20%
CbCrRGBHS II	**67.79%**	57.02%	**90.66%**	**82.04%**

Table 11. Accuracy results for CbCrRGBHS on VT-AAST database using 10 fold cross validation

	Precision	Recall	Specificity	Accuracy
CbCrRGBHS	42.47%	65.28%	87.34%	84.58%
CbCrRGBHS I	44.53%	63.91%	**88.06%**	84.91%
CbCrRGBHS II	**47.13%**	**66.09%**	87.91%	**86.18%**

Table 12. Accuracy results for CbCrRGBHS on UCD database using combination of networks

	Precision	Recall	Specificity	Accuracy
AND	**70.52%**	57.87%	**93.15%**	**84.11%**
OR	61.50%	**66.43%**	86.89%	81.64%
VOTE	65.88%	61.54%	90.39%	83.00%

Table 13. Accuracy results for CbCrRGBHS on VT-AAST database using combination of networks

	Precision	Recall	Specificity	Accuracy
AND	**53.11%**	63.54%	**93.57%**	**89.81%**
OR	44.17%	**72.32%**	88.19%	86.21%
VOTE	47.55%	67.26%	90.83%	87.88%

Table 14. Accuracy results for CbCrRGBHS on UCD database using combination of networks after applying filling the holes and opening method

	Precision	Recall	Specificity	Accuracy
AND	**71.93%**	62.66%	**93.01%**	**85.23%**
OR	63.17%	**71.24%**	86.20%	82.37%
VOTE	67.23%	66.93%	90.07%	84.14%

In neural networks, using more than one hidden layer usually not only decreases the performance rate, but also increases the training and testing time (Tesauro, 1992). The reason is that by increasing the number of layers, it becomes too difficult to infer the conditional distribution of the hidden activities (Hinton *et al.*, 2006). A

Table 15. Accuracy results for CbCrRGBHS on VT-AAST database using combination of networks after applying filling the holes and opening method

	Precision	Recall	Specificity	Accuracy
AND	**52.99%**	67.42%	**93.00%**	**89.80%**
OR	44.25%	**76.56%**	87.41%	86.05%
VOTE	47.52%	71.66%	90.07%	87.76%

Table 16. Accuracy results for other methods on UCD database

	Precision	Recall	Specificity	Accuracy
Gaussian	54.96%	66.82%	81.12%	77.46%
Chen	63.75%	51.13%	89.98%	80.02%
Kovac	62.51%	**69.09%**	85.71%	81.45%
Kong	37.47%	14.58%	**91.61%**	71.87%
CbCrRGBHS	63.19%	55.55%	88.85%	80.31%
CbCrRGBHS-VOTE	**67.23%**	66.93%	90.07%	**84.14%**

Table 17. Accuracy results for other methods on VT-AAST database

	Precision	Recall	Specificity	Accuracy
Gaussian	30.00%	60.37%	79.84%	77.40%
Chen	31.62%	54.59%	83.10%	79.53%
Kovac	31.81%	65.02%	80.05%	78.17%
Kong	45.97%	29.51%	**95.03%**	86.83%
CbCrRGBHS	42.47%	65.28%	87.34%	84.58%
CbCrRGBHS-VOTE	**47.52%**	**71.66%**	90.07%	**87.76%**

greedy layer-wise unsupervised learning algorithm has been constructed for Deep Belief Networks (DBN) by Hinton *et al.* (2006). This is based on the concept that learning and combining a number of simpler models can be as effective as learning a complicated model. In the greedy algorithm, each model receives a different representation of the data (Hinton *et al.*, 2006). A non-linear transformation is applied to the input vectors, which produces output vectors for the next model. The upper layers of the DBN contain abstract concepts of the inputs and the lower layer represents the low-level features of the input. The classifier will first learn the low-level features, and then by combining this information it learns the abstract concepts (Hinton *et al.*, 2006).

The structure of the multiple layers of the generative model include directed connections with the exception of the top two layers, which have undirected connections. Considering W_0 as the weight between the first and second layer in the model, the goal is to learn W_0, and once W_0 has been learned, higher-level data at the first hidden layer can be generated using W_0^T (Hinton *et al.*, 2006). The generative model can be trained using the following algorithm (Hinton *et al.*, 2006):

1. By using the assumption that all the weight matrices are tight, learn W_0.
2. After W_0 is learned, freeze W_0, and W_0^T is used in the first hidden layer in order to infer factorial approximate posterior distributions over the states of the variables.
3. In the final stage, all the higher weight matrices are tied to each other, except W_0, which is untied from other weight matrices. A Restricted Boltzmann Machine (RBM) model of the higher-level data is learned. These data were produced by using W_0^T to transform the original data.

A DBN can consist of several RBM networks. A RBM is a special kind of Boltzmann Machine with the difference that the nodes in each layer are not connected to each other (Hinton *et al.*, 2006). For generating data, Gibbs sampling can be applied between layers. The algorithm uses the states of the units in one layer to update the units in other layers in parallel. The updating continues until the system has reached its equilibrium distribution (Hinton *et al.*, 2006). There are several methods for generating data, including contrastive divergence, which is a fast method for generating data using Gibbs sampling (Maryaz & Hinton, 2001). The contrastive divergence learning is based on minimizing the differences between divergences. Hinton *et al.* (2006) and Bengio, *et al.* (2007) have performed experiments on the MNIST database using deep learning methods. The MNIST database is a handwritten digits database containing 60,000 samples for training and 10,000 samples for testing. Hinton *et al.* (2006) and Bengio, *et al.* (2007) have reported their results on the MNIST database using different techniques, demonstrating that deep learning has much better performance, compared to that of the other techniques.

The auto encoder approach has also been used as the deep learning structure (Hinton & Salakhutdinov, 2006). Approximately 75% of samples were used for training and the remaining for validation. Hidden layers with different number of neurons were examined, while three hidden layers were used in the structure. The results were evaluated using the UCD and VT-AAST databases (Abdallah *et al.*, 2007a) (Abdallah *et al.*, 2007b).

Different Auto encoders with dissimilar number of nodes in the hidden layers were considered in this experiment. The number of nodes in the hidden layers ranged from 250 to 500 with a 50 interval between each experiment. The best results occurred when the number of nodes in the hidden layer was 450 (Hajiarbabi & Agah, 2015). The other observation is that there is a tradeoff between recall with precision, accuracy, and specificity. The reason is that to have higher recall, which is detecting more skin pixels correctly, the probability to detect more non-skin pixels as human skin is higher, which will reduce the precision, and vice versa.

In detecting faces, there may be some parts of the skin inside the skin components that have not been detected as human skin. In addition, there could be some small pixels from the background that have been considered as human skin. In order to increase the skin detection rate, some morphological operations such as filling the holes and opening were applied to the images (Hajiarbabi &Agah, 2014).

Table 18 demonstrates the result of using deep learning (Auto encoder) along with the other methods discussed, using the UCD database. Skin detection using deep learning shows improved results in terms of recall and accuracy. Table 19 presents the result of different methods when applied to the VT-AAST.

Figure 2 and Figure 3 illustrate some of the experimental results on images from the UCD database. The first image shows the original image from the database and the second image shows the result of applying deep learning method for detecting the skin, followed by filling the holes, and opening methods on the result. Figure 4 and Figure 5 illustrate some of the results on the images in the VT-AAST database.

Table 18. Accuracy results for other methods on UCD database

	Precision	Recall	Specificity	Accuracy
Gaussian	54.96%	66.82%	81.12%	77.46%
Chen	63.75%	51.13%	89.98%	80.02%
Kovac	62.51%	69.09%	85.71%	81.45%
Kong	37.47%	14.58%	91.61%	71.87%
Neural Network	71.30%	60.25%	**93.43%**	82.36%
Deep learning	**65.81%**	**70.17%**	88.68%	**82.93%**

Table 19. Accuracy results for other methods on VT-AAST database

	Precision	Recall	Specificity	Accuracy
Gaussian	30.00%	60.37%	79.84%	77.40%
Chen	31.62%	54.59%	83.10%	79.53%
Kovac	31.81%	65.02%	80.05%	78.17%
Kong	45.97%	29.51%	95.03%	86.83%
Neural Network	**54.26%**	59.07%	**93.36%**	88.56%
Deep learning	46.05%	**75.38%**	90.15%	**88.81%**

Figure 2. Skin detection using deep learning, experimental results on UCD database

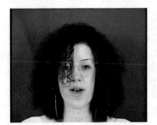

TEXTURE SEGMENTATION

The skin detection algorithm works well when the color of the environment does not affect the color of the face. As mentioned before, the color of some objects and other things in the nature—such as the color of sand, rock, or soil—can be identical to that of the human skin. In such cases, the skin detection algorithm may not detect the skin pixel correctly. A number of features have been used in order to distinguish between the human skin and other objects. The color of two objects may be similar; however, there are other characteristics that can be used to distinguish between the two objects. One such example is the texture of the two objects. The texture of rock differs from the texture of sand; and we can detect them easily even if they have the same color. One method for texture segmentation is to use the co-occurrence matrix (Shapiro & Stockman, 2000). Co-occurrence matrix C is a two

Figure 3. Skin detection using deep learning, experimental results on UCD database

Figure 4. Skin detection using deep learning, experimental results on VT-AAST database

Figure 5. Skin detection using deep learning, experimental results on VT-AAST database

dimensional array which shows the number that value i co-occurs with value j. for example $C(0,1)$ looks at the right pixel and counts the occurrences of the pattern in the image (Shapiro & Stockman, 2000).

By calculating the co-occurrences matrix, the properties of the texture are computed. However, this information cannot be used to classify textures. Important information should be extracted from the co-occurrence matrix, including:

$$Energy = \sum_i \sum_j N_d^2 \left(i, j\right)$$

$$Entropy = -\sum_i \sum_j N_d \left(i, j\right) log_2 N_d \left(i, j\right)$$

$$Contrast = \sum_i \sum_j \left(i - j\right)^2 N_d \left(i, j\right)$$

$$Homogeneity = \sum_i \sum_j \frac{N_d \left(i, j\right)}{1 + \left|i - j\right|}$$

$$Correlation = \frac{\sum_i \sum_j \left(i - \mu_i\right)\left(j - \mu_j\right) N_d \left(i, j\right)}{\sigma_i \sigma_j}$$

$N_d \left(i\right)$ and $N_d \left(j\right)$ are defined by:

$$N_d \left(i\right) = \sum_j N_d \left(i, j\right)$$

$$N_d \left(j\right) = \sum_i N_d \left(i, j\right)$$

In addition to these features, some other features were also selected by the authors which correspond to image color. These include the Cb, Cr, H and S components of the YCbCr and HSV color spaces. For training purposes patches were collected from different datasets, such as Textures.com and Describable Textures Dataset (DTD) (Cimpoi *et al.*, 2014) and other images from the Web. The Textures.com site contains 120,984 images from different categories, such as fabric, wood, metal etc. The Describable Textures Dataset contains 5,640 images from 47 different categories. There are 120 images for each category. Image sizes range between 300x300 and 640x640.

The test were done using different sizes of patches chosen from datasets and the size 20 by 20 showed better results, so 20 by 20 patches were used for the experiment. Figure 6 shows a number of patches from the human skin.

The color information Cb, Cr, H and S, combined with Energy, Entropy, Contrast, Homogeneity and Correlation from the co-occurrence matrix—built from the grey scale image—were used by the authors.

For the training, approximately 10,000 patches were used from human skin, along with 30,000 patches from objects, specifically those whose color were similar to that of human skin color. The Support Vector Machine (SVM) with radial basis function as kernel was used for training. Because of the large size of the input, SVM seemed to be a better structure than either neural network or deep learning. The classifier managed to classify the objects, as reported in Table 20.

For testing, total of 10,000 patches were selected from the Web and other datasets; and the results are shown in Table 21.

Figure 6. Human skin texture

Table 20. Accuracy results for training textures samples

	Precision	Recall	Specificity	Accuracy
Texture (SVM)	98.98%	99.40%	98.98%	99.30%

Table 21. Accuracy results for testing textures samples

	Precision	Recall	Specificity	Accuracy
Texture (SVM)	96.46%	95.26%	96.41%	95.83%

It was determined that texture segmentation technique can be used along with the skin detection. If the system chooses a part as human skin, the texture segmentation can verify the selection, or if the texture differs from human skin, the part can be rejected.

FACE DETECTION

The Rowley and Viola-Jones methods search all areas of an image in order to find faces. As the result, such approaches may not be time-efficient. A much faster method is to divide the image into two parts, the ones that contain human skin and those that do not. After this step, the search for finding human face would be restricted to those areas that just contain human skins. Therefore, face detection using color images can be faster compared to other approaches (Hajiarbabi & Agah, 2015). However, due to lack of comprehensive comparative evaluation between different methods, comparing face detection using color images with other methods is not simple (Hjelmas & Kee Low, 2001). In face detection using color images, there are not many color databases, and also most of the tests using Viola-Jones and Rowley methods have been done on gray scale images. Unlike Viola-Jones and Rowley methods that need a window to be moved pixel by pixel on the entire image, face detection using color does not need to move a window pixel by pixel over the entire image, except for some small parts of the image. Some works such as (Chandrappa *et al.*, 2011) have also stated that the color-based methods is faster compared to other methods.

The idea of face detection using color images is that, the skin pixels from the other parts of the image can be separated, and then by using some information, the face can be detected from other parts of the body. In (Hajiarbabi & Agah, 2014) a method for face detection has been proposed based on skin segmentation.

Another method for face detection is to detect the eyes and the lip, and then detect the face based on the locations of the eyes and the lip. For eyes and lip detection, we have proposed a rule-based method. The rule-based methods are faster, compared to other methods. In the eyes' area of a face, there is a high contrast, as dark iris is surrounded by white sclera, which is again surrounded by black eyelashes. This characteristic was used in order to determine suitable rules for finding eyes in a color image. For this reason, first the portions of the face that are darker are selected. Experimentally, that operation was performed on more than 300 images, choosing the pixels where $R<100$, $G<100$, and $B<100$, seemed to produce the best results. Using these equations, most portions of the face are ignored, but all the dark places in the face which do not belong to eye and that may belong to other parts such has eyebrows and eyelashes are selected.

In the next step, the components which remain are those where neighbor pixels have a saturation—the S value in HSV color space—of less than 0.12. These pixels are added to the previous components. This results in the white part of the face, which is the sclera, to be added to the previously selected parts. The last step is choosing those components, which have the expansion by applying the saturation rule. After this step, there will remain just two or three components among the face component. The eyes components are usually larger than the other components and so can be easily detected.

In the detection of the lips, two different conditions should be considered. For those who wear lipstick, their lips are quite distinct from other portions of their face. These lips can be easily detected utilizing the HSV color space by using the equations:

$$H>0.94, 0.3<S<0.7, V>0.65$$

For the cases of without lipstick, the lips can be detected using the equations:

$$H<0.03, 0.3<S<0.7, V>0.65, G<110, B<110$$

These two equations are combined using the OR operation.

After applying these rules to the skin portion on the image, some components are found, with the largest component belonging to the lips.

For the testing purposes, selected photos from the Georgia Tech Face database were used. Tests were done on 400 images. Among all images, the detection rate was 86.5% for finding both eyes, 7% for finding one eye, and 6.5% where no eyes were detected. The major challenge for eyes was mainly due to some problem with skin detection. Additionally, in some images the eyes were closed. For lip detection, the detection rate was 96.5%. Figure 7 shows some samples for eye detection, the first image is the real image, and the second image shows the possible places for eyes in the image. The white fragments are the parts that were added by using saturation less than 0.12 to the previously selected parts. The third image shows the detected

Figure 7. Results for eye detection from Georgia Tech database

eyes. Figure 8 shows some samples for lip detection. The second image shows the parts that were accepted after applying the rules for finding the location of the lips.

As mentioned previously, because the results of the Rowley and Viola-Jones methods have been reported for grey scale images, it is not straight forward to compare the results of face detection using color images with the Rowley and Viola-Jones methods. However, with some mathematical expressions it can be shown that face detection using color images is indeed faster.

Considering an m*n image, for the Rowley method, the window size which is used to move over the image is 20*20 (Rowley *et al.*, 1998). Therefore the number of operations on the pixel will be:

$$400 * (m\text{-}19) (n\text{-}19)$$

In that equation, 400 represents the size of the window and $(m\text{-}19)(n\text{-}19)$ represents the number of windows which are needed to cover the entire image. Additionally, the image is subsampled several times, each time with the coefficient 1.2 (Rowley *et al.*, 1998). Henceforth, the total number of operations would be:

$$400 * (m\text{-}19) (n\text{-}19) + 400 (m/1.2 \text{-}19) (n/1.2 \text{-}19) + \ldots$$

Each window is applied to a receptive field neural network, which needs significant computation to determine if the component contains a face (Rowley *et al.*, 1998). At the worst case, each pixel is processed many more than 400 times. That is 400 times for the original image, 333 times with probability of 83.33% in the first subsampling and so on.

For the Viola-Jones method, a 24*24 window is moved over the image. Approximately 200 features with different size (s*t which s and t can be around 5 and 10) are applied to the windows (Viola & Jones, 2001). The operations for Viola-Jones method are:

Figure 8. Results for lip detection from Georgia Tech database

200 (m-23) (n-23) s t

where 200 is the number of features which are used to be placed on the image, s*t is the average size of each feature and (m-23) (n-23) is the number of the windows used to cover the entire image. Similar to the Rowley method, the Viola-Jones method also used subsampling in order to find faces where sizes are fewer than 24*24. Using the Viola-Jones method, the scaling is 1.25 and is done for 11 times (Viola & Jones, 2001), resulting in the total operations of:

$$[200 \ (m\text{-}23) \ (n\text{-}23) \ s \ t] + [200 \ (m/1.25\text{-}23) \ (n/1.25\text{-}23) \ s \ t] + \dots$$

However, the Viola-Jones method uses several techniques in order the speed up the operations. Integral image and cascade of classifiers are two such techniques that are used in the Viola-Jones method (Viola & Jones, 2001). In (Viola & Jones, 2001) it has been mentioned that the Viola-Jones method is 15 times faster than the Rowley method.

In face detection using color images, the total operations which are needed for skin detection is $5mn$. The reason is that each pixel is applied to five different neural networks. These quantities of operations are just for the skin detection phase. The time and operation for the face detection phase are not as high, because the detection phase is just applied to the components. In addition, for face detection using color images there is no need for subsampling.

A comparison between face detection using color images and the Rowley method shows that face detection using color images is at least 80 times faster. Additionally, the neural network used in the Rowley method is much more complicated and requires more time compared to neural network which is used in face detection using color images. By comparing the speeds between Viola-Jones and Rowley method, it can be seen that face detection using color images is 3 to 4 times faster than the Viola-Jones method.

Figure 9 shows the results for lip detection using the UCD database. The first image is the real image, the second image is the result after applying the face detection algorithm, the third image shows the detected skin using HSV color space, the forth image displays the possible place for lips, and the fifth image shows the lips that were detected.

Figure 10 shows the result of applying the eye detection algorithm to the UCD database. The first image shows the real image, the second image is the result after applying the skin detection algorithm, the third image shows the parts of the skin where R<100, G<100, and B<100, the forth image shows the possible places for the eyes, and the fifth image shows the detected eyes.

Figure 9. Results on UCD database

As stated, another method to find faces in an image is to use the location of the eyes and lips in the image. Figure 11 shows an image from the Georgia Tech database. The triangle between the eyes and lips shows the place of the face in the image. In order to draw a rectangle around the face, the distance between the eyes and lips can be used as a measure of the rectangle. The face width and length are usually two and two and half times of this distance, respectively.

In such systems, the next step after face detection is face recognition. The most popular methods are appearance-based methods (Hajiarbabi *et al.*, 2008). Other feature extraction methods such as Discrete Cosine Transform have also been used in face recognition (Hajiarbabi *et al.*, 2007).

Figure 10. Results on UCD database

Figure 11. Results for face detection on the Georgia Tech database

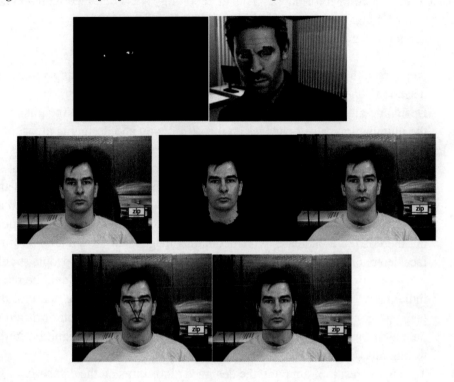

CONCLUSION

In this work, a number of novel methods had been discussed in the fields of skin detection, texture segmentation, and face detection in color images. A combination of neural networks was designed and developed in order to detect the human skin. The designed networks increase the detection rate of human skin compared to that of the other methods in this field. In face detection utilizing skin color, it is very important to detect the human skin correctly because it affects the face detection phase. Using combination of networks increases the time of skin detection phase, while improving the performance. The increase in time can be addressed by using parallel processors. Deep learning was another method that was used for skin detection. The results show that deep learning has better performance in terms of recall and accuracy, compared to other methods which include rule based methods, Gaussian method, and neural network. Although, deep learning's computational complexity may not be better than other methods, but it's much better performance makes it a more suitable method for detecting human skin pixels. In addition, an algorithm was proposed, implemented, and evaluated in order to locate the eyes and lips in an image using color information. This methodology was combined with another method for finding faces in the images using the locations of eyes and lips.

Potential future research directions of this work can include:

1. Applying other machine learning and deep learning methods to the skin detection phase.
2. Designing algorithms that reduce the effect of illumination on the image, as the illumination causes changes on the skin. Using and designing algorithms that reduce the effect of illumination can increase the detection rate of skin detection phase, which can improve the detection rate in the face detection phase.
3. Building a database for face detection and face recognition. Among the databases that are available, most of them are black and white. There are some good databases in face detection and some databases in the face recognition, but there is not a database, which contains images that are suitable for both face detection and face recognition. In this case, around 40-50 people should be chosen from different ages and races. Around 10 images should be taken individually; while these images are to be used for the training phase of the face recognition system. Around 100 images from combination of different people in the database will be used for the detection and recognition in the testing phase.
4. Testing the result of applying the designed algorithms on the database.

REFERENCES

Abdallah, A. S., Abbott, A. L., & El-Nasr, M. A. (2007a). A New Face Detection Technique using 2D DCT and Self Organizing Feature Map. *Proceedings of World Academy of Science. Engineering and Technology, 21*, 15–19.

Abdallah, A. S., El-Nasr, M. A., & Abbott, A. C. (2007b). A New Colour Image Database for Benchmarking of Automatic Face Detection and Human Skin Segmentation Techniques. *Proceedings of World Academy of Science. Engineering and Technology, 20*, 353–357.

Al-Mohair, H., Saleh, J., & Suandi, S. (2012). Human skin color detection: A review on neural network perspective. *International Journal of Innovative Computing, Information, & Control, 8*(12), 8115–8131.

Alshehri, S. (2012). Neural Networks Performance for Skin Detection. *Journal of Emerging Trends in Computing and Information Sciences, 3*(12), 1582–1585.

Brancati, N., De Pietro, G., Frucci, M., & Gallo, L. (2016). Human Skin Detection through Correlation Rules between the YCb and YCr Subspaces based on Dynamic Color Clustering. *Computer Vision and Image Understanding*, *155*, 33–42. doi:10.1016/j.cviu.2016.12.001

Chandrappa, D. N., Ravishankar, M., & RameshBabu, D. R. (2011). Face detection in color images using skin color model algorithm based on skin color information. *2011 3rd international conference on electronics computer technology (ICECT)*, 254–258.

Chen, H., Huang, C., & Fu, C. (2008). *Hybrid-boost learning for multi-pose face detection and facial expression recognition. In Pattern Recognition society* (Vol. 41, pp. 1173–1185). Elsevier.

Chiang, C., Tai, W., Yang, M., Huang, Y., & Huang, C. (2003). A novel method for detecting lips, eyes and faces in real time. *Real-Time Imaging*, *9*(4), 277–287. doi:10.1016/j.rti.2003.08.003

Chin, S., Seng, K., Ang, L., & Lim, K. (2009). New lips detection and tracking system. *Proceedings of the international multiconference of engineers and computer scientists*, 1.

Cimpoi, M., Maji, S., Kokkinos, I., Mohamed, S., & Vedaldi, A. (2014). *Describing Textures in the Wild, Computer Vision and Pattern Recognition*. CVPR.

Das, P., Sarkar, A., Halder, S., Kundu, D., Ghosh, S., & Das Gupta, S. (2015). *A Novel Approach towards detecting Faces and Gender using skin Segmentation and Template Matching. In Signal Processing and Integrated Networks* (pp. 431–436). SPIN.

Describable Textures Dataset (DTD). (2017). Retrieved from https://www.robots.ox.ac.uk/~vgg/data/dtd/

Doukim, C. A., Dargham, J. A., Chekima, A., & Omatu, S. (2010). Combining neural networks for skin detection. *Signal and Image Processing: an International Journal*, *1*(2), 1–11. doi:10.5121/sipij.2010.1201

Elgammal, A., Muang, C., & Hu, D. (2009). Skin Detection – a Short Tutorial. In Encyclopedia of Biometrics. Springer-Verlag Berlin Heidelberg.

Fink, B., Grammer, G., & Matts, P. J. (2006). Visible skin color distribution plays a role in the perception of age, attractiveness, and health in female faces. *Evolution and Human Behavior*, *27*(6), 433–442. doi:10.1016/j.evolhumbehav.2006.08.007

Fleck, M. M., Forsyth, D. A., & Bregler, C. (1996). Finding naked people. *Proceedings of the European Conference on Computer Vision (ECCV)*, 593–602.

Gondaliya, D., Kamothi, P., Fudnawala, V., Patal, K., Patal, H., & Naik, S. (2015). Review on Human Face Detection based on Skin Color and Edge Information. *International Journal of Engineering Science and Technology*, 7(1), 12–20.

Grace, J., & Reshmi, K. (2015, March). *Face recognition in surveillance system.* Innovations in information, Embedded and Communication Systems (ICIIECS), Coimbatore, India. Retrieved from http://www.anefian.com/research/face_reco.htm

Hajiarbabi, M., & Agah, A. (2014). Human Skin Color Detection using Neural Networks. *Journal of Intelligent Systems*, 24(4), 425–436.

Hajiarbabi, M., & Agah, A. (2014). Face Detection in color images using skin segmentation, *Journal of Automation. Mobile Robotics and Intelligent Systems*, 8(3), 41–51. doi:10.14313/JAMRIS_3-2014/26

Hajiarbabi, M., & Agah, A. (2015). Face recognition using canonical correlation, discrimination power and fractional multiple exemplar discriminant analyses, *Journal of Automation. Mobile Robotics and Intelligent Systems*, 9(4), 18–27. doi:10.14313/JAMRIS_4-2015/29

Hajiarbabi, M., & Agah, A. (2015). Techniques for skin, face, eye and lip detection using skin segmentation in color images. *International Journal of Computer Vision and Image Processing*, 5(2).

Hajiarbabi, M., & Agah, A. (2015). Human skin detection in color images using deep learning. *International Journal of Computer Vision and Image Processing*, 5(2).

Hajiarbabi, M., Askari, J., Sadri, S., & Saraee, M. (2007). Face Recognition Using Discrete Cosine Transform plus Linear Discriminant Analysis. *IEEE Conference WCE 2007/ICSIE2007*, 1, 652–655.

Hajiarbabi, M., Askari, J., Sadri, S., & Saraee, M. (2008). A New Linear Appearance-based Method in face Recognition. *Advances in Communication Systems and Electrical Engineering Lecture Notes in Electrical Engineering*, 4, 579–587. doi:10.1007/978-0-387-74938-9_39

Hassaballah, M., Murakami, K., & Ido, S. (2011). An automative eye detection method for gray intensity facial images. *International Journal of Computer Science Issues,* 8(2), 272–282.

Hinton, G., & Salakhutdinov, R. (2006). Reducing the dimensionality of data with neural networks. *Science, 313*(5786), 504–507. doi:10.1126/science.1127647 PMID:16873662

Hinton, G. E., Osindero, S., & The, Y. (2006). A fast learning algorithm for deep belief nets. *Neural Computation, 18*(7), 1527–1554. doi:10.1162/neco.2006.18.7.1527 PMID:16764513

Hjelmas, E., & Kee Low, B. (2001). Face Detection: A Survey. *Computer Vision and Image Understanding, 83*(3), 236–274. doi:10.1006/cviu.2001.0921

Kalbkhani, H., & Amirani, M. (2012). An efficient algorithm for lip segmentation in color face images based on local information. *Journal of World's Electrical Engineering and Technology, 1*(1), 12–16.

Khan, I., Abdullah, H., & Bin Zainal, M. (2013). Efficient eyes and mouth detection algorithm using combination of Viola Jones and skin color pixel detection. *International Journal of Engineering and Applied Sciences, 3*(4), 51–60.

Khedekar, P., Walunj, S., Sul, S., Sonune, P., Tiwari, D., & Phalke, D. A. (2016). Scale Adaptive Face Detection and Tracking for Controlling Computer Functions. *International Journal of Engineering Science and Computing, 6*(4), 4608–4612.

Kong, W., & Zhe, S. (2007). Multi-face detection based on down sampling and modified subtractive clustering for color images. *Journal of Zhejiang University, 8*(1), 72–78. doi:10.1631/jzus.2007.A0072

Kovac, J., Peer, P., & Solina, F. (2003). Human Skin Color Clustering for Face Detection. *EUROCON 2003. Computer as a Tool. The IEEE Region, 8*(2), 144–148.

Maryaz, G., & Hinton, G. E. (2001). Recognizing hand-written digits using hierarchical products of experts. *IEEE Transactions on Pattern Analysis and Machine Intelligence, 24,* 180–197.

Peng, K., Chen, L., Ruan, S., & Kukharev, G. (2005). A robust algorithm for eye detection on gray intensity face without spectacles. *Journal of Computer Science and Technology, 5*(3), 127–132.

Rajpathak, T., Kumar, R., & Schwartz, E. (2009). *Eye detection using morphological and color image processing.* Florida Conference on Recent Advances in Robotics.

Rowley, H., Baluja, S., & Kanade, T. (1998). Neural network-based face detection. *IEEE Pattern Analysis and Machine Intelligence, 20*(1), 22–38. doi:10.1109/34.655647

Seow, M., Valaparla, D., & Asari, V. (2003). Neural network based skin color model for face detection. *Proceedings of the 32nd Applied Imagery Pattern Recognition Workshop (AIPR'03)*, 141–145. doi:10.1109/AIPR.2003.1284262

Shapiro, L., & Stockman, G. (2000). *Computer Vision*. Upper Saddle River, NJ: Prentice Hall.

Sidbe, D., Montesinos, P., & Janaqi, S. (2006). A simple and efficient eye detection method in color images. *International conference image and vision computing*, 385–390.

Singh, S., Chauhan, D. S., Vatsa, M., & Singh, R. (2003). A Robust Skin Color Based Face Detection Algorithm. *Tamkang Journal of Science and Engineering*, 6(4), 227–234.

Soetedjo, A. (2011). Eye detection based on color and shape features. *International Journal of Advanced Computer Science and Applications, 3*(5), 17–22.

Tesauro, G. (1992). Practical issues in temporal difference learning. *Machine Learning, 8*(3-4), 257–277. doi:10.1007/BF00992697

Viola, P., & Jones, M. J. (2001). Robust real-time object detection. *Proceedings of IEEE Workshop on Statistical and Computational Theories of Vision.*

Wu, Y., & Ai, X. (2008). Face detection in color images using Adaboost algorithm based on skin color information. *2008 Workshop on Knowledge Discovery and Data Mining*, 339–342. doi:10.1109/WKDD.2008.148

Yang, G., Li, H., Zhang, L., & Cao, Y. (2010). Research on a skin color detection algorithm based on self-adaptive skin color mode. *International Conference on Communications and Intelligence Information Security*, 266–270. doi:10.1109/ ICCIIS.2010.67

Zuo, H., Fan, H., Blasch, E., & Ling, H. (2017). Combining Convolutional and Recurrent Neural Networks for Human Skin Detection. *IEEE Signal Processing Letters, 24*(3), 289–293. doi:10.1109/LSP.2017.2654803

Chapter 9

A Secured Contactless Fingerprint Verification Method Using a Minutiae Matching Technique

Tahirou Djara
Université d'Abomey-Calavi, Benin

Marc Kokou Assogba
Université d'Abomey-Calavi, Benin

Antoine Vianou
Université d'Abomey-Calavi, Benin

ABSTRACT

Most matching or verification phases of fingerprint systems use minutiae types and orientation angle to find matched minutiae pairs from the input and template fingerprints. Unfortunately, due to some non-linear distortions, like excessive pressure and fingers twisting during enrollment, this process can cause the minutiae features to be distorted from the original. The authors are interested in a fingerprint matching method using contactless images for fingerprint verification. After features extraction, they compute Euclidean distances between template minutiae (bifurcation and ending points) and input image minutiae. They compute then after bifurcation ridges orientation angles and ending point orientations. In the decision stage, they analyze the similarity between templates. The proposed algorithm has been tested on a set of 420 fingerprint images. The verification accuracy is found to be acceptable and the experimental results are promising. Future work will enhance the proposed verification method by a new template protection technique.

DOI: 10.4018/978-1-5225-5628-2.ch009

INTRODUCTION

Biometric authentication has received extensive attention over the past decade with increasing demands in automated personal identification as fingerprints are assumed to be unique across individuals, and fingers of the same individual (Pankanti et al., 2002). However, contact based fingerprint systems have some drawbacks due to skin elasticity, inconsistent finger placement, contact pressure, small sensing area, environment conditions and sensor noise. Additionally, problems like skin conditions (e.g. dirty or wet) and contagious diseases spreading make the use of contact based scanners not very safe (Yin et al., 2016). Another major risk in the contact-based systems is the possibility of chemical or bacteriological attacks. This risk is increasingly increased with the development of international terrorism nowadays. We are then interested in a fingerprint matching method using contactless images for fingerprint verification.

Depending on the application context, a biometric system may be called either a verification system or an identification system (Maltoni et al., 2003; AlMahafzah et al., 2012). A verification system authenticates a person's identity by comparing the captured biometric reference template pre-stored in the system. It conducts one-to-one comparison to confirm whether the claim of identity by the individual is true. An identification system recognizes an individual by searching the entire enrollment template database for a match. It conducts one-to-many comparisons to establish if the individual is present in the database and if so, returns the identifier of the enrollment reference that matched.

Fingerprint matching techniques can be coarsely classified into three categories, namely minutiae-based matching (Jain et al., 1997; Medina-pérez et al., 2012), image-based matching (A. Qader et al.,2006; Ito et al., 2009; Jain et al., 2000, Sha et al., 2003) and hybrid matching technique (Khalila et al., 2010; Kumar et al., 2012). Minutiae-based matching essentially consists of finding the alignment between the template and the input minutiae feature sets that result in the maximum number of minutiae pairings.

In this paper, we present a contactless fingerprint verification method using a minutiae matching technique, based on the alignment between template images acquired by a contactless system and input images acquired by the same way. Contactless images have been acquired and stored in a database during an enrollment step. The first stage in an Automatic Fingerprint Verification procedure is to extract minutiae from fingerprints. In our contactless fingerprint verification system, we have implemented a minutia extraction algorithm which has been presented in (Djara et al., 2010). The extracted features are ridge bifurcation, ridge ending and ridges orientations. Authors in (Kumar et al., 2012;He et al., 2002; Virk&Maini, 2012) determine orientations using horizontal axis.

Most of the matching or verification of the fingerprint verification systems use minutiae types and orientation angle to find matched minutiae pairs from the input and template fingerprints (Tiko&Kuosmanen, 2003). Thus, accuracy of the verification stage largely depends on the minutiae extraction process. Unfortunately, due to some non-linear distortion, like excessive pressure and twisting of fingers during enrollment, this process can cause the minutiae features to be distorted from the original. Some authors have used the Smallest Minimum Sum of Closest Euclidean Distance of bifurcation points to improve the accuracy of fingerprint verification (Bhowmik et al., 2009).

To overcome those drawbacks, we work on contactless fingerprint images. After features extraction, we compute Euclidean distances between template minutiae and input image minutiae. We compute then after ridges bifurcation orientations and the ridgesending orientations. In the decision stage, we analyze the similarity between templates. Our algorithm has been tested by computing various similarity scores.

In section 2 we present a literature review oriented on the biometric systems security in general and the special case of contactless fingerprint systems. In section 3 the experimental condition i.e. the contactless enrollment. Feature representation is presented in section 4. Ridge bifurcation and Ridge ending similarity are described in Section 5. Section 6 presents our minutiae matching algorithm. Section 7 presents the experimental results. Section 8 presents our outlook for the future and section 9 concludes the paper.

BACKGROUND

Biometric verification systems in general are subject to spoofing attacks in order to bypass them. These attacks are perfect from day to day and require appropriate measures. Several techniques are proposed to deal with these attacks and to secure the biometric systems. The proposed solutions can be divided into two main categories, palliative solutions and preventive solutions (Marasco et al., 2015). Each category can be divided into two types (hardware types and software types). There are two main methods of spoofing (Mojtaba M, 2010): Co-operative spoofing and non-Cooperative spoofing. Attacks are made by exploiting vulnerability points located at five levels of the biometric system (Javier G, 2014). It is:

1. **Presentation Attacks:** Reproduction of biometric modality is presented at the inputs.
2. Sensor is bypassed and previously stored data is hacked and used.
3. The set of extracted features are replaced with the false sets.

4.   The matcher is corrupted and sample is matched with the false set.
5.   The final match is altered by an attacker.

Indeed, security holes have been identified in all biometric systems. Thus Jain et al. in September 2007 have listed the vulnerabilities in the form of fishbone.

The contactless verification system presented in this paper makes it possible to limit the possibilities of reproduction of the fingerprint because the system avoids leaving traces at the image acquisition step. In addition, the contactless system allows the implementation of the 3D technique which offers better security. The 3D technique allows the sensor to differentiate between a finger and an image of the finger. This technique also improves the recognition algorithm (Kumar&Kwong, 2015; Yin et al., 2016) and offers good resistance to software level attacks. The finger vivacity recognition techniques also make it possible to fight against the reproduction (Matsumoto et al., 2002). One of the major challenges of fingerprint verification is the improvement of recognition accuracy. Several works have been carried out in this direction. In 2013, (Labati et al., 2013) proposed a neural network-based approach for the rotation effects reduction. This approach has reduced the ERR of existing biometric systems from 3.04% to 2.20%. In the fingerprint recognition process, the minutiae detection phase is very important for the overall performance of the system. Thus, (Liu et al., 2016) proposed a 3-step approach to improving image quality in the detection of minutiae of the contactless fingerprint. In addition, contactless fingerprint images often contain noises and have low contrast. To solve this problem, (Yin et al., 2016) proposed a method for intrinsic image decomposition and guided image

Figure 1. List of fishbone vulnerabilities (Jain et al, 2007)

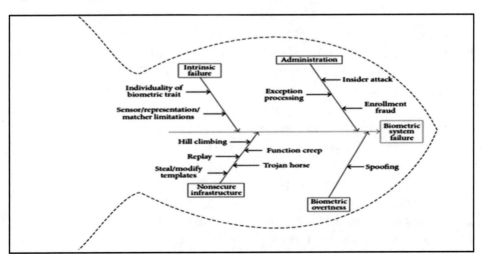

filtering. All that techniques can contribute to improve the contactless systems. In this paper we focus on the minutiae matching technique.

CONTACTLESS ENROLLMENT

After the tragic attacks of September 11, 2001, the need for improved and reliable fingerprint recognition technology drastically increased. Despite the known deficiencies and drawbacks of contact-based fingerprinting, this method is still deployed. Although contactless methods are known for producing distortion free fingerprints, this is a rather new technological development, and very few universities are involved in their development. Among authors interested by contactless fingerprint development, we have (Parziale et al., 2006; Hiew et al.,2007;Mil'shtein et al., 2008). Other authors present in an academic work, recent applications in contactless fingerprint (Milshtein et al., 2011; Pillai&Milshtein, 2012; Labati et al., 2013; Liu et al., 2016; Yin et al., 2016; Arora et al., 2016).

Acquisition Protocol

We have developed a Contactless Biometric Fingerprint Software (CBFS) for the acquisition and processing of our images. The contactless fingerprint acquisition system consists of this CBFS to visualize the sharpness of the finger before capture, a webcam for taking digital photo, and lighting equipment. The user is asked to put his finger in a fixed position, the reverse of his finger on the indicated place and his palm faces the camera. We use a medium-resolution webcam (Logitech Pro9000), driven by an interface as shown in Figure 2. In order to limit travel, a rectangular area is defined on the interface of the camera which will contain the finger before capture (area marked "1"). The acquired images are PNG format and have a size of 640x640. Figure 2-(a) shows the system and Figure 2-(b) shows a screenshot of the user's interface.

In acquisition stage, it is important to acquire images but also to represent them in a proper format. For that, we use the following soft wares:

- ij.process, an ImageJ package for image processing,
- Jama, (Java Matrix) package for linear algebra methods implementation,
- DSJ (Direct Show Java), a Microsoft API for the Webcam management,
- Java programming language,
- SQL language for database management.

Figure 2. Contactless fingerprint acquisition system and Screenshot of CBFS

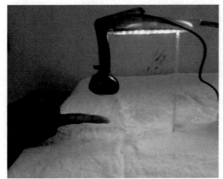

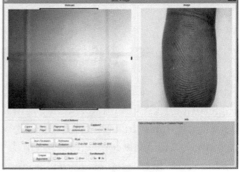

(a) Contactless fingerprint acquisition system

(b) User's interface

Figure 3. User's interface

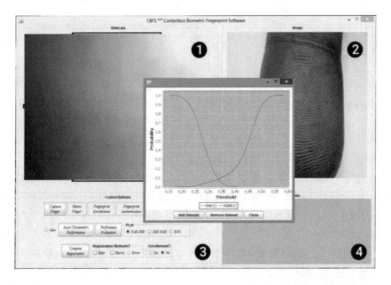

In the previous figure, the area marked "1" is used to present the finger for capture while the area marked "2" is used to show the captured image. The button "Insert Parameters Performances" is used to extract and save image signatures.

The distance between the camera and the finger, and the resolution of the output image are two important parameters in contactless image acquisition. In fact, many distances have been tested, and we find the optimum one is 8cm between the camera and the finger. In our experiment, the camera ensures a resolution of 360 dpi.

Figure 5 shows in (a) and (b) two fingerprints images acquired by a contact of sensor, while Figure 4 shows in (a) and (b) two images obtained using our camera. We notice that, a paramount advantage of contactless image acquisition is that a large image area can be captured quickly compared touch based systems.

Figure 4. Two different acquisitions of the same finger obtained by our webcam

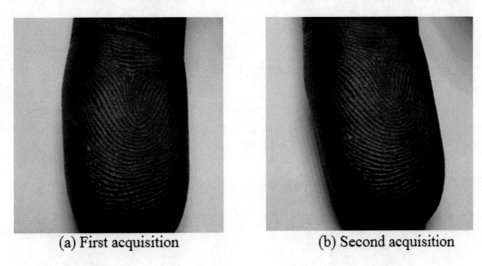

(a) First acquisition　　　　　　　　　　(b) Second acquisition

Figure 5. Two different acquisitions of the same finger obtained by contact-based system (FVC2004 DB1)

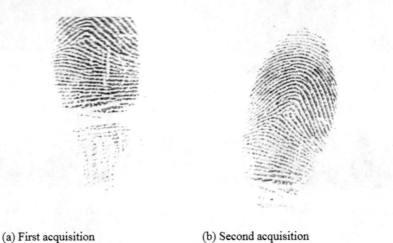

(a) First acquisition　　　　　　　　(b) Second acquisition

Pre-Processing Phase

Pre-processing plays a significant role in improving image contrast. We have used histogram equalization for image enhancement. Figure 6.a shows a contactless acquisition fingerprint image while Figure 6.b shows the enhanced image of Figure 6.a. Figure 6.c and 6.d show respectively the histogram of Figure 6.a and Figure 6.b. Images from webcam experiments are Red-Green-Blue color images. The image is converted to grey scale image using the CBFS.

FEATURE CHARACTERISATION

The used features are bifurcation points and ending points (Figures 8 and 9). In order to get the streaks in the image of fingerprint, a photometric adaptive threshold

Figure 6. Images and histograms

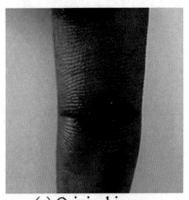

(a) Original image

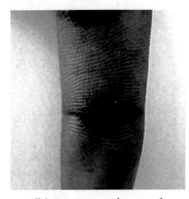

(b) Image enhanced

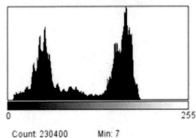

Count: 230400   Min: 7
Mean: 110.169   Max: 214
StdDev: 56.466   Mode: 168 (4893)

(c) Histogram of (a)

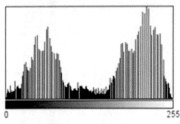

Count: 230400   Min: 0
Mean: 135.925   Max: 255
StdDev: 74.907   Mode: 215 (4893)

(d) Histogram of (b)

method has been developed and presented in (Djara et al., 2010). Two thresholds are defined i.e. S_s .and S_h corresponding to the mean of a square framework and the mean of a hexagonal framework. A pixel P is deleted or not by comparing its value with S_s .and S_h . Here we introduce the foreground regions extraction before streaks extraction. The extraction phase of the streaks is linked to the extraction foreground regions. For this purpose, we have applied a filter to the image in order to define its contour. Then a binary mask is subsequently applied to the image filter, which allows to have an image defining the contour of the fingerprint. This contour image is used for the extraction of foreground regions (see Figure 7).

The image from the photometric adaptive threshold is skeletonized in order to get minutiae (bifurcation points and ending points). The minutiae are extracted by scanning the local neighborhood of each ridge pixel in the image using a 3×3 window of Table 1. The crossing number (CN) is then computed, which is defined as half the sum of the differences between pairs of adjacent pixels in the eight-neighborhood as presented in (Arcelli & Baja, 1984; Mehtre, 1993). We have:

$$CN = \frac{1}{2}\sum_{i=1}^{8}\left|P_i - P_{i-1}\right|, \quad P_8 = P_0. \tag{1}$$

Figure 7. Main steps of the extraction of the foreground regions

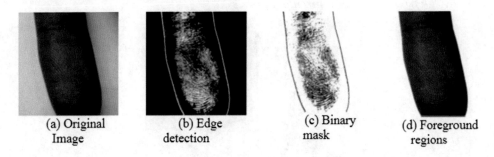

| (a) Original Image | (b) Edge detection | (c) Binary mask | (d) Foreground regions |

Table 1. 3×3 operation window

P_1	P_2	P_3
P_8	P	P_4
P_7	P_6	P_5

If $CN = 1$ then the ridge pixel is a ridge ending, while if $CN = 3$ the ridge pixel is a ridge bifurcation otherwise it is a non-minutiae point.

Ridge Bifurcation Orientation Characterization

In our approach, for bifurcation points we define a window W of size S*S and of central pixel the minutiae points. We count 3 points P_1, P_2, and P_3 around the perimeter of the window as shown in Figure 8.

For a given bifurcation point B_j, we compute the orientations as being (Equations 2, 3 and 4):

$$\theta_{1j} = Arccos\left(\frac{\overrightarrow{B_jP_1}.\overrightarrow{B_jP_2}}{B_jP_1 \times B_jP_2} \right) \tag{2}$$

$$\theta_{2j} = Arccos\left(\frac{\overrightarrow{B_jP_2}.\overrightarrow{B_jP_3}}{B_jP_2 \times B_jP_3} \right) \tag{3}$$

Figure 8. Orientations of bifurcation points

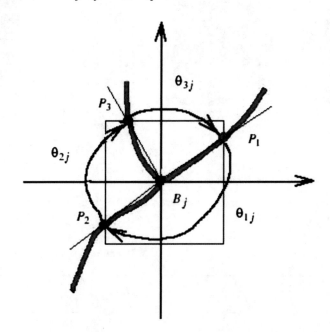

$$\theta_{3j} = Arccos \left(\frac{\overrightarrow{B_jP_3}.\overrightarrow{B_jP_1}}{B_jP_3 \times B_jP_1} \right) \tag{4}$$

(.) stands for the scalar product.

($\times$) stands for the ordinary multiplication.

For an image with M validated bifurcation points, we build a matrix of M rows and 5 columns. Each point is represented by a row in the matrix. The columns represent the coordinates and the angles between them are the branches.

$$\begin{pmatrix} x_1 & y_1 & \theta_{11} & \theta_{21} & \theta_{31} \\ \dots & \dots & \dots & \dots & \dots \\ x_M & y_M & \theta_{1M} & \theta_{2M} & \theta_{3M} \end{pmatrix} \tag{5}$$

Ridge Ending Orientation Characterization

We define two concentric windows $W_1 F_0$ and $W_2 F_1$ of central point the ridge ending point and for size S_1 and S_2. On the perimeter of $F_1 W_1$ we have a point P_1 and on the perimeter of $W_2 F_0$ we have a point $P_2 P_0$ as shown on figure 9. For a given ending point T_i, the orientation is defined as the angle between vectors.

$$\theta_i = Arccos \left(\frac{\overrightarrow{T_iP_0}.\overrightarrow{T_iP_1}}{T_iP_0 \times T_iP_1} \right) \tag{6}$$

(.) stands for the scalar product.

($\times$) stands for the ordinary multiplication.

For an image with N validated ending points, we build a matrix of N rows and 3 columns. Each row of the matrix represents an ending points. The columns represent the coordinates of the point and the angle of the branch.

$$\begin{pmatrix} x_1 & y_1 & \theta_1 \\ \dots & \dots & \dots \\ x_N & y_N & \theta_{1N} \end{pmatrix} \tag{7}$$

Figure 9. Orientation of ridge ending points

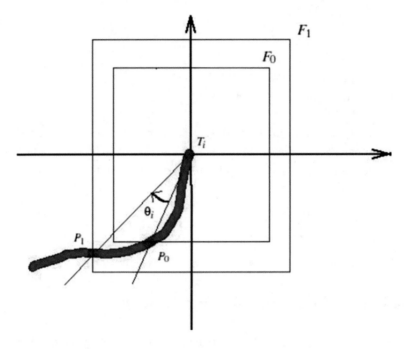

RIDGE BIFURCATION AND RIDGE ENDING SIMILARITY

In this section, we introduce the ridge bifurcation (Rb) and the ridge ending points (Re) similarity (Rb-Re Similarity). Let $I_t(Rb)$ and $I_{t+d}(Rb)$ be the template and query fingerprint Rb sets respectively. Let $I_t(Re)$ and $I_{t+d}(Re)$ be the template and query fingerprint Re sets respectively. We have:

$$I_t(b) = \{b_1, b_2, \ldots, b_M\} b_j = \left(x_j, y_j, \theta_{1j}, \theta_{2j}, \theta_{3j}\right); \quad j \in \left[1 \ldots M\right] \tag{8}$$

$$I_{t+d}(b) = \{b'_1, b'_2, \ldots, b'_{M'}\} b'_P = \left(x'_p, y'_p, \theta'_{1p}, \theta'_{2p}, \theta'_{3p}\right); \quad p \in \left[1 \ldots M'\right] \tag{9}$$

$$I_t(t) = \{t_1, t_2, \ldots, t_N\} t_i = \left(x_i, y_i, \theta_i\right); \quad i \in \left[1 \ldots N\right] \tag{10}$$

$$I_{t+d}(t) = \{t'_1, t'_2, \ldots, t'_{N'}\} t'_q = (x'_q, y'_q, \theta'_q); \quad q \in [1 \ldots N'] \tag{11}$$

where b_j and b'_p represent respectively the jth and the pth row of matrix of the Rb. t_i and t'_q represent respectively the ith and q^{th} row of matrix of the Re. It is assumed, that there is correspondence between b_j and b'_q if the Euclidean distance (ed) between them is smaller than a given tolerance d_0 and orientation differences (od) of their respective angles are smaller than angular tolerances $\theta_0, \alpha_0, \beta_0$:

$$ed(b_j, b'_p) = \sqrt{(x_j - x'_p)^2 + (y_j - y'_p)^2} \leq d_0 \quad and \tag{12}$$

$$\begin{cases} od(b_j, b'_p)_1 = min\left(\left|\theta_{1j} - \theta'_{1j}\right|, 360 - \left|\theta_{1j} - \theta'_{1j}\right|\right) \leq \theta_0 \\ \qquad\qquad and \\ od(b_j, b'_p)_2 = min\left(\left|\theta_{2j} - \theta'_{2j}\right|, 360 - \left|\theta_{2j} - \theta'_{2j}\right|\right) \leq \alpha_0 \\ \qquad\qquad or \\ od(b_j, b'_p)_3 = min\left(\left|\theta_{3j} - \theta'_{3j}\right|, 360 - \left|\theta_{3j} - \theta'_{3j}\right|\right) \leq \beta_0 \end{cases} \tag{13}$$

By the same way, we assume that there is a correspondence between t_i and t'_q if the euclidean distance (ed) between them is smaller than a given tolerance d_0 and the orientation difference (od) between them is smaller than an angular tolerance θ_0.

$$ed(t_i, t'_q) = \sqrt{(x_i - x'_q)^2 + (y_i - y'_q)^2} \leq d_0 \quad and \tag{14}$$

$$od(t_i, t'_q) = min\left(\left|\theta_i - \theta'_q\right|, 360 - \left|\theta_i - \theta'_q\right|\right) \leq \theta_0 \tag{15}$$

MINUTIAE MATCHING

The nature of the deformation between our images is a rigid transformation expressed by:

$$
\begin{pmatrix} x' \\ y' \\ 1 \end{pmatrix} = \begin{pmatrix} u_0 & u_1 & u_2 \\ v_0 & v_1 & v_2 \\ 0 & 0 & 1 \end{pmatrix} \begin{pmatrix} x \\ y \\ 1 \end{pmatrix} \tag{16}
$$

with

$$
\begin{aligned}
&u_0 = \cos(\theta) \quad u_1 = -\sin(\theta) \quad u_2 = \left(1 - \cos(\theta)\right)x_0 + y_0 \sin(\theta) + t_x \cos(\theta) - t_y \sin(\theta) \\
&v_0 = \sin(\theta) \quad v_1 = \cos(\theta) \quad v_2 = \left(1 - \cos(\theta)\right)x_0 + y_0 \sin(\theta) + t_x \sin(\theta) + t_y \cos(\theta)
\end{aligned} \tag{17}
$$

where $M_0 \begin{pmatrix} x_0 \\ y_0 \end{pmatrix}$ is the center of rotation, θ the angle of rotation, $\begin{pmatrix} t_x \\ t_y \end{pmatrix}$ the coordinates of the translation vector and $M'\begin{pmatrix} x' \\ y' \end{pmatrix}$, the transform of $M\begin{pmatrix} x \\ y \end{pmatrix}$.

In the research phase of the best deformation, the correspondence between the sets of control points is obtained by calculating the descriptor vector of Zernike moments on a window of size $L \times L$ centered at each point, taking into account ridges bifurcations. Comparison of correlation coefficients between the descriptors vectors of Zernike moments helps define the corresponding points. The estimation of parameters of the existing deformation between the images is performed using RANSAC algorithm (Random SAmple Consensus) that suppresses wrong matches. The correspondence between these two sets of control points is obtained by following these steps:

- Subdivide each image into thumbnail size $L \times L$ centered on each point B_i.
- For each thumbnail centered on this point B_i, construct the descriptor vector of Zernike moments M_z as follows:

$$
M_z = \left(\left| z_{11} \right|, \ldots, \left| z_{pq} \right|, \ldots, \left| z_{55} \right| \right) \tag{18}
$$

where $\left| z_{pq} \right|$ is the module of Zernike moments. We have used as the highest order of moments 5 after several experimental trials. Although the higher order moments are the fine details of the image, they are more sensitive to noise than lower order moments. The Zernike moment of order p with repetition q for a continuous image function $f(x, y)$, that vanishes outside the unit disk is:

$$Z_{pq} = \frac{p+1}{\pi} \iint\limits_{x^2+y^2 \leq 1} V_{pq}^*(\rho, \theta) f(x, y) \, dx \, dy \tag{19}$$

If F is the digital image of f, the above equation becomes:

$$Z_{pq} = \frac{p+1}{\pi} \sum_{x=1}^{N} \sum_{y=1}^{N} V_{pq}^*(\rho, \theta) F(x, y) \tag{20}$$

with

$$V_{pq}(\rho, \theta) = R_{pq}(\rho) e^{iq\theta} \tag{21}$$

where R_{pq} is the Zernike radial polynomials of order p with repetition q in (ρ, θ) polar coordinates given by:

$$R_{pq}(\rho) = \sum_{s=0}^{\frac{p-|q|}{2}} \frac{(-1)^s (p-s)!}{s! \left(\dfrac{p+|q|}{2} - s \right)! \left(\dfrac{p-|q|}{2} - s \right)!} \rho^{p-2s} \tag{22}$$

In the above equation p is a non-negative integer, ($p \geq 0$), and q positive and negative integers subject to the constraints:

$$\begin{cases} p - |q| \; is \; even \\ |q| \leq p \end{cases} \tag{23}$$

where V_{pq}^* denote complex conjugate of V_{pq}, $\rho = \sqrt{x^2 + y^2} \leq 1$ and $\theta = tan^{-1}\left(\dfrac{y}{x} \right)$.

- For any point r_i of the reference image, we suppose that its corresponding e_i of input image is from a set of points located within a certain radius R_0 around r_i. The radius R_0 limits the search for corresponding and therefore, dramatically reduces the number of comparisons to achieve in order to find out the corresponding points.
- The matching process is performed by calculating the correlation coefficients between the two descriptor vectors. The corresponding points are those which give the maximum value of correlation coefficients.

The correlation coefficient between two vectors of the features $X\left(x_1,\ldots,x_n\right)$ and $Y\left(y_1,\ldots,y_n\right)$ is given by the following formula:

$$C = \frac{\sum_{i=1}^{n}\left(x_i - \overline{x}\right)\left(y_i - \overline{y}\right)}{\sqrt{\sum_{i=1}^{n}\left(x_i - \overline{x}\right)^2} \times \sqrt{\sum_{i=1}^{n}\left(y_i - \overline{y}\right)^2}} \tag{24}$$

Figure 10. Determining the corresponding e_i (of input image) of a point r_i (of the reference image)

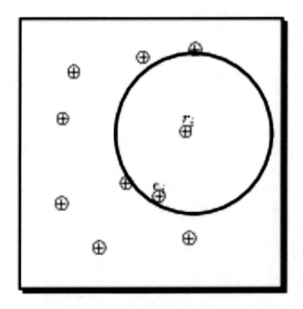

where $\bar{x}$ and $\bar{y}$ are averages of the two vectors X and Y respectively. If C is 0, the two vectors are not correlated. The two vectors are better correlated when C is far from 0 (near -1 or 1).

Once the sets of points $I_t(.)$ and $I_{t+d}(.)$ are aligned by applying the model of deformation given by Equation 16, the algorithm "Rb-Re Similarity" starts. The formal algorithm is the following (see figure 11).

Figure 11. Rb-Re Similarity

1: Let n_0 be the maximum number of matching minutiae computed after performing all fingerprint rigid transformation.
2: Let n_1 be the maximum number of matching Rb computed after performing all fingerprint rigid transformation.
3: Let n_2 be the maximum number of matching Re computed after performing all fingerprint rigid transformation.
4: **for** $i \leftarrow 1, M$ **do**
5:     **for** $j \leftarrow 1, M'$ **do**
6:         **if** RBSIMILARITY(b_i, b'_j) **then**
7:             $n_1 \leftarrow n_1 + 1$.
8:             *break.*
9:         **end if**
10:     **end for**
11: **end for**
12: **for** $i \leftarrow 1, N$ **do**
13:     **for** $j \leftarrow 1, N'$ **do**
14:         **if** RESIMILARITY(t_i, t'_j) **then**
15:             $n_2 \leftarrow n_2 + 1$.
16:             *break.*
17:         **end if**
18:     **end for**
19: **end for**
20: $n_0 \leftarrow n_1 + n_2$.
21: **function** RBSIMILARITY(a, b)
22:     **if** $ed(a,b) \leq d_0$ && ($od(a,b)_1 \leq \theta_0$ && ($od(a,b)_2 \leq \alpha_0 \parallel od(a,b)_3 \leq \beta_0$)) **then**
23:         **return** *true*
24:     **else**
25:         **return** *false*
26:     **end if**
27: **end function**
28: **function** RESIMILARITY(a, b)
29:     **if** $ed(a,b) \leq d_0$ && $od(a,b) \leq \theta_0$ **then**
30:         **return** *true*
31:     **else**
32:         **return** *false*
33:     **end if**
34: **end function**

The purpose of a match algorithm is to evaluate the similarity of two fingerprints, and to judge whether they belong to the same finger or not. In our method, the similarity value is computed using the formula presented by Galy (2005):

$$MS = \frac{N}{\max\left(N_{I_t}, N_{I_{t+d}}\right)} \tag{25}$$

where N_{I_t} and $N_{I_{t+d}}$ are the template and query fingerprint minutiae sets respectively, and N is the amount of matching minutiae pairs.

We created a database (available in http://refod.net/images/Fingerprint/DB2.zip) containing 420 prints with 28 different sets of fingers, each with 15 acquisitions.

Let F_{ij} be the jth fingerprint sample of the ith finger and T_{ij} the corresponding template ($1 \leq i \leq n; 1 \leq j \leq m$). The template T_{ij} are computed from the corresponding F_{ij} and stored on a disk by our platform

For matching, we perform the following operations:

1. **Genuine Matching (GM):** Each fingerprint template T_{ij} is matched against the fingerprint images F_{ik} ($k \neq j$) and the corresponding Genuine Matching Score gms_{ijk} are stored.

2. **Impostor Matching (IM):** Each fingerprint template T_{k1} is matched against the fingerprint images from different fingers F_{ij} (i > k) and the corresponding Impostor Matching Score ims_{ik} are stored.

The number of matching is defined in each case:

Case 1: $NGRA = \left\| \left\{ gms_{ijk}, i \in [1 \ldots n], 1 \leq j \neq k \leq m \right\} \right\| = n * m * (m - 1)$. In our case NGRA = 5880. NGRA is the Number of Genuine Recognition Attempts.

Case 2:
$$NIRA = \left\| \left\{ ims_{ik}, i \in [1 \ldots n], 1 \leq j \neq k \leq m \right\} \right\| = m \left[(n - 1) + (n - 2) + \ldots + 1 \right].$$
In our case NIRA = 5670. NIRA is the Number of Imposter Recognition Attempts.

The GM distribution and the IM distribution are computed and graphically reported to show how the algorithm differentiates the classes. The FMR (False

Match Rate) and FNMR(False Non-Match Rate) curves are computed from the above distributions for the threshold t ranking from 0 to 1.

The pairs (FMR(t), FNMR(t)) are plotted for the same value of t to obtained a ROC (Receiver Operating Characteristics) curve.

FMR(t) and FNMR(t) are defined by:

$$FMR(t) = \frac{card\left\{ims_{ik} \, / \, ims_{ik} \geq t\right\}}{NIRA} \tag{26}$$

$$FNMR(t) = \frac{card\left\{gms_{ik} \, / \, gms_{ijk} < t\right\}}{NGRA} \tag{27}$$

card denote the cardinality of a given set, FMR(t) denotes the percentage of $ims_{ik} \geq t$ and FNMR(t) denotes the percentage of $gms_{ijk} < t$.

EXPERIMENTAL RESULTS

Figure 12, shows in (a) GM and IM distributions. In (b) and (c) FMR-FNMR curves and ROC are respectively represented. We evaluate the algorithm performance by using Equal Error Rate (EER) where FMR = FNMR. We notice from figure 12-(b) that FMR and FNMR values are respectively 7.64% and 6.46% at a threshold (**th**) value of 0.33.

From the database, we achieved an EER to the order of 7.05%. The matching time is approximately 0.6s. The performance of our algorithm is acceptable. The results can be improved ensuring that the database does not contain such poor quality fingerprint images.

FUTURE RESEARCH DIRECTIONS

In a future work, the performance of our algorithms can be improved by taking into account the 3D fingerprint identification presented in (Ajay & Kwong, 2015; Hong Kong Polytechnic, 2013; Wang et al., 2010). We can also enhance our sensor by using a camera with flash instead of having a separate light device. The same sensor equipped with flash can be used to acquire the image of the face in the perspective of a multimodal system. This would result in a substantial saving for

Figure 12. GM-IM, FMR-FNMR curves and ROC

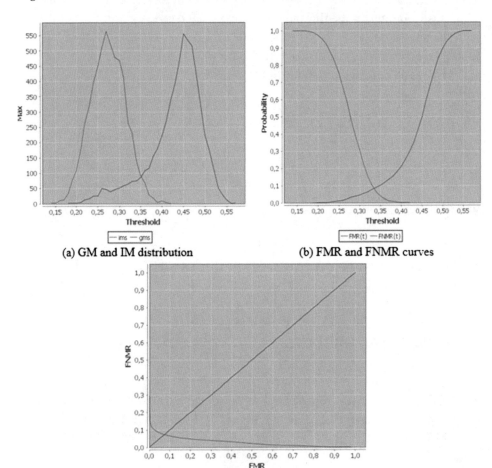

(a) GM and IM distribution   (b) FMR and FNMR curves

(c) FNMR = f(FMR)

the operational system to be developed. The biometric verification system proposed in this paper is based on the only fingerprint modality; it is a monomodal system. However, monomodal biometric systems have three main limitations: a limitation in terms of performance (physical characteristics variation), a limitation in terms of universality of use (absence of certain biometrics) and a limitation in terms of fraud detection (identity theft) (AlMahafzah et al., 2012; Allano, 2009; Ross, 2007). These limitations can be reduced or even eliminated by the joint use of several biometric systems which then form a multimodal biometric system. The contactless fingerprint can therefore be combined with the face in order to improve the performance, robustness and universality of the system to be developed. Since face recognition is by nature contactless, we will develop a fully contactless multimodal biometric system. Particular emphasis will be placed on the method of the scores fusion for the two modalities to be used.It will be the fusion of scores in a sequential approach adapted to the user. In all cases described above, the extracted features will be stored in a database for future comparisons. It will then raise the problem of protecting these stored templates against spoofing actions. One of the vulnerability levels of biometric verification systems is the ability to modify the template. To ensure the protection of the templates, the most used approach is the rigid transformation which performs a translation and a rotation (Moudjahdi et al., 2012) without modifying feature characteristics. This rigid transformation approach that uses the Hausdroff distance (Ali and Prakash, 2015) poses the problem of the security of the person to be authenticated. Indeed, in this approach, the parameters of transformation are provided by man. As a result, there is a risk that these parameters will be forgotten in the case of a memory disorder such as Alzheimer's. On the other hand, the individual who wants to authenticate can be attacked in order to remove the template protection settings. To eliminate these risks, we propose an innovative technique which consists in having the parameters of protection of the template provided by the computer. The implementation of this technique consists in first determining the coordinates of the center of mass of the registered biometric image. In a second step, the area of interest of size $N \times M$ having the characteristic points of the image is defined. The third and fourth steps will be respectively the computation of the Zernike Moment and the various associated modules. In the fifth and last step, a random choice will be made among the modules calculated to obtain the distance do.

CONCLUSION

In this paper, we investigated a fingerprint matching algorithm with only minutiae information as an approach for a supervised contactless biometric system. In this new context, our experiments show that fingerprint images can be well matched using the minutiae matching method. The performance of the algorithm is evaluated through a created database using the CBFS. As shown, we have led 5880 comparisons intra-class (Number of Genuine Recognition Attempts) and 5670 comparisons inter-class (Number of Imposter Recognition Attempts). The illustration of the results available in the contact context shows that the performance of our algorithms is acceptable. The results are encouraging with an Equal Error Rate around 7.05%.

Compared to the contact-based fingerprint verification method, the contactless method offers greater ease of use for users. The sensor used for acquiring the contactless image is very affordable. We will implement our algorithm for secure digital borrows contactless and define other original algorithm digitals fingerprint security without contact using the sphere of Pointcarré.

REFERENCES

Ali, S. S., & Prakash, S. (2015). Enhanced fingerprint Shell. *Signal Processing and Integrated Networks (SPIN), 2015 2nd International Conference on.* doi:10.1109/SPIN.2015.7095438

Allano, L. (2009). *La Biométrie multimodale: stratégies de fusion de scores et mesures de dépendance appliquées aux bases de personnes virtuelles* (Thèse de doctorat). Institut National des Télécommunications Paris.

AlMahafzah, H., & AlRwashdeh, M. Z. (2012). A survey of multibiometric systems. *International Journal of Computers and Applications, 43*(15).

Arcelli, C., & Di Baja, G. S. (1985). A width-independent fast thinning algorithm. *IEEE Transactions on Pattern Analysis and Machine Intelligence, 4*(7), 463–474. doi:10.1109/TPAMI.1985.4767685 PMID:21869284

Bhowmik, U. K., Ashrafi, A., & Adhami, R. R. (2009). A Fingerprint Verification Algorithm Using the Smallest Minimum Sum of Closest Euclidean Distance. In *Electrical, Communications, and Computers, 2009.CONIELECOMP 2009. International Conference on* (pp. 90-95). IEEE. doi:10.1109/CONIELECOMP.2009.57

Djara, T., Assogba, M. K., & Nait-Ali, A. (2010). Caractérisation spatiale des empreintes de l'index en analyse biométrique. *Actes du CARI 2010*, 501-508.

Galbally, J., Fierrez, J., Ortega-Garcia, J., & Cappelli, R. (2014). Fingerprint Anti-spoofing in Biometric Systems. In S. Marcel, M. Nixon, & S. Li (Eds.), *Handbook of Biometric Anti-Spoofing. Advances in Computer Vision and Pattern Recognition.* London: Springer. doi:10.1007/978-1-4471-6524-8_3

Galy, N. (2005). *Etude d'un système complet de reconnaissance d'empreintes digitales pour un capteur microsystème à balayage* (Thesis). Institut National Polytechnique de Grenoble - INPG.

He, Y., Tian, J., Luo, X., & Zhang, T. (2002). Image enhancement and minutiae matching in fingerprint verification. *Pattern Recognition Letters*, 1349–1360.

Hiew, B., Teoh, A., & Pang, Y. (2007). Touch-less fingerprint recognition system. *ICB, LNCS, 3832*, 24–29.

Ito, K., & Morita, A. (2009). A fingerprint recognition algorithm using phase-based image matching for low quality fingerprints. IEEE.

Jain, A., Lin Hong, , & Bolle, R. (1997). On-line fingerprint verification. *IEEE Transactions on Pattern Analysis and Machine Intelligence, 19*(4), 302–314. doi:10.1109/34.587996

Jain, A., Prabhakar, S., Hong, L., & Pankanti, S. (2000). Filterbank-based fingerprint matching. *IEEE Transactions on Image Processing, 9*(5), 846–859. doi:10.1109/83.841531 PMID:18255456

Khalila, M. S., Mohamada, D., Khanb, M. K., & Al-Nuzailia, Q. (2010). Fingerprint verification using statistical descriptors. *Digital Signal Processing, 20*(4), 1264–1273. doi:10.1016/j.dsp.2009.12.002

Kumar, A., & Kwong, C. (2015, March). Towards contactless, low-cost, and accurate 3D fingerprint identification. *IEEE Transactions on Pattern Analysis and Machine Intelligence, 37*(3), 681–696. doi:10.1109/TPAMI.2014.2339818 PMID:26353269

Kumar, R., Chandra, P., & Hanmandlu, M. (2012). Statistical descriptors for fingerprint matching. *International Journal of Computers and Applications, 59*(16), 24–27. doi:10.5120/9633-4361

Labati, R. D., Genovese, A., & Piuri, V. (2013). Fabio Scotti Contactless fingerprint recognition: A neural approach for perspective and rotation effects reduction. *Computational Intelligence in Biometrics and Identity Management (CIBIM), 2013 IEEE Workshop on.*

Liu, X., Pedersen, M., Charrier, C., Cheikh, F. A., & Bours, P. (2016). *An improved 3-step contactless fingerprint image enhancement approach for minutia detecting.* IEEE.

Maltoni, D., Maio, D., Jai, A. K., & Prabhakar, A. (2003). *Handbook of fingerprint recognition* (2nd ed.). Springer.

Marasco, E., & Ross, A. (2015). A Survey on anti-spoofing schemes for fingerprint recognition systems. *ACM Computing Surveys, 47*(2).

Matsumoto, T., Matsumoto, H., Yamada, K., & Ho-shino, S. (2002). Impact of artificial "gummy" fingers on fingerprint systems. SPIE, 4677.

Medina-pérez, M. A., & Gracia-Barroto, M. (2012). al, Improving fingerprint verification using minutiae triplets. *Pattern Recognition*, 3418–3437.

Mehtre, B. M. (1993). Fingerprint image analysis for automatic identification. *Machine Vision and Applications*, 6(2), 124–139. doi:10.1007/BF01211936

Mil'shtein, S., Palma, J., Liessner, C., Baier, M., Pillai, A., & Shendye, A. (2008). *Line scanner for biometric applications*. Traitement du Signal.

Milshtein, S., Pillai, A., Kunnil, V. O., Baier, M., & Bustos, P. (2011). Applications of Contactless Fingerprinting, Recent Application in Biometric. In Tech.

Mojtaba, M. W. B. (2010, January). Liveness and Spoofing in Fingerprint Identification Issues and Challenges. Academic Press.

Moujahdi, C., Ghouzali, S., Mikram, M., Rziza, M., & Bebis, G. (2012). Spiral cube for biometric template protection. In *Imageand Signal Processing* (Vol. 7340, pp. 235–244). Springer. doi:10.1007/978-3-642-31254-0_27

Pankanti, S., Prabhakar, S., & Jain, A. (2002). On the individuality of fingerprints. *IEEE Trans. Pattern Anal.*, 24(8), 1010–1025. doi:10.1109/TPAMI.2002.1023799

Parziale, G., Santana, E.-D., & Hauke, R. (2006). The surround imager: A multi-camera touchless device to acquire 3d rolled-equivalent fingerprints. *ICB, LNCS*, 3832, 244–250.

Pillai, A., & Mil'shtein, S. (2012). Can Contactless fingerprint be compared to existing database? *Homeland Security (HST), 2012 IEEE Conference on Technologies for*.

Qader, H. A. (2006). *Fingerprint recognition using zernike moments*. Internationnal Arab Journal of Information Technology.

Ross, A. (2007). An introduction to multibiometrics. *Proc. of the 15th European Signal Processing Conference (EUSIPCO)*.

Sha, L. F., Zhao, F., & Tang, X. O. (2003). Improved fingercode for filterbank-based fingerprint matching. *International Conference on Image Processing, 2*, 895-898.

The Hong Kong Polytechnic University 3D Fingerprint Images Database. (2013). Retrieved from http://www.comp.polyu.edu.hk/~csajaykr/3Dfingerprint.htm

Tico & Kuosmanen. (2003). Fingerprint matching using an orientation-based minutia descriptor. *IEEE Trans. PAMI.*, 25(8), 1009-1014.

Virk & Maini. (2012). Fingerprint image enhancement and minutiae matching in fingerprint verification. *Journal of Computing Technologies*.

Wang, Y., Lau, D. L., & Hassebrook, L. G. (2010). Fit-sphere unwrapping and performance analysis of 3D fingerprints. *Applied Optics*, *49*(4), 592–600. doi:10.1364/AO.49.000592 PMID:20119006

Yin, X., Hu, J., & Xu, J. (2016). Contactless fingerprint enhancement via intrinsic image decomposition and guided image filtering. *Industrial Electronics and Applications (ICIEA), 2016 IEEE 11th Conference on.*

Related References

To continue our tradition of advancing academic research, we have compiled a list of recommended IGI Global readings. These references will provide additional information and guidance to further enrich your knowledge and assist you with your own research and future publications.

Adeyemo, O. (2013). The nationwide health information network: A biometric approach to prevent medical identity theft. In *User-driven healthcare: Concepts, methodologies, tools, and applications* (pp. 1636–1649). Hershey, PA: IGI Global. doi:10.4018/978-1-4666-2770-3.ch081

Adler, M., & Henman, P. (2009). Justice beyond the courts: The implications of computerisation for procedural justice in social security. In A. Martínez & P. Abat (Eds.), *E-justice: Using information communication technologies in the court system* (pp. 65–86). Hershey, PA: IGI Global. doi:10.4018/978-1-59904-998-4.ch005

Aflalo, E., & Gabay, E. (2013). An information system for coping with student dropout. In L. Tomei (Ed.), *Learning tools and teaching approaches through ICT advancements* (pp. 176–187). Hershey, PA: IGI Global. doi:10.4018/978-1-4666-2017-9.ch016

Ahmed, M. A., Janssen, M., & van den Hoven, J. (2012). Value sensitive transfer (VST) of systems among countries: Towards a framework. *International Journal of Electronic Government Research*, 8(1), 26–42. doi:10.4018/jegr.2012010102

Aikins, S. K. (2008). Issues and trends in internet-based citizen participation. In G. Garson & M. Khosrow-Pour (Eds.), *Handbook of research on public information technology* (pp. 31–40). Hershey, PA: IGI Global. doi:10.4018/978-1-59904-857-4.ch004

Aikins, S. K. (2009). A comparative study of municipal adoption of internet-based citizen participation. In C. Reddick (Ed.), *Handbook of research on strategies for local e-government adoption and implementation: Comparative studies* (pp. 206–230). Hershey, PA: IGI Global. doi:10.4018/978-1-60566-282-4.ch011

Aikins, S. K. (2012). Improving e-government project management: Best practices and critical success factors. In *Digital democracy: Concepts, methodologies, tools, and applications* (pp. 1314–1332). Hershey, PA: IGI Global. doi:10.4018/978-1-4666-1740-7.ch065

Akabawi, M. S. (2011). Ghabbour group ERP deployment: Learning from past technology failures. In E. Business Research and Case Center (Ed.), Cases on business and management in the MENA region: New trends and opportunities (pp. 177-203). Hershey, PA: IGI Global. doi:10.4018/978-1-60960-583-4.ch012

Akabawi, M. S. (2013). Ghabbour group ERP deployment: Learning from past technology failures. In *Industrial engineering: Concepts, methodologies, tools, and applications* (pp. 933–958). Hershey, PA: IGI Global. doi:10.4018/978-1-4666-1945-6.ch051

Akbulut, A. Y., & Motwani, J. (2008). Integration and information sharing in e-government. In G. Putnik & M. Cruz-Cunha (Eds.), *Encyclopedia of networked and virtual organizations* (pp. 729–734). Hershey, PA: IGI Global. doi:10.4018/978-1-59904-885-7.ch096

Akers, E. J. (2008). Technology diffusion in public administration. In G. Garson & M. Khosrow-Pour (Eds.), *Handbook of research on public information technology* (pp. 339–348). Hershey, PA: IGI Global. doi:10.4018/978-1-59904-857-4.ch033

Al-Shafi, S. (2008). Free wireless internet park services: An investigation of technology adoption in Qatar from a citizens' perspective. *Journal of Cases on Information Technology, 10*(3), 21–34. doi:10.4018/jcit.2008070103

Al-Shafi, S., & Weerakkody, V. (2009). Implementing free wi-fi in public parks: An empirical study in Qatar. *International Journal of Electronic Government Research, 5*(3), 21–35. doi:10.4018/jegr.2009070102

Aladwani, A. M. (2002). Organizational actions, computer attitudes and end-user satisfaction in public organizations: An empirical study. In C. Snodgrass & E. Szewczak (Eds.), *Human factors in information systems* (pp. 153–168). Hershey, PA: IGI Global. doi:10.4018/978-1-931777-10-0.ch012

Aladwani, A. M. (2002). Organizational actions, computer attitudes, and end-user satisfaction in public organizations: An empirical study. *Journal of Organizational and End User Computing, 14*(1), 42–49. doi:10.4018/joeuc.2002010104

Allen, B., Juillet, L., Paquet, G., & Roy, J. (2005). E-government and private-public partnerships: Relational challenges and strategic directions. In M. Khosrow-Pour (Ed.), *Practicing e-government: A global perspective* (pp. 364–382). Hershey, PA: IGI Global. doi:10.4018/978-1-59140-637-2.ch016

Alshawaf, A., & Knalil, O. E. (2008). IS success factors and IS organizational impact: Does ownership type matter in Kuwait? *International Journal of Enterprise Information Systems, 4*(2), 13–33. doi:10.4018/jeis.2008040102

Ambali, A. R. (2009). Digital divide and its implication on Malaysian e-government: Policy initiatives. In H. Rahman (Ed.), *Social and political implications of data mining: Knowledge management in e-government* (pp. 267–287). Hershey, PA: IGI Global. doi:10.4018/978-1-60566-230-5.ch016

Amoretti, F. (2007). Digital international governance. In A. Anttiroiko & M. Malkia (Eds.), *Encyclopedia of digital government* (pp. 365–370). Hershey, PA: IGI Global. doi:10.4018/978-1-59140-789-8.ch056

Amoretti, F. (2008). Digital international governance. In A. Anttiroiko (Ed.), *Electronic government: Concepts, methodologies, tools, and applications* (pp. 688–696). Hershey, PA: IGI Global. doi:10.4018/978-1-59904-947-2.ch058

Amoretti, F. (2008). E-government at supranational level in the European Union. In A. Anttiroiko (Ed.), *Electronic government: Concepts, methodologies, tools, and applications* (pp. 1047–1055). Hershey, PA: IGI Global. doi:10.4018/978-1-59904-947-2.ch079

Amoretti, F. (2008). E-government regimes. In A. Anttiroiko (Ed.), *Electronic government: Concepts, methodologies, tools, and applications* (pp. 3846–3856). Hershey, PA: IGI Global. doi:10.4018/978-1-59904-947-2.ch280

Amoretti, F. (2009). Electronic constitution: A Braudelian perspective. In F. Amoretti (Ed.), *Electronic constitution: Social, cultural, and political implications* (pp. 1–19). Hershey, PA: IGI Global. doi:10.4018/978-1-60566-254-1.ch001

Amoretti, F., & Musella, F. (2009). Institutional isomorphism and new technologies. In M. Khosrow-Pour (Ed.), *Encyclopedia of information science and technology* (2nd ed.; pp. 2066–2071). Hershey, PA: IGI Global. doi:10.4018/978-1-60566-026-4.ch325

Andersen, K. V., & Henriksen, H. Z. (2007). E-government research: Capabilities, interaction, orientation, and values. In D. Norris (Ed.), *Current issues and trends in e-government research* (pp. 269–288). Hershey, PA: IGI Global. doi:10.4018/978-1-59904-283-1.ch013

Anderson, K. V., & Henriksen, H. Z. (2005). The first leg of e-government research: Domains and application areas 1998-2003. *International Journal of Electronic Government Research*, *1*(4), 26–44. doi:10.4018/jegr.2005100102

Anttiroiko, A. (2009). Democratic e-governance. In M. Khosrow-Pour (Ed.), *Encyclopedia of information science and technology* (2nd ed.; pp. 990–995). Hershey, PA: IGI Global. doi:10.4018/978-1-60566-026-4.ch158

Association, I. R. (2010). *Networking and telecommunications: Concepts, methodologies, tools and applications* (Vols. 1–3). Hershey, PA: IGI Global. doi:10.4018/978-1-60566-986-1

Association, I. R. (2010). *Web-based education: Concepts, methodologies, tools and applications* (Vols. 1–3). Hershey, PA: IGI Global. doi:10.4018/978-1-61520-963-7

Baker, P. M., Bell, A., & Moon, N. W. (2009). Accessibility issues in municipal wireless networks. In C. Reddick (Ed.), *Handbook of research on strategies for local e-government adoption and implementation: Comparative studies* (pp. 569–588). Hershey, PA: IGI Global. doi:10.4018/978-1-60566-282-4.ch030

Becker, S. A., Keimer, R., & Muth, T. (2010). A case on university and community collaboration: The sci-tech entrepreneurial training services (ETS) program. In S. Becker & R. Niebuhr (Eds.), *Cases on technology innovation: Entrepreneurial successes and pitfalls* (pp. 68–90). Hershey, PA: IGI Global. doi:10.4018/978-1-61520-609-4.ch003

Becker, S. A., Keimer, R., & Muth, T. (2012). A case on university and community collaboration: The sci-tech entrepreneurial training services (ETS) program. In Regional development: Concepts, methodologies, tools, and applications (pp. 947-969). Hershey, PA: IGI Global. doi:10.4018/978-1-4666-0882-5.ch507

Bernardi, R. (2012). Information technology and resistance to public sector reforms: A case study in Kenya. In T. Papadopoulos & P. Kanellis (Eds.), *Public sector reform using information technologies: Transforming policy into practice* (pp. 59–78). Hershey, PA: IGI Global. doi:10.4018/978-1-60960-839-2.ch004

Bernardi, R. (2013). Information technology and resistance to public sector reforms: A case study in Kenya. In *User-driven healthcare: Concepts, methodologies, tools, and applications* (pp. 14–33). Hershey, PA: IGI Global. doi:10.4018/978-1-4666-2770-3.ch002

Bolívar, M. P., Pérez, M. D., & Hernández, A. M. (2012). Municipal e-government services in emerging economies: The Latin-American and Caribbean experiences. In Y. Chen & P. Chu (Eds.), *Electronic governance and cross-boundary collaboration: Innovations and advancing tools* (pp. 198–226). Hershey, PA: IGI Global. doi:10.4018/978-1-60960-753-1.ch011

Borycki, E. M., & Kushniruk, A. W. (2010). Use of clinical simulations to evaluate the impact of health information systems and ubiquitous computing devices upon health professional work. In S. Mohammed & J. Fiaidhi (Eds.), *Ubiquitous health and medical informatics: The ubiquity 2.0 trend and beyond* (pp. 552–573). Hershey, PA: IGI Global. doi:10.4018/978-1-61520-777-0.ch026

Borycki, E. M., & Kushniruk, A. W. (2011). Use of clinical simulations to evaluate the impact of health information systems and ubiquitous computing devices upon health professional work. In *Clinical technologies: Concepts, methodologies, tools and applications* (pp. 532–553). Hershey, PA: IGI Global. doi:10.4018/978-1-60960-561-2.ch220

Buchan, J. (2011). Developing a dynamic and responsive online learning environment: A case study of a large Australian university. In B. Czerkawski (Ed.), *Free and open source software for e-learning: Issues, successes and challenges* (pp. 92–109). Hershey, PA: IGI Global. doi:10.4018/978-1-61520-917-0.ch006

Buenger, A. W. (2008). Digital convergence and cybersecurity policy. In G. Garson & M. Khosrow-Pour (Eds.), *Handbook of research on public information technology* (pp. 395–405). Hershey, PA: IGI Global. doi:10.4018/978-1-59904-857-4.ch038

Burn, J. M., & Loch, K. D. (2002). The societal impact of world wide web - Key challenges for the 21st century. In A. Salehnia (Ed.), *Ethical issues of information systems* (pp. 88–106). Hershey, PA: IGI Global. doi:10.4018/978-1-931777-15-5.ch007

Burn, J. M., & Loch, K. D. (2003). The societal impact of the world wide web-Key challenges for the 21st century. In M. Khosrow-Pour (Ed.), *Advanced topics in information resources management* (Vol. 2, pp. 32–51). Hershey, PA: IGI Global. doi:10.4018/978-1-59140-062-2.ch002

Related References

Bwalya, K. J., Du Plessis, T., & Rensleigh, C. (2012). The "quicksilver initiatives" as a framework for e-government strategy design in developing economies. In K. Bwalya & S. Zulu (Eds.), *Handbook of research on e-government in emerging economies: Adoption, e-participation, and legal frameworks* (pp. 605–623). Hershey, PA: IGI Global. doi:10.4018/978-1-4666-0324-0.ch031

Cabotaje, C. E., & Alampay, E. A. (2013). Social media and citizen engagement: Two cases from the Philippines. In S. Saeed & C. Reddick (Eds.), *Human-centered system design for electronic governance* (pp. 225–238). Hershey, PA: IGI Global. doi:10.4018/978-1-4666-3640-8.ch013

Camillo, A., Di Pietro, L., Di Virgilio, F., & Franco, M. (2013). Work-groups conflict at PetroTech-Italy, S.R.L.: The influence of culture on conflict dynamics. In B. Christiansen, E. Turkina, & N. Williams (Eds.), *Cultural and technological influences on global business* (pp. 272–289). Hershey, PA: IGI Global. doi:10.4018/978-1-4666-3966-9.ch015

Capra, E., Francalanci, C., & Marinoni, C. (2008). Soft success factors for m-government. In A. Anttiroiko (Ed.), *Electronic government: Concepts, methodologies, tools, and applications* (pp. 1213–1233). Hershey, PA: IGI Global. doi:10.4018/978-1-59904-947-2.ch089

Cartelli, A. (2009). The implementation of practices with ICT as a new teaching-learning paradigm. In A. Cartelli & M. Palma (Eds.), *Encyclopedia of information communication technology* (pp. 413–417). Hershey, PA: IGI Global. doi:10.4018/978-1-59904-845-1.ch055

Charalabidis, Y., Lampathaki, F., & Askounis, D. (2010). Investigating the landscape in national interoperability frameworks. *International Journal of E-Services and Mobile Applications*, 2(4), 28–41. doi:10.4018/jesma.2010100103

Charalabidis, Y., Lampathaki, F., & Askounis, D. (2012). Investigating the landscape in national interoperability frameworks. In A. Scupola (Ed.), *Innovative mobile platform developments for electronic services design and delivery* (pp. 218–231). Hershey, PA: IGI Global. doi:10.4018/978-1-4666-1568-7.ch013

Chen, I. (2005). Distance education associations. In C. Howard, J. Boettcher, L. Justice, K. Schenk, P. Rogers, & G. Berg (Eds.), *Encyclopedia of distance learning* (pp. 599–612). Hershey, PA: IGI Global. doi:10.4018/978-1-59140-555-9.ch087

Chen, I. (2008). Distance education associations. In L. Tomei (Ed.), *Online and distance learning: Concepts, methodologies, tools, and applications* (pp. 562–579). Hershey, PA: IGI Global. doi:10.4018/978-1-59904-935-9.ch048

Chen, Y. (2008). Managing IT outsourcing for digital government. In A. Anttiroiko (Ed.), *Electronic government: Concepts, methodologies, tools, and applications* (pp. 3107–3114). Hershey, PA: IGI Global. doi:10.4018/978-1-59904-947-2.ch229

Chen, Y., & Dimitrova, D. V. (2006). Electronic government and online engagement: Citizen interaction with government via web portals. *International Journal of Electronic Government Research*, 2(1), 54–76. doi:10.4018/jegr.2006010104

Chen, Y., & Knepper, R. (2005). Digital government development strategies: Lessons for policy makers from a comparative perspective. In W. Huang, K. Siau, & K. Wei (Eds.), *Electronic government strategies and implementation* (pp. 394–420). Hershey, PA: IGI Global. doi:10.4018/978-1-59140-348-7.ch017

Chen, Y., & Knepper, R. (2008). Digital government development strategies: Lessons for policy makers from a comparative perspective. In H. Rahman (Ed.), *Developing successful ICT strategies: Competitive advantages in a global knowledge-driven society* (pp. 334–356). Hershey, PA: IGI Global. doi:10.4018/978-1-59904-654-9. ch017

Cherian, E. J., & Ryan, T. W. (2014). Incongruent needs: Why differences in the iron-triangle of priorities make health information technology adoption and use difficult. In C. El Morr (Ed.), *Research perspectives on the role of informatics in health policy and management* (pp. 209–221). Hershey, PA: IGI Global. doi:10.4018/978-1-4666-4321-5.ch012

Cho, H. J., & Hwang, S. (2010). Government 2.0 in Korea: Focusing on e-participation services. In C. Reddick (Ed.), *Politics, democracy and e-government: Participation and service delivery* (pp. 94–114). Hershey, PA: IGI Global. doi:10.4018/978-1-61520-933-0.ch006

Chorus, C., & Timmermans, H. (2010). Ubiquitous travel environments and travel control strategies: Prospects and challenges. In M. Wachowicz (Ed.), *Movement-aware applications for sustainable mobility: Technologies and approaches* (pp. 30–51). Hershey, PA: IGI Global. doi:10.4018/978-1-61520-769-5.ch003

Chuanshen, R. (2007). E-government construction and China's administrative litigation act. In A. Anttiroiko & M. Malkia (Eds.), *Encyclopedia of digital government* (pp. 507–510). Hershey, PA: IGI Global. doi:10.4018/978-1-59140-789-8.ch077

Ciaghi, A., & Villafiorita, A. (2012). Law modeling and BPR for public administration improvement. In K. Bwalya & S. Zulu (Eds.), *Handbook of research on e-government in emerging economies: Adoption, e-participation, and legal frameworks* (pp. 391–410). Hershey, PA: IGI Global. doi:10.4018/978-1-4666-0324-0.ch019

Ciaramitaro, B. L., & Skrocki, M. (2012). mHealth: Mobile healthcare. In B. Ciaramitaro (Ed.), Mobile technology consumption: Opportunities and challenges (pp. 99-109). Hershey, PA: IGI Global. doi:10.4018/978-1-61350-150-4.ch007

Comite, U. (2012). Innovative processes and managerial effectiveness of e-procurement in healthcare. In A. Manoharan & M. Holzer (Eds.), *Active citizen participation in e-government: A global perspective* (pp. 206–229). Hershey, PA: IGI Global. doi:10.4018/978-1-4666-0116-1.ch011

Cordella, A. (2013). E-government success: How to account for ICT, administrative rationalization, and institutional change. In J. Gil-Garcia (Ed.), *E-government success factors and measures: Theories, concepts, and methodologies* (pp. 40–51). Hershey, PA: IGI Global. doi:10.4018/978-1-4666-4058-0.ch003

Cropf, R. A. (2009). ICT and e-democracy. In M. Khosrow-Pour (Ed.), *Encyclopedia of information science and technology* (2nd ed.; pp. 1789–1793). Hershey, PA: IGI Global. doi:10.4018/978-1-60566-026-4.ch281

Cropf, R. A. (2009). The virtual public sphere. In M. Pagani (Ed.), *Encyclopedia of multimedia technology and networking* (2nd ed.; pp. 1525–1530). Hershey, PA: IGI Global. doi:10.4018/978-1-60566-014-1.ch206

D'Abundo, M. L. (2013). Electronic health record implementation in the United States healthcare industry: Making the process of change manageable. In V. Wang (Ed.), *Handbook of research on technologies for improving the 21st century workforce: Tools for lifelong learning* (pp. 272–286). Hershey, PA: IGI Global. doi:10.4018/978-1-4666-2181-7.ch018

Damurski, L. (2012). E-participation in urban planning: Online tools for citizen engagement in Poland and in Germany. *International Journal of E-Planning Research*, *1*(3), 40–67. doi:10.4018/ijepr.2012070103

de Almeida, M. O. (2007). E-government strategy in Brazil: Increasing transparency and efficiency through e-government procurement. In M. Gascó-Hernandez (Ed.), *Latin America online: Cases, successes and pitfalls* (pp. 34–82). Hershey, PA: IGI Global. doi:10.4018/978-1-59140-974-8.ch002

de Juana Espinosa, S. (2008). Empirical study of the municipalitites' motivations for adopting online presence. In A. Anttiroiko (Ed.), *Electronic government: Concepts, methodologies, tools, and applications* (pp. 3593–3608). Hershey, PA: IGI Global. doi:10.4018/978-1-59904-947-2.ch262 de Souza Dias, D. (2002). Motivation for using information technology. In C. Snodgrass & E. Szewczak (Eds.), *Human factors in information systems* (pp. 55–60). Hershey, PA: IGI Global. doi:10.4018/978-1-931777-10-0.ch005

Demediuk, P. (2006). Government procurement ICT's impact on the sustainability of SMEs and regional communities. In S. Marshall, W. Taylor, & X. Yu (Eds.), *Encyclopedia of developing regional communities with information and communication technology* (pp. 321–324). Hershey, PA: IGI Global. doi:10.4018/978-1-59140-575-7.ch056

Devonshire, E., Forsyth, H., Reid, S., & Simpson, J. M. (2013). The challenges and opportunities of online postgraduate coursework programs in a traditional university context. In B. Tynan, J. Willems, & R. James (Eds.), *Outlooks and opportunities in blended and distance learning* (pp. 353–368). Hershey, PA: IGI Global. doi:10.4018/978-1-4666-4205-8.ch026

Di Cerbo, F., Scotto, M., Sillitti, A., Succi, G., & Vernazza, T. (2007). Toward a GNU/Linux distribution for corporate environments. In S. Sowe, I. Stamelos, & I. Samoladas (Eds.), *Emerging free and open source software practices* (pp. 215–236). Hershey, PA: IGI Global. doi:10.4018/978-1-59904-210-7.ch010

Diesner, J., & Carley, K. M. (2005). Revealing social structure from texts: Meta-matrix text analysis as a novel method for network text analysis. In V. Narayanan & D. Armstrong (Eds.), *Causal mapping for research in information technology* (pp. 81–108). Hershey, PA: IGI Global. doi:10.4018/978-1-59140-396-8.ch004

Dologite, D. G., Mockler, R. J., Bai, Q., & Viszhanyo, P. F. (2006). IS change agents in practice in a US-Chinese joint venture. In M. Hunter & F. Tan (Eds.), *Advanced topics in global information management* (Vol. 5, pp. 331–352). Hershey, PA: IGI Global. doi:10.4018/978-1-59140-923-6.ch015

Drnevich, P., Brush, T. H., & Luckock, G. T. (2011). Process and structural implications for IT-enabled outsourcing. *International Journal of Strategic Information Technology and Applications*, 2(4), 30–43. doi:10.4018/jsita.2011100103

Dwivedi, A. N. (2009). *Handbook of research on information technology management and clinical data administration in healthcare* (Vols. 1–2). Hershey, PA: IGI Global. doi:10.4018/978-1-60566-356-2

Elbeltagi, I., McBride, N., & Hardaker, G. (2006). Evaluating the factors affecting DSS usage by senior managers in local authorities in Egypt. In M. Hunter & F. Tan (Eds.), *Advanced topics in global information management* (Vol. 5, pp. 283–307). Hershey, PA: IGI Global. doi:10.4018/978-1-59140-923-6.ch013

Eom, S., & Fountain, J. E. (2013). Enhancing information services through public-private partnerships: Information technology knowledge transfer underlying structures to develop shared services in the U.S. and Korea. In J. Gil-Garcia (Ed.), *E-government success around the world: Cases, empirical studies, and practical recommendations* (pp. 15–40). Hershey, PA: IGI Global. doi:10.4018/978-1-4666-4173-0.ch002

Esteves, T., Leuenberger, D., & Van Leuven, N. (2012). Reaching citizen 2.0: How government uses social media to send public messages during times of calm and times of crisis. In K. Kloby & M. D'Agostino (Eds.), *Citizen 2.0: Public and governmental interaction through web 2.0 technologies* (pp. 250–268). Hershey, PA: IGI Global. doi:10.4018/978-1-4666-0318-9.ch013

Estevez, E., Fillottrani, P., Janowski, T., & Ojo, A. (2012). Government information sharing: A framework for policy formulation. In Y. Chen & P. Chu (Eds.), *Electronic governance and cross-boundary collaboration: Innovations and advancing tools* (pp. 23–55). Hershey, PA: IGI Global. doi:10.4018/978-1-60960-753-1.ch002

Ezz, I. E. (2008). E-governement emerging trends: Organizational challenges. In A. Anttiroiko (Ed.), *Electronic government: Concepts, methodologies, tools, and applications* (pp. 3721–3737). Hershey, PA: IGI Global. doi:10.4018/978-1-59904-947-2.ch269

Fabri, M. (2009). The Italian style of e-justice in a comparative perspective. In A. Martínez & P. Abat (Eds.), *E-justice: Using information communication technologies in the court system* (pp. 1–19). Hershey, PA: IGI Global. doi:10.4018/978-1-59904-998-4.ch001

Fagbe, T., & Adekola, O. D. (2010). Workplace safety and personnel well-being: The impact of information technology. *International Journal of Green Computing*, *1*(1), 28–33. doi:10.4018/jgc.2010010103

Fagbe, T., & Adekola, O. D. (2011). Workplace safety and personnel well-being: The impact of information technology. In *Global business: Concepts, methodologies, tools and applications* (pp. 1438–1444). Hershey, PA: IGI Global. doi:10.4018/978-1-60960-587-2.ch509

Farmer, L. (2008). Affective collaborative instruction with librarians. In S. Kelsey & K. St.Amant (Eds.), *Handbook of research on computer mediated communication* (pp. 15–24). Hershey, PA: IGI Global. doi:10.4018/978-1-59904-863-5.ch002

Favier, L., & Mekhantar, J. (2007). Use of OSS by local e-administration: The French situation. In K. St.Amant & B. Still (Eds.), *Handbook of research on open source software: Technological, economic, and social perspectives* (pp. 428–444). Hershey, PA: IGI Global. doi:10.4018/978-1-59140-999-1.ch033

Fernando, S. (2009). Issues of e-learning in third world countries. In M. Khosrow-Pour (Ed.), *Encyclopedia of information science and technology* (2nd ed.; pp. 2273–2277). Hershey, PA: IGI Global. doi:10.4018/978-1-60566-026-4.ch360

Filho, J. R., & dos Santos, J. R. Jr. (2009). Local e-government in Brazil: Poor interaction and local politics as usual. In C. Reddick (Ed.), *Handbook of research on strategies for local e-government adoption and implementation: Comparative studies* (pp. 863–878). Hershey, PA: IGI Global. doi:10.4018/978-1-60566-282-4.ch045

Fletcher, P. D. (2004). Portals and policy: Implications of electronic access to U.S. federal government information services. In A. Pavlichev & G. Garson (Eds.), *Digital government: Principles and best practices* (pp. 52–62). Hershey, PA: IGI Global. doi:10.4018/978-1-59140-122-3.ch004

Fletcher, P. D. (2008). Portals and policy: Implications of electronic access to U.S. federal government information services. In A. Anttiroiko (Ed.), *Electronic government: Concepts, methodologies, tools, and applications* (pp. 3970–3979). Hershey, PA: IGI Global. doi:10.4018/978-1-59904-947-2.ch289

Forlano, L. (2004). The emergence of digital government: International perspectives. In A. Pavlichev & G. Garson (Eds.), *Digital government: Principles and best practices* (pp. 34–51). Hershey, PA: IGI Global. doi:10.4018/978-1-59140-122-3.ch003

Franzel, J. M., & Coursey, D. H. (2004). Government web portals: Management issues and the approaches of five states. In A. Pavlichev & G. Garson (Eds.), *Digital government: Principles and best practices* (pp. 63–77). Hershey, PA: IGI Global. doi:10.4018/978-1-59140-122-3.ch005

Gaivéo, J. M. (2013). Security of ICTs supporting healthcare activities. In M. Cruz-Cunha, I. Miranda, & P. Gonçalves (Eds.), *Handbook of research on ICTs for human-centered healthcare and social care services* (pp. 208–228). Hershey, PA: IGI Global. doi:10.4018/978-1-4666-3986-7.ch011

Garson, G. D. (1999). *Information technology and computer applications in public administration: Issues and trends*. Hershey, PA: IGI Global. doi:10.4018/978-1-87828-952-0

Garson, G. D. (2003). Toward an information technology research agenda for public administration. In G. Garson (Ed.), *Public information technology: Policy and management issues* (pp. 331–357). Hershey, PA: IGI Global. doi:10.4018/978-1-59140-060-8.ch014

Related References

Garson, G. D. (2004). The promise of digital government. In A. Pavlichev & G. Garson (Eds.), *Digital government: Principles and best practices* (pp. 2–15). Hershey, PA: IGI Global. doi:10.4018/978-1-59140-122-3.ch001

Garson, G. D. (2007). An information technology research agenda for public administration. In G. Garson (Ed.), *Modern public information technology systems: Issues and challenges* (pp. 365–392). Hershey, PA: IGI Global. doi:10.4018/978-1-59904-051-6.ch018

Gasco, M. (2007). Civil servants' resistance towards e-government development. In A. Anttiroiko & M. Malkia (Eds.), *Encyclopedia of digital government* (pp. 190–195). Hershey, PA: IGI Global. doi:10.4018/978-1-59140-789-8.ch028

Gasco, M. (2008). Civil servants' resistance towards e-government development. In A. Anttiroiko (Ed.), *Electronic government: Concepts, methodologies, tools, and applications* (pp. 2580–2588). Hershey, PA: IGI Global. doi:10.4018/978-1-59904-947-2.ch190

Ghere, R. K. (2010). Accountability and information technology enactment: Implications for social empowerment. In E. Ferro, Y. Dwivedi, J. Gil-Garcia, & M. Williams (Eds.), *Handbook of research on overcoming digital divides: Constructing an equitable and competitive information society* (pp. 515–532). Hershey, PA: IGI Global. doi:10.4018/978-1-60566-699-0.ch028

Gibson, I. W. (2012). Simulation modeling of healthcare delivery. In A. Kolker & P. Story (Eds.), *Management engineering for effective healthcare delivery: Principles and applications* (pp. 69–89). Hershey, PA: IGI Global. doi:10.4018/978-1-60960-872-9.ch003

Gil-Garcia, J. R. (2007). Exploring e-government benefits and success factors. In A. Anttiroiko & M. Malkia (Eds.), *Encyclopedia of digital government* (pp. 803–811). Hershey, PA: IGI Global. doi:10.4018/978-1-59140-789-8.ch122

Gil-Garcia, J. R., & González Miranda, F. (2010). E-government and opportunities for participation: The case of the Mexican state web portals. In C. Reddick (Ed.), *Politics, democracy and e-government: Participation and service delivery* (pp. 56–74). Hershey, PA: IGI Global. doi:10.4018/978-1-61520-933-0.ch004

Goldfinch, S. (2012). Public trust in government, trust in e-government, and use of e-government. In Z. Yan (Ed.), *Encyclopedia of cyber behavior* (pp. 987–995). Hershey, PA: IGI Global. doi:10.4018/978-1-4666-0315-8.ch081

Goodyear, M. (2012). Organizational change contributions to e-government project transitions. In S. Aikins (Ed.), *Managing e-government projects: Concepts, issues, and best practices* (pp. 1–21). Hershey, PA: IGI Global. doi:10.4018/978-1-4666-0086-7.ch001

Gordon, S., & Mulligan, P. (2003). Strategic models for the delivery of personal financial services: The role of infocracy. In S. Gordon (Ed.), *Computing information technology: The human side* (pp. 220–232). Hershey, PA: IGI Global. doi:10.4018/978-1-93177-752-0.ch014

Gordon, T. F. (2007). Legal knowledge systems. In A. Anttiroiko & M. Malkia (Eds.), *Encyclopedia of digital government* (pp. 1161–1166). Hershey, PA: IGI Global. doi:10.4018/978-1-59140-789-8.ch175

Graham, J. E., & Semich, G. W. (2008). Integrating technology to transform pedagogy: Revisiting the progress of the three phase TUI model for faculty development. In L. Tomei (Ed.), *Adapting information and communication technologies for effective education* (pp. 1–12). Hershey, PA: IGI Global. doi:10.4018/978-1-59904-922-9.ch001

Grandinetti, L., & Pisacane, O. (2012). Web services for healthcare management. In D. Prakash Vidyarthi (Ed.), *Technologies and protocols for the future of internet design: Reinventing the web* (pp. 60–94). Hershey, PA: IGI Global. doi:10.4018/978-1-4666-0203-8.ch004

Groenewegen, P., & Wagenaar, F. P. (2008). VO as an alternative to hierarchy in the Dutch police sector. In G. Putnik & M. Cruz-Cunha (Eds.), *Encyclopedia of networked and virtual organizations* (pp. 1851–1857). Hershey, PA: IGI Global. doi:10.4018/978-1-59904-885-7.ch245

Gronlund, A. (2001). Building an infrastructure to manage electronic services. In S. Dasgupta (Ed.), *Managing internet and intranet technologies in organizations: Challenges and opportunities* (pp. 71–103). Hershey, PA: IGI Global. doi:10.4018/978-1-878289-95-7.ch006

Gronlund, A. (2002). Introduction to electronic government: Design, applications and management. In Å. Grönlund (Ed.), *Electronic government: Design, applications and management* (pp. 1–21). Hershey, PA: IGI Global. doi:10.4018/978-1-930708-19-8.ch001

Gupta, A., Woosley, R., Crk, I., & Sarnikar, S. (2009). An information technology architecture for drug effectiveness reporting and post-marketing surveillance. In J. Tan (Ed.), *Medical informatics: Concepts, methodologies, tools, and applications* (pp. 631–646). Hershey, PA: IGI Global. doi:10.4018/978-1-60566-050-9.ch047

Hallin, A., & Lundevall, K. (2007). mCity: User focused development of mobile services within the city of Stockholm. In I. Kushchu (Ed.), Mobile government: An emerging direction in e-government (pp. 12-29). Hershey, PA: IGI Global. doi:10.4018/978-1-59140-884-0.ch002

Hallin, A., & Lundevall, K. (2009). mCity: User focused development of mobile services within the city of Stockholm. In S. Clarke (Ed.), Evolutionary concepts in end user productivity and performance: Applications for organizational progress (pp. 268-280). Hershey, PA: IGI Global. doi:10.4018/978-1-60566-136-0.ch017

Hallin, A., & Lundevall, K. (2009). mCity: User focused development of mobile services within the city of Stockholm. In D. Taniar (Ed.), Mobile computing: Concepts, methodologies, tools, and applications (pp. 3455-3467). Hershey, PA: IGI Global. doi:10.4018/978-1-60566-054-7.ch253

Hanson, A. (2005). Overcoming barriers in the planning of a virtual library. In M. Khosrow-Pour (Ed.), *Encyclopedia of information science and technology* (pp. 2255–2259). Hershey, PA: IGI Global. doi:10.4018/978-1-59140-553-5.ch397

Haque, A. (2008). Information technology and surveillance: Implications for public administration in a new word order. In T. Loendorf & G. Garson (Eds.), *Patriotic information systems* (pp. 177–185). Hershey, PA: IGI Global. doi:10.4018/978-1-59904-594-8.ch008

Hauck, R. V., Thatcher, S. M., & Weisband, S. P. (2012). Temporal aspects of information technology use: Increasing shift work effectiveness. In J. Wang (Ed.), *Advancing the service sector with evolving technologies: Techniques and principles* (pp. 87–104). Hershey, PA: IGI Global. doi:10.4018/978-1-4666-0044-7.ch006

Hawk, S., & Witt, T. (2006). Telecommunications courses in information systems programs. *International Journal of Information and Communication Technology Education, 2*(1), 79–92. doi:10.4018/jicte.2006010107

Helms, M. M., Moore, R., & Ahmadi, M. (2009). Information technology (IT) and the healthcare industry: A SWOT analysis. In J. Tan (Ed.), *Medical informatics: Concepts, methodologies, tools, and applications* (pp. 134–152). Hershey, PA: IGI Global. doi:10.4018/978-1-60566-050-9.ch012

Hendrickson, S. M., & Young, M. E. (2014). Electronic records management at a federally funded research and development center. In J. Krueger (Ed.), *Cases on electronic records and resource management implementation in diverse environments* (pp. 334–350). Hershey, PA: IGI Global. doi:10.4018/978-1-4666-4466-3.ch020

Henman, P. (2010). Social policy and information communication technologies. In J. Martin & L. Hawkins (Eds.), *Information communication technologies for human services education and delivery: Concepts and cases* (pp. 215–229). Hershey, PA: IGI Global. doi:10.4018/978-1-60566-735-5.ch014

Hismanoglu, M. (2011). Important issues in online education: E-pedagogy and marketing. In U. Demiray & S. Sever (Eds.), *Marketing online education programs: Frameworks for promotion and communication* (pp. 184–209). Hershey, PA: IGI Global. doi:10.4018/978-1-60960-074-7.ch012

Ho, K. K. (2008). The e-government development, IT strategies, and portals of the Hong Kong SAR government. In A. Anttiroiko (Ed.), *Electronic government: Concepts, methodologies, tools, and applications* (pp. 715–733). Hershey, PA: IGI Global. doi:10.4018/978-1-59904-947-2.ch060

Holden, S. H. (2003). The evolution of information technology management at the federal level: Implications for public administration. In G. Garson (Ed.), *Public information technology: Policy and management issues* (pp. 53–73). Hershey, PA: IGI Global. doi:10.4018/978-1-59140-060-8.ch003

Holden, S. H. (2007). The evolution of federal information technology management literature: Does IT finally matter? In G. Garson (Ed.), *Modern public information technology systems: Issues and challenges* (pp. 17–34). Hershey, PA: IGI Global. doi:10.4018/978-1-59904-051-6.ch002

Holland, J. W. (2009). Automation of American criminal justice. In M. Khosrow-Pour (Ed.), *Encyclopedia of information science and technology* (2nd ed.; pp. 300–302). Hershey, PA: IGI Global. doi:10.4018/978-1-60566-026-4.ch051

Holloway, K. (2013). Fair use, copyright, and academic integrity in an online academic environment. In *Digital rights management: Concepts, methodologies, tools, and applications* (pp. 917–928). Hershey, PA: IGI Global. doi:10.4018/978-1-4666-2136-7.ch044

Horiuchi, C. (2005). E-government databases. In L. Rivero, J. Doorn, & V. Ferraggine (Eds.), *Encyclopedia of database technologies and applications* (pp. 206–210). Hershey, PA: IGI Global. doi:10.4018/978-1-59140-560-3.ch035

Horiuchi, C. (2006). Creating IS quality in government settings. In E. Duggan & J. Reichgelt (Eds.), *Measuring information systems delivery quality* (pp. 311–327). Hershey, PA: IGI Global. doi:10.4018/978-1-59140-857-4.ch014

Hsiao, N., Chu, P., & Lee, C. (2012). Impact of e-governance on businesses: Model development and case study. In *Digital democracy: Concepts, methodologies, tools, and applications* (pp. 1407–1425). Hershey, PA: IGI Global. doi:10.4018/978-1-4666-1740-7.ch070

Huang, T., & Lee, C. (2010). Evaluating the impact of e-government on citizens: Cost-benefit analysis. In C. Reddick (Ed.), *Citizens and e-government: Evaluating policy and management* (pp. 37–52). Hershey, PA: IGI Global. doi:10.4018/978-1-61520-931-6.ch003

Hunter, M. G., Diochon, M., Pugsley, D., & Wright, B. (2002). Unique challenges for small business adoption of information technology: The case of the Nova Scotia ten. In S. Burgess (Ed.), *Managing information technology in small business: Challenges and solutions* (pp. 98–117). Hershey, PA: IGI Global. doi:10.4018/978-1-930708-35-8.ch006

Hurskainen, J. (2003). Integration of business systems and applications in merger and alliance: Case metso automation. In T. Reponen (Ed.), *Information technology enabled global customer service* (pp. 207–225). Hershey, PA: IGI Global. doi:10.4018/978-1-59140-048-6.ch012

Iazzolino, G., & Pietrantonio, R. (2011). The soveria.it project: A best practice of e-government in southern Italy. In D. Piaggesi, K. Sund, & W. Castelnovo (Eds.), *Global strategy and practice of e-governance: Examples from around the world* (pp. 34–56). Hershey, PA: IGI Global. doi:10.4018/978-1-60960-489-9.ch003

Imran, A., & Gregor, S. (2012). A process model for successful e-government adoption in the least developed countries: A case of Bangladesh. In F. Tan (Ed.), *International comparisons of information communication technologies: Advancing applications* (pp. 321–350). Hershey, PA: IGI Global. doi:10.4018/978-1-61350-480-2.ch014

Inoue, Y., & Bell, S. T. (2005). Electronic/digital government innovation, and publishing trends with IT. In M. Khosrow-Pour (Ed.), *Encyclopedia of information science and technology* (pp. 1018–1023). Hershey, PA: IGI Global. doi:10.4018/978-1-59140-553-5.ch180

Islam, M. M., & Ehsan, M. (2013). Understanding e-governance: A theoretical approach. In M. Islam & M. Ehsan (Eds.), *From government to e-governance: Public administration in the digital age* (pp. 38–49). Hershey, PA: IGI Global. doi:10.4018/978-1-4666-1909-8.ch003

Jaeger, B. (2009). E-government and e-democracy in the making. In M. Khosrow-Pour (Ed.), *Encyclopedia of information science and technology* (2nd ed.; pp. 1318–1322). Hershey, PA: IGI Global. doi:10.4018/978-1-60566-026-4.ch208

Jain, R. B. (2007). Revamping the administrative structure and processes in India for online diplomacy. In A. Anttiroiko & M. Malkia (Eds.), *Encyclopedia of digital government* (pp. 1418–1423). Hershey, PA: IGI Global. doi:10.4018/978-1-59140-789-8.ch217

Jain, R. B. (2008). Revamping the administrative structure and processes in India for online diplomacy. In A. Anttiroiko (Ed.), *Electronic government: Concepts, methodologies, tools, and applications* (pp. 3142–3149). Hershey, PA: IGI Global. doi:10.4018/978-1-59904-947-2.ch233

Jauhiainen, J. S., & Inkinen, T. (2009). E-governance and the information society in periphery. In C. Reddick (Ed.), *Handbook of research on strategies for local e-government adoption and implementation: Comparative studies* (pp. 497–514). Hershey, PA: IGI Global. doi:10.4018/978-1-60566-282-4.ch026

Jensen, M. J. (2009). Electronic democracy and citizen influence in government. In C. Reddick (Ed.), *Handbook of research on strategies for local e-government adoption and implementation: Comparative studies* (pp. 288–305). Hershey, PA: IGI Global. doi:10.4018/978-1-60566-282-4.ch015

Jiao, Y., Hurson, A. R., Potok, T. E., & Beckerman, B. G. (2009). Integrating mobile-based systems with healthcare databases. In J. Erickson (Ed.), *Database technologies: Concepts, methodologies, tools, and applications* (pp. 484–504). Hershey, PA: IGI Global. doi:10.4018/978-1-60566-058-5.ch031

Joia, L. A. (2002). A systematic model to integrate information technology into metabusinesses: A case study in the engineering realms. In F. Tan (Ed.), *Advanced topics in global information management* (Vol. 1, pp. 250–267). Hershey, PA: IGI Global. doi:10.4018/978-1-930708-43-3.ch016

Jones, T. H., & Song, I. (2000). Binary equivalents of ternary relationships in entity-relationship modeling: A logical decomposition approach. *Journal of Database Management, 11*(2), 12–19. doi:10.4018/jdm.2000040102

Juana-Espinosa, S. D. (2007). Empirical study of the municipalitites' motivations for adopting online presence. In L. Al-Hakim (Ed.), *Global e-government: Theory, applications and benchmarking* (pp. 261–279). Hershey, PA: IGI Global. doi:10.4018/978-1-59904-027-1.ch015

Jun, K., & Weare, C. (2012). Bridging from e-government practice to e-government research: Past trends and future directions. In K. Bwalya & S. Zulu (Eds.), *Handbook of research on e-government in emerging economies: Adoption, e-participation, and legal frameworks* (pp. 263–289). Hershey, PA: IGI Global. doi:10.4018/978-1-4666-0324-0.ch013

Junqueira, A., Diniz, E. H., & Fernandez, M. (2010). Electronic government implementation projects with multiple agencies: Analysis of the electronic invoice project under PMBOK framework. In J. Cordoba-Pachon & A. Ochoa-Arias (Eds.), *Systems thinking and e-participation: ICT in the governance of society* (pp. 135–153). Hershey, PA: IGI Global. doi:10.4018/978-1-60566-860-4.ch009

Juntunen, A. (2009). Joint service development with the local authorities. In C. Reddick (Ed.), *Handbook of research on strategies for local e-government adoption and implementation: Comparative studies* (pp. 902–920). Hershey, PA: IGI Global. doi:10.4018/978-1-60566-282-4.ch047

Kamel, S. (2001). *Using DSS for crisis management.* Hershey, PA: IGI Global. doi:10.4018/978-1-87828-961-2.ch020

Kamel, S. (2006). DSS for strategic decision making. In M. Khosrow-Pour (Ed.), *Cases on information technology and organizational politics & culture* (pp. 230–246). Hershey, PA: IGI Global. doi:10.4018/978-1-59904-411-8.ch015

Kamel, S. (2009). The software industry in Egypt as a potential contributor to economic growth. In M. Khosrow-Pour (Ed.), *Encyclopedia of information science and technology* (2nd ed.; pp. 3531–3537). Hershey, PA: IGI Global. doi:10.4018/978-1-60566-026-4.ch562

Kamel, S., & Hussein, M. (2008). Xceed: Pioneering the contact center industry in Egypt. *Journal of Cases on Information Technology*, *10*(1), 67–91. doi:10.4018/jcit.2008010105

Kamel, S., & Wahba, K. (2003). The use of a hybrid model in web-based education: "The Global campus project. In A. Aggarwal (Ed.), *Web-based education: Learning from experience* (pp. 331–346). Hershey, PA: IGI Global. doi:10.4018/978-1-59140-102-5.ch020

Kardaras, D. K., & Papathanassiou, E. A. (2008). An exploratory study of the e-government services in Greece. In G. Garson & M. Khosrow-Pour (Eds.), *Handbook of research on public information technology* (pp. 162–174). Hershey, PA: IGI Global. doi:10.4018/978-1-59904-857-4.ch016

Kassahun, A. E., Molla, A., & Sarkar, P. (2012). Government process reengineering: What we know and what we need to know. In *Digital democracy: Concepts, methodologies, tools, and applications* (pp. 1730–1752). Hershey, PA: IGI Global. doi:10.4018/978-1-4666-1740-7.ch086

Khan, B. (2005). Technological issues. In B. Khan (Ed.), *Managing e-learning strategies: Design, delivery, implementation and evaluation* (pp. 154–180). Hershey, PA: IGI Global. doi:10.4018/978-1-59140-634-1.ch004

Khasawneh, A., Bsoul, M., Obeidat, I., & Al Azzam, I. (2012). Technology fears: A study of e-commerce loyalty perception by Jordanian customers. In J. Wang (Ed.), *Advancing the service sector with evolving technologies: Techniques and principles* (pp. 158–165). Hershey, PA: IGI Global. doi:10.4018/978-1-4666-0044-7.ch010

Khatibi, V., & Montazer, G. A. (2012). E-research methodology. In A. Juan, T. Daradoumis, M. Roca, S. Grasman, & J. Faulin (Eds.), *Collaborative and distributed e-research: Innovations in technologies, strategies and applications* (pp. 62–81). Hershey, PA: IGI Global. doi:10.4018/978-1-4666-0125-3.ch003

Kidd, T. (2011). The dragon in the school's backyard: A review of literature on the uses of technology in urban schools. In L. Tomei (Ed.), *Online courses and ICT in education: Emerging practices and applications* (pp. 242–257). Hershey, PA: IGI Global. doi:10.4018/978-1-60960-150-8.ch019

Kidd, T. T. (2010). My experience tells the story: Exploring technology adoption from a qualitative perspective - A pilot study. In H. Song & T. Kidd (Eds.), *Handbook of research on human performance and instructional technology* (pp. 247–262). Hershey, PA: IGI Global. doi:10.4018/978-1-60566-782-9.ch015

Kieley, B., Lane, G., Paquet, G., & Roy, J. (2002). e-Government in Canada: Services online or public service renewal? In Å. Grönlund (Ed.), Electronic government: Design, applications and management (pp. 340-355). Hershey, PA: IGI Global. doi:10.4018/978-1-930708-19-8.ch016

Kim, P. (2012). "Stay out of the way! My kid is video blogging through a phone!": A lesson learned from math tutoring social media for children in underserved communities. In *Wireless technologies: Concepts, methodologies, tools and applications* (pp. 1415–1428). Hershey, PA: IGI Global. doi:10.4018/978-1-61350-101-6.ch517

Kirlidog, M. (2010). Financial aspects of national ICT strategies. In S. Kamel (Ed.), *E-strategies for technological diffusion and adoption: National ICT approaches for socioeconomic development* (pp. 277–292). Hershey, PA: IGI Global. doi:10.4018/978-1-60566-388-3.ch016

Kisielnicki, J. (2006). Transfer of information and knowledge in the project management. In E. Coakes & S. Clarke (Eds.), *Encyclopedia of communities of practice in information and knowledge management* (pp. 544–551). Hershey, PA: IGI Global. doi:10.4018/978-1-59140-556-6.ch091

Related References

Kittner, M., & Van Slyke, C. (2006). Reorganizing information technology services in an academic environment. In M. Khosrow-Pour (Ed.), *Cases on the human side of information technology* (pp. 49–66). Hershey, PA: IGI Global. doi:10.4018/978-1-59904-405-7.ch004

Knoell, H. D. (2008). Semi virtual workplaces in German financial service enterprises. In P. Zemliansky & K. St.Amant (Eds.), *Handbook of research on virtual workplaces and the new nature of business practices* (pp. 570–581). Hershey, PA: IGI Global. doi:10.4018/978-1-59904-893-2.ch041

Koh, S. L., & Maguire, S. (2009). Competing in the age of information technology in a developing economy: Experiences of an Indian bank. In S. Koh & S. Maguire (Eds.), *Information and communication technologies management in turbulent business environments* (pp. 326–350). Hershey, PA: IGI Global. doi:10.4018/978-1-60566-424-8.ch018

Kollmann, T., & Häsel, M. (2009). Competence of information technology professionals in internet-based ventures. In I. Lee (Ed.), *Electronic business: Concepts, methodologies, tools, and applications* (pp. 1905–1919). Hershey, PA: IGI Global. doi:10.4018/978-1-60566-056-1.ch118

Kollmann, T., & Häsel, M. (2009). Competence of information technology professionals in internet-based ventures. In A. Cater-Steel (Ed.), *Information technology governance and service management: Frameworks and adaptations* (pp. 239–253). Hershey, PA: IGI Global. doi:10.4018/978-1-60566-008-0.ch013

Kollmann, T., & Häsel, M. (2010). Competence of information technology professionals in internet-based ventures. In *Electronic services: Concepts, methodologies, tools and applications* (pp. 1551–1565). Hershey, PA: IGI Global. doi:10.4018/978-1-61520-967-5.ch094

Kraemer, K., & King, J. L. (2006). Information technology and administrative reform: Will e-government be different? *International Journal of Electronic Government Research*, 2(1), 1–20. doi:10.4018/jegr.2006010101

Kraemer, K., & King, J. L. (2008). Information technology and administrative reform: Will e-government be different? In D. Norris (Ed.), *E-government research: Policy and management* (pp. 1–20). Hershey, PA: IGI Global. doi:10.4018/978-1-59904-913-7.ch001

Lampathaki, F., Tsiakaliaris, C., Stasis, A., & Charalabidis, Y. (2011). National interoperability frameworks: The way forward. In Y. Charalabidis (Ed.), *Interoperability in digital public services and administration: Bridging e-government and e-business* (pp. 1–24). Hershey, PA: IGI Global. doi:10.4018/978-1-61520-887-6.ch001

Lan, Z., & Scott, C. R. (1996). The relative importance of computer-mediated information versus conventional non-computer-mediated information in public managerial decision making. *Information Resources Management Journal, 9*(1), 27–0. doi:10.4018/irmj.1996010103

Law, W. (2004). *Public sector data management in a developing economy.* Hershey, PA: IGI Global. doi:10.4018/978-1-59140-259-6.ch034

Law, W. K. (2005). Information resources development challenges in a cross-cultural environment. In M. Khosrow-Pour (Ed.), *Encyclopedia of information science and technology* (pp. 1476–1481). Hershey, PA: IGI Global. doi:10.4018/978-1-59140-553-5.ch259

Law, W. K. (2009). Cross-cultural challenges for information resources management. In M. Khosrow-Pour (Ed.), *Encyclopedia of information science and technology* (2nd ed.; pp. 840–846). Hershey, PA: IGI Global. doi:10.4018/978-1-60566-026-4.ch136

Law, W. K. (2011). Cross-cultural challenges for information resources management. In *Global business: Concepts, methodologies, tools and applications* (pp. 1924–1932). Hershey, PA: IGI Global. doi:10.4018/978-1-60960-587-2.ch704

Malkia, M., & Savolainen, R. (2004). eTransformation in government, politics and society: Conceptual framework and introduction. In M. Malkia, A. Anttiroiko, & R. Savolainen (Eds.), eTransformation in governance: New directions in government and politics (pp. 1-21). Hershey, PA: IGI Global. doi:10.4018/978-1-59140-130-8.ch001

Mandujano, S. (2011). Network manageability security. In D. Kar & M. Syed (Eds.), *Network security, administration and management: Advancing technology and practice* (pp. 158–181). Hershey, PA: IGI Global. doi:10.4018/978-1-60960-777-7.ch009

Marich, M. J., Schooley, B. L., & Horan, T. A. (2012). A normative enterprise architecture for guiding end-to-end emergency response decision support. In M. Jennex (Ed.), *Managing crises and disasters with emerging technologies: Advancements* (pp. 71–87). Hershey, PA: IGI Global. doi:10.4018/978-1-4666-0167-3.ch006

Related References

Markov, R., & Okujava, S. (2008). Costs, benefits, and risks of e-government portals. In G. Putnik & M. Cruz-Cunha (Eds.), *Encyclopedia of networked and virtual organizations* (pp. 354–363). Hershey, PA: IGI Global. doi:10.4018/978-1-59904-885-7.ch047

Martin, N., & Rice, J. (2013). Evaluating and designing electronic government for the future: Observations and insights from Australia. In V. Weerakkody (Ed.), *E-government services design, adoption, and evaluation* (pp. 238–258). Hershey, PA: IGI Global. doi:10.4018/978-1-4666-2458-0.ch014

i.   Martinez, A. C. (2008). Accessing administration's information via internet in Spain. In F. Tan (Ed.), *Global information technologies: Concepts, methodologies, tools, and applications* (pp. 2558–2573). Hershey, PA: IGI Global. doi:10.4018/978-1-59904-939-7.ch186

Mbarika, V. W., Meso, P. N., & Musa, P. F. (2006). A disconnect in stakeholders' perceptions from emerging realities of teledensity growth in Africa's least developed countries. In M. Hunter & F. Tan (Eds.), *Advanced topics in global information management* (Vol. 5, pp. 263–282). Hershey, PA: IGI Global. doi:10.4018/978-1-59140-923-6.ch012

Mbarika, V. W., Meso, P. N., & Musa, P. F. (2008). A disconnect in stakeholders' perceptions from emerging realities of teledensity growth in Africa's least developed countries. In F. Tan (Ed.), *Global information technologies: Concepts, methodologies, tools, and applications* (pp. 2948–2962). Hershey, PA: IGI Global. doi:10.4018/978-1-59904-939-7.ch209

Means, T., Olson, E., & Spooner, J. (2013). Discovering ways that don't work on the road to success: Strengths and weaknesses revealed by an active learning studio classroom project. In A. Benson, J. Moore, & S. Williams van Rooij (Eds.), *Cases on educational technology planning, design, and implementation: A project management perspective* (pp. 94–113). Hershey, PA: IGI Global. doi:10.4018/978-1-4666-4237-9.ch006

Melitski, J., Holzer, M., Kim, S., Kim, C., & Rho, S. (2008). Digital government worldwide: An e-government assessment of municipal web sites. In G. Garson & M. Khosrow-Pour (Eds.), *Handbook of research on public information technology* (pp. 790–804). Hershey, PA: IGI Global. doi:10.4018/978-1-59904-857-4.ch069

Memmola, M., Palumbo, G., & Rossini, M. (2009). Web & RFID technology: New frontiers in costing and process management for rehabilitation medicine. In L. Al-Hakim & M. Memmola (Eds.), *Business web strategy: Design, alignment, and application* (pp. 145–169). Hershey, PA: IGI Global. doi:10.4018/978-1-60566-024-0.ch008

Meng, Z., Fahong, Z., & Lei, L. (2008). Information technology and environment. In Y. Kurihara, S. Takaya, H. Harui, & H. Kamae (Eds.), *Information technology and economic development* (pp. 201–212). Hershey, PA: IGI Global. doi:10.4018/978-1-59904-579-5.ch014

Mentzingen de Moraes, A. J., Ferneda, E., Costa, I., & Spinola, M. D. (2011). Practical approach for implementation of governance process in IT: Information technology areas. In N. Shi & G. Silvius (Eds.), *Enterprise IT governance, business value and performance measurement* (pp. 19–40). Hershey, PA: IGI Global. doi:10.4018/978-1-60566-346-3.ch002

Merwin, G. A. Jr, McDonald, J. S., & Odera, L. C. (2008). Economic development: Government's cutting edge in IT. In M. Raisinghani (Ed.), *Handbook of research on global information technology management in the digital economy* (pp. 1–37). Hershey, PA: IGI Global. doi:10.4018/978-1-59904-875-8.ch001

Meso, P., & Duncan, N. (2002). Can national information infrastructures enhance social development in the least developed countries? An empirical investigation. In M. Dadashzadeh (Ed.), *Information technology management in developing countries* (pp. 23–51). Hershey, PA: IGI Global. doi:10.4018/978-1-931777-03-2.ch002

Meso, P. N., & Duncan, N. B. (2002). Can national information infrastructures enhance social development in the least developed countries? In F. Tan (Ed.), *Advanced topics in global information management* (Vol. 1, pp. 207–226). Hershey, PA: IGI Global. doi:10.4018/978-1-930708-43-3.ch014

Middleton, M. (2008). Evaluation of e-government web sites. In G. Garson & M. Khosrow-Pour (Eds.), *Handbook of research on public information technology* (pp. 699–710). Hershey, PA: IGI Global. doi:10.4018/978-1-59904-857-4.ch063

Mingers, J. (2010). Pluralism, realism, and truth: The keys to knowledge in information systems research. In D. Paradice (Ed.), *Emerging systems approaches in information technologies: Concepts, theories, and applications* (pp. 86–98). Hershey, PA: IGI Global. doi:10.4018/978-1-60566-976-2.ch006

Related References

Mital, K. M. (2012). ICT, unique identity and inclusive growth: An Indian perspective. In A. Manoharan & M. Holzer (Eds.), *E-governance and civic engagement: Factors and determinants of e-democracy* (pp. 584–612). Hershey, PA: IGI Global. doi:10.4018/978-1-61350-083-5.ch029

Mizell, A. P. (2008). Helping close the digital divide for financially disadvantaged seniors. In F. Tan (Ed.), *Global information technologies: Concepts, methodologies, tools, and applications* (pp. 2396–2402). Hershey, PA: IGI Global. doi:10.4018/978-1-59904-939-7.ch173

Molinari, F., Wills, C., Koumpis, A., & Moumtzi, V. (2011). A citizen-centric platform to support networking in the area of e-democracy. In H. Rahman (Ed.), *Cases on adoption, diffusion and evaluation of global e-governance systems: Impact at the grass roots* (pp. 282–302). Hershey, PA: IGI Global. doi:10.4018/978-1-61692-814-8.ch014

Molinari, F., Wills, C., Koumpis, A., & Moumtzi, V. (2013). A citizen-centric platform to support networking in the area of e-democracy. In H. Rahman (Ed.), *Cases on progressions and challenges in ICT utilization for citizen-centric governance* (pp. 265–297). Hershey, PA: IGI Global. doi:10.4018/978-1-4666-2071-1.ch013

Monteverde, F. (2010). The process of e-government public policy inclusion in the governmental agenda: A framework for assessment and case study. In J. Cordoba-Pachon & A. Ochoa-Arias (Eds.), *Systems thinking and e-participation: ICT in the governance of society* (pp. 233–245). Hershey, PA: IGI Global. doi:10.4018/978-1-60566-860-4.ch015

Moodley, S. (2008). Deconstructing the South African government's ICT for development discourse. In A. Anttiroiko (Ed.), *Electronic government: Concepts, methodologies, tools, and applications* (pp. 622–631). Hershey, PA: IGI Global. doi:10.4018/978-1-59904-947-2.ch053

Moodley, S. (2008). Deconstructing the South African government's ICT for development discourse. In C. Van Slyke (Ed.), *Information communication technologies: Concepts, methodologies, tools, and applications* (pp. 816–825). Hershey, PA: IGI Global. doi:10.4018/978-1-59904-949-6.ch052

Mora, M., Cervantes-Perez, F., Gelman-Muravchik, O., Forgionne, G. A., & Mejia-Olvera, M. (2003). DMSS implementation research: A conceptual analysis of the contributions and limitations of the factor-based and stage-based streams. In G. Forgionne, J. Gupta, & M. Mora (Eds.), *Decision-making support systems: Achievements and challenges for the new decade* (pp. 331–356). Hershey, PA: IGI Global. doi:10.4018/978-1-59140-045-5.ch020

Mörtberg, C., & Elovaara, P. (2010). Attaching people and technology: Between e and government. In S. Booth, S. Goodman, & G. Kirkup (Eds.), *Gender issues in learning and working with information technology: Social constructs and cultural contexts* (pp. 83–98). Hershey, PA: IGI Global. doi:10.4018/978-1-61520-813-5. ch005

Murphy, J., Harper, E., Devine, E. C., Burke, L. J., & Hook, M. L. (2011). Case study: Lessons learned when embedding evidence-based knowledge in a nurse care planning and documentation system. In A. Cashin & R. Cook (Eds.), *Evidence-based practice in nursing informatics: Concepts and applications* (pp. 174–190). Hershey, PA: IGI Global. doi:10.4018/978-1-60960-034-1.ch014

Mutula, S. M. (2013). E-government's role in poverty alleviation: Case study of South Africa. In H. Rahman (Ed.), *Cases on progressions and challenges in ICT utilization for citizen-centric governance* (pp. 44–68). Hershey, PA: IGI Global. doi:10.4018/978-1-4666-2071-1.ch003

Nath, R., & Angeles, R. (2005). Relationships between supply characteristics and buyer-supplier coupling in e-procurement: An empirical analysis. *International Journal of E-Business Research*, *1*(2), 40–55. doi:10.4018/jebr.2005040103

Nissen, M. E. (2006). Application cases in government. In M. Nissen (Ed.), *Harnessing knowledge dynamics: Principled organizational knowing & learning* (pp. 152–181). Hershey, PA: IGI Global. doi:10.4018/978-1-59140-773-7.ch008

Norris, D. F. (2003). Leading-edge information technologies and American local governments. In G. Garson (Ed.), *Public information technology: Policy and management issues* (pp. 139–169). Hershey, PA: IGI Global. doi:10.4018/978-1-59140-060-8.ch007

Norris, D. F. (2008). Information technology among U.S. local governments. In G. Garson & M. Khosrow-Pour (Eds.), *Handbook of research on public information technology* (pp. 132–144). Hershey, PA: IGI Global. doi:10.4018/978-1-59904-857-4.ch013

Northrop, A. (1999). The challenge of teaching information technology in public administration graduate programs. In G. Garson (Ed.), *Information technology and computer applications in public administration: Issues and trends* (pp. 1–22). Hershey, PA: IGI Global. doi:10.4018/978-1-87828-952-0.ch001

Northrop, A. (2003). Information technology and public administration: The view from the profession. In G. Garson (Ed.), *Public information technology: Policy and management issues* (pp. 1–19). Hershey, PA: IGI Global. doi:10.4018/978-1-59140-060-8.ch001

Northrop, A. (2007). Lip service? How PA journals and textbooks view information technology. In G. Garson (Ed.), *Modern public information technology systems: Issues and challenges* (pp. 1–16). Hershey, PA: IGI Global. doi:10.4018/978-1-59904-051-6.ch001

Null, E. (2013). Legal and political barriers to municipal networks in the United States. In A. Abdelaal (Ed.), *Social and economic effects of community wireless networks and infrastructures* (pp. 27–56). Hershey, PA: IGI Global. doi:10.4018/978-1-4666-2997-4.ch003

Okunoye, A., Frolick, M., & Crable, E. (2006). ERP implementation in higher education: An account of pre-implementation and implementation phases. *Journal of Cases on Information Technology, 8*(2), 110–132. doi:10.4018/jcit.2006040106

Olasina, G. (2012). A review of egovernment services in Nigeria. In A. Tella & A. Issa (Eds.), *Library and information science in developing countries: Contemporary issues* (pp. 205–221). Hershey, PA: IGI Global. doi:10.4018/978-1-61350-335-5.ch015

Orgeron, C. P. (2008). A model for reengineering IT job classes in state government. In G. Garson & M. Khosrow-Pour (Eds.), *Handbook of research on public information technology* (pp. 735–746). Hershey, PA: IGI Global. doi:10.4018/978-1-59904-857-4.ch066

Owsinski, J. W., & Pielak, A. M. (2011). Local authority websites in rural areas: Measuring quality and functionality, and assessing the role. In Z. Andreopoulou, B. Manos, N. Polman, & D. Viaggi (Eds.), *Agricultural and environmental informatics, governance and management: Emerging research applications* (pp. 39–60). Hershey, PA: IGI Global. doi:10.4018/978-1-60960-621-3.ch003

Owsiński, J. W., Pielak, A. M., Sęp, K., & Stańczak, J. (2014). Local web-based networks in rural municipalities: Extension, density, and meaning. In Z. Andreopoulou, V. Samathrakis, S. Louca, & M. Vlachopoulou (Eds.), *E-innovation for sustainable development of rural resources during global economic crisis* (pp. 126–151). Hershey, PA: IGI Global. doi:10.4018/978-1-4666-4550-9.ch011

Pagani, M., & Pasinetti, C. (2008). Technical and functional quality in the development of t-government services. In A. Anttiroiko (Ed.), *Electronic government: Concepts, methodologies, tools, and applications* (pp. 2943–2965). Hershey, PA: IGI Global. doi:10.4018/978-1-59904-947-2.ch220

Pani, A. K., & Agrahari, A. (2005). On e-markets in emerging economy: An Indian experience. In M. Khosrow-Pour (Ed.), *Advanced topics in electronic commerce* (Vol. 1, pp. 287–299). Hershey, PA: IGI Global. doi:10.4018/978-1-59140-819-2.ch015

Papadopoulos, T., Angelopoulos, S., & Kitsios, F. (2011). A strategic approach to e-health interoperability using e-government frameworks. In A. Lazakidou, K. Siassiakos, & K. Ioannou (Eds.), *Wireless technologies for ambient assisted living and healthcare: Systems and applications* (pp. 213–229). Hershey, PA: IGI Global. doi:10.4018/978-1-61520-805-0.ch012

Papadopoulos, T., Angelopoulos, S., & Kitsios, F. (2013). A strategic approach to e-health interoperability using e-government frameworks. In *User-driven healthcare: Concepts, methodologies, tools, and applications* (pp. 791–807). Hershey, PA: IGI Global. doi:10.4018/978-1-4666-2770-3.ch039

Papaleo, G., Chiarella, D., Aiello, M., & Caviglione, L. (2012). Analysis, development and deployment of statistical anomaly detection techniques for real e-mail traffic. In T. Chou (Ed.), *Information assurance and security technologies for risk assessment and threat management: Advances* (pp. 47–71). Hershey, PA: IGI Global. doi:10.4018/978-1-61350-507-6.ch003

Papp, R. (2003). Information technology & FDA compliance in the pharmaceutical industry. In M. Khosrow-Pour (Ed.), *Annals of cases on information technology* (Vol. 5, pp. 262–273). Hershey, PA: IGI Global. doi:10.4018/978-1-59140-061-5.ch017

Parsons, T. W. (2007). Developing a knowledge management portal. In A. Tatnall (Ed.), *Encyclopedia of portal technologies and applications* (pp. 223–227). Hershey, PA: IGI Global. doi:10.4018/978-1-59140-989-2.ch039

Passaris, C. E. (2007). Immigration and digital government. In A. Anttiroiko & M. Malkia (Eds.), *Encyclopedia of digital government* (pp. 988–994). Hershey, PA: IGI Global. doi:10.4018/978-1-59140-789-8.ch148

Pavlichev, A. (2004). The e-government challenge for public administration. In A. Pavlichev & G. Garson (Eds.), *Digital government: Principles and best practices* (pp. 276–290). Hershey, PA: IGI Global. doi:10.4018/978-1-59140-122-3.ch018

Penrod, J. I., & Harbor, A. F. (2000). Designing and implementing a learning organization-oriented information technology planning and management process. In L. Petrides (Ed.), *Case studies on information technology in higher education: Implications for policy and practice* (pp. 7–19). Hershey, PA: IGI Global. doi:10.4018/978-1-878289-74-2.ch001

Planas-Silva, M. D., & Joseph, R. C. (2011). Perspectives on the adoption of electronic resources for use in clinical trials. In M. Guah (Ed.), *Healthcare delivery reform and new technologies: Organizational initiatives* (pp. 19–28). Hershey, PA: IGI Global. doi:10.4018/978-1-60960-183-6.ch002

Pomazalová, N., & Rejman, S. (2013). The rationale behind implementation of new electronic tools for electronic public procurement. In N. Pomazalová (Ed.), *Public sector transformation processes and internet public procurement: Decision support systems* (pp. 85–117). Hershey, PA: IGI Global. doi:10.4018/978-1-4666-2665-2.ch006

Postorino, M. N. (2012). City competitiveness and airport: Information science perspective. In M. Bulu (Ed.), *City competitiveness and improving urban subsystems: Technologies and applications* (pp. 61–83). Hershey, PA: IGI Global. doi:10.4018/978-1-61350-174-0.ch004

Poupa, C. (2002). Electronic government in Switzerland: Priorities for 2001-2005 - Electronic voting and federal portal. In Å. Grönlund (Ed.), *Electronic government: Design, applications and management* (pp. 356–369). Hershey, PA: IGI Global. doi:10.4018/978-1-930708-19-8.ch017

Powell, S. R. (2010). Interdisciplinarity in telecommunications and networking. In *Networking and telecommunications: Concepts, methodologies, tools and applications* (pp. 33–40). Hershey, PA: IGI Global. doi:10.4018/978-1-60566-986-1.ch004

Priya, P. S., & Mathiyalagan, N. (2011). A study of the implementation status of two e-governance projects in land revenue administration in India. In M. Shareef, V. Kumar, U. Kumar, & Y. Dwivedi (Eds.), *Stakeholder adoption of e-government services: Driving and resisting factors* (pp. 214–230). Hershey, PA: IGI Global. doi:10.4018/978-1-60960-601-5.ch011

Prysby, C., & Prysby, N. (2000). Electronic mail, employee privacy and the workplace. In L. Janczewski (Ed.), *Internet and intranet security management: Risks and solutions* (pp. 251–270). Hershey, PA: IGI Global. doi:10.4018/978-1-878289-71-1.ch009

Prysby, C. L., & Prysby, N. D. (2003). Electronic mail in the public workplace: Issues of privacy and public disclosure. In G. Garson (Ed.), *Public information technology: Policy and management issues* (pp. 271–298). Hershey, PA: IGI Global. doi:10.4018/978-1-59140-060-8.ch012

Prysby, C. L., & Prysby, N. D. (2007). You have mail, but who is reading it? Issues of e-mail in the public workplace. In G. Garson (Ed.), *Modern public information technology systems: Issues and challenges* (pp. 312–336). Hershey, PA: IGI Global. doi:10.4018/978-1-59904-051-6.ch016

Radl, A., & Chen, Y. (2005). Computer security in electronic government: A state-local education information system. *International Journal of Electronic Government Research, 1*(1), 79–99. doi:10.4018/jegr.2005010105

Rahman, H. (2008). Information dynamics in developing countries. In C. Van Slyke (Ed.), *Information communication technologies: Concepts, methodologies, tools, and applications* (pp. 104–114). Hershey, PA: IGI Global. doi:10.4018/978-1-59904-949-6.ch008

Ramanathan, J. (2009). Adaptive IT architecture as a catalyst for network capability in government. In P. Saha (Ed.), *Advances in government enterprise architecture* (pp. 149–172). Hershey, PA: IGI Global. doi:10.4018/978-1-60566-068-4.ch007

Ramos, I., & Berry, D. M. (2006). Social construction of information technology supporting work. In M. Khosrow-Pour (Ed.), *Cases on information technology: Lessons learned* (Vol. 7, pp. 36–52). Hershey, PA: IGI Global. doi:10.4018/978-1-59140-673-0.ch003

Ray, D., Gulla, U., Gupta, M. P., & Dash, S. S. (2009). Interoperability and constituents of interoperable systems in public sector. In V. Weerakkody, M. Janssen, & Y. Dwivedi (Eds.), *Handbook of research on ICT-enabled transformational government: A global perspective* (pp. 175–195). Hershey, PA: IGI Global. doi:10.4018/978-1-60566-390-6.ch010

Reddick, C. G. (2007). E-government and creating a citizen-centric government: A study of federal government CIOs. In G. Garson (Ed.), *Modern public information technology systems: Issues and challenges* (pp. 143–165). Hershey, PA: IGI Global. doi:10.4018/978-1-59904-051-6.ch008

Reddick, C. G. (2010). Citizen-centric e-government. In C. Reddick (Ed.), *Homeland security preparedness and information systems: Strategies for managing public policy* (pp. 45–75). Hershey, PA: IGI Global. doi:10.4018/978-1-60566-834-5.ch002

Reddick, C. G. (2010). E-government and creating a citizen-centric government: A study of federal government CIOs. In C. Reddick (Ed.), *Homeland security preparedness and information systems: Strategies for managing public policy* (pp. 230–250). Hershey, PA: IGI Global. doi:10.4018/978-1-60566-834-5.ch012

Reddick, C. G. (2010). Perceived effectiveness of e-government and its usage in city governments: Survey evidence from information technology directors. In C. Reddick (Ed.), *Homeland security preparedness and information systems: Strategies for managing public policy* (pp. 213–229). Hershey, PA: IGI Global. doi:10.4018/978-1-60566-834-5.ch011

Reddick, C. G. (2012). Customer relationship management adoption in local governments in the United States. In S. Chhabra & M. Kumar (Eds.), *Strategic enterprise resource planning models for e-government: Applications and methodologies* (pp. 111–124). Hershey, PA: IGI Global. doi:10.4018/978-1-60960-863-7.ch008

Reeder, F. S., & Pandy, S. M. (2008). Identifying effective funding models for e-government. In A. Anttiroiko (Ed.), *Electronic government: Concepts, methodologies, tools, and applications* (pp. 1108–1138). Hershey, PA: IGI Global. doi:10.4018/978-1-59904-947-2.ch083

Riesco, D., Acosta, E., & Montejano, G. (2003). An extension to a UML activity graph from workflow. In L. Favre (Ed.), *UML and the unified process* (pp. 294–314). Hershey, PA: IGI Global. doi:10.4018/978-1-93177-744-5.ch015

Ritzhaupt, A. D., & Gill, T. G. (2008). A hybrid and novel approach to teaching computer programming in MIS curriculum. In S. Negash, M. Whitman, A. Woszczynski, K. Hoganson, & H. Mattord (Eds.), *Handbook of distance learning for real-time and asynchronous information technology education* (pp. 259–281). Hershey, PA: IGI Global. doi:10.4018/978-1-59904-964-9.ch014

Roche, E. M. (1993). International computing and the international regime. *Journal of Global Information Management, 1*(2), 33–44. doi:10.4018/jgim.1993040103

Rocheleau, B. (2007). Politics, accountability, and information management. In G. Garson (Ed.), *Modern public information technology systems: Issues and challenges* (pp. 35–71). Hershey, PA: IGI Global. doi:10.4018/978-1-59904-051-6.ch003

Rodrigues Filho, J. (2010). E-government in Brazil: Reinforcing dominant institutions or reducing citizenship? In C. Reddick (Ed.), *Politics, democracy and e-government: Participation and service delivery* (pp. 347–362). Hershey, PA: IGI Global. doi:10.4018/978-1-61520-933-0.ch021

Rodriguez, S. R., & Thorp, D. A. (2013). eLearning for industry: A case study of the project management process. In A. Benson, J. Moore, & S. Williams van Rooij (Eds.), Cases on educational technology planning, design, and implementation: A project management perspective (pp. 319-342). Hershey, PA: IGI Global. doi:10.4018/978-1-4666-4237-9.ch017

Roman, A. V. (2013). Delineating three dimensions of e-government success: Security, functionality, and transformation. In J. Gil-Garcia (Ed.), *E-government success factors and measures: Theories, concepts, and methodologies* (pp. 171–192). Hershey, PA: IGI Global. doi:10.4018/978-1-4666-4058-0.ch010

Ross, S. C., Tyran, C. K., & Auer, D. J. (2008). Up in smoke: Rebuilding after an IT disaster. In H. Nemati (Ed.), *Information security and ethics: Concepts, methodologies, tools, and applications* (pp. 3659–3675). Hershey, PA: IGI Global. doi:10.4018/978-1-59904-937-3.ch248

Ross, S. C., Tyran, C. K., Auer, D. J., Junell, J. M., & Williams, T. G. (2005). Up in smoke: Rebuilding after an IT disaster. *Journal of Cases on Information Technology*, 7(2), 31–49. doi:10.4018/jcit.2005040103

Roy, J. (2008). Security, sovereignty, and continental interoperability: Canada's elusive balance. In T. Loendorf & G. Garson (Eds.), *Patriotic information systems* (pp. 153–176). Hershey, PA: IGI Global. doi:10.4018/978-1-59904-594-8.ch007

Rubeck, R. F., & Miller, G. A. (2009). vGOV: Remote video access to government services. In A. Scupola (Ed.), Cases on managing e-services (pp. 253-268). Hershey, PA: IGI Global. doi:10.4018/978-1-60566-064-6.ch017

Saekow, A., & Boonmee, C. (2011). The challenges of implementing e-government interoperability in Thailand: Case of official electronic correspondence letters exchange across government departments. In Y. Charalabidis (Ed.), *Interoperability in digital public services and administration: Bridging e-government and e-business* (pp. 40–61). Hershey, PA: IGI Global. doi:10.4018/978-1-61520-887-6.ch003

Saekow, A., & Boonmee, C. (2012). The challenges of implementing e-government interoperability in Thailand: Case of official electronic correspondence letters exchange across government departments. In *Digital democracy: Concepts, methodologies, tools, and applications* (pp. 1883–1905). Hershey, PA: IGI Global. doi:10.4018/978-1-4666-1740-7.ch094

Sagsan, M., & Medeni, T. (2012). Understanding "knowledge management (KM) paradigms" from social media perspective: An empirical study on discussion group for KM at professional networking site. In M. Cruz-Cunha, P. Gonçalves, N. Lopes, E. Miranda, & G. Putnik (Eds.), *Handbook of research on business social networking: Organizational, managerial, and technological dimensions* (pp. 738–755). Hershey, PA: IGI Global. doi:10.4018/978-1-61350-168-9.ch039

Sahi, G., & Madan, S. (2013). Information security threats in ERP enabled e-governance: Challenges and solutions. In *Enterprise resource planning: Concepts, methodologies, tools, and applications* (pp. 825–837). Hershey, PA: IGI Global. doi:10.4018/978-1-4666-4153-2.ch048

Sanford, C., & Bhattacherjee, A. (2008). IT implementation in a developing country municipality: A sociocognitive analysis. *International Journal of Technology and Human Interaction*, 4(3), 68–93. doi:10.4018/jthi.2008070104

Schelin, S. H. (2003). E-government: An overview. In G. Garson (Ed.), *Public information technology: Policy and management issues* (pp. 120–138). Hershey, PA: IGI Global. doi:10.4018/978-1-59140-060-8.ch006

Schelin, S. H. (2004). Training for digital government. In A. Pavlichev & G. Garson (Eds.), *Digital government: Principles and best practices* (pp. 263–275). Hershey, PA: IGI Global. doi:10.4018/978-1-59140-122-3.ch017

Schelin, S. H. (2007). E-government: An overview. In G. Garson (Ed.), *Modern public information technology systems: Issues and challenges* (pp. 110–126). Hershey, PA: IGI Global. doi:10.4018/978-1-59904-051-6.ch006

Schelin, S. H., & Garson, G. (2004). Theoretical justification of critical success factors. In G. Garson & S. Schelin (Eds.), *IT solutions series: Humanizing information technology: Advice from experts* (pp. 4–15). Hershey, PA: IGI Global. doi:10.4018/978-1-59140-245-9.ch002

Scime, A. (2002). Information systems and computer science model curricula: A comparative look. In M. Dadashzadeh, A. Saber, & S. Saber (Eds.), *Information technology education in the new millennium* (pp. 146–158). Hershey, PA: IGI Global. doi:10.4018/978-1-931777-05-6.ch018

Scime, A. (2009). Computing curriculum analysis and development. In M. Khosrow-Pour (Ed.), *Encyclopedia of information science and technology* (2nd ed.; pp. 667–671). Hershey, PA: IGI Global. doi:10.4018/978-1-60566-026-4.ch108

Scime, A., & Wania, C. (2008). Computing curricula: A comparison of models. In C. Van Slyke (Ed.), *Information communication technologies: Concepts, methodologies, tools, and applications* (pp. 1270–1283). Hershey, PA: IGI Global. doi:10.4018/978-1-59904-949-6.ch088

Seidman, S. B. (2009). An international perspective on professional software engineering credentials. In H. Ellis, S. Demurjian, & J. Naveda (Eds.), *Software engineering: Effective teaching and learning approaches and practices* (pp. 351–361). Hershey, PA: IGI Global. doi:10.4018/978-1-60566-102-5.ch018

Seifert, J. W. (2007). E-government act of 2002 in the United States. In A. Anttiroiko & M. Malkia (Eds.), *Encyclopedia of digital government* (pp. 476–481). Hershey, PA: IGI Global. doi:10.4018/978-1-59140-789-8.ch072

Seifert, J. W., & Relyea, H. C. (2008). E-government act of 2002 in the United States. In A. Anttiroiko (Ed.), *Electronic government: Concepts, methodologies, tools, and applications* (pp. 154–161). Hershey, PA: IGI Global. doi:10.4018/978-1-59904-947-2.ch013

Seufert, S. (2002). E-learning business models: Framework and best practice examples. In M. Raisinghani (Ed.), *Cases on worldwide e-commerce: Theory in action* (pp. 70–94). Hershey, PA: IGI Global. doi:10.4018/978-1-930708-27-3.ch004

Shareef, M. A., & Archer, N. (2012). E-government service development. In M. Shareef, N. Archer, & S. Dutta (Eds.), *E-government service maturity and development: Cultural, organizational and technological perspectives* (pp. 1–14). Hershey, PA: IGI Global. doi:10.4018/978-1-60960-848-4.ch001

Shareef, M. A., & Archer, N. (2012). E-government initiatives: Review studies on different countries. In M. Shareef, N. Archer, & S. Dutta (Eds.), *E-government service maturity and development: Cultural, organizational and technological perspectives* (pp. 40–76). Hershey, PA: IGI Global. doi:10.4018/978-1-60960-848-4.ch003

Shareef, M. A., Kumar, U., & Kumar, V. (2011). E-government development: Performance evaluation parameters. In M. Shareef, V. Kumar, U. Kumar, & Y. Dwivedi (Eds.), *Stakeholder adoption of e-government services: Driving and resisting factors* (pp. 197–213). Hershey, PA: IGI Global. doi:10.4018/978-1-60960-601-5.ch010

Shareef, M. A., Kumar, U., Kumar, V., & Niktash, M. (2012). Electronic-government vision: Case studies for objectives, strategies, and initiatives. In M. Shareef, N. Archer, & S. Dutta (Eds.), *E-government service maturity and development: Cultural, organizational and technological perspectives* (pp. 15–39). Hershey, PA: IGI Global. doi:10.4018/978-1-60960-848-4.ch002

Shukla, P., Kumar, A., & Anu Kumar, P. B. (2013). Impact of national culture on business continuity management system implementation. *International Journal of Risk and Contingency Management*, 2(3), 23–36. doi:10.4018/ijrcm.2013070102

Shulman, S. W. (2007). The federal docket management system and the prospect for digital democracy in U S rulemaking. In G. Garson (Ed.), *Modern public information technology systems: Issues and challenges* (pp. 166–184). Hershey, PA: IGI Global. doi:10.4018/978-1-59904-051-6.ch009

Simonovic, S. (2007). Problems of offline government in e-Serbia. In A. Anttiroiko & M. Malkia (Eds.), *Encyclopedia of digital government* (pp. 1342–1351). Hershey, PA: IGI Global. doi:10.4018/978-1-59140-789-8.ch205

Simonovic, S. (2008). Problems of offline government in e-Serbia. In A. Anttiroiko (Ed.), *Electronic government: Concepts, methodologies, tools, and applications* (pp. 2929–2942). Hershey, PA: IGI Global. doi:10.4018/978-1-59904-947-2.ch219

Related References

Singh, A. M. (2005). Information systems and technology in South Africa. In M. Khosrow-Pour (Ed.), *Encyclopedia of information science and technology* (pp. 1497–1502). Hershey, PA: IGI Global. doi:10.4018/978-1-59140-553-5.ch263

Singh, S., & Naidoo, G. (2005). Towards an e-government solution: A South African perspective. In W. Huang, K. Siau, & K. Wei (Eds.), *Electronic government strategies and implementation* (pp. 325–353). Hershey, PA: IGI Global. doi:10.4018/978-1-59140-348-7.ch014

Snoke, R., & Underwood, A. (2002). Generic attributes of IS graduates: An analysis of Australian views. In F. Tan (Ed.), *Advanced topics in global information management* (Vol. 1, pp. 370–384). Hershey, PA: IGI Global. doi:10.4018/978-1-930708-43-3.ch023

Sommer, L. (2006). Revealing unseen organizations in higher education: A study framework and application example. In A. Metcalfe (Ed.), *Knowledge management and higher education: A critical analysis* (pp. 115–146). Hershey, PA: IGI Global. doi:10.4018/978-1-59140-509-2.ch007

Song, H., Kidd, T., & Owens, E. (2011). Examining technological disparities and instructional practices in English language arts classroom: Implications for school leadership and teacher training. In L. Tomei (Ed.), *Online courses and ICT in education: Emerging practices and applications* (pp. 258–274). Hershey, PA: IGI Global. doi:10.4018/978-1-60960-150-8.ch020

Speaker, P. J., & Kleist, V. F. (2003). Using information technology to meet electronic commerce and MIS education demands. In A. Aggarwal (Ed.), *Web-based education: Learning from experience* (pp. 280–291). Hershey, PA: IGI Global. doi:10.4018/978-1-59140-102-5.ch017

Spitler, V. K. (2007). Learning to use IT in the workplace: Mechanisms and masters. In M. Mahmood (Ed.), *Contemporary issues in end user computing* (pp. 292–323). Hershey, PA: IGI Global. doi:10.4018/978-1-59140-926-7.ch013

Stellefson, M. (2011). Considerations for marketing distance education courses in health education: Five important questions to examine before development. In U. Demiray & S. Sever (Eds.), *Marketing online education programs: Frameworks for promotion and communication* (pp. 222–234). Hershey, PA: IGI Global. doi:10.4018/978-1-60960-074-7.ch014

Straub, D. W., & Loch, K. D. (2006). Creating and developing a program of global research. *Journal of Global Information Management*, *14*(2), 1–28. doi:10.4018/jgim.2006040101

Straub, D. W., Loch, K. D., & Hill, C. E. (2002). Transfer of information technology to the Arab world: A test of cultural influence modeling. In M. Dadashzadeh (Ed.), *Information technology management in developing countries* (pp. 92–134). Hershey, PA: IGI Global. doi:10.4018/978-1-931777-03-2.ch005

Straub, D. W., Loch, K. D., & Hill, C. E. (2003). Transfer of information technology to the Arab world: A test of cultural influence modeling. In F. Tan (Ed.), *Advanced topics in global information management* (Vol. 2, pp. 141–172). Hershey, PA: IGI Global. doi:10.4018/978-1-59140-064-6.ch009

Suki, N. M., Ramayah, T., Ming, M. K., & Suki, N. M. (2013). Factors enhancing employed job seekers intentions to use social networking sites as a job search tool. In A. Mesquita (Ed.), *User perception and influencing factors of technology in everyday life* (pp. 265–281). Hershey, PA: IGI Global. doi:10.4018/978-1-4666-1954-8.ch018

Suomi, R. (2006). Introducing electronic patient records to hospitals: Innovation adoption paths. In T. Spil & R. Schuring (Eds.), *E-health systems diffusion and use: The innovation, the user and the use IT model* (pp. 128–146). Hershey, PA: IGI Global. doi:10.4018/978-1-59140-423-1.ch008

Swim, J., & Barker, L. (2012). Pathways into a gendered occupation: Brazilian women in IT. *International Journal of Social and Organizational Dynamics in IT*, *2*(4), 34–51. doi:10.4018/ijsodit.2012100103

Tarafdar, M., & Vaidya, S. D. (2006). Adoption and implementation of IT in developing nations: Experiences from two public sector enterprises in India. In M. Khosrow-Pour (Ed.), *Cases on information technology planning, design and implementation* (pp. 208–233). Hershey, PA: IGI Global. doi:10.4018/978-1-59904-408-8.ch013

Tarafdar, M., & Vaidya, S. D. (2008). Adoption and implementation of IT in developing nations: Experiences from two public sector enterprises in India. In G. Garson & M. Khosrow-Pour (Eds.), *Handbook of research on public information technology* (pp. 905–924). Hershey, PA: IGI Global. doi:10.4018/978-1-59904-857-4.ch076

Thesing, Z. (2007). Zarina thesing, pumpkin patch. In M. Hunter (Ed.), *Contemporary chief information officers: Management experiences* (pp. 83–94). Hershey, PA: IGI Global. doi:10.4018/978-1-59904-078-3.ch007

Thomas, J. C. (2004). Public involvement in public administration in the information age: Speculations on the effects of technology. In M. Malkia, A. Anttiroiko, & R. Savolainen (Eds.), *eTransformation in governance: New directions in government and politics* (pp. 67–84). Hershey, PA: IGI Global. doi:10.4018/978-1-59140-130-8.ch004

Treiblmaier, H., & Chong, S. (2013). Trust and perceived risk of personal information as antecedents of online information disclosure: Results from three countries. In F. Tan (Ed.), *Global diffusion and adoption of technologies for knowledge and information sharing* (pp. 341–361). Hershey, PA: IGI Global. doi:10.4018/978-1-4666-2142-8.ch015

van Grembergen, W., & de Haes, S. (2008). IT governance in practice: Six case studies. In W. van Grembergen & S. De Haes (Eds.), *Implementing information technology governance: Models, practices and cases* (pp. 125–237). Hershey, PA: IGI Global. doi:10.4018/978-1-59904-924-3.ch004

van Os, G., Homburg, V., & Bekkers, V. (2013). Contingencies and convergence in European social security: ICT coordination in the back office of the welfare state. In M. Cruz-Cunha, I. Miranda, & P. Gonçalves (Eds.), *Handbook of research on ICTs and management systems for improving efficiency in healthcare and social care* (pp. 268–287). Hershey, PA: IGI Global. doi:10.4018/978-1-4666-3990-4.ch013

Velloso, A. B., Gassenferth, W., & Machado, M. A. (2012). Evaluating IBMEC-RJ's intranet usability using fuzzy logic. In M. Cruz-Cunha, P. Gonçalves, N. Lopes, E. Miranda, & G. Putnik (Eds.), *Handbook of research on business social networking: Organizational, managerial, and technological dimensions* (pp. 185–205). Hershey, PA: IGI Global. doi:10.4018/978-1-61350-168-9.ch010

Villablanca, A. C., Baxi, H., & Anderson, K. (2009). Novel data interface for evaluating cardiovascular outcomes in women. In A. Dwivedi (Ed.), *Handbook of research on information technology management and clinical data administration in healthcare* (pp. 34–53). Hershey, PA: IGI Global. doi:10.4018/978-1-60566-356-2.ch003

Villablanca, A. C., Baxi, H., & Anderson, K. (2011). Novel data interface for evaluating cardiovascular outcomes in women. In *Clinical technologies: Concepts, methodologies, tools and applications* (pp. 2094–2113). Hershey, PA: IGI Global. doi:10.4018/978-1-60960-561-2.ch806

Virkar, S. (2011). Information and communication technologies in administrative reform for development: Exploring the case of property tax systems in Karnataka, India. In J. Steyn, J. Van Belle, & E. Mansilla (Eds.), *ICTs for global development and sustainability: Practice and applications* (pp. 127–149). Hershey, PA: IGI Global. doi:10.4018/978-1-61520-997-2.ch006

Virkar, S. (2013). Designing and implementing e-government projects: Actors, influences, and fields of play. In S. Saeed & C. Reddick (Eds.), *Human-centered system design for electronic governance* (pp. 88–110). Hershey, PA: IGI Global. doi:10.4018/978-1-4666-3640-8.ch007

Wallace, A. (2009). E-justice: An Australian perspective. In A. Martínez & P. Abat (Eds.), *E-justice: Using information communication technologies in the court system* (pp. 204–228). Hershey, PA: IGI Global. doi:10.4018/978-1-59904-998-4.ch014

Wang, G. (2012). E-democratic administration and bureaucratic responsiveness: A primary study of bureaucrats' perceptions of the civil service e-mail box in Taiwan. In K. Kloby & M. D'Agostino (Eds.), *Citizen 2.0: Public and governmental interaction through web 2.0 technologies* (pp. 146–173). Hershey, PA: IGI Global. doi:10.4018/978-1-4666-0318-9.ch009

Wangpipatwong, S., Chutimaskul, W., & Papasratorn, B. (2011). Quality enhancing the continued use of e-government web sites: Evidence from e-citizens of Thailand. In V. Weerakkody (Ed.), *Applied technology integration in governmental organizations: New e-government research* (pp. 20–36). Hershey, PA: IGI Global. doi:10.4018/978-1-60960-162-1.ch002

Wedemeijer, L. (2006). Long-term evolution of a conceptual schema at a life insurance company. In M. Khosrow-Pour (Ed.), *Cases on database technologies and applications* (pp. 202–226). Hershey, PA: IGI Global. doi:10.4018/978-1-59904-399-9.ch012

Whybrow, E. (2008). Digital access, ICT fluency, and the economically disadvantages: Approaches to minimize the digital divide. In F. Tan (Ed.), *Global information technologies: Concepts, methodologies, tools, and applications* (pp. 1409–1422). Hershey, PA: IGI Global. doi:10.4018/978-1-59904-939-7.ch102

Whybrow, E. (2008). Digital access, ICT fluency, and the economically disadvantages: Approaches to minimize the digital divide. In C. Van Slyke (Ed.), *Information communication technologies: Concepts, methodologies, tools, and applications* (pp. 764–777). Hershey, PA: IGI Global. doi:10.4018/978-1-59904-949-6.ch049

Wickramasinghe, N., & Geisler, E. (2010). Key considerations for the adoption and implementation of knowledge management in healthcare operations. In M. Saito, N. Wickramasinghe, M. Fuji, & E. Geisler (Eds.), *Redesigning innovative healthcare operation and the role of knowledge management* (pp. 125–142). Hershey, PA: IGI Global. doi:10.4018/978-1-60566-284-8.ch009

Wickramasinghe, N., & Geisler, E. (2012). Key considerations for the adoption and implementation of knowledge management in healthcare operations. In *Organizational learning and knowledge: Concepts, methodologies, tools and applications* (pp. 1316–1328). Hershey, PA: IGI Global. doi:10.4018/978-1-60960-783-8.ch405

Wickramasinghe, N., & Goldberg, S. (2007). A framework for delivering m-health excellence. In L. Al-Hakim (Ed.), *Web mobile-based applications for healthcare management* (pp. 36–61). Hershey, PA: IGI Global. doi:10.4018/978-1-59140-658-7.ch002

Wickramasinghe, N., & Goldberg, S. (2008). Critical success factors for delivering m-health excellence. In N. Wickramasinghe & E. Geisler (Eds.), *Encyclopedia of healthcare information systems* (pp. 339–351). Hershey, PA: IGI Global. doi:10.4018/978-1-59904-889-5.ch045

Wyld, D. (2009). Radio frequency identification (RFID) technology. In J. Symonds, J. Ayoade, & D. Parry (Eds.), *Auto-identification and ubiquitous computing applications* (pp. 279–293). Hershey, PA: IGI Global. doi:10.4018/978-1-60566-298-5.ch017

Yaghmaei, F. (2010). Understanding computerised information systems usage in community health. In J. Rodrigues (Ed.), *Health information systems: Concepts, methodologies, tools, and applications* (pp. 1388–1399). Hershey, PA: IGI Global. doi:10.4018/978-1-60566-988-5.ch088

Yee, G., El-Khatib, K., Korba, L., Patrick, A. S., Song, R., & Xu, Y. (2005). Privacy and trust in e-government. In W. Huang, K. Siau, & K. Wei (Eds.), *Electronic government strategies and implementation* (pp. 145–190). Hershey, PA: IGI Global. doi:10.4018/978-1-59140-348-7.ch007

Yeh, S., & Chu, P. (2010). Evaluation of e-government services: A citizen-centric approach to citizen e-complaint services. In C. Reddick (Ed.), *Citizens and e-government: Evaluating policy and management* (pp. 400–417). Hershey, PA: IGI Global. doi:10.4018/978-1-61520-931-6.ch022

Young-Jin, S., & Seang-tae, K. (2008). E-government concepts, measures, and best practices. In A. Anttiroiko (Ed.), *Electronic government: Concepts, methodologies, tools, and applications* (pp. 32–57). Hershey, PA: IGI Global. doi:10.4018/978-1-59904-947-2.ch004

Yun, H. J., & Opheim, C. (2012). New technology communication in American state governments: The impact on citizen participation. In K. Bwalya & S. Zulu (Eds.), *Handbook of research on e-government in emerging economies: Adoption, e-participation, and legal frameworks* (pp. 573–590). Hershey, PA: IGI Global. doi:10.4018/978-1-4666-0324-0.ch029

Zhang, N., Guo, X., Chen, G., & Chau, P. Y. (2011). User evaluation of e-government systems: A Chinese cultural perspective. In F. Tan (Ed.), *International enterprises and global information technologies: Advancing management practices* (pp. 63–84). Hershey, PA: IGI Global. doi:10.4018/978-1-60960-605-3.ch004

Zuo, Y., & Hu, W. (2011). Trust-based information risk management in a supply chain network. In J. Wang (Ed.), *Supply chain optimization, management and integration: Emerging applications* (pp. 181–196). Hershey, PA: IGI Global. doi:10.4018/978-1-60960-135-5.ch013

Compilation of References

Abdallah, A. S., Abbott, A. L., & El-Nasr, M. A. (2007a). A New Face Detection Technique using 2D DCT and Self Organizing Feature Map. *Proceedings of World Academy of Science. Engineering and Technology*, *21*, 15–19.

Abdallah, A. S., El-Nasr, M. A., & Abbott, A. C. (2007b). A New Colour Image Database for Benchmarking of Automatic Face Detection and Human Şkin Segmentation Techniques. *Proceedings of World Academy of Science. Engineering and Technology*, *20*, 353–357.

Aharon, M., Elad, M., & Bruckstein, A. (2006). K-SVD: An algorithm for designing overcomplete dictionaries for sparse representation. *IEEE Transactions on Signal Processing*, *54*(11), 4311–4322. doi:10.1109/TSP.2006.881199

Aldoma, A., Tombari, F., Di Stefano, L., & Vincze, M. (2012). A global hypotheses verification method for 3d object recognition. *Computer Vision–ECCV*, *2012*, 511–524.

Ali, S. S., & Prakash, S. (2015). Enhanced fingerprint Shell. *Signal Processing and Integrated Networks (SPIN), 2015 2nd International Conference on*. doi:10.1109/SPIN.2015.7095438

Allano, L. (2009). *La Biométrie multimodale: stratégies de fusion de scores et mesures de dépendance appliquées aux bases de personnes virtuelles* (Thèse de doctorat). Institut National des Télécommunications Paris.

AlMahafzah, H., & AlRwashdeh, M. Z. (2012). A survey of multibiometric systems. *International Journal of Computers and Applications*, *43*(15).

Almazan, J., Gordo, A., Fornés, A., & Valveny, E. (2013). Handwritten word spotting with corrected attributes. *Proceedings of the IEEE International Conference on Computer Vision*, 1017-1024.

Almazan, J., Gordo, A., Fornés, A., & Valveny, E. (2014). Segmentation-free word spotting with exemplar svms. *Pattern Recognition*, *47*(12), 3967–3978. doi:10.1016/j.patcog.2014.06.005

Al-Mohair, H., Saleh, J., & Suandi, S. (2012). Human skin color detection: A review on neural network perspective. *International Journal of Innovative Computing, Information, & Control*, *8*(12), 8115–8131.

Alsabti, K., Ranka, S., & Singh, V. (1997). *An Efficient K-Means Clustering Algorithm*. Electrical Engineering and Computer Science.

Alshehri, S. (2012). Neural Networks Performance for Skin Detection. *Journal of Emerging Trends in Computing and Information Sciences, 3*(12), 1582–1585.

Aneja, D., & Rawat, T. K. (2013). Fuzzy Clustering Algorithms for Effective Medical Image Segmentation. *International Journal of Intelligent Systems and Applications, 5*(11), 55–61. doi:10.5815/ijisa.2013.11.06

Angelova, A., Krizhevsky, A., Vanhoucke, V., Ogale, A. S., & Ferguson, D. (2015, September). *Real-Time Pedestrian Detection with Deep Network Cascades* (Vol. 2). BMVC. doi:10.5244/C.29.32

Arcelli, C., & Di Baja, G. S. (1985). A width-independent fast thinning algorithm. *IEEE Transactions on Pattern Analysis and Machine Intelligence, 4*(7), 463–474. doi:10.1109/TPAMI.1985.4767685 PMID:21869284

Arrospide, J., Salgado, L., & Marinas, J. (2013). HOG-like gradient-based descriptor for visual vehicle detection. *Intelligent Vehicles Symposium (IV)*, 223-228.

Audras, C., Comport, A. I., Meilland, M., & Rives, P. 2011. Real-time dense RGBD localisation and mapping. In *Australian Conference on Robotics and Automation*. Monash University.

Bataineh, K. M., Najia, M., & Saqera, M. (2011). A Comparison Study between Various Fuzzy Clustering Algorithms. *Jordan Journal of Mechanical and Industrial Engineering, 5*(4), 335–343.

Bauer, S., Wasza, J., Haase, S., Marosi, N., & Hornegger, J. (2011). Multi-modal surface registration for markerless initial patient setup in radiation therapy using Microsoft's Kinect sensor. *Computer Vision Workshops (ICCV Workshops), 2011 IEEE International Conference on*, 1175–1181.

Bay, H., Tuytelaars, T., & Van Gool, L. (2006). Surf: Speeded up robust features. In *European conference on computer vision*, Springer Berlin Heidelberg.

Bay, H., Ess, A., Tuytelaars, T., & Van Gool, L. (2008, June). Speeded-up robust features (surf). *Computer Vision and Image Understanding, 110*(3), 346–359. doi:10.1016/j.cviu.2007.09.014

Bengio, Y., Courville, A., & Vincent, P. (2013). Representation learning: A review and new perspectives. *IEEE Transactions on Pattern Analysis and Machine Intelligence, 35*(8), 1798–1828. doi:10.1109/TPAMI.2013.50 PMID:23787338

Besl, P. J., & McKay, N. D. (1992). A method for registration of 3-D shapes. *IEEE Transactions on Pattern Analysis and Machine Intelligence, 14*(2), 239–256. doi:10.1109/34.121791

Bhowmik, U. K., Ashrafi, A., & Adhami, R. R. (2009). A Fingerprint Verification Algorithm Using the Smallest Minimum Sum of Closest Euclidean Distance. In *Electrical, Communications, and Computers, 2009. CONIELECOMP 2009. International Conference on* (pp. 90-95). IEEE. doi:10.1109/CONIELECOMP.2009.57

Bicchi, A., & Kumar, V. (2000). Robotic grasping and contact: A review. In *Robotics and Automation, 2000. Proceedings. ICRA'00. IEEE International Conference on* (vol. 1, pp. 348–353). IEEE. doi:10.1109/ROBOT.2000.844081

Bilgin, G., Ertürk, S., & Yildirim, T. (2011). Segmentation of Hyperspectral Images via Subtractive Clustering and Cluster Validation Using One-Class Support Vector Machines. *IEEE Transactions on Geoscience and Remote Sensing*, 49(8), 2936–2944. doi:10.1109/TGRS.2011.2113186

Bohg, J., Morales, A., Asfour, T., & Kragic, D. (2014). Data-driven grasp synthesisa survey. *IEEE Transactions on Robotics*, 30(2), 289–309. doi:10.1109/TRO.2013.2289018

Borges, P. V. K., Conci, N., & Cavallaro, A. (2013). Video-based human behavior understanding: A survey. *IEEE Transactions on Circuits and Systems for Video Technology*, 23(11), 1993–2008. doi:10.1109/TCSVT.2013.2270402

Bosch, A., Zisserman, A., & Munoz, X. (2007, July). Representing shape with a spatial pyramid kernel. In *Proceedings of the 6th ACM international conference on Image and video retrieval* (pp. 401-408). ACM. doi:10.1145/1282280.1282340

Boudissa, A., Tan, J. K., Kim, H., Shinomiya, T., & Ishikawa, S. (2013). A novel pedestrian detector on low-resolution images: Gradient LBP using patterns of oriented edges. *IEICE Transactions on Information and Systems*, 96(12), 2882–2887. doi:10.1587/transinf.E96.D.2882

Brancati, N., De Pietro, G., Frucci, M., & Gallo, L. (2016). Human Skin Detection through Correlation Rules between the YCb and YCr Subspaces based on Dynamic Color Clustering. *Computer Vision and Image Understanding*, 155, 33–42. doi:10.1016/j.cviu.2016.12.001

Brar, G. S. (2007). An Efficient Data Clustering Algorithm Using Fuzzy Logic For Control Of A Multi Compressor System. *IETECH Journal of Electrical Analysis*, 1(2), 130–136.

Bronstein, A., Bronstein, M., & Ovsjanikov, M. (2010). 3d features, surface descriptors, and object descriptors. *3D Imaging, Analysis, and Applications*.

Bro, R., & Smilde, A. K. (2014). Principal component analysis. *Analytical Methods*, 6(9), 2812–2831. doi:10.1039/C3AY41907J

Brunnstrom, K., Eklundh, J., & Uhlin, T. (1996). Active Fixation for Scene Exploration. *International Journal of Computer Vision*, 17(2). doi:10.1007/BF00058749

Buades, A., Coll, B., & Morel, J. M. (2005, June). A non-local algorithm for image denoising. In *Computer Vision and Pattern Recognition, 2005. CVPR 2005. IEEE Computer Society Conference on* (Vol. 2, pp. 60-65). IEEE. doi:10.1109/CVPR.2005.38

Campbell, R. J., & Flynn, P. J. (2001). A survey of free-form object representation and recognition techniques. *Computer Vision and Image Understanding*, 81(2), 166–210. doi:10.1006/cviu.2000.0889

Cao, L., Liu, Z., & Huang, T. S. (2010, June). Cross-dataset action detection. In Computer vision and pattern recognition (CVPR), 2010 IEEE conference on (pp. 1998-2005). IEEE. doi:10.1109/CVPR.2010.5539875

Carcagnì, P., Del Coco, M., Leo, M., & Distante, C. (2015). Facial expression recognition and histograms of oriented gradients: A comprehensive study. *SpringerPlus*, *4*(1), 645. doi:10.1186/s40064-015-1427-3 PMID:26543779

Carson, C., Belongie, S., Greenspan, H., & Malik, J. (2002). Blobworld: Image Segmentation Using Expectation Maximisation and Its Application to Image Querying. *IEEE Transactions on Pattern Analysis and Machine Intelligence*, *24*(8), 1026–1038. doi:10.1109/TPAMI.2002.1023800

Cazorla, M., Viejo, D., & Pomares, C. (2010). Study of the SR4000 camera. In *Workshop of Physical Agents*. Red de Agentes Físicos.

Chan, J., Ziftci, C., & Forsyth, D. (2006). Searching off-line arabic documents. *Computer Vision and Pattern Recognition, 2*, 1455-1462. doi:10.1109/CVPR.2006.269

Chandrappa, D. N., Ravishankar, M., & RameshBabu, D. R. (2011). Face detection in color images using skin color model algorithm based on skin color information. *2011 3rd international conference on electronics computer technology (ICECT)*, 254–258.

Chane, C. S., Schu¨tze, R., Boochs, F., & Marzani, F. S. (2013). Registration of 3D and Multispectral Data for the Study of Cultural Heritage Surfaces. *Sensors (Basel)*, *13*(1), 1004–1020. doi:10.3390/s130101004 PMID:23322103

Chang, H., Lee, H. D., & Overill, R. (2014). Human-centric security service and its application in smart space. *Security and Communication Networks*, *7*(10), 1439–1440.

Chang, P., Shen, J., & Cheung, S.-C. (2013). A Robust RGB-D SLAM System for 3D Environment with Planar Surfacess. *Proc. of the IEEE International Conference on Image Processing*.

Chaumette, F. (2004). Image moments: A general and useful set of features for visual servoing. *IEEE Transactions on Robotics*, *20*(4), 713–723. doi:10.1109/TRO.2004.829463

Chen, Qin, & Jia. (2008). *A Weighted Mean Substractive Clustering Algorithm*. Academic Press.

Chen, Y., & Medioni, G. (1991). Object modeling by registration of multiple range images. *Proceedings IEEE International Conference on Robotics and Automation*, 2724-2729. doi:10.1109/ROBOT.1991.132043

Chen, B. J., Shu, H. Z., Zhang, H., Chen, G., Toumoulin, C., Dillenseger, J. L., & Luo, L. M. (2012). Quaternion Zernike moments and their invariants for color image analysis and object recognition. *Signal Processing*, *92*(2), 308–318. doi:10.1016/j.sigpro.2011.07.018

Cheng, Z., Qin, L., Huang, Q., Yan, S., & Tian, Q. (2014). Recognizing human group action by layered model with multiple cues. *Neurocomputing*, *136*, 124–135. doi:10.1016/j.neucom.2014.01.019

Chen, H., Huang, C., & Fu, C. (2008). *Hybrid-boost learning for multi-pose face detection and facial expression recognition. In Pattern Recognition society* (Vol. 41, pp. 1173–1185). Elsevier.

Chiang, C., Tai, W., Yang, M., Huang, Y., & Huang, C. (2003). A novel method for detecting lips, eyes and faces in real time. *Real-Time Imaging, 9*(4), 277–287. doi:10.1016/j.rti.2003.08.003

Chin, S., Seng, K., Ang, L., & Lim, K. (2009). New lips detection and tracking system. *Proceedings of the international multiconference of engineers and computer scientists, 1.*

Choi, W., Shahid, K., & Savarese, S. (2009, September). What are they doing?: Collective activity classification using spatio-temporal relationship among people. In *Computer Vision Workshops (ICCV Workshops), 2009 IEEE 12th International Conference on* (pp. 1282-1289). IEEE.

Choujaa, D., & Dulay, N. (2008, December). Tracme: Temporal activity recognition using mobile phone data. In *Embedded and Ubiquitous Computing, 2008. EUC'08. IEEE/IFIP International Conference on* (Vol. 1, pp. 119-126). IEEE.

Cimpoi, M., Maji, S., Kokkinos, I., Mohamed, S., & Vedaldi, A. (2014). *Describing Textures in the Wild, Computer Vision and Pattern Recognition.* CVPR.

Ciocca, G., Cusano, C., & Schettini, R. (2015). Image orientation detection using LBP-based features and logistic regression. *Multimedia Tools and Applications, 74*(9), 3013–3034. doi:10.1007/s11042-013-1766-4

Collins, R. T., Lipton, A. J., Kanade, T., Fujiyoshi, H., Duggins, D., Tsin, Y., ... & Wixson, L. (2000). A system for video surveillance and monitoring. *VSAM final report*, 1-68.

Collobert, R., & Weston, J. (2008, July). A unified architecture for natural language processing: Deep neural networks with multitask learning. In *Proceedings of the 25th international conference on Machine learning* (pp. 160-167). ACM. doi:10.1145/1390156.1390177

Comport, A. I., Malis, E., & Rives, P. (2007). Accurate Quadrifocal Tracking for Robust 3D Visual Odometry. *Robotics and Automation, 2007 IEEE International Conference on*, 40–45.

Corona, C., & Llanes-santiago, O. (2018). An Approach to Fault Diagnosis Using Fuzzy Clustering. Conference of the European Society for Fuzzy Logic and Technology, 641. doi:10.1007/978-3-319-66830-7

Corvee, E., & Bremond, F. (2010, August). Body parts detection for people tracking using trees of histogram of oriented gradient descriptors. *Advanced Video and Signal Based Surveillance, Seventh IEEE International Conference*, 469-475. doi:10.1109/AVSS.2010.51

Dabov, K., Foi, A., Katkovnik, V., & Egiazarian, K. (2007). Video denoising by sparse 3D transform-domain collaborative filtering. In *European Signal Processing Conference (Vol. 149)*. Tampere, Finland: Academic Press.

Dabov, K., Foi, A., Katkovnik, V., & Egiazarian, K. (2006, January). Image denoising with block-matching and 3 D filtering. *Proceedings of the Society for Photo-Instrumentation Engineers, 6064*(30), 606414–606414. doi:10.1117/12.643267

Dai, X., Zhang, H., Liu, T., Shu, H., & Luo, L. (2014). Legendre moment invariants to blur and affine transformation and their use in image recognition. *Pattern Analysis & Applications*, *17*(2), 311–326. doi:10.1007/s10044-012-0273-y

Dalal, N., & Triggs, B. (2005, June). Histograms of oriented gradients for human detection. In *Computer Vision and Pattern Recognition, 2005. CVPR 2005. IEEE Computer Society Conference on* (Vol. 1, pp. 886-893). IEEE. doi:10.1109/CVPR.2005.177

Dalton, L., Ballarin, V., & Brun, M. (2009). Clustering Algorithms: On Learning, Validation, Performance, and Applications to Genomics. *Current Genomics*, *10*(6), 430–445. doi:10.2174/138920209789177601 PMID:20190957

Das, P., Sarkar, A., Halder, S., Kundu, D., Ghosh, S., & Das Gupta, S. (2015). *A Novel Approach towards detecting Faces and Gender using skin Segmentation and Template Matching. In Signal Processing and Integrated Networks* (pp. 431–436). SPIN.

Dave, R. N. (1993). Robust Fuzzy Clustering Algorithms. *IEEE International Conference on Fuzzy Systems*, 1281–86. doi:10.1109/FUZZY.1993.327577

Davison, A. J. (2003). Real-time simultaneous localisation and mapping with a single camera. In *Proceedings of the ninth ieee international conference on computer vision* (vol. 2, pp. 1403). Washington, DC: IEEE Computer Society. doi:10.1109/ICCV.2003.1238654

Davison, A. J., Reid, I. D., Molton, N. D., & Stasse, O. (2007, June). Monoslam: Real-time single camera slam. *IEEE Transactions on Pattern Analysis and Machine Intelligence*, *29*(6), 1052–1067. doi:10.1109/TPAMI.2007.1049 PMID:17431302

Dellaert, F., Burgard, W., Fox, D., & Thrun, S. (1999). Using the CONDENSATION algorithm for robust, vision-based mobile robot localization. In *Proceedings. 1999 IEEE computer society conference on computer vision and pattern recognition (cat. no pr00149)* (Vol. 2, pp. 588–594). Fort Collins, CO: IEEE Comput. Soc. doi:10.1109/CVPR.1999.784976

Deniz, O., Bueno, G., Salido, J., & De la Torre, F. (2011). Face recognition using histograms of oriented gradients. *Pattern Recognition Letters*, *32*(12), 1598–1603. doi:10.1016/j.patrec.2011.01.004

Describable Textures Dataset (DTD). (2017). Retrieved from https://www.robots.ox.ac.uk/~vgg/data/dtd/

Dhanachandra, N., & Chanu, Y. J. (2017). A Survey on Image Segmentation Methods Using Clustering Techniques. *European Journal of Engineering Research and Science*, *2*(1), 15–20. doi:10.24018/ejers.2017.2.1.237

Dhanachandra, N., Manglem, K., & Chanu, Y. J. (2015). Image Segmentation Using K -Means Clustering Algorithm and Subtractive Clustering Algorithm. *Procedia Computer Science*, *54*, 764–771. doi:10.1016/j.procs.2015.06.090

Diankov, R. (2010). *Automated Construction of Robotic Manipulation Programs* (PhD thesis). Carnegie Mellon University, Robotics Institute.

Diankov, R., & Kuffner, J. (2008). *Openrave: A planning architecture for autonomous robotics.* Robotics Institute, Pittsburgh, PA, Tech. Rep. CMU-RI-TR-08-34, 79

Díaz-Pernil, D., Peña-Cantillana, F., & Gutiérrez-Naranjo, M. A. (2014). Skeletonizing Digital Images with Cellular Automata. In P. Rosin, A. Adamatzky, & X. Sun (Eds.), *Cellular Automata in Image Processing and Geometry. Emergence, Complexity and Computation* (Vol. 10). Cham: Springer.

Diplaros, Vlassis, & Gevers. (2007). A Spatially Constrained Generative Model and an EM Algorithm for Image Segmentation. *IEEE Transactions on Neural Networks, 18*(3), 798–808. doi:10.1109/TNN.2007.891190

Dissanayake, M., Newman, P., Clark, S., Durrant-Whyte, H. F., & Csorba, M. (2001). A solution to the simultaneous localization and map building (SLAM) problem. Robotics and Automation. *IEEE Transactions on, 17*(3), 229–241.

Djara, T., Assogba, M. K., & Nait-Ali, A. (2010). Caractérisation spatiale des empreintes de l'index en analyse biométrique. *Actes du CARI 2010*, 501-508.

Do, T. T., & Kijak, E. (2012). Face recognition using co-occurrence histograms of oriented gradients. *Acoustics, Speech and Signal Processing (ICASSP), IEEE International Conference on*, 1301-1304. doi:10.1109/ICASSP.2012.6288128

Dobhal, T., Shitole, V., Thomas, G., & Navada, G. (2015). Human activity recognition using binary motion image and deep learning. *Procedia Computer Science, 58*, 178–185. doi:10.1016/j.procs.2015.08.050

Do, C. B., & Batzoglou, S. (2008). What Is the Expectation Maximization Algorithm? *Nature Biotechnology, 26*(8), 897–899. doi:10.1038/nbt1406 PMID:18688245

Dogaru, R., & Dogaru, I. (2014). Cellular Automata for Efficient Image and Video Compression. In Cellular Automata in Image Processing and Geometry (pp. 1-23). Springer International Publishing. doi:10.1007/978-3-319-06431-4_1

Dollar, P., Wojek, C., Schiele, B., & Perona, P. (2012). Pedestrian detection: An evaluation of the state of the art. *IEEE Transactions on Pattern Analysis and Machine Intelligence, 34*(4), 743–761. doi:10.1109/TPAMI.2011.155 PMID:21808091

Dorian, G.-L., & Juan, D. T. (2012). Bags of binary words for fast place recognition in image sequences. IEEE Transactions on Robotics.

Dougherty, Barrera, Brun, Kim, Cesar, Chen, … Trent. (2002). Inference from Clustering with Application to Gene-Expression Microarrays. *Journal of Computational Biology , 9*(1), 105–26. doi:10.1089/10665270252833217

Doukim, C. A., Dargham, J. A., Chekima, A., & Omatu, S. (2010). Combining neural networks for skin detection. *Signal and Image Processing: an International Journal, 1*(2), 1–11. doi:10.5121/sipij.2010.1201

Druon, S., Aldon, M.-J., & Crosnier, A. (2006). Color Constrained ICP for Registration of Large Unstructured 3D Color Data Sets. *Information Acquisition, 2006 IEEE International Conference on*, 249–255.

Duan, L., Guan, T., & Yang, B. (2009). Registration Combining Wide and Narrow Baseline Feature Tracking Techniques for Markerless AR Systems. *Sensors (Basel)*, *9*(12), 10097–10116. doi:10.3390/s91210097 PMID:22303164

Dubey & Mushrif. (2016). FCM Clustering Algorithms for Segmentation of Brain MR Images. *Advances in Fuzzy Systems*, *2016*(2013), 1–15.

Duraiswamy, K., & Valli Mayil, V. (2008). Similarity Matrix Based Session Clustering by Sequence Alignment Using Dynamic Programming. *Computer and Information Science*, *1*(3), 66–72. doi:10.5539/cis.v1n3p66

Ekvall, S., & Kragic, D. (2007). Learning and evaluation of the approach vector for automatic grasp generation and planning. In *Robotics and Automation, 2007 IEEE International Conference on* (pp. 4715–4720). IEEE. doi:10.1109/ROBOT.2007.364205

Elgammal, A., Muang, C., & Hu, D. (2009). Skin Detection – a Short Tutorial. In Encyclopedia of Biometrics. Springer-Verlag Berlin Heidelberg.

Endres, F., Hess, J., Engelhard, N., Sturm, J., Cremers, D., & Burgard, W. (2012). An Evaluation of the {RGB-D SLAM} System. *Proc. of the IEEE International Conference on Robotics and Automation (ICRA)*. doi:10.1109/ICRA.2012.6225199

Engel, J., Koltun, V., & Cremers, D. (2016). *Direct sparse odometry*. CoRR.

Engel, J., Schops, T., & Cremers, D. (2014, September). *LSD-SLAM: Large Scale Direct Monocular SLAM*. In European conference on computer vision, Zurich, Switzerland.

Fernandez, S., Graves, A., & Schmidhuber, J. (2007). An application of recurrent neural networks to discriminative keyword spotting. *Artificial Neural Networks*, 220–229.

Fink, B., Grammer, G., & Matts, P. J. (2006). Visible skin color distribution plays a role in the perception of age, attractiveness, and health in female faces. *Evolution and Human Behavior*, *27*(6), 433–442. doi:10.1016/j.evolhumbehav.2006.08.007

Fischer, A., Keller, A., Frinken, V., & Bunke, H. (2010). HMM-based word spotting in handwritten documents using subword models. *Pattern recognition (icpr), International conference*, 3416-3419. doi:10.1109/ICPR.2010.834

Fischler, M. A., & Bolles, R. C. (1981, June). Random sample consensus: A paradigm for model fitting with applications to image analysis and automated cartography. *Communications of the ACM*, *24*(6), 381–395. doi:10.1145/358669.358692

Fleck, M. M., Forsyth, D. A., & Bregler, C. (1996). Finding naked people. *Proceedings of the European Conference on Computer Vision (ECCV)*, 593–602.

Flohr, F., & Gavrila, D. (2013). PedCut: an iterative framework for pedestrian segmentation combining shape models and multiple data cues. BMVC. doi:10.5244/C.27.66

Flusser, J., Zitova, B., & Suk, T. (2009). *Moments and moment invariants in pattern recognition*. John Wiley & Sons. doi:10.1002/9780470684757

Forster, C., Pizzoli, M., & Scaramuzza, D. (2014). SVO: Fast semi-direct monocular visual odometry. IEEE international conference on robotics and automation (icra). doi:10.1109/ICRA.2014.6906584

Forsyth, D., & Ponce, J. (2011). *Computer vision: a modern approach*. Upper Saddle River, NJ: Prentice Hall.

Frinken, V., Fischer, A., & Bunke, H. (2010). A novel word spotting algorithm using bidirectional long short-term memory neural networks. Artificial Neural Networks in Pattern Recognition, 185-196. doi:10.1007/978-3-642-12159-3_17

Frinken, V., Fischer, A., Manmatha, R., & Bunke, H. (2011). A novel word spotting method based on recurrent neural networks. *Pattern Analysis and Machine Intelligence. IEEE Transactions on*, *34*(2), 211–224.

Galbally, J., Fierrez, J., Ortega-Garcia, J., & Cappelli, R. (2014). Fingerprint Anti-spoofing in Biometric Systems. In S. Marcel, M. Nixon, & S. Li (Eds.), *Handbook of Biometric Anti-Spoofing. Advances in Computer Vision and Pattern Recognition*. London: Springer. doi:10.1007/978-1-4471-6524-8_3

Galy, N. (2005). *Etude d'un système complet de reconnaissance d'empreintes digitales pour un capteur microsystème à balayage* (Thesis). Institut National Polytechnique de Grenoble - INPG.

Gao, S., Tsang, I. W. H., Chia, L. T., & Zhao, P. (2010, June). Local features are not lonely–Laplacian sparse coding for image classification. In *Computer Vision and Pattern Recognition (CVPR), 2010 IEEE Conference on* (pp. 3555-3561). IEEE. doi:10.1109/CVPR.2010.5539943

Gao, Y., & Yang, J. (2014). The Application of Cellular Automaton in Medical Semiautomatic Segmentation. In P. Rosin, A. Adamatzky, & X. Sun (Eds.), *Cellular Automata in Image Processing and Geometry. Emergence, Complexity and Computation* (Vol. 10). Cham: Springer. doi:10.1007/978-3-319-06431-4_9

Garcia-Garcia, A., Orts-Escolano, S., Garcia-Rodriguez, J., & Cazorla, M. (2016). Interactive 3d object recognition pipeline on mobile gpgpu computing platforms using low-cost rgb-d sensors. *Journal of Real-Time Image Processing*, 1–20.

Garcia-Garcia, A., Orts-Escolano, S., Oprea, S., Garcia-Rodriguez, J., Azorin-Lopez, J., Saval-Calvo, M., & Cazorla, M. (2017). Multi-sensor 3d object dataset for object recognition with full pose estimation. *Neural Computing & Applications*, *28*(5), 941–952. doi:10.1007/s00521-016-2224-9

Geismann, P., & Knoll, A. (2010). Speeding up HOG and LBP features for pedestrian detection by multiresolution techniques. *Advances in Visual Computing*, 243-252.

Gil, A., Mozos, O., Ballesta, M., & Reinoso, O. (2010). A comparative evaluation of interest point detectors and local descriptors for visual SLAM. *Machine Vision and Applications, 21*(6), 905–920. doi:10.1007/s00138-009-0195-x

Godin, G., Rioux, M., & Baribeau, R. (1994). Three-dimensional registration using range and intensity information. *Proc. SPIE, 2350*, 279-290. doi:10.1117/12.189139

Gomb, P. (2009). Detection of Interest Points on 3D Data: Extending the Harris Operator. In Computer Recognition Systems 3. Springer Berlin Heidelberg.

Gondaliya, D., Kamothi, P., Fudnawala, V., Patal, K., Patal, H., & Naik, S. (2015). Review on Human Face Detection based on Skin Color and Edge Information. *International Journal of Engineering Science and Technology, 7*(1), 12–20.

Gonzàlez, J., Moeslund, T. B., & Wang, L. (2012). Semantic Understanding of Human Behaviors in Image Sequences: From video-surveillance to video-hermeneutics. *Computer Vision and Image Understanding, 116*(3), 305–306. doi:10.1016/j.cviu.2012.01.001

Gonzalez, R., & Woods, R. (2002). *Digital Image Processing*. Prentice Hall. doi:10.1016/0734-189X(90)90171-Q

Gorelick, L., Blank, M., Shechtman, E., Irani, M., & Basri, R. (2007). Actions as space-time shapes. *IEEE Transactions on Pattern Analysis and Machine Intelligence, 29*(12), 2247–2253. doi:10.1109/TPAMI.2007.70711 PMID:17934233

Grace, J., & Reshmi, K. (2015, March). *Face recognition in surveillance system*. Innovations in information, Embedded and Communication Systems (ICIIECS), Coimbatore, India. Retrieved from http://www.anefian.com/research/face_reco.htm

Guo, L. J., & Zhao, J. Y. (2008, December). Specific human detection from surveillance video based on color invariant moments. In *Intelligent Information Technology Application, 2008. IITA'08. Second International Symposium on* (Vol. 2, pp. 331-335). IEEE. doi:10.1109/IITA.2008.326

Guo, Y., Bennamoun, M., Sohel, F., Lu, M., & Wan, J. (2014). 3d object recognition in cluttered scenes with local surface features: A survey. *IEEE Transactions on Pattern Analysis and Machine Intelligence, 36*(11), 2270–2287. doi:10.1109/TPAMI.2014.2316828 PMID:26353066

Hajiarbabi, M., & Agah, A. (2014). Face Detection in color images using skin segmentation, *Journal of Automation. Mobile Robotics and Intelligent Systems, 8*(3), 41–51. doi:10.14313/JAMRIS_3-2014/26

Hajiarbabi, M., & Agah, A. (2014). Human Skin Color Detection using Neural Networks. *Journal of Intelligent Systems, 24*(4), 425–436.

Hajiarbabi, M., & Agah, A. (2015). Face recognition using canonical correlation, discrimination power and fractional multiple exemplar discriminant analyses, *Journal of Automation. Mobile Robotics and Intelligent Systems, 9*(4), 18–27. doi:10.14313/JAMRIS_4-2015/29

Hajiarbabi, M., & Agah, A. (2015). Human skin detection in color images using deep learning. *International Journal of Computer Vision and Image Processing*, 5(2).

Hajiarbabi, M., & Agah, A. (2015). Techniques for skin, face, eye and lip detection using skin segmentation in color images. *International Journal of Computer Vision and Image Processing*, 5(2).

Hajiarbabi, M., Askari, J., Sadri, S., & Saraee, M. (2007). Face Recognition Using Discrete Cosine Transform plus Linear Discriminant Analysis. *IEEE Conference WCE 2007/ICSIE2007*, 1, 652–655.

Hajiarbabi, M., Askari, J., Sadri, S., & Saraee, M. (2008). A New Linear Appearance-based Method in face Recognition. *Advances in Communication Systems and Electrical Engineering Lecture Notes in Electrical Engineering*, 4, 579–587. doi:10.1007/978-0-387-74938-9_39

Hanna, K. J., & Hoyos, H. T. (2017). *U.S. Patent Application No. 15/477,633*. Retrieved from https://www.microsoft.com/en-us/download/details.aspx?id=52315

Hartley, R., & Zisserman, A. (2003). *Multiple view geometry in computer vision* (2nd ed.). New York: Cambridge University Press.

Hassaballah, M., Murakami, K., & Ido, S. (2011). An automative eye detection method for gray intensity facial images. *International Journal of Computer Science Issues, 8*(2), 272–282.

Henry, P., Krainin, M., Herbst, E., Ren, X., & Fox, D. (2010). Rgbd mapping: Using depth cameras for dense 3d modeling of indoor environments. RGB-D: Advanced Reasoning with Depth Cameras Workshop in conjunction with RSS.

Hetzel, G., Leibe, B., Levi, P., & Schiele, B. (2001). 3D Object Recognition from Range Images using Local Feature Histograms. In *CVPR* (vol. 2, pp. 394–399). IEEE Computer Society. doi:10.1109/CVPR.2001.990988

He, Y., Tian, J., Luo, X., & Zhang, T. (2002). Image enhancement and minutiae matching in fingerprint verification. *Pattern Recognition Letters*, 1349–1360.

Hiew, B., Teoh, A., & Pang, Y. (2007). Touch-less fingerprint recognition system. *ICB, LNCS, 3832*, 24–29.

Hinton, G. E., Osindero, S., & The, Y. (2006). A fast learning algorithm for deep belief nets. *Neural Computation, 18*(7), 1527–1554. doi:10.1162/neco.2006.18.7.1527 PMID:16764513

Hinton, G., & Salakhutdinov, R. (2006). Reducing the dimensionality of data with neural networks. *Science, 313*(5786), 504–507. doi:10.1126/science.1127647 PMID:16873662

Hjelmas, E., & Kee Low, B. (2001). Face Detection: A Survey. *Computer Vision and Image Understanding, 83*(3), 236–274. doi:10.1006/cviu.2001.0921

Hou, J., Gao, H., & Li, X. (2016). DSets-DBSCAN : A Parameter-Free Clustering Algorithm. *IEEE Transactions on Image Processing, 25*(7), 3182–3193. doi:10.1109/TIP.2016.2559803 PMID:28113183

Huang, F. J., Boureau, Y. L., & LeCun, Y. (2007, June). Unsupervised learning of invariant feature hierarchies with applications to object recognition. In *Computer Vision and Pattern Recognition, 2007. CVPR'07. IEEE Conference on* (pp. 1-8). IEEE.

Huang, A. S., Bachrach, A., Henry, P., Krainin, M., Maturana, D., Fox, D., & Roy, N. (2011). *Visual Odometry and Mapping for Autonomous Flight Using an RGB-D Camera. Int. Symposium on Robotics Research (ISRR)*, Flagstaff, AZ.

Huang, L., Yin, F., Chen, Q. H., & Liu, C. L. (2013). Keyword spotting in unconstrained handwritten Chinese documents using contextual word model. *Image and Vision Computing*, *31*(12), 958–968. doi:10.1016/j.imavis.2013.10.003

Huang, Z., Bao, Y., Dong, W., Lu, X., & Duan, H. (2014). Online treatment compliance checking for clinical pathways. *Journal of Medical Systems*, *38*(10), 123. doi:10.1007/s10916-014-0123-0 PMID:25149871

Hu, M. K. (1962). Visual pattern recognition by moment invariants. *I.R.E. Transactions on Information Theory*, *8*(2), 179–187. doi:10.1109/TIT.1962.1057692

Ioannidis, K., Sirakoulis, G. C., & Andreadis, I. (2014). Cellular Automata for Image Resizing. In P. Rosin, A. Adamatzky, & X. Sun (Eds.), *Cellular Automata in Image Processing and Geometry. Emergence, Complexity and Computation* (Vol. 10). Cham: Springer.

Ito, K., & Morita, A. (2009). A fingerprint recognition algorithm using phase-based image matching for low quality fingerprints. IEEE.

Izadi, S., Kim, D., Hilliges, O., Molyneaux, D., Newcombe, R. A., Kohli, P., . . . Fitzgibbon, A. W. (2011a). KinectFusion: Real-time 3D reconstruction and interaction using a moving depth camera. UIST, 559–568.

Izadi, S., Newcombe, R. A., Kim, D., Hilliges, O., Molyneaux, D., Hodges, S., . . . Fitzgibbon, A. W. (2011b). KinectFusion: Real-time dynamic 3D surface reconstruction and interaction. SIGGRAPH Talks, 23:1-23:1.

Jacob, G. M., & Das, S. (2017). Moving Object Segmentation for Jittery Videos, by Clustering of Stabilized Latent Trajectories. *Image and Vision Computing*, *64*, 10–22. doi:10.1016/j.imavis.2017.05.002

Jain, R., & Doermann, D. (2012). Logo retrieval in document images. *Document analysis systems (das), 10th iapr international workshop on*, 135-139. doi:10.1109/DAS.2012.54

Jain, A., Lin Hong, , & Bolle, R. (1997). On-line fingerprint verification. *IEEE Transactions on Pattern Analysis and Machine Intelligence*, *19*(4), 302–314. doi:10.1109/34.587996

Jain, A., Prabhakar, S., Hong, L., & Pankanti, S. (2000). Filterbank-based fingerprint matching. *IEEE Transactions on Image Processing*, *9*(5), 846–859. doi:10.1109/83.841531 PMID:18255456

Jarek, S. (1994). Seeded Region Growing. *IEEE Transactions on Pattern Analysis and Machine Intelligence*, *16*(6), 641–647. doi:10.1109/34.295913

Jiji, G. (2015). Hybrid Data Clustering Approach Using K-Means And Flower Pollination Algorithm. *Advanced Computational Intelligence: An International Journal*, *2*(2), 15–25.

Johnson, A. E., & Hebert, M. (1997). Surface registration by matching oriented points. *3-D Digital Imaging and Modeling, 1997. Proceedings., International Conference on Recent Advances in*, 121–128.

Kalbkhani, H., & Amirani, M. (2012). An efficient algorithm for lip segmentation in color face images based on local information. *Journal of World's Electrical Engineering and Technology*, *1*(1), 12–16.

Kamon, I., Flash, T., & Edelman, S. (1996). Learning to grasp using visual information. In *Robotics and Automation, 1996. Proceedings., 1996 IEEE International Conference on* (vol. 3, pp. 2470–2476). IEEE. doi:10.1109/ROBOT.1996.506534

Kanungo, T., Mount, D. M., Netanyahu, N. S., Piatko, C. D., Silverman, R., & Wu, A. Y. (2002). An Efficient K-Means Clustering Algorithm: Analysis and Implementation. *IEEE Transactions on Pattern Analysis and Machine Intelligence*, *24*(7), 881–892. doi:10.1109/TPAMI.2002.1017616

Kaur, P. (2011). *Kernelized Type-2 Fuzzy C-Means Clustering Algorithm in Segmentation of Noisy Medical Images*. IEEE. doi:10.1109/RAICS.2011.6069361

Kerl, C., Sturm, J., & Cremers, D. (2013). Robust Odometry Estimation for RGB-D Cameras. *Proc. of the IEEE Int. Conf. on Robotics and Automation (ICRA)*.

Kessentini, Y., Chatelain, C., & Paquet, T. (2013). Word spotting and regular expression detection in handwritten documents. *International Conference on Document Analysis and Recognition (ICDAR)*, 516-520. doi:10.1109/ICDAR.2013.109

Khalila, M. S., Mohamada, D., Khanb, M. K., & Al-Nuzailia, Q. (2010). Fingerprint verification using statistical descriptors. *Digital Signal Processing*, *20*(4), 1264–1273. doi:10.1016/j.dsp.2009.12.002

Khan, I., Abdullah, H., & Bin Zainal, M. (2013). Efficient eyes and mouth detection algorithm using combination of Viola Jones and skin color pixel detection. *International Journal of Engineering and Applied Sciences*, *3*(4), 51–60.

Khan, M. (2013). Image Segmentation Methods: A Comparative Study. *International Journal of Soft Computing and Engineering*, *3*(4), 84–92. doi:10.1117/1.2762250

Khanmohammadi, S., Adibeig, N., & Shanehbandy, S. (2017). An Improved Overlapping K-Means Clustering Method for Medical Applications. *Expert Systems with Applications*, *67*, 12–18. doi:10.1016/j.eswa.2016.09.025

Khayyat, M., Lam, L., & Suen, C. Y. (2014). Learning-based word spotting system for Arabic handwritten documents. *Pattern Recognition*, *47*(3), 1021–1030. doi:10.1016/j.patcog.2013.08.014

Khedekar, P., Walunj, S., Sul, S., Sonune, P., Tiwari, D., & Phalke, D. A. (2016). Scale Adaptive Face Detection and Tracking for Controlling Computer Functions. *International Journal of Engineering Science and Computing*, 6(4), 4608–4612.

Khoshelham, K., & Elberink, S. O. (2012). Accuracy and Resolution of Kinect Depth Data for Indoor Mapping Applications. *Sensors (Basel)*, *12*(2), 1437–1454. doi:10.3390/s120201437 PMID:22438718

Klein, G., & Murray, D. (2007). Parallel tracking and mapping for small ar workspaces. In *Proceedings of the 2007 6th IEEE and ACM international symposium on mixed and augmented reality* (pp. 1–10). Washington, DC: IEEE Computer Society.

Ko, B. C., Kim, D. Y., Jung, J. H., & Nam, J. Y. (2013). Three-level cascade of random forests for rapid human detection. *Optical Engineering (Redondo Beach, Calif.)*, *52*(2), 027204–027204. doi:10.1117/1.OE.52.2.027204

Koch, R. (1993). *Dynamic 3D Scene Analysis through Synthesis Feedback Control*. Academic Press.

Kong, W., & Zhe, S. (2007). Multi-face detection based on down sampling and modified subtractive clustering for color images. *Journal of Zhejiang University*, *8*(1), 72–78. doi:10.1631/jzus.2007.A0072

Koser, K., & Koch, R. (2007). Perspectively Invariant Normal Features. *Computer Vision, 2007. ICCV 2007. IEEE 11th International Conference on*, 1–8. doi:10.1109/ICCV.2007.4408837

Kotoulas, L., & Andreadis, I. (2005, October). Image analysis using moments. *5th Int. Conf. on Technology and Automation*, 360364.

Kovac, J., Peer, P., & Solina, F. (2003). Human Skin Color Clustering for Face Detection. *EUROCON 2003. Computer as a Tool. The IEEE Region*, 8(2), 144–148.

Kramer, J., Parker, M., Burrus, N., Echtler, F., & Herrera, D. (2012). Object Modeling and Detection. Hacking the Kinect, 173–206. doi:10.1007/978-1-4302-3868-3_9

Kroemer, O., Detry, R., Piater, J., & Peters, J. (2010). Combining active learning and reactive control for robot grasping. *Robotics and Autonomous Systems*, *58*(9), 1105–1116. doi:10.1016/j.robot.2010.06.001

Kumar, A., & Kwong, C. (2015, March). Towards contactless, low-cost, and accurate 3D fingerprint identification. *IEEE Transactions on Pattern Analysis and Machine Intelligence*, *37*(3), 681–696. doi:10.1109/TPAMI.2014.2339818 PMID:26353269

Kumar, R., Chandra, P., & Hanmandlu, M. (2012). Statistical descriptors for fingerprint matching. *International Journal of Computers and Applications*, *59*(16), 24–27. doi:10.5120/9633-4361

Küng, O., Strecha, C., Beyeler, A., Zufferey, J.-C., Floreano, D., Fua, P., & Gervaix, F. (2011). The accuracy of automatic photogrammetric techniques on ultra-light uav imagery. ISPRS -. *The International Archives of the Photogrammetry, Remote Sensing and Spatial Information Sciences*, *38*(C22), 125–130.

Kuryloski, P., Giani, A., Giannantonio, R., Gilani, K., Gravina, R., Seppa, V. P., . . . Yang, A. Y. (2009, June). DexterNet: An open platform for heterogeneous body sensor networks and its applications. In *Wearable and Implantable Body Sensor Networks, 2009. BSN 2009. Sixth International Workshop on* (pp. 92-97). IEEE.

Kushwah, A. (2017). A Review: An Optimized Technique For Image Segmentation. *International Journal of Advanced Research in Computer Science, 8*(5), 1375–1380.

Labati, R. D., Genovese, A., & Piuri, V. (2013). Fabio Scotti Contactless fingerprint recognition: A neural approach for perspective and rotation effects reduction. *Computational Intelligence in Biometrics and Identity Management (CIBIM), 2013 IEEE Workshop on.*

Labbe, M., & Michaud, F. (2014). Online global loop closure detection for large scale multi-session graph-based SLAM. *2014 IEEE/RSJ international conference on intelligent robots and systems,* 2661–2666. doi:10.1109/IROS.2014.6942926

Labbe, M., & Michaud, F. (2011). Memory management for real-time appearance-based loop closure detection. In *IROS* (pp. 1271–1276). IEEE. doi:10.1109/IROS.2011.6094602

Lam, A., Sato, I., & Sato, Y. (2012, November). Denoising hyperspectral images using spectral domain statistics. In *Pattern Recognition (ICPR), 2012 21st International Conference on* (pp. 477-480). IEEE.

Lan, T., Wang, Y., Yang, W., Robinovitch, S. N., & Mori, G. (2012). Discriminative latent models for recognizing contextual group activities. *IEEE Transactions on Pattern Analysis and Machine Intelligence, 34*(8), 1549–1562. doi:10.1109/TPAMI.2011.228 PMID:22144516

Laptev, I., Marszalek, M., Schmid, C., & Rozenfeld, B. (2008, June). Learning realistic human actions from movies. In *Computer Vision and Pattern Recognition, 2008. CVPR 2008. IEEE Conference on* (pp. 1-8). IEEE. doi:10.1109/CVPR.2008.4587756

Lavrenko, V., Rath, T. M., & Manmatha, R. (2004). Holistic word recognition for handwritten historical documents. *Document Image Analysis for Libraries, 2004. Proceedings. First International Workshop on,* 278-287. doi:10.1109/DIAL.2004.1263256

LeCun, Y., Bengio, Y., & Hinton, G. (2015). Deep learning. *Nature, 521*(7553), 436–444. doi:10.1038/nature14539 PMID:26017442

Lee, Bullmore, & Frangou. (2010). Quantitative Evaluation of Simulated Functional Brain Networks in Graph Theoretical Analysis. *Deep-Sea Research Part II,* 1–32. doi:10.1016/j.dsr2.2010.12.006

Lee, H., Pham, P., Largman, Y., & Ng, A. Y. (2009b). Unsupervised feature learning for audio classification using convolutional deep belief networks. Advances in neural information processing systems, 1096-1104.

Lee, M. A., & Bruce, L. M. (2010, July). Applying cellular automata to hyperspectral edge detection. In *Geoscience and Remote Sensing Symposium (IGARSS), 2010 IEEE International* (pp. 2202-2205). IEEE. doi:10.1109/IGARSS.2010.5652717

Lee, H. F., Siddiqui, M. K., Rafibakhsh, N., Gong, J., & Gordon, C. (2012). Analysis of XBOX Kinect Sensor Data for Use on Construction Sites. *Depth Accuracy and Sensor Interference Assessment. Ch.*, *86*, 848–857.

Lee, H., Grosse, R., Ranganath, R., & Ng, A. Y. (2009a, June). Convolutional deep belief networks for scalable unsupervised learning of hierarchical representations. In *Proceedings of the 26th annual international conference on machine learning* (pp. 609-616). ACM. doi:10.1145/1553374.1553453

Lepetit, V., Moreno-Noguer, F., & Fua, P. (2009, February). Epnp: An accurate o(n) solution to the pnp problem. *International Journal of Computer Vision*, *81*(2), 155–166.

Li, He, & Wen. (2015). Dynamic Particle Swarm Optimization and K-Means Clustering Algorithm for Image Segmentation. *Optik - International Journal for Light and Electron Optics*, *126*(24), 4817–22. doi:.10.1016/j.ijleo.2015.09.127

Li, M., Suohai, F., & Runzhu, F. (2016). A Hybrid Method for Image Segmentation Based on Artificial Fish Swarm Algorithm and Fuzzy -Means Clustering. *A Hybrid for Image Segmentation Based on Artificial Fish Swarm Algorithm and Fuzzy-Means Clustering*, 1–13. http://www.emis.de/journals/HOA/CMMM/Volume4_2/459642.abs.html

Liao, C. S., Choi, J. H., Zhang, D., Chan, S. H., & Cheng, J. X. (2015). Denoising stimulated Raman spectroscopic images by total variation minimization. *The Journal of Physical Chemistry C*, *119*(33), 19397–19403. doi:10.1021/acs.jpcc.5b06980 PMID:26955400

Liao, S. X., & Pawlak, M. (1996). On image analysis by moments. *IEEE Transactions on Pattern Analysis and Machine Intelligence*, *18*(3), 254–266. doi:10.1109/34.485554

Li, J., & Lewis, H. W. (2016). Fuzzy Clustering Algorithms — Review of the Applications. *2016 IEEE International Conference on Smart Cloud (SmartCloud)*, 282–88. doi:10.1109/SmartCloud.2016.14

Liu, H., Xu, T., Wang, X., & Qian, Y. (2013, January). Related HOG Features for Human Detection Using Cascaded Adaboost and SVM Classifiers. MMM, (2), 345-355. doi:10.1007/978-3-642-35728-2_33

Liu, X., Bourennane, S., & Fossati, C. (2012). Denoising of hyperspectral images using the PARAFAC model and statistical performance analysis. *IEEE Transactions on Geoscience and Remote Sensing*, *50*(10), 3717–3724. doi:10.1109/TGRS.2012.2187063

Liu, X., Pedersen, M., Charrier, C., Cheikh, F. A., & Bours, P. (2016). *An improved 3-step contactless fingerprint image enhancement approach for minutia detecting*. IEEE.

López-Fandiño, J., Quesada-Barriuso, P., Heras, D. B., & Argüello, F. (2015). Efficient ELM-based techniques for the classification of hyperspectral remote sensing images on commodity GPUs. *IEEE Journal of Selected Topics in Applied Earth Observations and Remote Sensing*, *8*(6), 2884–2893. doi:10.1109/JSTARS.2014.2384133

Lourakis, M. I. A., & Argyros, A. A. (2009, March). Sba: a software package for generic sparse bundle adjustment. *ACM Trans. Math. Softw.*, *36*(1), 2:1–2:30.

Lowe, D. G. (2004, November). Distinctive image features from scale-invariant keypoints. *International Journal of Computer Vision, 60*(2), 91–110. doi:10.1023/B:VISI.0000029664.99615.94

Loy, C. C. (2010). *Activity understanding and unusual event detection in surveillance videos* (Doctoral dissertation). Queen Mary University of London.

Lucas, B. D., & Kanade, T. (1981). An Iterative Image Registration Technique with an Application to Stereo Vision. Academic Press.

Lu, F., & Milios, E. (1997, October). Globally consistent range scan alignment for environment mapping. *Autonomous Robots, 4*(4), 333–349. doi:10.1023/A:1008854305733

Luisier, F., & Blu, T. (2008). SURE-LET multichannel image denoising: Interscale orthonormal wavelet thresholding. *IEEE Transactions on Image Processing, 17*(4), 482–492. doi:10.1109/TIP.2008.919370 PMID:18390357

Lukac, P., Hudec, R., Benco, M., Kamencay, P., Dubcova, Z., & Zachariasova, M. (2011). Simple Comparison of Image Segmentation Algorithms Based on Evaluation Criterion. *Proceedings of 21st International Conference, Radioelektronika 2011, 1*, 233–36. doi:10.1109/RADIOELEK.2011.5936406

Luo, R. C., Chou, Y. T., Liao, C. T., Lai, C. C., & Tsai, A. C. (2007, November). NCCU security warrior: An intelligent security robot system. In *Industrial Electronics Society, 2007. IECON 2007. 33rd Annual Conference of the IEEE* (pp. 2960-2965). IEEE.

Määttä, T., Härmä, A., & Aghajan, H. (2010, August). On efficient use of multi-view data for activity recognition. In *Proceedings of the Fourth ACM/IEEE International Conference on Distributed Smart Cameras* (pp. 158-165). ACM. doi:10.1145/1865987.1866012

Maggioni, M., Katkovnik, V., Egiazarian, K., & Foi, A. (2013). Nonlocal transform-domain filter for volumetric data denoising and reconstruction. *IEEE Transactions on Image Processing, 22*(1), 119–133. doi:10.1109/TIP.2012.2210725 PMID:22868570

Mahjoub & Kalti. (2011). Image Segmentation by EM Algorithm Based on Adaptive Distance. *International Journal of Advanced Computer Science and Applications*, 19–25.

Maintz, T. (2005). *Segmentation*. Digital and Medical Image Processing. Retrieved from http://www.cs.uu.nl/docs/vakken/ibv/reader/chapter10.pdf

Maltoni, D., Maio, D., Jai, A. K., & Prabhakar, A. (2003). *Handbook of fingerprint recognition* (2nd ed.). Springer.

Manmatha, R., Han, C., & Riseman, E. M. (1996). Word spotting: A new approach to indexing handwriting. *Computer Vision and Pattern Recognition*, 631-637. doi:10.1109/CVPR.1996.517139

Manmatha, R., & Rath, T. (2003). Indexing of handwritten historical documents-recent progress. *Proceedings 2003 Symposium on Document Image Understanding Technology*, 77-86.

Marasco, E., & Ross, A. (2015). A Survey on anti-spoofing schemes for fingerprint recognition systems. *ACM Computing Surveys, 47*(2).

Mardiris, V., & Chatzis, V. (2014). Image Processing Algorithms Implementation Using Quantum Cellular Automata. In P. Rosin, A. Adamatzky, & X. Sun (Eds.), *Cellular Automata in Image Processing and Geometry. Emergence, Complexity and Computation* (Vol. 10). Cham: Springer. doi:10.1007/978-3-319-06431-4_4

Marszalek, M., Laptev, I., & Schmid, C. (2009, June). Actions in context. In *Computer Vision and Pattern Recognition, 2009. CVPR 2009. IEEE Conference on* (pp. 2929-2936). IEEE. doi:10.1109/CVPR.2009.5206557

Marti, U. V., & Bunke, H. (2002). The IAM-database: An English sentence database for offline handwriting recognition. *International Journal on Document Analysis and Recognition, 5*(1), 39–46. doi:10.1007/s100320200071

Maryaz, G., & Hinton, G. E. (2001). Recognizing hand-written digits using hierarchical products of experts. *IEEE Transactions on Pattern Analysis and Machine Intelligence, 24*, 180–197.

Masood, S., Sharif, M., Masood, A., Yasmin, M., & Raza, M. (2015). A Survey on Medical Image Segmentation. *Current Medical Imaging Reviews, 11*(1), 3–14. doi:10.2174/15734056 1101150423103441

Masuda, T., Sakaue, K., & Yokoya, N. (1996). Registration and Integration of Multiple Range Images for 3-D Model Construction. *Proceedings of the 1996 International Conference on Pattern Recognition (ICPR '96)*, 879. doi:10.1109/ICPR.1996.546150

Matikainen, P., Pillai, P., Mummert, L., Sukthankar, R., & Hebert, M. (2011, March). Prop-free pointing detection in dynamic cluttered environments. In *Automatic Face & Gesture Recognition and Workshops (FG 2011), 2011 IEEE International Conference on* (pp. 374-381). IEEE. doi:10.1109/FG.2011.5771428

Matko, D. (2002). Direct Fuzzy Model-Reference Adaptive Control. *International Journal of Intelligent Systems, 17*, 943–963. doi:10.1002/int.10054

Matsumoto, T., Matsumoto, H., Yamada, K., & Ho-shino, S. (2002). Impact of artificial "gummy" fingers on fingerprint systems. SPIE, 4677.

McCann, S. (2005). *3d reconstruction from multiple images*. Academic Press.

Medina-pérez, M. A., & Gracia-Barroto, M. (2012). al, Improving fingerprint verification using minutiae triplets. *Pattern Recognition*, 3418–3437.

Mehtre, B. M. (1993). Fingerprint image analysis for automatic identification. *Machine Vision and Applications, 6*(2), 124–139. doi:10.1007/BF01211936

Mendel, J. M., John, R. I., Liu, F., Mendel, J. M., John, R. I., & Liu, F. (2006). Interval Type-2 Fuzzy Logic Systems Made Simple. *IEEE Transactions on Fuzzy Systems, 14*(6), 808–821. doi:10.1109/TFUZZ.2006.879986

Mercimek, M., Gulez, K., & Mumcu, T. V. (2005). Real object recognition using moment invariants. *Sadhana*, *30*(6), 765–775. doi:10.1007/BF02716709

Mil'shtein, S., Palma, J., Liessner, C., Baier, M., Pillai, A., & Shendye, A. (2008). *Line scanner for biometric applications*. Traitement du Signal.

Miller, A. T., & Allen, P. K. (2004). Graspit! a versatile simulator for robotic grasping. *IEEE Robotics & Automation Magazine*, *11*(4), 110–122. doi:10.1109/MRA.2004.1371616

Milshtein, S., Pillai, A., Kunnil, V. O., Baier, M., & Bustos, P. (2011). Applications of Contactless Fingerprinting, Recent Application in Biometric. In Tech.

Minetto, R., Thome, N., Cord, M., Leite, N. J., & Stolfi, J. (2013). T-HOG: An effective gradient-based descriptor for single line text regions. *Pattern Recognition*, *46*(3), 1078–1090. doi:10.1016/j.patcog.2012.10.009

Minoofam, S. A. H., Dehshibi, M. M., Bastanfard, A., & Shanbehzadeh, J. (2014). Pattern Formation Using Cellular Automata and L-Systems: A Case Study in Producing Islamic Patterns. In P. Rosin, A. Adamatzky, & X. Sun (Eds.), *Cellular Automata in Image Processing and Geometry. Emergence, Complexity and Computation* (Vol. 10). Cham: Springer. doi:10.1007/978-3-319-06431-4_12

Mojtaba, M. W. B. (2010, January). Liveness and Spoofing in Fingerprint Identification Issues and Challenges. Academic Press.

Morse, B. S. (2000). Lecture 18: Segmentation (Region Based). Brigham Young University.

Moujahdi, C., Ghouzali, S., Mikram, M., Rziza, M., & Bebis, G. (2012). Spiral cube for biometric template protection. In *Imageand Signal Processing* (Vol. 7340, pp. 235–244). Springer. doi:10.1007/978-3-642-31254-0_27

Mur-Artal, R., Montiel, J. M. M., & Tardos, J. D. (2015). *Orb-slam: a versatile and accurate monocular slam system*. CoRR, abs/1502.00956.

Naik, D., & Shah, P. (1993). A Review on Image Segmentation Techniques. *Pattern Recognition*, *26*(9), 1277–1294. doi:10.1016/0031-3203(93)90135-J

Neverova, N. (2016). *Deep learning for human motion analysis* (Doctoral dissertation). INSA Lyon.

Newcombe, R. A., & Davison, A. J. (2010). Live dense reconstruction with a single moving camera. IEEE conference on computer vision and pattern recognition. doi:10.1109/CVPR.2010.5539794

Newcombe, R. A., Izadi, S., Hilliges, O., Molyneaux, D., Kim, D., Davison, A. J., . . . Fitzgibbon, A. W. (2011). KinectFusion: Real-time dense surface mapping and tracking. ISMAR, 127–136.

Newcombe, R. A., Lovegrove, S. J., & Davison, A. J. (2011). Dtam: dense tracking and mapping in real-time. In *Proceedings of the 2011 international conference on computer vision* (pp. 2320–2327). Washington, DC: IEEE Computer Society. doi:10.1109/ICCV.2011.6126513

Newell, A. J., & Griffin, L. D. (2011). Multiscale histogram of oriented gradient descriptors for robust character recognition. *Document Analysis and Recognition, International Conference on,* 1085-1089. doi:10.1109/ICDAR.2011.219

Ngiam, J., Chen, Z., Koh, P. W., & Ng, A. Y. (2011). Learning deep energy models. *Proceedings of the 28th International Conference on Machine Learning (ICML-11),* 1105-1112.

Nguyen, D. T., Ogunbona, P. O., & Li, W. (2013). A novel shape-based non-redundant local binary pattern descriptor for object detection. *Pattern Recognition, 46*(5), 1485–1500. doi:10.1016/j.patcog.2012.10.024

Nigam, S., Deb, K., & Khare, A. (2013, May). Moment invariants based object recognition for different pose and appearances in real scenes. In *Informatics, Electronics & Vision (ICIEV), 2013 International Conference on* (pp. 1-5). IEEE. doi:10.1109/ICIEV.2013.6572697

Nigam, S., Khare, M., Srivastava, R. K., & Khare, A. (2013, April). An effective local feature descriptor for object detection in real scenes. In *Information & Communication Technologies (ICT), 2013 IEEE Conference on* (pp. 244-248). IEEE. doi:10.1109/CICT.2013.6558098

Nigam, S., & Khare, A. (2015). Multiresolution approach for multiple human detection using moments and local binary patterns. *Multimedia Tools and Applications, 74*(17), 7037–7062. doi:10.1007/s11042-014-1951-0

Nigam, S., & Khare, A. (2016). Integration of moment invariants and uniform local binary patterns for human activity recognition in video sequences. *Multimedia Tools and Applications, 75*(24), 17303–17332. doi:10.1007/s11042-015-3000-z

Ning, J., Zhang, L., Zhang, D., & Wu, C. (2009). Robust object tracking using joint color-texture histogram. *International Journal of Pattern Recognition and Artificial Intelligence, 23*(07), 1245–1263. doi:10.1142/S0218001409007624

Ning, J., Zhang, L., Zhang, D., & Wu, C. (2012). Robust mean-shift tracking with corrected background-weighted histogram. *IET Computer Vision, 6*(1), 62–69. doi:10.1049/iet-cvi.2009.0075

Nowicki, M., & Skrzypczyski, P. (2013). Robust Registration of Kinect Range Data for Sensor Motion Estimation. *Proceedings of the 8th International Conference on Computer Recognition Systems CORES 2013,* 835–844. doi:10.1007/978-3-319-00969-8_82

Otsu, N. (1979). A Threshold Selection Method from Gray-Level Histograms. *IEEE Transactions on Systems, Man, and Cybernetics, 20*(1), 62–66. doi:10.1109/TSMC.1979.4310076

Pang, Y., Yuan, Y., Li, X., & Pan, J. (2011). Efficient HOG human detection. *Signal Processing, 91*(4), 773–781. doi:10.1016/j.sigpro.2010.08.010

Pankanti, S., Prabhakar, S., & Jain, A. (2002). On the individuality of fingerprints. *IEEE Trans. Pattern Anal., 24*(8), 1010–1025. doi:10.1109/TPAMI.2002.1023799

Papavassiliou, V., Stafylakis, T., Katsouros, V., & Carayannis, G. (2010). Handwritten document image segmentation into text lines and words. *Pattern Recognition, 43*(1), 369–377. doi:10.1016/j.patcog.2009.05.007

Park, Y., Moon, S., & Suh, I. H. (2016). *Tracking Human-like Natural Motion Using Deep Recurrent Neural Networks.* arXiv preprint arXiv:1604.04528

Parziale, G., Santana, E.-D., & Hauke, R. (2006). The surround imager: A multi-camera touchless device to acquire 3d rolled-equivalent fingerprints. *ICB, LNCS, 3832,* 244–250.

Peng, B., Zhang, L., & Zhang, D. (2012). A Survey of Graph Theoretical Approaches to Image Segmentation. *Pattern Recognition, 46*(3), 1020–1038. doi:10.1016/j.patcog.2012.09.015

Peng, K., Chen, L., Ruan, S., & Kukharev, G. (2005). A robust algorithm for eye detection on gray intensity face without spectacles. *Journal of Computer Science and Technology, 5*(3), 127–132.

Peng, Y., Meng, D., Xu, Z., Gao, C., Yang, Y., & Zhang, B. (2014). Decomposable nonlocal tensor dictionary learning for multispectral image denoising. In *Proceedings of the IEEE Conference on Computer Vision and Pattern Recognition* (pp. 2949-2956). IEEE. doi:10.1109/CVPR.2014.377

Pietikäinen, M., Hadid, A., Zhao, G., & Ahonen, T. (2011). *Computer vision using local binary patterns* (Vol. 40). Springer. doi:10.1007/978-0-85729-748-8

Pillai, A., & Mil'shtein, S. (2012). Can Contactless fingerprint be compared to existing database? *Homeland Security (HST), 2012 IEEE Conference on Technologies for.*

Plaza, J., Plaza, A. J., & Barra, C. (2009). Multi-channel morphological profiles for classification of hyperspectral images using support vector machines. *Sensors (Basel), 9*(1), 196–218. doi:10.3390/s90100196 PMID:22389595

Pomerleau, F., Colas, F., Siegwart, R., & Magnenat, S. (2013). Comparing ICP variants on real-world data sets. *Autonomous Robots, 34*(3), 133–148. doi:10.1007/s10514-013-9327-2

Porikli, F., Bremond, F., Dockstader, S. L., Ferryman, J., Hoogs, A., Lovell, B. C., ... Venetianer, P. L. (2013). Video surveillance: Past, present, and now the future (DSP Forum). *IEEE Signal Processing Magazine, 30*(3), 190–198. doi:10.1109/MSP.2013.2241312

Portilla, J., Strela, V., Wainwright, M. J., & Simoncelli, E. P. (2003). Image denoising using scale mixtures of Gaussians in the wavelet domain. *IEEE Transactions on Image Processing, 12*(11), 1338–1351. doi:10.1109/TIP.2003.818640 PMID:18244692

Pottmann, H., Leopoldseder, S., & Hofer, M. (2002). Simultaneous registration of multiple views of a 3D object. Intl. Archives of the Photogrammetry, Remote Sensing and Spatial Information Sciences, 34(3A), 265–270.

Prasantha, H. S. (2010). Medical Image Segmentation. *Medical Image Segmentation, 2*(4), 1209–1218. doi:10.1201/9781420090413-c10

Priego, B., Veganzones, M. A., Chanussot, J., Amiot, C., Prieto, A., & Duro, R. (2013, September). Spatio-temporal cellular automata-based filtering for image sequence denoising: Application to fluoroscopic sequences. In *Image Processing (ICIP), 2013 20th IEEE International Conference on* (pp. 548-552). IEEE.

Pulli, K. (1999). Multiview registration for large data sets. *Proc. Second International Conference on 3-D Digital Imaging and Modeling*, 160–168. doi:10.1109/IM.1999.805346

Qader, H. A. (2006). *Fingerprint recognition using zernike moments*. Internationnal Arab Journal of Information Technology.

Raguram, R., Frahm, J.-M., & Pollefeys, M. (2008). A Comparative Analysis of RANSAC Techniques Leading to Adaptive Real-Time Random Sample Consensus. Lecture Notes in Computer Science, 5303, 500–513. doi:10.1007/978-3-540-88688-4_37

Rajpathak, T., Kumar, R., & Schwartz, E. (2009). *Eye detection using morphological and color image processing*. Florida Conference on Recent Advances in Robotics.

Rangkuti, A. H., Rasjid, Z. E., Imaduddin, M., Chandra, A. S., & Chancra, D. (2015). Face Skin Disease Recognation Using Fuzzy Subtractive Clustering Algorithm. *Journal of Theoretical and Applied Information Technology*, *73*(1), 174–182.

Rath, T. M., Lavrenko, V., & Manmatha, R. (2003). *A statistical approach to retrieving historical manuscript images without recognition* (No. CIIR-MM-42). Space and Naval Warfare Systems Center.

Rath, T. M., Lavrenko, V., & Manmatha, R. (2003). *Retrieving historical manuscripts using shape*. Massachusetts Univ Amherst Center For Intelligent Information Retrieval. doi:10.21236/ADA477875

Rath, T. M., & Manmatha, R. (2007). Word spotting for historical documents. *International Journal on Document Analysis and Recognition*, *9*(2-4), 139–152. doi:10.1007/s10032-006-0027-8

Ravi, S., & Khan, A. M. (2012). Operators Used In Edge Detection Computation : A Case Study. *International International Journal of Applied Engineering Research*, *7*(11), 7–12.

Ren, H., Heng, C. K., Zheng, W., Liang, L., & Chen, X. (2010). Fast object detection using boosted co-occurrence histograms of oriented gradients. *Image Processing (ICIP), 17th IEEE International Conference*, 2705-2708. doi:10.1109/ICIP.2010.5651963

Renard, N., Bourennane, S., & Blanc-Talon, J. (2008). Denoising and dimensionality reduction using multilinear tools for hyperspectral images. *IEEE Geoscience and Remote Sensing Letters*, *5*(2), 138–142. doi:10.1109/LGRS.2008.915736

Rifai, S., Vincent, P., Muller, X., Glorot, X., & Bengio, Y. (2011). Contractive auto-encoders: Explicit invariance during feature extraction. *Proceedings of the 28th international conference on machine learning (ICML-11)*, 833-840.

Rodriguez, M. D., Ahmed, J., & Shah, M. (2008, June). Action mach a spatio-temporal maximum average correlation height filter for action recognition. In *Computer Vision and Pattern Recognition, 2008. CVPR 2008. IEEE Conference on* (pp. 1-8). IEEE. doi:10.1109/CVPR.2008.4587727

Rodriguez, J. A., & Perronnin, F. (2008). Local gradient histogram features for word spotting in unconstrained handwritten documents. *International Conference on Frontiers in Handwriting Recognition*, 7-12.

Rodriguez-Serrano, J. A., Perronnin, F., Sánchez, G., & Lladós, J. (2010). Unsupervised writer adaptation of whole-word HMMs with application to word-spotting. *Pattern Recognition Letters*, *31*(8), 742–749. doi:10.1016/j.patrec.2010.01.007

Rosin, P. L., & Sun, X. (2014). Edge Detection Using Cellular Automata. In P. Rosin, A. Adamatzky, & X. Sun (Eds.), *Cellular Automata in Image Processing and Geometry. Emergence, Complexity and Computation* (Vol. 10). Cham: Springer.

Ross, A. (2007). An introduction to multibiometrics. *Proc. of the 15th European Signal Processing Conference (EUSIPCO)*.

Rosten, E., & Drummond, T. (2006). Machine learning for high-speed corner detection. In *Proceedings of the 9th European conference on computer vision* (pp. 430–443). Springer-Verlag. doi:10.1007/11744023_34

Rothacker, L., Rusinol, M., & Fink, G. A. (2013). Bag-of-features HMMs for segmentation-free word spotting in handwritten documents. *Document Analysis and Recognition (ICDAR), 12th International Conference IEEE*,1305-1309. doi:10.1109/ICDAR.2013.264

Rothfeder, J. L., Feng, S., & Rath, T. M. (2003). Using corner feature correspondences to rank word images by similarity. *Computer Vision and Pattern Recognition Workshop*, 3, 30-30. doi:10.1109/CVPRW.2003.10021

Rowley, H., Baluja, S., & Kanade, T. (1998). Neural network-based face detection. *IEEE Pattern Analysis and Machine Intelligence*, *20*(1), 22–38. doi:10.1109/34.655647

Rublee, E., Rabaud, V., Konolige, K., & Bradski, G. (2011). Orb: an efficient alternative to sift or surf. In *Proceedings of the 2011 international conference on computer vision* (pp. 2564–2571). Washington, DC: IEEE Computer Society. doi:10.1109/ICCV.2011.6126544

Rudin, L. I., Osher, S., & Fatemi, E. (1992). Nonlinear total variation based noise removal algorithms. *Physica D. Nonlinear Phenomena*, *60*(1-4), 259–268. doi:10.1016/0167-2789(92)90242-F

Rusinkiewicz, S., & Levoy, M. (2001). Efficient variants of the ICP algorithm. *Proc. Third International Conference on 3-D Digital Imaging and Modeling*, 145–152. doi:10.1109/IM.2001.924423

Rusinol, M., Aldavert, D., Toledo, R., & Llados, J. (2011). Browsing heterogeneous document collections by a segmentation-free word spotting method. *Document Analysis and Recognition (ICDAR), International Conference*, 63-67. doi:10.1109/ICDAR.2011.22

Rusinol, M., Aldavert, D., Toledo, R., & Llados, J. (2015). Efficient segmentation-free keyword spotting in historical document collections. *Pattern Recognition, 48*(2), 545–555. doi:10.1016/j. patcog.2014.08.021

Rusu, R. B., Blodow, N., & Beetz, M. (2009). Fast Point Feature Histograms (FPFH) for 3D registration. *Robotics and Automation, 2009. ICRA '09. IEEE International Conference on,* 3212–3217.

Rutakemwa, M. M. (2013). A PSO-Based Substractive Data Clustering Algorithm. *International Journal of Research in Computer Science, 3*(1), 19–25. doi:10.7815/ijorcs.31.2013.057

Saidani, A., Kacem Echi, A., & Belaid, A. (2015). Arabic/Latin and Machine-printed/Handwritten Word Discrimination using HOG-based Shape Descriptor. *ELCVIA: electronic letters on computer vision and image analysis,* 0001-23.

Salmon, J., Harmany, Z., Deledalle, C. A., & Willett, R. (2014). Poisson noise reduction with non-local PCA. *Journal of Mathematical Imaging and Vision, 48*(2), 279–294. doi:10.1007/s10851-013-0435-6

Salvi, J., Matabosch, C., Fofi, D., & Forest, J. (2007). A review of recent range image registration methods with accuracy evaluation. *Image and Vision Computing, 25*(5), 578–596. doi:10.1016/j. imavis.2006.05.012

Sandhya, H. (2017). A Survey on Clustering Algorithms Used to Perform Image Segmentation. *International Journal of Advance Research Ideas and Innovations in Technology, 3*(1), 655–661.

Saval-Calvo, M., Azorin-Lopez, J., & Fuster-Guillo, A. (2013). Model-Based Multi-view Registration for RGB-D Sensors. Lecture Notes in Computer Science, 7903, 496–503. doi:10.1007/978-3-642-38682-4_53

Schroth, G., Hilsenbeck, S., Huitl, R., Schweiger, F., & Steinbach, E. (2011). Exploiting text-related features for content-based image retrieval. *Multimedia (ISM), IEEE International Symposium,* 77-84.

Schuldt, C., Laptev, I., & Caputo, B. (2004, August). Recognizing human actions: a local SVM approach. In *Pattern Recognition, 2004. ICPR 2004. Proceedings of the 17th International Conference on (Vol. 3,* pp. 32-36). IEEE. doi:10.1109/ICPR.2004.1334462

Senthilkumaran, N., & Rajesh, R. (2009). Edge Detection Techniques for Image Segmentation–a Survey of Soft Computing Approaches. *International Journal of Recent Trends in Engineering and Technology, 1*(2), 250–254. doi:10.1109/ARTCom.2009.219

Seow, M., Valaparla, D., & Asari, V. (2003). Neural network based skin color model for face detection. *Proceedings of the 32nd Applied Imagery Pattern Recognition Workshop (AIPR'03),* 141–145. doi:10.1109/AIPR.2003.1284262

Sha, L. F., Zhao, F., & Tang, X. O. (2003). Improved fingercode for filterbank-based fingerprint matching. *International Conference on Image Processing, 2,* 895-898.

Shapiro, L., & Stockman, G. (2000). *Computer Vision*. Upper Saddle River, NJ: Prentice Hall.

Shekhar, R., & Jawahar, C. V. (2012). Word image retrieval using bag of visual words. *Document Analysis Systems (DAS), 2012 10th IAPR International Workshop,* 297-301. doi:10.1109/DAS.2012.96

Shen, J., Su, P.-C., Cheung, S. S., & Zhao, J. (2013, September). Virtual Mirror Rendering With Stationary RGB-D Cameras and Stored 3-D Background. *Image Processing. IEEE Transactions on, 22*(9), 3433–3448. PMID:23782808

Shen, J., Yang, W., & Sun, C. (2013). Real-time human detection based on gentle MILBoost with variable granularity HOG-CSLBP. *Neural Computing & Applications, 23*(7-8), 1937–1948. doi:10.1007/s00521-012-1153-5

Shu, C., Ding, X., & Fang, C. (2011). Histogram of the oriented gradient for face recognition. *Tsinghua Science and Technology, 16*(2), 216–224. doi:10.1016/S1007-0214(11)70032-3

Sidbe, D., Montesinos, P., & Janaqi, S. (2006). A simple and efficient eye detection method in color images. *International conference image and vision computing,* 385–390.

Simon, D. A. (1996). *Fast and accurate shape-based registration* (Ph.D. thesis). Carnegie Mellon University.

Singh, S., Velastin, S. A., & Ragheb, H. (2010, August). Muhavi: A multicamera human action video dataset for the evaluation of action recognition methods. In *Advanced Video and Signal Based Surveillance (AVSS), 2010 Seventh IEEE International Conference on* (pp. 48-55). IEEE. doi:10.1109/AVSS.2010.63

Singh, S., Chauhan, D. S., Vatsa, M., & Singh, R. (2003). A Robust Skin Color Based Face Detection Algorithm. *Tamkang Journal of Science and Engineering, 6*(4), 227–234.

Sivic, J., & Zisserman, A. (2003, October). Video Google: A text retrieval approach to object matching in videos. *Proceedings of the international conference on computer vision, 2,* 1470–1477. doi:10.1109/ICCV.2003.1238663

Sjoerds, Z., Stufflebeam, S. M., Veltman, D. J., Van den Brink, W., Penninx, B. W. J. H., & Douw, L. (2017). Loss of Brain Graph Network Efficiency in Alcohol Dependence. *Addiction Biology, 22*(2), 523–534. doi:10.1111/adb.12346 PMID:26692359

Skibbe, H., Reisert, M., Schmidt, T., Brox, T., Ronneberger, O., & Burkhardt, H. (2012). Fast rotation invariant 3D feature computation utilizing efficient local neighborhood operators. *IEEE Transactions on Pattern Analysis and Machine Intelligence, 34*(8), 1563–1575. doi:10.1109/TPAMI.2011.263 PMID:22201055

Smith, D. J., & Harvey, R. W. (2011). Document Retrieval Using SIFT Image Features. *J. UCS, 17*(1), 3–15.

Soetedjo, A. (2011). Eye detection based on color and shape features. *International Journal of Advanced Computer Science and Applications, 3*(5), 17–22.

Sonka, M., Hlavac, V., & Boyle, R. (2014). *Image processing, analysis, and machine vision.* Cengage Learning.

Souvenir, R., & Babbs, J. (2008, June). Learning the viewpoint manifold for action recognition. In *Computer Vision and Pattern Recognition, 2008. CVPR 2008. IEEE Conference on* (pp. 1-7). IEEE. doi:10.1109/CVPR.2008.4587552

Srihari, S. N., Huang, C., & Srinivasan, H. (2005). Search engine for handwritten documents. *Proceedings of the Society for Photo-Instrumentation Engineers, 5676,* 66–75. doi:10.1117/12.585883

Srihari, S. N., Srinivasan, H., Babu, P., & Bhole, C. (2005). Handwritten arabic word spotting using the cedarabic document analysis system. *Proc. Symposium on Document Image Understanding Technology,* 123-132.

Srihari, S. N., Srinivasan, H., Haung, C., & Shetty, S. (2006). Spotting words in Latin, Devanagari and Arabic scripts. *Vivek: Indian Journal of Artificial Intelligence, 16*(3), 2–9.

Steder, B., Rusu, R. B., Konolige, K., & Burgard, W. (2010). NARF: 3D range image features for object recognition. In: Workshop on Defining and Solving Realistic Perception Problems in Personal Robotics. *IEEE/RSJ Int. Conf. on Intelligent Robots and Systems (IROS).*

Steinbrucker, F., Sturm, J., & Cremers, D. (2011). Real-time visual odometry from dense RGB-D images. *Computer Vision Workshops (ICCV Workshops), 2011 IEEE International Conference on,* 719–722. doi:10.1109/ICCVW.2011.6130321

Storn, R., & Price, K. (1997). Differential evolution–a simple and efficient heuristic for global optimization over continuous spaces. *Journal of Global Optimization, 11*(4), 341–359. doi:10.1023/A:1008202821328

Strasdat, H., Davison, A. J., Montiel, J. M. M., & Konolige, K. (2011). Double window optimisation for constant time visual slam. In *Proceedings of the 2011 international conference on computer vision* (pp. 2352–2359). Washington, DC: IEEE Computer Society. doi:10.1109/ICCV.2011.6126517

Strasdat, H., Montiel, J. M. M., & Davison, A. J. (2012, February). Editors choice article: visual slam: why filter? *Image and Vision Computing, 30*(2), 65–77. doi:10.1016/j.imavis.2012.02.009

Stückler, J., & Behnke, S. (2012). *Model Learning and Real-Time Tracking Using Multi-Resolution Surfel Maps.* AAAI.

Su, B., Lu, S., Tian, S., Lim, J. H., & Tan, C. L. (2014). Character recognition in natural scenes using convolutional co-occurrence hog. *22nd International Conference on Pattern Recognition,* 2926-2931. doi:10.1109/ICPR.2014.504

Suk, T., & Flusser, J. (2003). Combined blur and affine moment invariants and their use in pattern recognition. *Pattern Recognition, 36*(12), 2895–2907. doi:10.1016/S0031-3203(03)00187-0

Szegedy, C., Liu, W., Jia, Y., Sermanet, P., Reed, S., Anguelov, D., ... Rabinovich, A. (2015). Going deeper with convolutions. *Proceedings of the IEEE conference on computer vision and pattern recognition*, 1-9.

Tamas, L., & Goron, L. C. (2012). 3D map building with mobile robots. *Control Automation (MED), 2012 20th Mediterranean Conference on*, 134–139.

Tam, G. K. L., Cheng, Z.-Q., Lai, Y.-K., Langbein, F. C., Liu, Y., Marshall, D., ... Rosin, P. L. (2013). Registration of 3D Point Clouds and Meshes: A Survey from Rigid to Nonrigid. *Visualization and Computer Graphics. IEEE Transactions on, 19*(7), 1199–1217.

Tarabalka, Y., Chanussot, J., & Benediktsson, J. A. (2010). Segmentation and classification of hyperspectral images using watershed transformation. *Pattern Recognition, 43*(7), 2367–2379. doi:10.1016/j.patcog.2010.01.016

Tatiraju, Suman, & Mehta. (2008). Image Segmentation Using K-Means Clustering, EM and Normalized Cuts. *Department of EECS*. Retrieved from http://ares.utcluj.ro/psi/tsg/proiect/Tema4/image_segmentation_using_k-means_clustering.pdf

Terasawa, K., & Tanaka, Y. (2009). Slit style HOG feature for document image word spotting. *Document Analysis and Recognition, 10th International Conference*, 116-120.

Tesauro, G. (1992). Practical issues in temporal difference learning. *Machine Learning, 8*(3-4), 257–277. doi:10.1007/BF00992697

The Hong Kong Polytechnic University 3D Fingerprint Images Database. (2013). Retrieved from http://www.comp.polyu.edu.hk/~csajaykr/3Dfingerprint.htm

Thompson, M. A., Scott, I. R., Shah, P. L., Ohnstad, T. W., & Weldon, K. A. (2016). *U.S. Patent No. 9,269,215*. Washington, DC: U.S. Patent and Trademark Office.

Thontadari, C., & Prabhakar, C. J. (2016). Scale Space Co-Occurrence HOG Features for Word Spotting in Handwritten Document Images. *International Journal of Computer Vision and Image Processing, 6*(2), 71–86. doi:10.4018/IJCVIP.2016070105

Thontadari, C., & Prabhakar, C. J. (2017). Segmentation Based Word Spotting Method for Handwritten Documents. *International Journals of Advanced Research in Computer Science and Software Engineering., 7*(6), 35–40. doi:10.23956/ijarcsse/V7I6/0127

Thrun, S., Fox, D., Burgard, W., & Dellaert, F. (2001). Robust Monte Carlo localization for mobile robots. *Artificial Intelligence, 128*(1-2), 99–141. doi:10.1016/S0004-3702(01)00069-8

Thrun, S., & Montemerlo, M. (2006, May). The graph slam algorithm with applications to large-scale mapping of urban structures. *The International Journal of Robotics Research, 25*(5-6), 403–429. doi:10.1177/0278364906065387

Tian, S., Lu, S., Su, B., & Tan, C. L. (2013). Scene text recognition using co-occurrence of histogram of oriented gradients. *Document Analysis and Recognition, 12th International Conference on*, 912-916. doi:10.1109/ICDAR.2013.186

Tian, S., Bhattacharya, U., Lu, S., Su, B., Wang, Q., Wei, X., & Tan, C. L. (2015). Multilingual scene character recognition with co-occurrence of histogram of oriented gradients. *Pattern Recognition, 51*, 125–134. doi:10.1016/j.patcog.2015.07.009

Tico & Kuosmanen. (2003). Fingerprint matching using an orientation-based minutia descriptor. *IEEE Trans. PAMI., 25*(8), 1009-1014.

Tombari, F., Salti, S., & Di Stefano, L. (2010). Unique signatures of histograms for local surface description. In *European Conference on Computer Vision* (pp. 356–369). Springer. doi:10.1007/978-3-642-15558-1_26

Tralic, D., Rosin, P. L., Sun, X., & Grgic, S. (2014). Copy-Move Forgery Detection Using Cellular Automata. In P. Rosin, A. Adamatzky, & X. Sun (Eds.), *Cellular Automata in Image Processing and Geometry. Emergence, Complexity and Computation* (Vol. 10). Cham: Springer.

Tran, C., Doshi, A., & Trivedi, M. M. (2012). Modeling and prediction of driver behavior by foot gesture analysis. *Computer Vision and Image Understanding, 116*(3), 435–445. doi:10.1016/j.cviu.2011.09.008

Turk, G., & Levoy, M. (1994). Zippered polygon meshes from range images. *Proceedings of the 21st annual conference on Computer graphics and interactive techniques*, 311–318.

van Zijl, L. (2014). Content-Based Image Retrieval with Cellular Automata. In P. Rosin, A. Adamatzky, & X. Sun (Eds.), *Cellular Automata in Image Processing and Geometry. Emergence, Complexity and Computation* (Vol. 10). Cham: Springer.

Viejo, D., & Cazorla, M. (2008). 3D Model Based Map Building. *International Symposium on Robotics, ISR 2008*.

Viejo, D., & Cazorla, M. (2014). A robust and fast method for 6DoF motion estimation from generalized 3D data. *Autonomous Robots, 36*(4), 295–308. doi:10.1007/s10514-013-9354-z

Viola, P., & Jones, M. J. (2001). Robust real-time object detection. *Proceedings of IEEE Workshop on Statistical and Computational Theories of Vision*.

Virk & Maini. (2012). Fingerprint image enhancement and minutiae matching in fingerprint verification. *Journal of Computing Technologies*.

Vishwakarma, S., & Agrawal, A. (2013). A survey on activity recognition and behavior understanding in video surveillance. *The Visual Computer, 29*(10), 983–1009. doi:10.1007/s00371-012-0752-6

Vrigkas, M., Karavasilis, V., Nikou, C., & Kakadiaris, I. A. (2014). Matching mixtures of curves for human action recognition. *Computer Vision and Image Understanding, 119*, 27–40. doi:10.1016/j.cviu.2013.11.007

Vu, Q. D., & Chung, S. T. (2017, May). Real-time robust human tracking based on Lucas-Kanade optical flow and deep detection for embedded surveillance. In *Information and Communication Technology for Embedded Systems (IC-ICTES), 2017 8th International Conference of* (pp. 1-6). IEEE.

Wang, H. M., Guo, S. D., & Yu, D. H. (2004). A New CA Method for Image Processing Based on Morphology and Coordinate Logic. *Application Research of Computers, 1*, 81.

Wang, H., & Dong, Y. (2008). An Improved Image Segmentation Algorithm Based on Otsu Method. In *Proceedings of SPIE, 6625*, 1–8. doi:10.1117/12.790781

Wang, J., Yang, J., Yu, K., Lv, F., Huang, T., & Gong, Y. (2010). Locality-constrained linear coding for image classification. *Computer Vision and Pattern Recognition (CVPR), 2010 IEEE Conference*, 3360-3367.

Wang, Y., Huang, K., & Tan, T. (2007, June). Human activity recognition based on R transform. In *Computer Vision and Pattern Recognition, 2007. CVPR'07. IEEE Conference on* (pp. 1-8). IEEE. doi:10.1109/CVPR.2007.383505

Wang, J., Delabie, J., Aasheim, H., Smeland, E., & Myklebost, O. (2002). Clustering of the SOM Easily Reveals Distinct Gene Expression Patterns: Results of a Reanalysis of Lymphoma Study. *BMC Bioinformatics, 3*(1), 36. doi:10.1186/1471-2105-3-36 PMID:12445336

Wang, L., Shi, J., Song, G., & Shen, I. F. (2007, November). Object detection combining recognition and segmentation. In *Asian conference on computer vision* (pp. 189-199). Springer.

Wang, Y., Lau, D. L., & Hassebrook, L. G. (2010). Fit-sphere unwrapping and performance analysis of 3D fingerprints. *Applied Optics, 49*(4), 592–600. doi:10.1364/AO.49.000592 PMID:20119006

Wang, Y., & Mori, G. (2011). Hidden part models for human action recognition: Probabilistic versus max margin. *IEEE Transactions on Pattern Analysis and Machine Intelligence, 33*(7), 1310–1323. doi:10.1109/TPAMI.2010.214 PMID:21135448

Watanabe, T., Ito, S., & Yokoi, K. (2009). Co-occurrence histograms of oriented gradients for pedestrian detection. In *Advances in Image and Video Technology* (pp. 37–47). Springer Berlin Heidelberg. doi:10.1007/978-3-540-92957-4_4

Weik, S. (1997). Registration of 3-D partial surface models using luminance and depth information. *3-D Digital Imaging and Modeling, 1997. Proceedings., International Conference on Recent Advances in*, 93–100.

Weinland, D., Ronfard, R., & Boyer, E. (2006). Free viewpoint action recognition using motion history volumes. *Computer Vision and Image Understanding, 104*(2), 249–257. doi:10.1016/j.cviu.2006.07.013

Whelan, T., Johannsson, H., Kaess, M., Leonard, J. J., & McDonald, J. B. (2013a). Robust Real-Time Visual Odometry for Dense {RGB-D} Mapping. IEEE Intl. Conf. on Robotics and Automation, ICRA.

Whelan, T., Kaess, M., Fallon, M. F., Johannsson, H., Leonard, J. J., & McDonald, J. B. (2012). Kintinuous: Spatially Extended {K}inect{F}usion. RSS Workshop on RGB-D: Advanced Reasoning with Depth Cameras, Sydney, Australia.

Whelan, T., Kaess, M., Leonard, J. J., & McDonald, J. B. (2013b). Deformation-based Loop Closure for Large Scale Dense {RGB-D SLAM}. IEEE/RSJ Intl. Conf. on Intelligent Robots and Systems, IROS, Tokyo, Japan.

Wiliem, A., Madasu, V., Boles, W., & Yarlagadda, P. (2012). A suspicious behaviour detection using a context space model for smart surveillance systems. *Computer Vision and Image Understanding*, *116*(2), 194–209. doi:10.1016/j.cviu.2011.10.001

Wollmer, M., Eyben, F., Keshet, J., Graves, A., Schuller, B., & Rigoll, G. (2009). Robust discriminative keyword spotting for emotionally colored spontaneous speech using bidirectional LSTM networks. *Acoustics, Speech and Signal Processing, IEEE International Conference*, 3949-3952. doi:10.1109/ICASSP.2009.4960492

Wshah, S., Kumar, G., & Govindaraju, V. (2014). Statistical script independent word spotting in offline handwritten documents. *Pattern Recognition*, *47*(3), 1039–1050. doi:10.1016/j.patcog.2013.09.019

Wu, C., Clipp, B., Li, X., Frahm, J.-M., & Pollefeys, M. (2008). 3D model matching with Viewpoint-Invariant Patches (VIP). *Computer Vision and Pattern Recognition, 2008. CVPR 2008. IEEE Conference on*, 1–8.

Wu, Y., & Ai, X. (2008). Face detection in color images using Adaboost algorithm based on skin color information. *2008 Workshop on Knowledge Discovery and Data Mining*, 339–342. doi:10.1109/WKDD.2008.148

Xu, Q. (2017). *3D Body Tracking using Deep Learning*. Academic Press.

Yalniz, I. Z., & Manmatha, R. (2012). An efficient framework for searching text in noisy document images. *Document Analysis Systems (DAS), 10th IAPR International Workshop*, 48-52. doi:10.1109/DAS.2012.18

Yang, F., Ding, M., Zhang, X., Wu, Y., & Hu, J. (2013). Two Phase Non-Rigid Multi- Modal Image Registration Using Weber Local Descriptor-Based Similarity Metrics and Normalized Mutual Information. *Sensors (Basel)*, *13*(6), 7599–7617. doi:10.3390/s130607599 PMID:23765270

Yang, G., Li, H., Zhang, L., & Cao, Y. (2010). Research on a skin color detection algorithm based on self-adaptive skin color mode. *International Conference on Communications and Intelligence Information Security*, 266–270. doi:10.1109/ICCIIS.2010.67

Yang, M.-S., & Nataliani, Y. (2017). Robust-Learning Fuzzy c-Means Clustering Algorithm with Unknown Number of Clusters. *Pattern Recognition*, *71*, 45–59. doi:10.1016/j.patcog.2017.05.017

Yang, Y., & Huang, S. (2007). Image Segmentation By Fuzzy C-Means Clustering Algorithm With a Noval Penalty Term. *Computer Information*, *26*, 17–31.

Yanp, M.-S., & Wu, K.-L. (2003). A Novel Fuzzy Clustering Algorithm. *IEEE International Conference in Robotucs and Automation*, 647–52.

Yin, X., Hu, J., & Xu, J. (2016). Contactless fingerprint enhancement via intrinsic image decomposition and guided image filtering. *Industrial Electronics and Applications (ICIEA), 2016 IEEE 11th Conference on*.

Yumak, Z., Ren, J., Thalmann, N. M., & Yuan, J. (2014). Modelling multi-party interactions among virtual characters, robots, and humans. *Presence (Cambridge, Mass.)*, *23*(2), 172–190. doi:10.1162/PRES_a_00179

Yussiff, A. L., Yong, S. P., & Baharudin, B. B. (2014). Detecting people using histogram of oriented gradients: a step towards abnormal human activity detection. In *Advances in Computer Science and its Applications* (pp. 1145–1150). Berlin: Springer. doi:10.1007/978-3-642-41674-3_159

Zafar, M. H., & Ilyas, M. (2015). A Clustering Based Study of Classification Algorithms. *International Journal of Database Theory and Applications*, *8*(1), 11–22. doi:10.14257/ijdta.2015.8.1.02

Zajdel, W., Krijnders, J. D., Andringa, T., & Gavrila, D. M. (2007, September). CASSANDRA: audio-video sensor fusion for aggression detection. In *Advanced Video and Signal Based Surveillance, 2007. AVSS 2007. IEEE Conference on* (pp. 200-205). IEEE. doi:10.1109/AVSS.2007.4425310

Zanaty, E. A. (2012). Determining the Number of Clusters for Kernelized Fuzzy C-Means Algorithms for Automatic Medical Image Segmentation. *Egyptian Informatics Journal*, *13*(1), 39–58. doi:10.1016/j.eij.2012.01.004

Zeisl, B., Köser, K., & Pollefeys, M. (2013). Automatic Registration of RGBD Scans via Salient Directions. *Computer Vision, 2013. ICCV 2013. IEEE 16th International Conference on*.

Zhang, C. (2016). *Human Activity Analysis using Multi-modalities and Deep Learning* (Doctoral dissertation). The City College of New York.

Zhang, L., Choi, S.-I., & Park, S.-Y. (2011). Robust ICP Registration Using Biunique Correspondence. *3D Imaging, Modeling, Processing, Visualization and Trans-mission (3DIMPVT), 2011 International Conference on*, 80–85. doi:10.1109/3DIMPVT.2011.18

Zhang, D., & Lu, G. (2004). Review of shape representation and description techniques. *Pattern Recognition*, *37*(1), 1–19. doi:10.1016/j.patcog.2003.07.008

Zhang, J., Shan, Y., & Huang, K. (2015). ISEE Smart Home (ISH): Smart video analysis for home security. *Neurocomputing*, *149*, 752–766. doi:10.1016/j.neucom.2014.08.002

Zhang, J., & Tan, T. (2002). Brief review of invariant texture analysis methods. *Pattern Recognition*, *35*(3), 735–747. doi:10.1016/S0031-3203(01)00074-7

Zhang, L., Zhang, L., Mou, X., & Zhang, D. (2011). FSIM: A feature similarity index for image quality assessment. *IEEE Transactions on Image Processing*, *20*(8), 2378–2386. doi:10.1109/TIP.2011.2109730 PMID:21292594

Zhao, Y., & Belkasim, S. (2012). Multiresolution Fourier descriptors for multiresolution shape analysis. *IEEE Signal Processing Letters*, *19*(10), 692–695. doi:10.1109/LSP.2012.2210040

Zhou, S., Liu, Q., Guo, J., & Jiang, Y. (2012). ROI-HOG and LBP based human detection via shape part-templates matching. In Neural Information Processing (pp. 109-115). Springer Berlin/Heidelberg. doi:10.1007/978-3-642-34500-5_14

Zhu, Q., Yeh, M. C., Cheng, K. T., & Avidan, S. (2006). Fast human detection using a cascade of histograms of oriented gradients. In *Computer Vision and Pattern Recognition, 2006 IEEE Computer Society Conference on* (Vol. 2, pp. 1491-1498). IEEE.

Zinsser, T., Schmidt, J., & Niemann, H. (2003). A refined ICP algorithm for robust 3-D correspondence estimation. Image Processing, 2003. *ICIP 2003. Proceedings. 2003 International Conference on, 2.*

Zitová, B., & Flusser, J. (2003). Image registration methods: A survey. *Image and Vision Computing*, *21*(11), 977–1000. doi:10.1016/S0262-8856(03)00137-9

Zuo, H., Fan, H., Blasch, E., & Ling, H. (2017). Combining Convolutional and Recurrent Neural Networks for Human Skin Detection. *IEEE Signal Processing Letters*, *24*(3), 289–293. doi:10.1109/LSP.2017.2654803

About the Contributors

Jose Garcia-Rodriguez received his PhD degree, with specialization in Computer Vision and Neural Networks, from the University of Alicante (Spain). He is currently Associate Professor at the Department of Computer Technology of the University of Alicante. His research areas of interest include: computer vision, computational intelligence, machine learning, pattern recognition, robotics, man-machine interfaces, ambient intelligence, computational chemistry, and parallel and multicore architectures. He has authored +100 publications in journals, books and top conferences and revised papers for several journals, chairing special sessions in top conferences like WCCI, IJCNN or IWANN, organizing special issues in journals like Neural Processing Letters, and participating in program committees of several conferences including IJCNN, ICRA, ICANN, IWANN, KES, ICDP and many others. He is also member of international research organizations like INNS, IEICE and European Networks of Excellence HIPEAC and EuCog.

* * *

Arvin Agah is Associate Dean for Research and Graduate Programs in the School of Engineering and Professor of Electrical Engineering and Computer Science at the University of Kansas, which he joined in 1997. His research interests include applied artificial intelligence, bioengineering, autonomous robotics, and software engineering. He has edited two books and published over 170 refereed articles in these areas. Dr. Agah has been a co-investigator on projects that represent more than $33 million in research funding. He has supervised 16 Ph.D. students, 39 M.S. students, and 44 undergraduate research students. He has received multiple honors for his teaching excellence. He has been a researcher at the Bio-Robotics Division of Mechanical Engineering Laboratory in Tsukuba, Japan; IBM Los Angeles Scientific Center; and Xerox Research Center in Rochester, NY and El Segundo, CA. Dr. Agah received his B.A. in Computer Science with Highest Honors from the University of Texas at Austin, M.S. in Computer Science from Purdue University, and M.S. in Biomedical Engineering, and Ph.D. in Computer Science from the University of Southern California.

Marc Kokou Assogba received his PhD degree from Université Paris XII Val-de-Marne (now Université Paris-EstCreteil UPEC) in 1999. He is Lecturer at Université d'Abomey-Calavi in Republic of Benin since 2002. Prof. Assogba is very interested in Electronics, Medical Image Processing, Biometrics and Applied Computer Sciences. Prof Assogba is Director of Laboratoire d'Electrotechnique, de Télécommunication et d'Informatique Appliquée (LETIA).

Thontadari C. received his M.Sc degree in Computer Science from Kuvempu University, Karnataka, India in 2010. He is currently pursuing his Ph.D. in Kuvempu University, Karnataka, India. His research interests are Image and Document Image Processing, Computer Vision and Machine Vision.

Prabhakar C. J. received his Ph.D. degree in Computer Science and Technology from Gulbarga University, Gulbarga, Karnataka, India in 2009 and guided 6 scholars for Ph.D. He acted as principle investigator for various R&D Projects. He is currently working as Associate Professor in the Department of Computer Science and M.C.A, Kuvempu University, Karnataka, India. His research interests are Pattern Recognition, Computer Vision, Machine Vision and Video Processing. He published more than 100 research publications in various National, International peer reviewed journals and conferences. He has delivered key note addresses at various International conferences. He is serving as a reviewer for many International journals and member of TPC in International conferences.

Tahirou Djara is a Postdoctoral Research Assistant at the at the Polytechnic School of Abomey-Calavi located in the University of Abomey-Calavi, Bénin. His research interests include: biometrics, signal and image processing, computational intelligence, industrial applications and symbolical programming. He is member of the research laboratory: Laboratory of Electronics, Telecommunications and Applied Data Processing Technology (Laboratoire d'Electrotechnique de Télécommunication et d'Informatique Appliquée – LETIA/EPAC). He received the Ph.D. degree in signals and image processing from the University of Abomey-Calavi, in 2013. He is a consultant in quality assurance in higher education and consultant in the field of science and engineering technology.

Richard J. Duro received a M.S. degree in Physics from the University of Santiago de Compostela, Spain, in 1989, and a Ph.D. in Physics from the same University in 1992. He is currently a Full Professor in the Department of Computer Science and head of the Integrated Group for Engineering Research at the University of A Coruña. His research interests include higher order neural network structures, hyperspectral image and signal processing and autonomous and evolutionary robotics.

Andrés Fuster Guilló received the B.S. degree in Computer Science Engineering from Polytechnic University of Valencia (Spain) in 1995 and the PhD degree in Computer Science at the University of Alicante (Spain) in 2003. Since 1997, he has been a member of the faculty of the Department of "Computer Science Technology and Computation" at the University of Alicante, where he is currently a professor. He was Deputy Coordinator of the Polytechnic School at the University of Alicante for seven years and Director of the Secretariat for Information Technology at the University of Alicante for four years. During this period he has coordinated and participated in several strategic technology projects: Open University (transparency portal and open data), UACloud, Smart University, among others.

Mohammadreza Hajiarbabi is a Computer Science Ph.D. student at the University of Kansas.

Bhavneet Kaur received the B.Sc (H) degree in computer science from Delhi University and MCA degree from Sikkim Manipal University in 2014. She is currently working towards the Ph.D. degree in Computer Applications at Chandigarh University. Her research interests are digital image processing, computer vision, and computer graphics.

Jose María Cañas Plaza is associate professor at Universidad Rey Juan Carlos where he cofounded the RoboticsLab in 2000. He was member of Robot Learning Lab, at Carnegie Mellon University and visiting scientist at Georgia Institute of Technology. His interests are perception and control for autonomous robots and computer vision systems. He leads the JdeRobot open source framework for robotics

Alberto Martín Florido is part time professor at Universidad Rey Juan Carlos (Madrid, Spain) and Computer Vision Engineer at Geomni a bussines unit of Verisk Analytics. He is member of GSYC group. He collaborates as developer on JdeRobot, a free software framework for developing applications in robotics and computer vision. He received his MSc in Computer Vision from Universidad Rey Juan Carlos. During the summer of 2017 he was mentor of Google Summer of Code for a project of Deep Reinforcement Learning.

A. K. Misra has received Doctor of Philosophy from University of Allahabad in 1990. He has worked as a Professor in the Department of Computer Science and Engineering, M. N. N. I. T. Allahabad. Currently, he is an advisor of S. P. Memorial Institute of Technology, Allahabad. He has 40 years of teaching experience. He has published more than 80 research papers in refereed journals and conference proceedings and supervised 20 Ph.D. candidates. He is a member of IEEE, Fellow of Institution of Engineers, India and Life Member of Indian Society of Technical Education and Computer Society of India.

Swati Nigam has received M. Sc. and D. Phil. degree in Computer Science from Department of Electronics and Communication, University of Allahabad, India. She has been associated with University of Allahabad, Allahabad, India for 12 years. Currently, she is a Post Doctoral Researcher at the S. P. Memorial Institute of Technology, Kaushambi, Uttar Pradesh, India under SERB-DST scheme. She has received senior research fellowship of Council of Scientific and Industrial Research (CSIR), India. She is a professional member of IEEE and ACM. Her research interests include object detection, object tracking and human activity recognition.

Blanca Priego Torres received the title of Telecommunications Engineer in 2009 from the University of Granada, Spain. In 2011, she obtained the Master's Degree in Information and Communications Technologies in Mobile Networks from the University of A Coruña, Spain and a Ph.D. from the same University in 2017. She is currently working towards her Ph.D. as a member of the Integrated Group for Engineering Research at the University of A Coruña. Her research interests include multidimensional signal processing, new neural-network structures and hyperspectral image analysis applied to the Industrial and Naval Field.

Francisco Rivas Montero is a Researcher into Computer Vision group at Geomni, a Verisk Analytics Division. He received his MSc in Computer Vision from the Universidad Rey Juan Carlos where he is now part time professor at GSYC group. He is one of the main developers of JdeRobot, a software framework for developing applications in robotics and computer vision. He is currently doing his PhD on pedestrian detection using Deep Learning.

Meenakshi Sharma received MCA (H) and M.Tech in Computer Science and Engineering from Kurukshetra University. She has been awarded Ph.D. in Computer Science and Engineering from Kurukshetra University in 2012. Her research interests are Data compression, Digital Image Processing, and data warehousing.

Rajiv Singh is an Assistant Professor at the Department of Computer Science, Banasthali University. He has received M. Sc. and Doctor of Philosophy (D.Phil.) in Computer Science from University of Allahabad, Allahabad, India. His research areas of interests are information fusion, medical image processing, computer vision and information security. He has published more than fifteen papers in refereed conferences and journals. He has served as reviewer for reputed journals like Information Fusion, IEEE Transactions on Biomedical Engineering, IEEE Transactions on Image Processing, IET Image Processing and many conferences. He is a professional member of IEEE and ACM.

Antoine Vianou is a Ph.D.-Engineer in Energy and Electricity sciences. He has been graduated through many universities as the University of Dakar and the University of Evry Val d'Essonne. He is a Full Professor in Engineering Sciences and Technologies (E.S.T.). Pr. VIANOU is currently Chairman of the Sectoral Scientific Committee of E.S.T. of the Scientific Council of UAC in Benin and is also Director of the Laboratory of Thermophysic Characterization of Materials and Energy Mastering. He is the Director of the Doctoral School of Engineering Sciences in UAC. During his academic career, Professor VIANOU taught in several African Universities and in several French ones. He is author of over hundred articles in the fields of Engineering Sciences and Technologies. In addition, he received several honors in recognition for his professional career.

Index

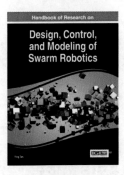

Stay Current on the Latest Emerging Research Developments

Become an IGI Global Reviewer for Authored Book Projects

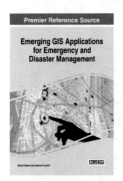

Premier Reference Source

Emerging GIS Applications for Emergency and Disaster Management

Premier Reference Source

Managerial Strategies and Green Solutions for Project Sustainability

Premier Reference Source

Comparative Approaches to Using R and Python for Statistical Data Analysis

Premier Reference Source

Solutions for High-Touch Communications in a High-Tech World

The overall success of an authored book project is dependent on quality and timely reviews.

In this competitive age of scholarly publishing, constructive and timely feedback significantly decreases the turnaround time of manuscripts from submission to acceptance, allowing the publication and discovery of progressive research at a much more expeditious rate. Several IGI Global authored book projects are currently seeking highly qualified experts in the field to fill vacancies on their respective editorial review boards:

Applications may be sent to:
development@igi-global.com

Applicants must have a doctorate (or an equivalent degree) as well as publishing and reviewing experience. Reviewers are asked to write reviews in a timely, collegial, and constructive manner. All reviewers will begin their role on an ad-hoc basis for a period of one year, and upon successful completion of this term can be considered for full editorial review board status, with the potential for a subsequent promotion to Associate Editor.

If you have a colleague that may be interested in this opportunity, we encourage you to share this information with them.

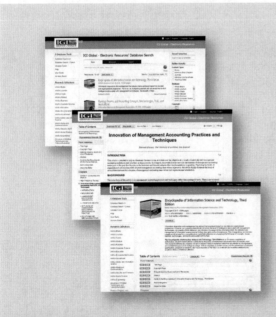

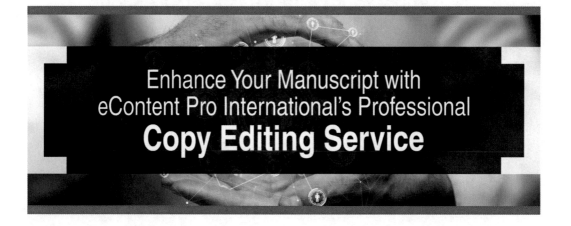

Information Resources Management Association

Advancing the Concepts & Practices of Information Resources Management in Modern Organizations

Become an IRMA Member

Members of the **Information Resources Management Association (IRMA)** understand the importance of community within their field of study. The Information Resources Management Association is an ideal venue through which professionals, students, and academicians can convene and share the latest industry innovations and scholarly research that is changing the field of information science and technology. Become a member today and enjoy the benefits of membership as well as the opportunity to collaborate and network with fellow experts in the field.

IRMA Membership Benefits:

- **One FREE Journal Subscription**

- **30% Off Additional Journal Subscriptions**

- **20% Off Book Purchases**

- Updates on the latest events and research on Information Resources Management through the IRMA-L listserv.

- Updates on new open access and downloadable content added to Research IRM.

- A copy of the Information Technology Management Newsletter twice a year.

- A certificate of membership.

IRMA Membership $195

Scan code or visit **irma-international.org** and begin by selecting your free journal subscription.

Membership is good for one full year.

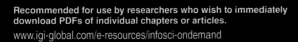

Printed in the United States
By Bookmasters